P9-CTA-955

THE POLITICS
OF LITERATURE

Dissenting Essays on the Teaching of English

THE POLITICS
OF LITERATURE

DISSENTING ESSAYS
ON THE TEACHING OF ENGLISH

EDITED BY

LOUIS KAMPF AND PAUL LAUTER

VINTAGE BOOKS
A Division of Random House, New York

FIRST VINTAGE BOOKS EDITION, January 1973
Copyright © 1970, 1972 by Random House, Inc.

All rights reserved under International and Pan-American
Copyright Conventions. Published in the United States by
Random House, Inc., New York, and simultaneously in
Canada by Random House of Canada Limited, Toronto.
Originally published by Pantheon Books, a division of
Random House, Inc., in May 1972.

Library of Congress Cataloging in Publication Data

The Politics of literature.

Includes bibliographical references.
1. English literature—Study and teaching—Addresses,
essays, lectures. I. Kampf, Louis, ed. II. Lauter,
Paul, ed.
[PR37.P6 1973]   820'.7   72–4342
ISBN 0–394–71820–8 (pbk.)

Permissions acknowledgments appear on pages ix–x.

Manufactured in the United States of America

For George Jackson

Editors' Note

We want to thank André Schiffrin of Pantheon Books. He waited a long time for this volume. The reward for his patience is not the book he expected. In spite of disagreements, he has been generous with his time, patient and helpful beyond duty. We have enjoyed working with him. What more could one ask of an editor and publisher?

ACKNOWLEDGMENTS

Acknowledgment is gratefully extended to the following for permission to include copyright material.

Atheneum Publishers, Inc.: For "Eating Poetry," from *Reasons for Moving* by Mark Strand. Copyright © 1966 by Mark Strand. Reprinted by permission of Atheneum Publishers. Appeared originally in *The New York Review of Books*. For "Shh! the Professor Is Sleeping," from *Green Business* by John N. Morris. Copyright © 1970 by John N. Morris. Reprinted by permission of Atheneum Publishers. For "Separation," from *The Moving Target* by W. S. Merwin. Copyright © 1963 by W. S. Merwin. Reprinted by permission of Atheneum Publishers.

Benson & Hedges: For quotation from advertisement for "Virginia Slims."

City Lights Books: For quotation from *The Teeth-Mother Naked at Last* by Robert Bly. Copyright © 1970 by Robert Bly.

Georgetown University Press: For "The Logic of Non-standard English" by William Labov. Reprinted from *Linguistics and the Teaching of Standard English to Speakers of Other Languages or Dialects* by James E. Alatis, ed. Copyright © 1969 by Georgetown University Press, Washington, D.C.

Alfred A. Knopf, Inc.: For "Impasse," from *The Panther and the Lash* by Langston Hughes. Copyright © 1967 by Arna Bontemps and George Houston Bass.

The Macmillan Company: For quotations from "Easter 1916" and "In Memory of Eva Gore-Booth and Con Markiewicz," from *Collected Poems* by William Butler Yeats. Copyright 1933 by The Macmillan Company, renewed 1961 by Bertha Georgie Yeats.

William Morrow & Company, Inc.: For "Nikki-Rosa," from *Black Feeling, Black Talk, Black Judgment* by Nikki Giovanni. Copyright © 1968, 1970 by Nikki Giovanni.

New Directions Publishing Corporation: For "Thought," from *Long Live Man* by Gregory Corso. Copyright © 1962 by New Directions Publishing Corporation. For quotation from "Life at War," from *The Sorrow Dance* by Denise Levertov. Copyright © 1966 by Denise Levertov Goodman.

Nipper Music Company and Doors Music Company: For quotation from "Twentieth Century Fox"—lyrics by The Doors. Copyright © 1966 Nipper Music Company, 1970 assigned to Doors Music Company. Used by permission of authors and publishers.

Random House, Inc.: For "Man on Wheels," from *Collected Poems* by Karl Shapiro. Copyright © 1968 by Karl Shapiro.

CONTENTS

THE POLITICS
OF LITERATURE

Dissenting Essays on the Teaching of English

INTRODUCTION

Louis Kampf and Paul Lauter

I

Consider our friend Martin, a college English teacher. He has been at it for seven years and things are not holding together. Under his feet, something is sliding. His students, when they come to class at all and if they enter a discussion—neither of which, for many, is usual—are inclined to divert it from Swift's *Modest Proposal* to last night's TV riots in Northern Ireland or to Bernadette Devlin's pregnancy or even to the bottle throwing in the Chicano quarter across the highway. At his back he hears the regents' mandate that academic freedom extends only to the legitimate and prescribed subject matter of the course—presumably eighteenth-century English literature—*not* to irrelevant political matters. And meanwhile his senior colleague, Professor Pillsbury, teaching similar courses, allows of little discussion, gives quizzes on the reading, has few attendance problems, and those of short duration, even offers to share a reliable lesson plan. When it comes to tests, to be sure, Pillsbury's students and his produce equally banal essays—nor do they seem, on comprehensive

3

exams, to have absorbed much different factual information. Martin's students seem less driven . . . but then they
don't show up all that often.

And he is up for tenure shortly. Since his classroom is
"private," he will be evaluated on rumor, maybe on attendance and grading, and on what he produces in the way of
articles about Crabbe, his dissertation subject. He has by
now even less interest in Crabbe than his students—he
would rather act in a production of *The Country Wife*. Or
even spend more time reading eighteenth-century slave
narratives and preparing classes that will involve his black
and Latin students—though on the whole they seem more
inclined to show up in Pillsbury's section than in his.
Nevertheless, three articles in four years won't promote
him.

And in all of this, somehow, the original impulse that
led him to the English classroom has faded. It's a job, now.
More papers to grade next year, with money tight, class size
going up, and fewer graduate assistants to take care of
freshmen. How distant, now, even without student riots,
the images of leisured, literary discussion among colleagues; distant, too, the sense of purpose toward students
"less fortunate," less lettered than he. Now the conversation is of multiplying disasters: student incompetence,
open admissions, degenerating standards, threatening legis-
lators, cutbacks, female studies, realty-tax hike, freeze on
promotions, breakdown in air conditioning. To his students, our friend Martin may begin to seem more rigid,
academic; he may indeed grasp at what he perceives as
"lesser evils" to stop his slide from a teaching career that
appeared dignified and meaningful into a life of drudgery,
paperwork, and meanness. Nevertheless, he means to do
good—and not just for himself. Only it doesn't work out.
The students remain angry, bored, or pedantic; the ad-
ministration oppressive or stodgy; the journals tedious;
the profession philistine.

What we want to explore here, and in much of this book, is how such a state of affairs developed and what might be done about it. Not only for Martin, who represents a minority, really, among English and foreign-language teachers. But for the greater number of women and men trying to cope as teachers at community colleges and high schools, those who have evaded teaching through editorial work, those students wondering what the point of literary study might be now that the job market has contracted. The classrooms and offices of literature departments abound with good intentions—and with bad feelings, defensiveness about the profession, self-apology, contempt for students. How did that contradiction come about? Who can resolve it? What can we teach or write about— and how—that will unify intention and action in our lives, and produce competent students?

It would be absurd to suggest that we have formulated answers to all those questions. We do think that more realistic appraisals of the history, function, and possibilities for literary study are available. And we think there are alternatives to self-hatred:

> At issue is not whether the college classroom should be political but whether it can make a contribution to human life equal to that of the sandbox and the monkey bars. . . . My sole claim to excellence as a teacher was in dramatizing for my students why they didn't need to like me very much.[1]

Or to self-righteous contempt for one's students:

> . . . in some ways, the semester was valuable because I learned something, if you didn't. . . . I learned that all this bull about "getting it together" or "working together" (be it for peace or a grade) is just that—bull. . . . Generally, this class has been the most silent, reticent, paranoid bunch of people in a group I have ever encountered. . . .
> You had an opportunity to find out something about

yourselves. This, by the way, is the crux of education. And as far as I can see, you found out very little.

You had an opportunity to explore ideas—on your own —and didn't. Most of the papers hashed over the usual cliché-ridden topics.[2]

Perhaps a way of moving toward an understanding of literary study neither contemptuous nor contemptible is to suggest that the first and last question teachers usually ask —What can we teach or write?—is itself misleading. For the issue is not, we believe, "What do I do Monday?" though the imperative for survival sometimes restricts us to that question, and though good teachers like John Holt and David Holbrook have provided often useful answers. Because the problems people experience as teachers or critics of literature are not primarily the products of their incompetence or lack of imagination but of the fundamental conflicts in our society. No set of magical formulas will resolve the contradictory pulls a sensitive teacher may feel from working-class students and conservative school administrators; nor can college teaching be significantly reformed until we understand the forces that continue to undermine it and to relegate each brave new study to limbo. In short, the difficulties young, and older, students and teachers of literature face are more political than pedagogical—or, rather, the problems of pedagogy are rooted in problems of politics. Their solution, we would argue, is also political. The issue is *what* politics, and beyond that, how are politics to be translated into literary practice.

Take the issue of grading, for example. Grading is a mainstay for socializing students in our competitive schools to our competitive economic system—the A's a relatively scarce commodity for which students are taught to scramble against each other. More directly, grades *are* money: students obtain not only scholarships but discounts in their auto insurance for maintaining averages of B or better. Not surprisingly, then, notions of grading a class collectively meet with official hostility. So does grading on the basis, not of what students get out of a course, but of what they contribute to the learning of others. Whereas a teacher who grades on a curve, whose effect is obviously to exacerbate competition, is never questioned. These are political matters, for they involve the issues of privatizing or collectivizing intellectual resources, competition or cooperation as norms. Just how political is illustrated, perhaps, by the fact that Paul Lauter was fired from his last teaching job at the University of Maryland for alleged "subversion of the grading system."

We should begin, then, with political questions: "What has made me feel so desperate about finding something *relevant* to teach?" Or "What is it outside my own limitations that prevents me from getting through to my students —or their getting through to me?" Or "Why does publish-or-perish persist, even though everyone responsible deplores it?" Or "How do I answer the regent who tells me to keep my politics out of his classrooms?" We would suggest that while teachers can indeed become more competent, can use livelier, more relevant material—works less biased by race or class or sex—solving the basic conflicts which now challenge literary study and the literary profession is integral with the struggle for socialism in the United States. What we shall propose in the pages that follow is that these conflicts arise from the roles culture and its bearers have played in bourgeois society and that our problem is, finally, to *change those roles* rather than merely the ways in which we play them.

Such considerations help explain what this book is not as well as what it tries to be. It is, for one thing, not intended to be representative of the literary critical practice of radicals in the United States; neither is it intended to *define* critical objectives or to serve as an exclusive example. We have made no attempt to gather a representative selection of "radical" literary criticism or scholarship.

This book has no domestic samples of the latest Marxist, structural, and Freudian modes so popular in French intellectual circles; it has no philological research on left-wing authors of the 1930s; there is no ideological analysis of an Odets play; nor do we include a survey of the political content of contemporary literature. Such gaps are not necessarily virtues; they do, however, point to our major concern: the specific social effects of literature. For this, our movement has few precedents, though William Empson and Kenneth Burke—both on the periphery of academic respectability—gave us useful, but often obscure, hints. It might be asked why there are no essays in this book on black literature or by black writers. The essays we print came out of the collective experience of a group of white literary intellectuals. The need during the past years for black radicals to work separately is well known, and has its source in the sharp differences of black and white social experience in the United States. A black version of this book would look very different. Indeed, as so often in the realm of politics, here blacks are way ahead of us: there are a substantial number of excellent studies available on the subjects of black culture and black literature. The essays in this book which deal with black culture (by William Labov, Wayne O'Neil, Barbara Kessel, and Florence Howe) do so primarily in terms of black language and literature's impact on whites.

Like the political situation of those on the left, the strategy of these essays remains uncertain. Their task is largely to clear away the underbrush; to begin opening some paths toward a different practice, different roles. Those were not our intentions when we began to work on the volume more than three years ago. But the political experience of those few years taught us—as it did many others in the radical movement—that high culture propagates the values of those who rule and therefore helps to maintain current social arrangements. We began to understand that our *insti-*

tutional roles as teachers, scholars, and critics of literature —the institutional role of literature itself—did not stand in critical opposition to the governing culture, but were expressions of it. The desire to clarify the social function of literature and culture and our changing perceptions of our own roles are at the core of many of these essays. And it is this desire which has impelled us and our comrades to deviate from our earlier intent of simply writing more committed, more "relevant," more overtly radical or Marxist critical essays.

Nearly all the contributors to this volume are people who have themselves been deeply transformed by the events of the past ten years: most of them have spent short periods in jail; nearly all have committed acts of civil disobedience in protest against the war and domestic oppressions; some participated in the Columbia or Harvard strikes; several have been fired for political reasons, and at least two cannot currently obtain teaching work; another is under suspension and facing academic trial. Some worked in the civil rights movement in Mississippi, teaching black grammar-school children; others in community organizing projects, working with high school kids, in draft resistance, Students for a Democratic Society (SDS), the New University Conference (NUC), women's liberation, the Revolutionary Union, and so forth. Participation in these movements for radical social change, whether on campus or off, changes first the pattern of one's day-to-day life, one's personal feelings and relationships, one's mode of work, and one's objectives for a career. It is difficult to communicate, as it is even more difficult to imagine, the profound ways in which active political work changes one's perceptions of social relations, of reality itself. It was no accident, for example, that the initial student rebellion at Berkeley was led by veterans of Mississippi Summer, and that it focused on issues both of political restriction and of educational irrelevance and bureaucratization.

We asked people to write for this volume because they are trying to define different cultural ends for literature and for learning. This task of redefinition has involved a common effort for all but one of the essayists and editors: over four years or more we have done common political work, both within and outside our profession. This work, the struggles we have engaged in together, the hours—days —spent on discussions, arguments, and analyses, the process of learning from each other and from our mistakes—these, not the world of professional criticism, have begun to define for us what is of literary value.

We wished initially to include a few papers on specific literary figures. We have, however, only a single, quite atypical specimen in Lillian Robinson's essay. We regard the lack of such staples of literary study less as a limitation than as an indication of certain problems both with that form itself and in our growth as critics.

In the first place, one major task we see for the kind of criticism we are learning to write is reconstructing the canon of what is studied and taught. T. S. Eliot is certainly right in arguing that each new work of art reconstructs, in part, your view of others. Reading slave narratives, Kate Chopin's novel *The Awakening,* Big Bill Haywood's *Autobiography,* or Rebecca Harding Davis's "Life in the Iron Mills" certainly forced on us some different understandings of Thoreau's political essays and of Melville's "Benito Cereno," of the heroines of Henry Adams's *Democracy* and Henry James's *Bostonians,* of the images of society in Howells and Dreiser.

But it hasn't been simply a matter of canon; rather more, of what questions we ask about literature or about a particular writer's work. For example, we thought, about half-way through our planning, of having Paul Lauter write an essay on Thoreau for the book. Here is his description of the process that left that essay still unwritten:

"I had done one some ten years ago ('Thoreau's Pro-

phetic Testimony') which argued that Thoreau was consistent in all his writings since, like a Hebrew prophet, he
was attempting to awaken and change his readers. Thus his
speeches supporting John Brown were not at odds with the
pacifism of 'Civil Disobedience' or with *Walden,* as had
been charged, but were sharper attempts to penetrate the
consciousness of a still-slumbering people. But lately it had
seemed to me less important to protect Thoreau's non-
violent consistency; indeed, what intrigued me was his development from the somewhat private 'Civil Disobedience,'
through the more directly political but frustrated 'Slavery
in Massachusetts,' and to the explicit commitment to
armed struggle in 'John Brown.' It seemed to me that an
essay tracing Thoreau's development along those lines
could also chart the changes in abolitionism, which seemed
to have receded as an idealistic reform movement during
the late forties—its energies channeled into electoral politics and diffused in utopian enterprises—to have faced a
strong proslavery resurgence, and finally to have moved,
through the insistence of certain blacks, in the direction of
armed resistance to the Fugitive Slave Act, and thus toward
Harpers Ferry and war. It seemed to me, in something of a
simple-minded way, that such an essay would be more
'relevant' than most literary studies, because it might tell
us something about the conditions and development of our
own movement as well as of Thoreau and abolitionism.

"It also became clear how little I—an English and
American literature Ph.D., NYU, Indiana, Yale—knew
about the dynamics of abolitionism, about Thoreau's real
relationships to the movement or to John Brown. I found
mainly that knowing the 'facts' and some of the scholarship, and coming to understand the dynamics of movements for social change today, I was too ignorant of mid-
nineteenth-century American society and politics, how they
really functioned, to judge the reliability of what I read.
And I found, too, speaking with friends and colleagues,

that they were no less ignorant, closed into their specialties, than I. My projected essay on 'Thoreau and the Abolitionist Movement—From "Civil Disobedience" to Armed Struggle,' narrowly as I'd conceived it, still began to take on the character of a long course of self-education.

"I was also reading Margaret Fuller, for the first time with any seriousness, in teaching an American literature course. I was struck with her development from the difficult and often private abstractions of the *Dial* period, through the increasingly concrete social concerns of *Woman in the Nineteenth Century,* to the deeply involved and passionate reports of the revolution in Italy. Wasn't her development, I began to wonder, rather like Thoreau's? If so, was it social practice, and of what sort, that produced changes in them as writers and participants in political movements? In contrast to Emerson, for example, who gradually faded off into a more remote, darker brooding privacy. And then I got fired."

That is not an insignificant element in the explanation of why the essay has not been written. In general, academic repression, entwining teachers in a prison of bureaucracy and procedure and cutting us off from students, has helped limit the re-establishment of a left-wing literary culture in the United States, despite the very promising critical writing of 1968–1969. But repression is only one and perhaps not the most important reason for a certain faltering of intellectual development during these intervening two or three years.

Events of 1968 confirmed for many of us and for our students the accelerating disintegration of American social and political institutions. In particular, what happened at the Democratic convention in Chicago marked a sharp escalation in the violence of repressive tactics a "bipartisan" war government was willing to use against white as well as black dissidents. At the same time, many of us involved in the protest movements against racism, the war, and sexism had come to think of ourselves more explicitly as socialists and had begun to try unifying our work, teaching and research, with our developing politics. But the pressure of events—the murders of Hampton and Clark, the extension of the war, Jackson State, Kent State—the pious indifference of so many of our colleagues, these objective realities made it increasingly difficult to sustain that dialectic between activist politics and intellectual work. Hindsight reveals some of the failures of street politics. It also suggests how necessary, in a nation largely indifferent to the destruction of Vietnam, it was to confront people with the unpleasant realities of the war—to say nothing of the repression and exploitation closer to home. Be that as it may, we didn't glorify ourselves as too busy making a revolution to write about it; we just found ourselves more and more in the meeting rooms and in the streets, often asking how intellectuals could join meaningfully in movements for change.

That we were uncertain of our roles as activists and intellectuals, that the process of redefining a socialist literary practice has been slow and tentative, isn't surprising. The institutions of the left, which might have helped stabilize our work, had been decimated by McCarthyism and internal division. The culture of American working people was largely homogenized by the mass media and submerged in schools. "American studies programs," for example, tacitly assumed that the disputatious writings of Puritan divines were more basic to the emergence of an American culture, therefore more worthy of study, than the songs and narratives of the struggle against slavery, the poetry of Wobbly organizers, or the writings of activist women of the last century. Moreover, the religious ideas studied were lifted from the social and political contexts in which they arose; it was hardly possible in such courses to consider the main thrust of Puritanism as a revolutionary challenge by a rising bourgeoisie against the economy and culture of feudalism. Such terms or concepts never entered the discussion. We will return below to the fallacy of isolating "literary history" or "the history of ideas" from historical reality. Here we wish only to note how the choices of subject and approach that characterized our education, together with McCarthyism and factionalism, thoroughly depoliticized classrooms, and, for the most part, the literary culture represented by the standard journals. Or, not "depoliticized," but removed from the range of "legitimate" or "important" discussion fundamental political, ideological, or cultural alternatives to bourgeois capitalism, and all but obliterated the struggles for life and power of people seeking such alternatives. Thus whole areas of knowledge, a range of approaches to literature and history, were excluded from our experience. In this respect, our education unfitted us to answer questions like those which might be clarified by Lauter's unwritten essay: for example, what the development of abolitionist writing could tell us about our movement, how social practice—if indeed it was that—changed the writing, even the style and lives, of intellectuals like Thoreau and Fuller. And in a sense, what we haven't done is a reflection of how difficult is the process of repoliticizing our intellectual lives—if we may describe it that way—of breaking out of the political narrowness to which we've been trained.

II

But why should we have wanted more "reconsiderations of literary figures" in the book? Why, indeed, should one want a book of literary criticism, however "dissenting"? The fact that we don't generally ask those questions, as if critical writing were as natural, or inevitable, as grass, tells something about the literary profession and its history. We want to understand more about that. For if radical literary essays when they are written—and we do feel they should

be—are to be more than the products of compulsive professionalism, they must serve ends distinct from those now
imposed upon students of literature. Why the pressure to
write? And to write about narrowly literary subjects? Why,
indeed, separate departments of English or German or even
"comparative" literature? Why literature departments at
all? There is nothing self-evident about the answers to
these questions either. They are rooted in the social history
of criticism, in the development of why, and how, literary
works came to be formally studied, written about, "taught"
in classrooms. And beyond that, in the distinctive roles
carriers of high culture have come to play in our systems
of mass education. In our literary culture, in our profession, in our colleges and schools, criticism and literary
scholarship have come to assume a central and exaggerated
position. The first question we must address is, How did
this condition come about?

The contours of criticism's historical development
should be clear enough, though they can hardly be perceived, never mind understood, if one sees criticism—and
literature—developing according to an internal dynamic
alone. The history of literary criticism is ordinarily studied
as a closed field: some critics at some time develop an
aspect of the theories of earlier critics; the former are then
found wanting by yet other critics, who proceed to improve
the product. At best, an occasional historian of criticism
will risk speculating that a given method—say, that of Romantic criticism—might have developed because a shift in
poetic practice challenged existing methodology. But even
such a measuring of critical theory against the poetry actually being written does not engage the important questions, those which would give criticism its practical definition: Who is criticism for? What does it do to (or for)
people who read it?

Literary criticism as we know it in the West has a short
history. Some literary historians choose to refer to the

treatises on rhetoric of Western antiquity and the Middle Ages as literary criticism. But this is to stretch a point: collections of citations illustrating rhetorical figures have their uses, but they do not add up to literary criticism. A large body of formal criticism, based on principles derived from Italian Renaissance commentators on Aristotle's *Poetics*, was published in France and England during the seventeenth century. Today this "neoclassical" criticism is barely recognizable as such, and is rarely read outside a classroom. The reasons are not that the best of it is insensitive to the works it considers, not that it lacks intelligence, and not that there isn't anything to be learned from it. These early critics are so distant in spirit because the function of criticism changed drastically during the eighteenth century. Neoclassical criticism, addressed to a comparatively small body of upper-class readers and spectators, was narrowly literary. Its method was to evaluate works in terms of their congruence to the "rules" of literary forms, rather than to explore the works' relationship to life. Ranking works on a scale was of importance, since to an elite and leisured audience poems or plays were diversions, artifacts separated from the rest of life. Diversions and artifacts are commodities which must be chosen amongst; they are measured readily only against other diversions and artifacts, and hence need to be evaluated in their own terms. The latter were given convenient expression by the neoclassical rules.

The growth of a large middle-class reading public during the eighteenth century changed all that. The market was glutted by publications intended to educate the middle classes to the culture they hoped to share with the older elites. The major critics of the eighteenth century—Dr. Johnson, Diderot, Lessing—functioned as educators. They sensitized their readers to the validity of some literature's representation of life—the justness, for example, of Richardson's rendering of ordinary emotions, or the realism of *The London Merchant*; they moved the evaluation of literature's conformity to an acceptable moral code nearer the center of literary experience; and they spelled out the contemporary pertinence of some older classics. Literature was conceived of by these critics in its widest sense: taken to include almost anything in print. Even David Hume or Adam Smith, whom we think of respectively as professional philosopher and economist, made no division between their critical writings on ethics, literature, politics, economics, or theory of knowledge: all were subsumed under the category of criticism, and all were subjects to be taught to those who needed to learn, and had the leisure to do so.

Criticism in the nineteenth century—that of Saint-Beuve, Arnold, and Emerson, for example—can best be understood as extending the educational role established for it a hundred years earlier. Arnold confirmed criticism's domestication of literature for the middle classes by institutionalizing the critical function as part of the school curriculum. Here the study of literature becomes one way of civilizing the children of the middle classes, of imposing or providing a cultural overlay that helped distinguish the bourgeoisie's young from their social "subordinates." Looked at from another point of view, civilizing might be seen as a process of smoothing out the happy barbarities of a fabulous Huck Finn or, more realistically, a softening of the harsh contours of the cash nexus, which increasingly dominated competitive bourgeois life during the nineteenth century.

While some such functions persist in our own culture, the role of formal criticism has clearly changed since Arnold. Commitment to the education of a general public has continued to be used to support and justify critical activity, but reality belies such claims. For even writers in the best cultural and political journals speak to small numbers of mainly professional readers. Too often, the knowledge such writers try to convey becomes the elevated gossip of the snob; at best, within a small circle, these critics do at least perform their traditional role.

The same cannot be said for the vast bulk of criticism and literary scholarship being ground out today. It has a function, but this is related to the institutional procedures of education rather than to the education of a social class. Nearly all criticism is written to fulfill professional requirements. The thousands of people who teach literature in the English and foreign-language departments of the country's colleges and universities must write articles and books if they are to be promoted, to attain professional recognition, and, saddest of all, to keep their self-respect, identity, and sense of purpose. The amount of critical writing this process has generated is overwhelming; its effect on the function of criticism has, however, been paradoxical: though the volume of critical writing keeps getting larger, the function of criticism is withering away. No one, including the compulsively dedicated scholar, can conceivably read—or even keep track of—any substantial portion of our critical surfeit. Who reads the stuff? Clearly, the only person who might glance at the latest articles on Swift's *Tale of A Tub*, for example, is another professional doing *his* thing on *A Tale of A Tub*. It has been seriously proposed within the Modern Language Association (MLA) that critical and scholarly journals should stop publication. Instead, their editorial boards should decide what articles are acceptable to the scholarly "community." Accepted work would then be stored in a computerized information-retrieval system in Washington, D.C., named ERIC. Now the overworked academic preparing his article on *A Tale of A Tub* need only write to the Keeper of ERIC, the appropriate card would be punched, the button pushed, and the précis would come pouring forth. Clearly, the traditional function of criticism has disappeared. Whatever purposes criticism might serve, the general or literary education of the middle classes—or of anyone else—is rarely one of them.

The primary function of writing literary criticism has, in short, become certifying college and university teachers of literature. The expansion of higher education (a subject to which we shall return), and the resulting pressure for certification procedures applicable to the increasing number of teachers, have been one important cause of this development. However, the effects of educational expansion on literary criticism would hardly have been of importance if literature and English had not previously become a part —most often a required one—of the college curriculum. Most people assume that such has always been the case. But in the United States, for example, literature courses first began to appear in college catalogues no more than a hundred years ago. The first doctorate in English in the United States was awarded at approximately the same time. These two developments are obviously related. The doctorate was (and is) one's ticket of entry to the guild of literature teachers. But ironically, the degree certifies neither one's capacity to teach the subject nor one's mastery of it. Rather, doctors of literature are declared competent in handling the tools of scholarship or of bureaucracy. And they must continue to illustrate that competence if they are to maintain their place in the profession.

How scholarship came to be the measure of educational competence, and how the German system of certification came to be accepted in the rest of Europe and in North America, are important questions which cannot be answered in this context. Of significance to us is that the methods and objectives of professional scholarship—its very way of structuring the field—have been imposed on the *teaching* of literature, and have thereby forced a shift in the nature of literary study itself. Studying literature as an autonomous, self-defined field is, from the point of view of professional specialists, convenient, even necessary. How are they to master Spenserian prosody and allegory—to borrow an example from Delany—if they must also understand the underlying economic and social struggles of Renaissance Europe, the balance of political forces in Elizabethan England, the ideological functions of *The Faerie Queene* in those struggles? Must they be Renaissance Men to teach Renaissance literature? Or what can Engels tell them of the condition of English workers that is significant in understanding Dickens's characters in *Hard Times*? Why, then, study Engels if you have Dickens in a nineteenth-century-novel course? We shall have more to say below about the isolation of literary study from other formal disciplines. We wish here only to emphasize one source—the demands of professionalism—of that artificial separation, common enough to most professions. And the distinctive significance of it for the experience most of us have of literature.

For nearly all the "respectable" literature read by most people is read in relationship to school and to formal education. Thus criticism in the traditional sense occurs almost exclusively in the classroom rather than in journals or salons. For both student and teacher this means, in fact, that literature is not apprehended as a civilizing force but is *studied* as one field in a body of formal knowledge.[3] Can the introduction of students to a formal discipline be called criticism? Traditional criticism tried to educate middle-class readers to a way of feeling, a set of moral valuations, a style of life and thought which served the readers' personal and class interests. Criticism therefore tried to relate the experience of literature more intimately to the rest of the readers' lives. Ellen Cantarow's essay shows how far removed such critical practice is from anything going on in a classroom. Making literature an object of formal study does not always kill the possibility of experiencing books, though it may do so; however, it removes the experience of literature from the here and now to some world of fantasy, or to the realm of an autonomous, disinterested aesthetic.

The notion of literature as fuel for one's fantasy life and the concept of an autonomous aesthetic are related both logically and historically.[4] Most teachers of literature do, in fact, accept one or the other or both not merely as legitimate pedagogical objectives but as laws of nature. The separation of literature from life, as Richard Ohmann points out in his essay, has defined the nobility of the literary experience for a society which pretends to value contemplation over action. This self-serving ideology justifies the teacher's critical activities in the classroom and in print. Should the blinders of self-interest be torn away, the removal of literature to an abstract realm of the aesthetic will be seen, on the one hand, not as ennobling literature but as reducing it to triviality; here literature becomes a spectator sport, a plaything for those with leisure, a source of cheap—though perhaps desperately needed—fantasies. One reads as one would watch, not participate in, a baseball game. On the other hand, ennobling such experience by describing it in the vocabulary of transcendental philosophy allows for the most entrancing philosophical and critical speculations. But confining what appear to be a society's serious and elevated pursuits to a realm utterly removed from everyday experience also reduces seriousness to triviality. Such "seriousness" becomes one more aesthetic game. In the context of our class-structured educational system, such games, as essays like Bruce Franklin's and Katherine Ellis's show, may become not merely self-serving for the faculty but injurious to the students.

We are faced with a set of paradoxes: never has more literary criticism been written, yet the civilizing function historically imputed to it has been withering away; more students are "taking" literature, yet the reading of books seems mostly irrelevant to their lives; the literary professions have never been larger nor wealthier, yet teaching and criticism seem often to have become instruments of oppression rather than of enlightenment. How, to echo Ohmann's essay, did the profession "get into this fix"?

One major factor we have mentioned has been the enormous expansion of higher education since the end of World War II, and the consequent growth of the academic professions. The more students, the more teachers; the latter, for reasons we have sketched, generate more projects, start more journals, and produce more articles fated to be swallowed by ERIC. Though funds have become tighter in the recent past, and the rate of growth has diminished, there is no danger of the process being reversed even if the rate of population growth itself levels off. The Carnegie Commission's recommendation that the population of community colleges be doubled by 1980 will most likely be carried out; the proportion of the appropriate age group going to college promises to go well past 50 percent during the coming years. Almost all the academic professions have been deeply affected by this growth, as "gentlemen scholars" have been replaced by entrepreneurs, and the art of criticism by the arts of grantsmanship and social climbing. The ideological dislocations within the literary profession are tied both to expansion of the education industry and to the peculiar roles "culture" courses play in it: English or literature courses are, after all, required nearly everywhere. Therefore, to understand the profession's "fix," one must understand why higher education, in spite of recent cutbacks, is still a growth industry, and the tension that expansion has produced. There is a substantial literature available on this subject. Here we can merely sketch out some of the reasons for expansion which are pertinent to our discussion.[5]

1. Demobilization at the end of World War II, then population growth made absorption of a vastly increased labor force an imperative if the society's stability was to be

maintained. Economic expansion is the obvious (and most profitable) way of creating the necessary jobs. But in spite of the economic boosters injected by the cold war, the economy did not (and still doesn't) expand enough without creating unacceptable levels of inflation. Such failures have produced an extremely high unemployment rate amongst the young: up to 20 percent for the age group between sixteen and twenty-one; 40 to 50 percent for blacks in that bracket. The level of unemployment would be even higher if it were not for the substantial numbers absorbed by the armed forces—and by higher education.[6]

2. One would anticipate that bringing vast new populations to colleges and universities might create severe social problems, since the new collegians would expect to move upward to more prestigious and better-paying jobs already occupied by people of different ethnic or class origins. Such prospective social dislocations are neutralized by various mechanisms, some subtle, others less so. Of the latter variety is "upgrading" educational requirements for jobs: some clerks now need two years of college instead of a high school diploma; some bookkeepers need accounting degrees instead of a one-year commercial course; some welfare workers need graduate work in addition to the usual B.A.; choice engineering jobs are available only to graduates of MIT and Cal Tech, whereas the graduates of less prestigious schools pick up the crumbs of the profession. In short, those newly entered on higher education find themselves running longer and harder through the academy to stay, relatively, where their parents were in the social order.

More subtle is the psychological mechanism generally referred to as "cooling out."[7] Working-class students who come to community colleges and the lesser branches of their state universities expecting room at the top are taught instead to reconcile themselves to what are presented as their own "inadequacies," then pressed to "lower their sights to more realistic levels": to becoming medical technicians rather than doctors; mechanics rather than engineers; if female, secretaries rather than editors or journalists. The professions, and the educational requirements for them, are made to appear impossibly distant, out of reach.

3. And so they are: whatever training in specific professional skills the colleges might provide, their institutional task is to make sure at least of separating ("differentiating" is the jargon) the work force. Indeed, Ivar Berg, a professor at the Columbia School of Business, has shown that the training provided by the schools rarely bears a close relationship to the specific mechanics of the jobs people are slated to perform. One should recall that free public high school education began in the United States, not primarily to provide people with concrete job skills, but to teach them the habits requisite for the factory or the office.[8] Schools, at all levels, teach the young to accept tasks, to perform them as prescribed, and to get them done on time; skepticism students might retain about the work they are asked to do is, they learn, to be put into mental parentheses.[9]

Such acceptance helps to maintain belief in the fundamental assumptions of the country's democratic creed: that all people have equal opportunities to obtain wealth, status, happiness. Increased access to higher education, we are assured, will widen the possibilities for social mobility. If working-class students, now blessed with admissions slips to the nearest community college (or even to an elite university which they probably won't attend because they can't afford to), fail to climb, they have no one to blame but themselves. The process of maneuvering students to internalize failure, described so forcefully by Barbara Kessel and Wayne O'Neil, becomes one of the functions "culture" courses serve in the academy. For such reasons, freshman composition has long been the major "flunk-out" course in big, "open-admissions" public universities. The people flunked, or put into "special-skills programs" from which they never emerge, are those who lack the veneer of middle-class language and culture. Calling them "culturally deprived"—or some such euphemism for oppressed —is part of the process of shifting onto them responsibility for the conditions of their class or race.

The social consequences of expanding higher education seem to be similarly paradoxical. Social stratification has clearly hardened since the turn of the century; the expanded educational system has provided a chief mechanism, not for upward mobility, but for keeping people in their place. The correlation between level of family income and the level of one's higher education is nearly absolute. In turn, the correlation between the prestige of the college one attends and one's expected lifetime income is no less absolute.[10] Individuals do occasionally break out of this pattern; a social class never can.

What then happens to the children of blue-collar workers, for instance, who are first-generation collegians? They tend to become part of the white-collar proletariat. Once placed in an office, their chances of moving up in this hierarchy are smaller than they were a generation or two ago, for administrative and executive jobs have also been upgraded. Ordinarily, these go to the graduates of the more prestigious graduate schools of business. To add insult to injury, in most states, owing to their regressive tax structures, those on the bottom half of the income scale contribute much more than their share for the higher education of the children of those on the top half of the scale. They do so even if some of their children wind up in college, since elite parts of a state's university system cost much more to run than the lesser campuses. More than insult is involved, of course: the requisition of funds through taxes for an expanded system of higher education fixes lower-income families more firmly than ever in their social class.

4. Education, or at any rate intellectual work, has gen-

erated a substantial part of the economic growth since
World War II, though the amount has generally been exaggerated. Classical and Keynesian economic models have
failed to account for nearly a third of the economic growth
of the last fifty years. To explain this anomaly in the relation of investment to expansion, bourgeois economists have
posited the notion of human capital development. Investment in people ("human capital"), mainly by giving them
more education, is said to account for the gap in the
models. If people are taken to be commodities, improving
the goods will naturally make them more valuable. As a
corollary, the theorists of human capital development and
most economists of education trace all difficulties in the
economy to insufficiencies in education. If black laborers
earn less than white ones, it is because the latter have had
more education. If the Southern states experience economic difficulties, it is owing to people's relatively low level
of education. If Third World countries cannot generate
enough economic growth—guess what? Such ideas have, of
course, been peddled with great vigor by educators, since it
serves their self-interest and the interests of their institutions. The relationship between education and productivity is, at best, obscure; it can be argued, for example,
that more education is partly an outgrowth rather than a
cause of increased productivity, a form of consumption like
tourism and fancy automobiles. Nevertheless, the wide acceptance by liberals of the concept of investment in human
capital through education has led to the rather casual ap-
propriation of huge sums of money to educational institutions. These appropriations have created the professional
opportunities, the style of life, which Ohmann and Franklin discuss in their essays; they have also been the source of
our profession's growth and therefore a source of the cultural fix we're in. Lately, difficulties in the economy have
forced a reduction in what had appeared to be inexhaust-
ible sources of funds. The educational system has become

incapable of absorbing all the Ph.D.'s it produces. Yet for most people in the profession, the benefits to be attained are still substantial, if the competition more intense.

The growth we have tried to describe has brought many Third World and lower-class students into higher education. Their presence has forced professors of language and literature to confront, with varying degrees of seriousness, what the meaning of the traditional literary culture, described by Ellis and Kessel, might be for students who have not been born to it. To teach the governing tradition to elite students is to transmit to them something already their property, something, as Sheila Delany suggests, which embodies their values. To hand this property to the new body of students is little more than a "lay-on": it may be a way of testing their cultural resourcefulness, and therefore their capacity to climb; most often it is a way of flunking them out of the race, and forcing them to view failure as a product of their own stupidity and gaucherie.

What we observe is a heightening of tensions within the academic world. On the one hand, teachers are often confronted with students' boredom, "stupidity," indifference, or outright hostility. Students from variously oppressed groups—blacks, Latins, and now women—coming into colleges in substantial numbers, demand that knowledge be organized, not around professorial specialties, tracking, or "cooling them out," but toward solving the problems they face in their lives. The essays by Kessel, Cantarow, and O'Neil indicate how antagonism between student and teacher is built into courses that lay on culture, that try to get students to produce, for reasons largely unarticulated or patently false ("How do you expect to be understood?"), particular "cultivated" responses to literature or language. On the other hand, teachers observe—despite the lip service paid to the importance of undergraduate instruction—that both professional advancement and escape from the conflicts of undergraduate teaching to the privileged position of conducting graduate seminars lie in devoting one's energies to an area of specialization acceptable to the profession. Specialties in the study of literature have traditionally been defined by the iron laws of chronology and genre, rather than feelings, ideas, social or psychological needs: people are expected to become experts on the late Renaissance or satire or English Romantic poetry and so forth. If they do, they can become chairmen of MLA "sections," editors of scholarly journals, holders of graduate professoriats. And they can extend their domains by spinning out a system of subspecialties around them. Any graduate student knows that the way to get a respectable job is to impress one's adviser with the promise of excellence and future scholarly productivity in his specialty. Professors, in turn, retreat even further into their fields, at best hiring still other "specialists" in "black" or "female" literature to answer the students' demands. But such expedients do not respond to the increasing need to understand and to change this society, especially among those oppressed by it. This is all familiar enough: specialization breeds privilege, privilege generates more specialization; both isolate teachers from the concerns of students and, often, of the society generally. And more: specialization, while it has helped to establish and maintain privilege, finally incapacitates us as teachers and as people. We read all the articles on Victorian prose, but can conceive no connection between Matthew Arnold and the disintegration of ghetto schools; we can point to the subtleties of Henry James's use of point of view, but cannot respond to the student furious over the denouement of *The Bostonians*. We are specialists who deny any relationship between our French classrooms, the draft, and the century of war on Vietnam—what has French culture to do with that? Nor does the retreat into specialization respond to the facts outlined above: the stringencies in the economy, the overproduction of educational workers, and the likelihood that the education industry has, for a time, passed the peak of its growth. Such factors combine to limit sharply the numbers of literary professionals who can in practice take the road to specialization, graduate teaching, grantsmanship. For most of us there are, in fact, no evasions of the classroom. And there, playing at specialist mostly aggravates the boredom and the tensions we have described.

For some, the alternatives implied in this analysis are discomforting. If professional dislocations and campus tensions are tied to the broadening of mass education, shouldn't we, then, follow the lead of Spiro Agnew toward cutting back on college enrollments, restricting admissions to his version of Jefferson's "natural aristocracy," reimposing the various cultural "screens" that used to bar the campus to all but tokens from racial minorities or working families? [11] Such a "solution," could it be carried out, might further pacify campuses by underlining for those students allowed onto them their privileged position and their investment in the system that has guaranteed such status. In that sense, it would place students in a position similar to that privileged faculty now occupy. On the other hand, its undemocratic and reactionary character aside, a departure from expanding mass education would kill the goose upon which most academics have in the last twenty-five years depended for golden eggs. And it would hardly pacify the excluded—to say the least. Nor would it meet the needs of the corporate elite, as seen in educational reports like those of the Committee for Economic Development or the Carnegie Commission or the Rockefeller Brothers, to deal with social dislocation by opening upward paths to some representatives of underclass groups. While mass education has helped to finance and accelerate professionalism and its attendant vices of inordinate publication and empire building; has helped produce the growing disparity between the concerns of professionals and those of students; and has even failed to be the touted

instrument for equalizing opportunity and social position
—abandoning mass education would solve neither professional nor social problems. On the contrary. There is no
returning to Matthew Arnold and the cultured man's bur-
den, nor to Jefferson.

Neither can we hold still where we are. The advice one
hears from faculty liberals is to lie low, not to rock the boat
in the face of increasing backlash from the right. Stick to
your professional specialty, avoid politics, defend academic
integrity, maintain standards. When a friend at a California university insisted that a woman be hired into his
all-male department, a colleague hissed, "The ship is going
down, and you're polishing the brass." But continuing to
do what we have done can only increase the distress to
which this book is largely a response. How will classrooms
be salvaged by more specialization? Or the continued substitution of professional imperatives for humane ones improve the quality of literary criticism? Or silence end the
subordination of women and blacks in the academy? The
voices preaching "peace, peace," when there is no peace in
America are, too often, the voices of academic tenure and
privilege: those who have already substituted professional
self-interest for the interests of students, who identify
what's good for America as what's good for the Faculty
Senate. For most of us, however, and for those whom privilege has not deadened to students and to literature, and to
the needs of communities excluded from the campus, the
problem isn't holding on to what we have, but finding how
to participate in change. Both self-interest and commitments to social justice lead, we would argue, toward alter-
ing our roles as students or critics of literature.

III

But how does one begin? With the separation of academic disciplines, for example. At once we recall the voice

of a colleague: "It's bad enough you want me to become a revolutionary, but you want me to be a sociologist as well. I've got enough trouble making sense of our curriculum." There's a certain justice in that plaint, since the departmental curriculum seems inescapable. Our observation, particularly of English departments in the United States, suggests that most have one common characteristic: steady change. But as often as not, circular change, in which the same basic elements are shifted about, given slightly differing weights, a "new curriculum" emerges, and lo and behold, the 1972 version matches—but for the "Black Literature" and "Images of Women" courses—almost precisely that of 1962. In itself, the impulse to change is healthy, since it probably reflects the perception many sensitive teachers have that they are not getting through to their students. For (and many of our readers can evoke the room and chairs and faces to fill out this scene) "If you let them take nothing but courses emphasizing close reading of texts, they can't understand why poets have different concerns or use different language—or even that Keats and Yeats wrote a hundred years apart." But on the other hand, "If you eliminate the requirement for genre courses, they don't have a critical vocabulary; you're forever having to stop to explain irony or point of view." "But don't you think it's a bit arbitrary to omit Blake from the eighteenth-century course?" "I mean, what if they haven't read *Huckleberry Finn* and *Moby Dick?*" "The dean just won't allow us to require more than thirty hours." And so into the evening. From which might emerge a choice between "Poetic Forms" and "Prose Fiction," a new requirement for at least one course titled "Studies in the Age of ———," and agreement to present at least one course a term in Yeats or Eliot or Joyce, and one, since they no longer quite fill that bill, in contemporary literature. "Next week, we should try to deal with the comprehensive exam . . ."

This is not, sadly, a parody. Nor is it without pain that one mocks it. For many good teachers find themselves trapped into this choice among bunks in the prison house. All of us have found that manipulation of the traditional elements of literature curricula—literary "history," genre, textual analysis—does not produce a "successful" undergraduate program. That fact, we would suggest, has little to do with the good will or, finally, the competence of individual teachers within a department; and the failures of the curriculum need not, therefore, be the occasion for personal guilt. As a number of the essays in this book show, it has rather to do with the social functions of culture and its transmission in this society.

For most of us, the arguments put forward to maintain the current divisions of knowledge and the traditional elements of the literature curriculum in fact contradict, rather than promote, our *own* interests as teachers and as people, keeping us trapped within the professional framework that makes every choice a Hobson's choice. Emerging from the sandbox politics of curriculum revision does, to some degree, entail becoming "revolutionaries" and "sociologists." The latter, in the sense that we would have to try, as a number of these essays do, to integrate our study of literature and culture with an understanding of the dynamics of class, economics, and history. The former, in the sense that such an understanding of society is developed, we believe, only in the process of trying to change it.

It was, we think, a growing consciousness of this last fact that helped lead to the uprisings in various professional associations during 1968–1969. Teachers and critics of literature could hardly escape the contrast between the sterility of their academic roles and the new sense of literary vocation discovered by writers increasingly active in the antiwar movement. Here was Denise Levertov reading her poems in a "sanctuary" for draft resisters:

> The same war
>
> continues.
> We have breathed the grits of it in, all our lives,
> our lungs are pocked with it,
> the mucous membrane of our dreams
> coated with it, the imagination
> filmed over with the gray filth of it.
>
> "Life at War"

There, Robert Bly, his hands evoking the terror of aircraft over Vietnam:

> Massive engines lift beautifully from the deck.
> Wings appear over the trees, wings with eight hundred rivets.
>
> Engines burning a thousand gallons of gasoline a minute sweep
>   over the huts with dirt floors.
> .   .   .   .
> Helicopters flutter overhead. The death-
> bee is coming. Supersabres
> like knots of neurotic energy sweep
> around and return.
> This is Hamilton's triumph.
> This is the advantage of a centralized bank.
>
> B-52's come from Guam. All the teachers
> die in flames. The hopes of Tolstoy fall asleep in the ant-heap.
> Do not ask for mercy.
>
> *The Teeth-Mother Naked at Last*

Or again, Allen Ginsberg leading the chants and songs at the Pentagon and in the streets of Chicago. Or Mitch Goodman striding up the aisle toward the National Book Award podium to denounce Vice-President Humphrey. Where did poetry *classrooms* connect with poetry that thus lived in the values and politics of people? What had our texts, our journals, our Modern Language Association to do with that?

The Little Bourgeois Cultural Revolution of MLA 1968 really began with the student sit-ins of 1960 and the organization of SNCC; Mississippi Freedom Summer, 1964; Berkeley 1965; and so down to the Columbia strike that spring, just prior to our meeting. American education, it hardly needed us to say, was in crisis. Just where in all the ferment, we wondered, were most literature teachers? To what extent could we further activate our friends and colleagues into the antiwar movement or into radical politics? Could the annual MLA convention—that job market and old boys' reunion—be used to focus the discontent people already felt with the profession, to gather and organize them, to move them into action? For some years prior, one or another of us had organized small meetings at the MLA convention of those seeking new directions in their teaching or research or politics. Now, if ever, the simmering could be brought to a boil.

Our initial thoughts about just what to do at the convention extended little further than "stirring things up." In Boston, at the convention of the American Sociological Association (ASA), we had observed that the focus of the whole meeting was the activity of the Sociology Liberation Movement, its hallway literature tables, its posters, its buttons and slogan: "Knowledge for Whom?" In Chicago, as the sociologists' convention progressed, police were busy bloodying demonstrators at yet another convention. The ASA voted to move its next meeting out of Chicago, setting a precedent that would be followed by other professional associations. It was clear that "No Chicago" would be an issue at the MLA meeting, but that was not our own primary concern.

In part, we wanted to put the professional association, with such weight as it had, into the propaganda scales against the war and repression of students and blacks. So we introduced into regular channels resolutions on the war, draft resistance, and repression, expecting at best that the debates—and a teach-in we later planned—would be educational. But we felt, correctly, that many of those attending had already decided about the war and racism and repression; the problem was not to propagandize, but to activate and recruit them. In the first place, we wanted to help people, help ourselves, work out the connections between politics, teaching, and scholarship. So we scheduled a "seminar" on "Student Rebellions and the Teaching of Literature." And we introduced yet another resolution calling for an end to government financial support of the American Authors Series—elaborate, multivolume, and often pedantic editions of the already established, white and male, American pantheon. If people saw such connections, they might be activated, even in small ways: sitting at our literature table, handing out leaflets, wearing our "Mother Language Association" button—with all its appeal to four or five types of ambiguity. And so activated, people might be recruited into organizational support. Some of us anticipated that we might emerge from the convention having made some useful propaganda, with a small group of people who had shared experiences and politics, and a mailing list of a few hundred sympathizers. Very few anticipated how far results would initially surpass those expectations.

Once we had begun to organize, meeting with a group of younger teachers and graduate students in New York, we made, in the fashion of the day, a set of demands on the nervous MLA: a table for literature, a meeting room for our seminar, a participant on a panel titled "The American Scholar and the Crisis of Our Culture." All granted. We held a large organizational meeting at Columbia the evening before the convention, and early next morning established our beachhead at the Americana. But in so obscure and remote a corner were we located that we decided to use our posters for directional signs. Florence Howe went around with masking tape putting up directional posters picturing Eldridge Cleaver with the inscription "I got my job through the MLA," and others saying "The Tygers of Wrath are Wiser than the Horses of Instruction," onto the marbled walls of the Americana's side entrance, near an MLA sign. Meanwhile, Louis Kampf and four or five others handed out leaflets, while the first MLA panel on the crisis in the universities began before a huge audience in the Imperial Ballroom. Leslie Fiedler was just launched on a plea to get cops off campus when word spread that the house dicks were harassing Kampf and other leafleteers. Kampf stands protecting "The Tygers of Wrath," which has already been ripped down once by an enraged hotel cop. The cop stands snarling and pushing at Kampf till he is pulled away by his buddy. Lauter races up to the MLA headquarters. "Look, they're harassing our people and pulling down our posters. And they're threatening to call the cops. You should come down and do something about it." "Sorry. That's the hotel's affair. We can't do anything about that." Lauter off again to the Imperial Ballroom. Fiedler finished. "Can I make an emergency announcement?" Granted. "Look, while we're here talking about keeping cops off campus, the hotel cops are attacking Louis Kampf downstairs. And they're calling the New York cops. We need some help."

Back at the side entrance: the Tac Squad has arrived. Bluecoats everywhere. Will Kampf move away from the poster? "No." "O.K., you're under arrest. And those two guys, too"—one of whom had replaced Kampf at the poster. "Get me a lawyer," Louis calls, as he's led away.

Upstairs once again. The panel on "The American Scholar and the Crisis of Our Culture" is just beginning. We caucus outside in the hall. Shall we disrupt the meeting? "How can they go on bullshitting?" "But Poirier has something good to say." "That's words." We decide finally to form a silent vigil line underneath the podium, facing the fifteen hundred people in the audience. The panel goes along. Henry Nash Smith, the president-elect of the MLA, welcomes us—makes him feel he's right back in Berkeley. Poirier cleverly attacks the language and content of the ballot sent out by the MLA office over whether or not to move from Chicago. At the end, Florence Howe is granted time to plan a response to the busts. She asks for bail and for a committee, mainly of department chairmen, to demand of the MLA that they force the hotel to free the three arrested. "They did nothing," she concludes. "As a matter of fact, it was I who put up the posters in the first place." "Will you turn yourself in?" a man shouts from the audience. "Of course," Howe says, "the first thing"—her irony lost on the distressed gentleman. We ask a few scholarly heavies to help us take containers for bail around—their jaws drop, but they are too embarrassed to say no.

At noon, the Tactics Committee, informally assembled the night before, meets in an upstairs room at the City Squire Motel. For most of us, these meetings, two or three a day, sometimes on for hours, people drifting in or out, but a core steadily together, provided the most important experience of the convention. We must have radiated outward from the group something of a spirit of unity and joy, so antithetical to the usual desperate privacy of MLA job-seeking or the banal jollity of publishers' parties. People took us for a tight-knit, even a "disciplined," group of friends and comrades; whereas in fact, most people who made up the Tactics Committee had never even known each other before, let alone worked together politically— four or five of us from Resist and the New University Conference aside. People who had never been political activists, who had never heard of Resist or NUC, came and stayed and worked. And others told us, afterward, how that experience had reshaped their own practice and hopes

as teachers, how it had helped to lead them out of professionalism into radical political work, and thus, often,
out of teaching.

On Saturday, the second day of the convention, five
hundred people turned out at the Hilton's Trianon Room
for a teach-in on Vietnam featuring Noam Chomsky, who
had that day been named as a co-conspirator in the Spock-
Coffin-Goodman-Ferber case. Many at the teach-in remained to debate what action to take to force the Americana through the MLA to drop charges against the three
arrested the day before. A march to the Americana lobby
ensued and there, with the hotel management in a fury,
the Tac Squad hovering outside, and baggage piled around,
Bruce Franklin chaired, in careful parliamentary style, a
negotiating session between fifty or a hundred demonstrators, many sitting in a tight circle, and the MLA brass.
MLA had claimed that the charges were dropped; they
hadn't been. MLA hadn't denounced the hotel for calling
the cops; why not? Were we sure that cops wouldn't be
called again? The brass stumbled, tried to talk quietly to
people they took for "leaders." Franklin suggested politely
that they talk up so that *all* the people could hear. Finally,
the "meeting" adjourned to a basement cul-de-sac near
our table, where the discussion broadened into MLA's
politics, or lack of them. It was not the first or last time that
the organization's folly provided the context of our questioning.

Next day at the business meeting, for example, we
found that our resolutions had not been put on the agenda;
they'd arbitrarily been shelved by the Resolutions Committee. The body voted to hear them, and all but the one
attacking the American Authors Series passed overwhelm-
ingly. But on that issue, all the old stalwarts of the organization rose to defend what was, after all, bread and butter. Never mind that they'd argued, some of them, against
MLA taking "political stands" on Vietnam or the repres-

sion of Eldridge Cleaver and Octavio Paz; this, in spite of the heavy government funding involved, wasn't "politics" —our motion was an attack on American culture, on scholarship, on progress in the humanities, and on the MLA itself. It was the only vote we lost.

The high point of the business meeting was, of course, the election of Louis Kampf as second vice-president, the culmination of a series of unpredictable but hilariously logical accidents: Kampf's arrest, the MLA's refusal actively to support him, its bumbling bureaucratic attempts to sidetrack the No Chicago movement and our "political" resolutions, the fact that the official "candidate" for second vice-president had already been installed according to the official program—but most of all, the concentrated desire of many people at the convention for change in the national politics they saw manifest in Chicago's streets, the professional politics they saw in the MLA hiring halls and official councils, in their own lives and teaching.

Looking back at those events after two more conventions, and from a very different campus scene, what strikes us most about MLA 1968 was the amount of political and intellectual energy our organizing helped to release. Out of the seminar, initially on "Student Rebellions and the Teaching of Literature," a number of small groups emerged, including one on women. Two members of that group, occasional participants in Tactics meetings, tentatively proposed toward the end of the business meeting a sense of the body motion to establish a Commission on the Status of Women, which has proved one of the most significant instruments in pressuring for change in the profession and in the literary curriculum. Many of us who had participated in Tactics meetings, high on our political successes, turned back to our criticism and teaching, seeing the distance between them and our radicalism. By June, many of the first drafts of the papers in this book had been prepared for a "professions" day of the 1969 NUC national convention in Iowa City. For many of us, that single day's session provided the intellectual excitement, the stimulant for integrating our teaching with our politics, that all the long years of graduate study and MLA professionalism had served to separate.

In that sense, this book is one product of MLA 1968. Or rather, of the movements for social change, whose energy got concentrated and focused into events at that convention and into most of these papers. We do not agree with everything in all of them—we think that Franklin is mistaken in his assessment of Stalin's analysis of world revolution, for example, and that Northrop Frye comes off rather worse than he should in some of the essays. But on the whole, the book emerged out of shared political experience, collective critical practice. And that, we think, is its strength.

IV

But MLA 1968 was a brief four days. Those critics and teachers who, through the force of events and the logic of their own experience, have come to see through the ideological pretensions of the profession are faced with having to rebuild their careers—indeed, their lives. Nothing less will enable them to join their professional pursuits to the political imperatives they feel.[12] Bringing about such an integration implies the development of a literary practice based on socialist principles. Tasks relating to the production and distribution of literature—writing, publishing, teaching, research—should be performed on an egalitarian and collective basis; their goal should be the fulfillment of general human needs, not the advancement of individual careers. Literature itself needs to become one strand in the fabric of a socialist culture. Building socialism, after all, involves not only a necessary change in political structures but a transformation of fundamental social relations—that is, of the culture. Literature and literary practice, in spite of the intentions of the practitioners of aestheticism, are weapons in maintaining or transforming the received order of social relations. Appropriating those weapons, making of them an integral part of the struggle for socialism, is at the heart of a socialist literary practice. How to develop such a practice: that is the problem facing us, not unsettling a paleolithic professional association, nor even creating a "radical" critical methodology.

In thinking how to move toward that practice, it is well to consider just how artificially *narrow,* in fact, the reading and experience of most of us literature teachers has been. Martha Vicinus's essay only begins to examine working-class writings in England; in the United States, we have a far more diverse people's literature often buried in obscure books and archives, in old periodicals, in songs, and in experiences which few professionals share. Until recently, old labor songs or poems, as well as the writings of blacks and most women, received scant attention. And even now, of the literally hundreds of slave narratives, only about a dozen are readily available, and the range of work and slave songs remains the province of specialists—and, of course, black people and their artists. Rebecca Harding Davis's "Life in the Iron Mills," [13] written by a woman and dealing with the struggles of working people, has, like the writings of many women, never found its way into courses or into the awareness of most teachers. To break out of our closed-in specialties, we might consider teaching courses like "Revolutionary Literature," "Imperialism," or "The Antislavery Struggle" [14]—in addition to courses in black, Chicano, or female studies—as much to educate ourselves as our students.

Such a course on "Revolutionary Literature" as is outlined in note 14 was taught by Paul Lauter at the University of Maryland, Baltimore County—from which he was fired. Bringing together such a set of books by no means guarantees the "relevance" of the course or even its interest to students. Of five sections taught over three terms, perhaps two or three were successful. The course seemed to work when one or another of two conditions obtained: first, when a significant proportion of the students and the instructor had been heavily involved in ongoing political work and could use the books and discussions to reflect on the significance of that work and its future direction. Cantarow's essay reports a similar perception regarding the relationship of classes to a "sanctuary" at MIT. Second, the course worked when the classroom itself became an arena for developing collective work (one of the central subjects of the course). In that case, students became deeply concerned with the meaning for their lives of Mao Tse-tung's *Talks at the Yenan Forum on Art and Literature* and William Hinton's *Fanshen*. Therefore they got involved in developing group projects on the books and decided to attempt a collective final exam. For them, the course became, among other things, an experience in learning how classrooms socialize us into private, competitive, individualistic modes of behavior and how ridden with problems and conflicts the attempt to break out of and change such social relations is. Thus their practice in the classroom was an enactment of corresponding difficulties described in great detail by Hinton, dramatized by Edmundo Desnoes and other writers of fiction, and theorized about by Mao. Only in the course of that practice could they begin fully to understand the meaning of their classroom texts, and in turn, the books helped to reveal the social, political, and economic sources of their own conflicts.

New curricular material is thus helpful, but not in itself enough. Few literary professionals are familiar—even as professionals—with Wobbly songs or slave narratives or women's writings, because they have not participated in the struggles of such people. Thus, when we read in Mao Tse-tung that the primary task for writers and artists is "to understand people and know them well," our tendency, even if we take the phrase seriously, is to put an academic's gloss on "understand" and "know," and thus to think of becoming specialists in folklore or popular culture. But the lives of oppressed people are only partly articulated in art forms, as they are partly in organizational forms like unions or workers' study groups.[15] It is difficult for literary intellectuals to conceive of "culture" as inclusive of anything other than formal artistic or intellectual productions, objects in museums or words in books. These are, after all, bread and butter. Anthropologists have had a much wider conception of the notion: the way people conduct their lives within societies and institutions. Historically, the narrowing of the notion of culture to "the best that has been thought or said" (or painted or composed) was part of the same development—the rise of a large middle-class reading public—which gave criticism its important social function. Criticism gave expression to and articulated the ideologies for those forces which determined what was culture, and what not. For the members of the middle classes, the ideologies and valuations taught them by criticism became valuable commodities to possess, distinguishing them from those lower in the social scale. Restricting culture to "reading artifacts," as Raymond Williams calls them, devalues the cultural activity of large social sectors. Indeed, it falsifies reality, for as Howe's and Labov's essays show so vividly, amongst working-class and black youth, for example, there is a rich verbal culture—yet few feel the need to write. To know such people "well," and especially to understand the roles artworks play in their lives, one cannot, we believe, remain isolated behind expertise and professional distance. Can one grasp the force of "Oh, Freedom"—"And before I be a slave,/I be buried in my grave"—never having sung it in churches like those in Ruleville, Mississippi? The person from whom we have learned most about the usually forgotten literature of working people, of the poor, and of women has spent but one of her fifty-eight years teaching in a college; but the literature about which she has taught us remains vivid and living for her, and she is able to talk about it with such intensity, precisely because it has never become an object of abstract study. Rather it is integral to a life devoted to organizing workers, to raising children, to fighting McCarthyism, to writing and to reading.

It may seem a hard prescription to propose that teachers of literature, trained by graduate school in detachment and privacy, should conceive as central to their *work* entering actively into political struggle. But one might consider that our classroom objective is to make literature a vital part of students' lives, rather than an antiquarian or formal study or a means of forcing them into feelings of "cultural deprivation." In other words, we want to change the relationship of students to literature in a classroom from that of passive consumption of culture to an active engagement with the emotions, ideas, politics, and sensibilities of writers and of others. When a book supports or challenges our own lives, we may convey the sense that what's at stake is not a job of laying on "monuments of unageing intellect" but a life-process in which books do shape what we see or hope for or do. But what life-process can enter a class on *Invisible Man* if the movement against racism penetrates our lives no further than the TV screen, and if our main concern in the book is Ellison's elaborate imagery of bird-shit?

It is not, to be sure, that curious and delightful classes cannot be built on such a subject. We've done so. And we don't discount their interest—at least to some students. But as we said a little earlier, the problem we are speaking to is not "how to be interesting on a book by a black" but "how to develop a socialist literary practice." And that, beyond engaging the literary work of oppressed people and of the socialist world, cannot, when one comes down to it, be separated from developing a socialist political practice.

In that context, we might ask how we—literary intellectuals—can better use our talents outside the classroom. Few of us know how to do agitational writing, though we have a vast revolutionary tradition to draw from. We have yet to learn a critical practice whose intention is to communicate with others, different from our peers in the profession. Indeed, the profession treats such attempts with condescension. One virtue of Franklin's essay is its openly propagandistic manner, its clear intent to agitate for a set of ideas in the most direct manner possible. We have been taught to be offended by the notion of propaganda, and shrink from it as by reflex. But all language use, as Kenneth Burke tells us, is rhetorical and therefore propagandistic. Before the rise of an autonomous aesthetic in the eighteenth century, hardly anyone would have questioned this. If we take ideas seriously enough to want to convince others of their pertinence, then the critical writing giving them expression must be agitational; if these ideas come out of socialist convictions, and out of a desire to join socialist theory with its practice, they should be made available to more than elites. This does not mean that we should generously condescend to "write down," but that the knowledge and mode of dialectic of nonacademics, as Labov and Kessel show, is different from ours. We too have something to learn before we can share those things we *do* know productively with most other people.

Two types of institutions are the major source of nearly everyone's experience of literature: the schools and the publishing houses. These institutions, in effect, function as criticism once did: they are the arbiters of taste; they advise people on the choice of books available to them.

Publishers, of course, create that choice. Ordinarily, they do so not for the edification of potential readers but for profit. Both the schools and the publishers have been instrumental in creating a situation in which people are not participants in a cultural enterprise but spectators at a performance. This condition is, of course, deeply embedded in the relationship (or lack of it) of work to leisure activity under capitalism. The spectator sports—including literature—the society provides for filling the periods during which people escape from their meaningless labor not only serve to divert workers from their difficulties they turn in a profit for the promoters (publishers, critics, professors) as well. We must begin the arduous process of transforming the institutions of literature. Their role as arbiter should be seized by people so they might learn once again, to participate in determining the directions their cultural lives are to take. Participation in the composition, performance, and distribution of literature, as Howe's essay suggests, should help to demystify the most oppressive of the received dogmas of the psychology of art: that there is a distinct and separate sense which waits to be pleased by beautiful artifacts during those times when the body is not at work. Surely, one objective of building socialism is the reconciliation of the division between the realm of work and the realm of beauty and play. Appropriating the institutions which reinforce this split is one way to begin. It is necessary to point out, however, that while publishers have profited from radical writings, and a few radicals—mainly blacks and women— have advanced their politics through the publishing industry, organizing for workers' control and to wrest political control of the industry from those who manage it has not really begun in the United States. Building socialist counterinstitutions—movement presses, community papers, street theaters, film collectives—remains useful and often provides liberating experience for academics. To be sure, established institutions try to absorb the best of the movement's work and thus deflect our attack from them. Yet socialist institutions must be organized both for their intrinsic value and as bases from which to carry forward the struggle to control social institutions.

But anticipating from such and similar political strategies the rapid development of various aspects of a socialist literary practice would be misleading for a number of reasons. The instance of literary criticism is revealing of some of them.

In the first place, commentary *on* literature develops dialectically in relation to events and to what poets, novelists, and dramatists are actually writing. Thus, ancillary to expectations of a radical literary criticism must be demands for a radical literature, or beyond that, a radical culture. In white America, a contemporary radical culture is just beginning to emerge—for example, writing that grows out of and speaks to the struggle to create a peaceable, egalitarian, and socialist United States. The powerful antiwar poems of Denise Levertov, Robert Bly, Galway Kinnell, Adrienne Rich, and others—and, of course, the fact of the war itself—these, not radical literary criticism, helped break the claim that self-absorbed, academic poets had maintained (despite the popular success of Allen Ginsberg, for example) over literature classrooms and literary journals. Also in the late sixties, white American writers began to find models for a political, and generally socialist, literature in the works of Pablo Neruda, Aimé Césaire, and Lu Hsun, among others. Closer to home, they could observe how black writing was much more fully integrated with the lives and struggles of black people. Much of the new black poetry—Etheridge Knight, the Last Poets, Nikki Giovanni, not to speak of prose writers like Malcolm X, Eldridge Cleaver, Bobby Seale, Anne Moody, George Jackson—most of these writings had to be understood as weapons in a struggle for liberation, just as

slave narratives, spirituals, and work songs had been before them. Poetry meant something different from what it
came out to be in a classroom when it was a means for
shaping the consciousness of one's fellow prison inmates,
when Seale could be arrested for reciting poems in the
streets, or when white poets gathered to "celebrate," and
thus to aid, abet, and encourage, draft resistance. As we
suggested above, literary practice in the United States has
changed vitally in the past five years, but we are only in the
first stages of developing a radical literary criticism, a program of radical literary study, especially among whites.

If criticism waits upon literary development, it also faces
a complex problem of self-definition. A number of the
essays in the first two sections of this volume attack the
notion that the function of the teacher or critic of literature is to raise the level of students' (readers') taste and
perception to that established by the "great traditions" of
Western civilization. The political meaning of that conception is analyzed in some detail by those essays, and we
need not repeat the arguments here. But developing in
concrete practice an alternative function for literary study,
and that in the midst of this bourgeois culture, is by no
means easy. Mao Tse-tung poses the alternatives this way:

> Consequently, prior to the task of educating the workers,
> peasants, and soldiers, there is the task of learning from
> them. This is even more true of raising standards. There
> must be a basis from which to raise. Take a bucket of
> water, for instance; where is it to be raised from if not
> from the ground? From mid air? From what basis, then,
> are literature and art to be raised? From the basis of the
> feudal classes? From the basis of the bourgeoisie? From
> the basis of the petty-bourgeois intellectuals? No, not
> from any of these; only from the basis of the masses of
> workers, peasants and soldiers. Nor does this mean rais-
> ing the workers, peasants and soldiers up to the "heights"
> of the feudal classes, the bourgeoisie, or the petty-
> bourgeois intellectuals; it means *raising the level of*

literature and art in the direction in which the workers,
peasants and soldiers are themselves advancing, in the
direction in which the proletariat is advancing.[16]

The essays by Labov and O'Neil lay out just how destructive the practice of supposedly raising black people to the
standards of white bourgeois language has been, and we
have touched on the conflicts such conceptions of teaching
have helped produce. But what, precisely, it will mean for
teachers in the United States to help "raise the level of
literature and art in the direction in which" oppressed and
exploited groups in this country are moving isn't at all
simple to define. In attacking "the courtly Muses of
Europe," Emerson undoubtedly performed some such
function for American nationalism; similarly, in prose
like his 1855 "Preface" and "Democratic Vistas," Whitman
tried to point the artistic directions an egalitarian democracy would entail. It is much easier to perform the traditional office of critic, to interpret a more or less fixed body
of material to students, to "lay on" them an established
tradition and its monuments than to try to criticize literature in its changing, complex relationships to movements
for social change, to aid and encourage people in their
struggle to articulate their needs, anger, vision. That last,
surely, "is no country for old men." In doing the first, one
has the security of a rich storekeeper filling sacks with
penny candy: there's lots, and it is nothing to you if the bag
breaks or if some sticks. But the last, as we've been insisting, demands at least the risks of participation in action
for change, commitment to a future yet to be shaped
rather than tenure in a past simply to be ordered. Those
of us who have left, or been driven out of, the literary
profession can't really anticipate when or whether we will
return, "settle down," have a job. What we're suggesting,
in short, is that there aren't any formulas—for career or
paper or classroom—for anyone who would, to borrow

another of Mao's phrases, "produce works which awaken the masses, fire them with enthusiasm and impel them to unite and struggle to transform their environment."

The tone of that quotation is, we need hardly point out, quite alien to most of us even as writers and readers of this book. And that fact points up a third reason that a radical criticism may be slow to develop in the United States. The confident tone of Mao's statement reflects both the demands and the hopes of revolutionary communism in China. Literature would teach people to struggle, to identify enemy and strength within and without, or it could have no place in that massive and consuming conflict. With us, the reading of literature can play some very different functions, as essays like those of Ellis, Delany, and Cantarow demonstrate. If Mao's phrase evokes, for some, a sneer, it may not be because they deplore the idea of accepting a political function for literature but because they perceive that, mostly, in our culture the reading of literature is pacifying, that it often separates people from action instead of leading them into it. That is by no means necessary, as Howe's essay suggests. But even "revolutionary literature," including Mao, or *Man's Fate*, or Malcolm's *Autobiography*, can become just another commodity, the latest rage after the thrill of *The Female Eunuch*, the sniffles of *Love Story*, or indeed, the ironies of Donne and the symbols of Yeats.

We would not be mistaken here. We don't propose that there are simple, direct, one-to-one relationships between literature and action, between the poem and the shaping of a reader's sensibilities. These papers argue that such relationships do exist, however, that they can be opened and explored. And further, that in our culture—white, Western, male, and bourgeois, for the most part—one primary effect of the processes of cultivation is to diminish people's desire or capacity to act for change. Ultimately, the test of this book is not how many golden phrases we have turned "to keep a drowsy Emperor awake." But rather, how helpful our writing becomes in creating a humane and socialist society.

NOTES

1 Richard Elman, "Growing Up Teacher," *Village Voice*, July 22, 1971, pp. 7, 8.

2 Henry F. Ottinger, "In Short, Why Did the Class Fail?" *New York Times*, July 22, 1971, p. 33. Interestingly enough, Ottinger's and Elman's articles appeared on the same day.

3 The gigantic growth of scholarship since the Renaissance should be chronicled and analyzed in terms of its social and ideological functions. Here we can merely mention the role the division of knowledge into fields and subfields has played in this growth. Though Hume took philosophy, the social sciences, and literary criticism to be parts of the general activity of criticism, *An Inquiry Concerning Human Understanding*, for example, naturally divides itself into several of the areas of philosophy: epistemology, ethics, philosophy of religion. Kant formalized these divisions, and in the process fixed philosophy as the specialized concern of professionals. His claim that he was aroused from his "dogmatic slumbers," not by his general experience, but by reading Hume is of significance: here the critical considerations of one field relate primarily to other critical considerations, not to everyday life.

4 Aesthetics as an area of philosophic speculation is no older than the eighteenth century. As Paul Oskar Kristeller has pointed out, Kant formalized his predecessors' confused speculations about "beauty," and thus gave the science of aesthetics the status of a formal discipline. In the *Critique of Judgment* he claims that aesthetic judgments are totally disinterested. Kant's positing of an autonomous and transcendental aesthetic realm was, in fact, descriptive of the activity of the artistic connoisseur. Such activity was available only to the wealthy and leisured, and did not become prominent until the seventeenth and eighteenth centuries. Kant's definition of aesthetic judgments as disinterested ones implied that the aesthetic experience (and the attendant act of impersonal criticism) was of the highest kind. This notion later emerges in German Romanticism as the concept of Imagination as a noble kind of fantasy.

5 In addition to the materials mentioned in notes 6 to 10, readers might want to see the following: Robert H. Connery, ed., *The*

Corporation and the Campus (New York: Praeger Publishers, 1970); M. Blaug, ed., *Economics of Education 1*, Modern Economics Series (Harmondsworth: Penguin Books, 1968); Ivar Berg, *Education and Jobs: The Great Training Robbery* (New York: Praeger Publishers, 1970); James O'Connor, "The University and the Political Economy," *Leviathan*, March 1969, pp. 14–15.

6 See, for example, Margaret and John Rowntree, "The Political Economy of Youth," Detroit, Radical Education Project, c. 1968, p. 21.

7 See Burton R. Clark, "The 'Cooling-Out' Function in Higher Education," *American Journal of Sociology*, Vol. 65 (May 1960), pp. 569–76. "In summary, the cooling-out process in higher education is one whereby systematic discrepancy between aspiration and avenue is covered over and stress for the individual and the system is minimized. . . . The general result of cooling-out processes is that society can continue to encourage maximum effort without major disturbance from unfulfilled promises and expectations."

8 See Michael B. Katz, *The Irony of Early School Reform* (Cambridge, Mass.: Harvard University Press, 1968), pp. 87–88 and elsewhere.

9 The processes of education described in these and subsequent paragraphs are analyzed in some detail in Florence Howe and Paul Lauter, "Schools in America—The Making of Jet Pilots," in Lauter and Howe, *The Conspiracy of the Young* (New York and Cleveland: World Publishing Co., 1970), pp. 206–54. See also Jules Henry, "Golden Rule Days: American Schoolrooms," in *Culture Against Man* (New York: Random House, 1963).

10 See Patricia Cayo Sexton, *Education and Income: Inequalities of Opportunity in Our Public Schools* (New York: Viking Press, Compass Books, 1962), and W. Lee Hansen and Burton A. Weisbrod, *Benefits, Costs, and Finance of Public Higher Education* (Chicago: Markham Publishing Co., 1969).

11 See, e.g., the vice-president's address, the main points of which we have summarized, of April 18, 1970, to a Republican fund-raising dinner in Des Moines, Iowa.

12 Soon after events at the MLA convention, Kampf received a letter commenting on his essay "The Scandal of Literary Scholarship" from which we quote the following:

> I am currently serving as Instructor at X. University, to whom I have contracted my soul in return for a Ph.D. My doctoral course work is finished. I need only to complete my scholarly exercise in irrelevance to earn my scarlet letter. I can hardly bring myself to do it, but I do have to eat. I have managed to keep my soul intact so far by organizing a self-education

group on racism—the group will flourish as a Free University course this spring quarter.

My problem is simple and I am sure you understand it:

1) If I do not finish the dissertation, I do not get a decent job.

2) If I do finish it, I get a decent job which will place me in the same dilemma I am presently in if I wish to keep the job—i.e., the department will require of me more exercises in irrelevancy.

3) I do not care about a dissertation. I do care about the ignorance on college campuses with regard to America's moral illnesses and their possible tragic consequences.

Faced with these three alternatives, what am I to do?

13 Only recently made available by The Feminist Press—P.O. Box 334, Old Westbury, New York 11568—after a hundred years of neglect.

14 Revolutionary Literature: Lu Hsun, *Selected Stories;* Contemporary Cuban Short Stories; André Malraux, *Man's Fate;* Ignazio Silone, *Bread and Wine;* Che Guevara, *Reflections on the Cuban Revolutionary War;* Ho Chi Minh, *Prison Diary;* Ramon Sender, *Seven Red Sundays;* Edmundo Desnoes, *Inconsolable Memories;* Mao Tse-tung, *Ten More Poems* and *Talks at the Yenan Forum on Literature and Art;* Bobby Seale, *Seize the Time;* Denise Levertov, *Relearning the Alphabet;* Marge Piercy, *Hard Loving;* William Hinton, *Fanshen.*

Imperialism: Conrad, *Nostromo;* Forster, *A Passage to India;* Lenin, *Imperialism: The Highest Stage of Capitalism;* Frantz Fanon, *The Wretched of the Earth;* General Giap, *People's War, People's Army;* Doris Lessing, *African Stories;* Vietnamese Studies #14: *Literature and National Liberation in South Vietnam;* Anh Duc, *Hon Dat;* George Orwell, "Shooting an Elephant"; Pablo Neruda, selections from poems translated by Robert Bly and James Wright; Robert Bly, ed., *Forty Poems Touching on Recent American History;* W. A. Williams, *The Tragedy of American Diplomacy.*

The Antislavery Struggle: Selected slave narratives by Pennington, William and Ellen Craft, W. W. Brown, Lunsford, Lane, etc.; David Walker's *Appeal;* Frederick Douglass, *My Bondage and My Freedom;* W. W. Brown, *Clotel;* Stowe, *Uncle Tom's Cabin;* selections from *The Liberator;* Emerson, "Emancipation in the West Indies"; Thoreau, "Slavery in Massachusetts" and "John Brown"; Melville, "Benito Cereno"; J. W. De Forest, *Miss Ravenel's Conversion;* T. W. Higginson, *Black Rebellion;* Whittier, selections from the poems; John Jay Chapman, *William Lloyd Garrison.*

15 The Hammonds, E. P. Thompson, Richard Hoggart, and Raymond Williams have given us a rich picture of the cultural role

played by working-class institutions in England. No work of similar stature and of equal political pertinence to the left yet exists about the United States. Melvyn Dubofsky's otherwise excellent book about the IWW, *We Shall Be All: A History of the Industrial Workers of the World* (Chicago: Quadrangle Books, 1969), sadly neglects the organization's cultural institutions. Blacks, however, have made an important beginning during recent years.

16 Mao Tse-tung, *Talks at the Yenan Forum on Literature and Art* (San Francisco: China Books, 1965), p. 17. Our italics.

I

"THY HAND,
GREAT ANARCH..."

NOTES ON THE LITERARY PROFESSION

WHY TEACH LITERATURE?

An Account of How I Came to Ask That Question

Ellen Cantarow

I. How Not to Teach It: Notes from the Margins
of a Wellesley Textbook

I was an undergraduate at Wellesley College from 1958 to 1962. One day I must write a thoroughgoing account of what it's like to be a student at a women's liberal arts college; I will have to reconstruct the experience with a friend, since I find I have repressed much of it. Its more general contours, though, are clear. There was the intense self-hatred, the contempt for the image deflected at us by the opinions of the outside world: Wellesley, young ladies' finishing school, ready purveyor of bevies of well-groomed, well-raised, sweet young things of fine background, good for weekend mixers at Harvard and MIT. There was, at the same time, the nearly fevered craving for what seemed a mecca of heterosexual cosmopolitan intellectualism— Cambridge: to which we escaped as often as we could via the MTA from Riverside Station, a ride that took over an hour to deposit us finally, awed and aimless, at the kiosk in the middle of Harvard Square. (From which we some-times wound up in a Harvard dormitory bedroom; sometimes in the Harvard library hunched over a book, furtively looking at the male students; sometimes at the Brattle movie theater; sometimes at the 47 Club, where Kweskin's band might be playing or Baez singing.) There was, finally, the educational reality that belied the finishing-school image. Wellesley, in truth, was at great pains to train professionals, just as Harvard was. Indeed, Wellesley would outharvard Harvard if she could, and she did: her grading policies were and still are notoriously severe. The central truth about education at Wellesley was that it didn't just belie our life experience as girls at an intellectual and moral suburb of the most prestigious male educational institution in America; it nullified that experience, rendered it invisible, as invisible as the life and person of the hero of Ralph Ellison's novel. To be very brief, we lived in a state of schizophrenia that we took to be normal.

When I go back over some of the books I used then, I find the kind of marginal comments you are likely to find in your own. Two years after getting out of college an increase of some kind of consciousness prompted me to erase many of those comments; not only did they blacken the books, but their intellectual impoverishment embarrassed me. Suppose I were to lend someone the books? This was a fantasy that moved me to erase some twenty pages of marginal notes, until wrist fatigue made me give up the chore. If borrowers there ever be, then, they will read the following lines from Wordsworth's *Prelude:*

> . . . some famed temple where of yore
> The Druids worshipped, or the antique walls
> Of that large abbey, where within the Vale
> Of Nightshade, to St. Mary's honour buildt,
> Stands yet a mouldering pile with fractured arch,
> Belfry, and images, and living trees;
> A holy scene!—Along the smooth green turf
> Our horses grazed. . . .

Next to this I have written, in commentary on the first few lines, the single word PERIOD, and next to the last lines, TONE CHANGE. Yet I remember having been moved by those lines, and having imagined Wordsworth's ruined abbey within its green, shadowed sanctuary. Had I ever been able to transcribe that emotion, I believe my teacher, an honest man of good intentions, would have been immensely pleased. But I couldn't; and my inability to do so meant that both of us, my good and honest teacher and I, were victims of the only pedagogy he seemed to know how to practice, through which was taught "the New Criticism." Some rare intelligences at Wellesley in fact achieved fame through the undergraduate literary magazine because they were able to transcribe the flame of feeling through the language of skilled technical appreciation. But their success only seemed to throw into starker relief the contours of the deficiencies of the rest of us, and of the failures of the teaching given us. For such rare successes implied that only a chosen few, an elite, really could appreciate literature; the additional implication was that they would go on to be the future academic professionals, the future teachers of other, future exceptions.[1]

To return to my Wellesley anthology, upon leafing back some pages to the section on Pope, my borrower would read the following lines:

> Nothing so true as what you once let fall,
> "Most Women have no Characters at all."

Next to this I have written, SPEAKER. TONE (DEFINE). And further down the page, THE EPISTLE—SKETCHES, PORTRAITS OF CHARACTERLESS CHARACTERS—this last evidently having been transcribed during the course of a lecture.

> Let then the Fair one beautifully cry
> In Magdalen's loose hair and lifted eye,
> Or drest in smiles of sweet Cecilia shine,
> With simp'ring Angels, Palms, and Harps divine . . .

Oh! those lines, over which I once pored with delight, delight at the sheer skill of the poetry . . . Even now, transcribing them at my typewriter, the old feelings of awe stir in me, awe at the very majesty and balance of Pope's writing. I needn't even look at the book: I know the verses by heart. In my book I have underlined "beautifully cry," and by underscorings I have reminded myself that the "*l*'s" of "loose" and "lifted" (to use the terminology of my undergraduate years), and the "long *i*'s" of "smiles" and "shine," and the "sibilants" of "sweet" and "Cecilia" do what was termed in my classes "bringing out the meaning." But in fact was this not true? Didn't the syntactical choices, the choice of not merely the correct but the brilliant poetic alternatives, bring out Pope's meaning? Indeed they did— "brought it out" so successfully that we were persuaded of the universal correctness of what the poetry actually was saying. Or rather, it is truer to say that we heard the poetry more as "music," and didn't really hear Pope's message at all.

That the lines moved me as poetry shows that I had learned something about poetry and the writing of it. In that way I suppose you might say my education had been a success: I had bumbled into Wellesley, an intellectually awkward, seventeen-year-old freshman, knowing little about reading except that it was something you did flopped out on your bed with a bag of potato chips beside you— and now I knew that there was poetry like Pope's, plays like Shakespeare's; that *Crime and Punishment* wasn't simply a murder thriller but a profound and noble murder thriller, and that the choice of the brilliant syntactical alternative, informed by the thoughts and feelings of the exceptional man, had made them so.

I am only half joking, mind you. I can't entirely deprecate my training. For example, that I was trained as a New Critic has enabled me to read, to look at films, to look at art, with a critical skepticism and with the ability to discern the ways in which technique bespeaks intent. On the other hand, I go back to the "Epistle on the Characters of Women," and the girl who dutifully wrote, beside the statement "Most Women have no Characters at all," SPEAKER. TONE (DEFINE). Where in my notes was that other girl, the girl who at once raged at being taken for "a typical Wellesley *girl*" and looked anxiously at her hair, her eyes, turning her head from side to side to judge effect before embarking on that wearisome hour's train ride to Harvard Square? Where was still another, whose energies, whose rebellion could in real life burst out only as a love affair, damaging to the soul and self-conception but oh so terribly sophisticated? Where was my friend who, horrified, afraid, ashamed ("I'll never be that, I'm not like that"), went to visit her mother in an asylum and never saw her parent's breakdown as having anything to do with what life really was like for all women? And where was I who listened, fascinated, angry, and commiserating, late one night in the dormitory when another friend, just returned from New York and an illegal abortion, told about it in resolutely terse statements, then broke down weeping? Where were we? We were nowhere. Rendered invisible. Most women, indeed, had no characters at all: how could nonpeople have characters? To tell the truth, I never really thought about what Pope's poem was saying about me, or about my friend's mother, or about my friend; the accidents of our lives were merely that—accidents, superficies even, aberrations, things that happened to us, not because we were women, but because we had stumbled into some wilderness the knowledge of which chaos would now better enable us to skirt it and lead "successful," "normal" lives. If someone had asked me, Well now, what do you as a woman think of these lines? I would have replied in the same vigorous irritation with which I replied to young men who asked me, Do you think of yourself as a typical Wellesley girl? "What does it have to do with me? Maybe it applies to some women, but I'm *different*."

During my four years at Wellesley I mastered the techniques of the New Criticism. Since that methodology is described at length elsewhere in this volume, I won't pursue it further. Instead I will tell briefly about some of the confusion and frustration to which my training gave rise. There was, for example, the fact to which I alluded earlier, that I did feel deeply moved by much of what I read in college. But when I tried to write formally about such feelings, a kind of paralysis set in. I learned early that I must write "It would seem that," "As it were," "It might appear," instead of "I think," "I feel." I was—we were, our students still are—trained in what is euphemistically called "objectivity." But is such criticism objective? Does it not leave unquestioned, for example, the sentiment that women are characterless? And does it not leave just as unquestioned Pope's sentiment elsewhere that great literature is written for and understandable by the privileged alone, that the rest of the world is vulgar?

I remember writing a paper in my senior year on that great drama of political jealousies and revenge, *Julius Caesar*. At the time I was pained and anxious to find that the play neither moved nor interested me. I was pained because the paper had been assigned, and there could be no refusal of the task. After weeks of frustrated attempts to begin the wretched job, I finally decided to venture on an experiment in critical writing: transcribing my confusion about the play. This I wrote out in honesty, with some introductory coy phrases into which I translated the embarrassment I felt. Unlike my other teacher, the one for this course, I am sorry to say, was neither a man of honesty nor one of good intentions. In class he was given to utterances about "humility" before the great master Shakespeare; his manner was gentle, even priestly. He had studied at Harvard with Douglas Bush, and his method, like his teacher's, was a laying on of facts in fine phraseology; a witty and informed cataloguing. On students' papers this man became a demon; his humility disappeared; his comments were often cruel, sarcastic. On my poor experiment he dashed the following angry words: "Your flatulence does not make your flippancy functional." You and I may now attribute this nastiness to pathology, but at the time the comment dismayed even while it infuriated me. My friends too were appalled, but there was nothing to be done. For one thing he was the teacher, and brooked no appeal; for another, we understood the "objective" message couched in the folds of the personal pathology: When writing about literature, don't write about your own experience or feelings.

Interestingly enough, we all felt that in respect to literature our feelings ought to count. We all admired our friend from Bogotá who left school to return to Colombia after several months of anger at what she saw more clearly—or more self-confidently?—than the rest of us as miseducation. "What does he mean, 'objective'?" she fumed on receiving a D for a paper on Thoreau in which she had written about her experience in the student movement in Colombia. "He's full of shit! What is reading literature about unless you relate it to your own life and what you feel?"

As I said, most of us suffered a kind of paralysis. "Criticism" finally meant writing about the stern tasks assigned you as classroom responsibility. What you felt about literature, what reflections on your own life certain poems might inspire in you, you wrote about in your diary if you kept one at all. In my senior year, since (in the language of the college guide) I had "maintained above a B average," I was entitled to write a thesis. A thesis! How could I refuse the honor? For it was an honor: it proved that we were grown-ups in criticism; it was the finishing fillip to an education geared to turn out future academic professionals. But when I had to choose a topic I was at a loss. On the one hand I was in a period of admiration for Wallace Stevens, but when I shyly confessed this proclivity to one of my teachers, he told me that, alas, so much already had been written about Stevens, why didn't I choose an author—more virgin, so to speak? I had just taken a course on Pope and Swift, and my teacher there, another soul not only honest but kind, divining in me a "talent for the eighteenth century," suggested I write on Fielding. At the time Fielding seemed to me a suitably recondite author, and the topic my teacher suggested—Fielding's irony —quite a respectable one, professionally speaking.

Fielding's irony, however, turned out to be a problem with which I was incapable of dealing, as I was with Fielding himself, who, having been made a professional responsibility, became incomparably remote and dull. There was, to cap all, the added embarrassment of having an adviser whom I had admired ever since I had taken his course on modern drama; his reflections were so vivid, so finely original! It seemed to me I must please him, though how I could do so escaped me, since my own thoughts seemed lumbering, pedestrian, uninspired. All of this, of course, owed much to the fact that I was a young woman student and he an older male teacher; the most personal exchange that I can recall taking place between us was an initial one when, invited to have coffee with him in Harvard Square, I arrived, awed and flustered, and he remarked, "You've changed your hairdo!"

It was a painful year. I dodged Fielding and the problems his irony presented until I couldn't any more, and then wrote a fifty-page, less than pedestrian commentary on his "technique," using among other sources Wayne Booth's *Rhetoric of Fiction*, which was modish at the time. Never did I perceive Fielding's irony as proceeding from any social circumstances, or Fielding's own political post as a place in which he might have acquired experience that tempered his literary attitudes. Nor did I even understand that most elementary of facts, that Fielding's irony broke down whenever he was moved to "benevolent" reflections. (Surely a useful study might be made of the relation between the irony of that author, his benevolence, and his attitudes about sex and social class.) Nor, of course, did I ever consider Fielding's female characters as anything other than parts of a jigsaw puzzle that might be reconciled by a studied urbanity to fit nicely into a discourse about "the comic epic in prose." Surely Sophia is a rather remarkable young woman for her time, and still more remarkable for a male author to have invented. All was device; all was a study of irony as one kind of literary device. And in my dull, harried pursuit of the "function" of such a device, I worried and bored myself, and undoubtedly my adviser as well.

Because this baby thesis was intended to resemble its mature counterpart as much as possible, I "defended" it. My defense was embarrassing, for I was asked by a professor who had never taught me but who was on my board what I felt made Fielding's writing particularly English. It was one of the more intelligent questions I was asked either in college or in graduate school: I failed to rise to the occasion. "What makes it—uh—particularly English?" I faltered. "Yes," the professor retorted, somewhat snappishly. "You know, what things in the writing deal with English national character, as opposed to American, let's say." Life . . . ? National character . . . ? I was at a loss: it seemed to me at once too simple and too obscure. "I'm not sure what you mean," I said. "Well," persisted the professor, "how about the fox-chases, Squire Western's estate . . . ?" This ping-pong match went on for another two minutes or so, whereupon the professor desisted. When told that I was to be a graduate student at Harvard the following year, she seemed surprised.

Surely she shouldn't have been. At Harvard—outside of Reuben Brower's courses, in which New Criticism was the prevailing doctrine—for the degree we had to master quantities of literature in pursuit of "literary history." "Literary history" was a concept that rested on a vacuous but absolutely authoritarian notion of historical explanation. You were given to understand that literary rules and "standards" originated in something called "the development of genres." The logical practice following from this theory was studying all the works comprised in any given "genre." This pseudo-explanation of historical development reminds me of the joke about the man who, on asking the sage at the top of the mountain what holds up the world, is told, "An elephant." "But what holds up the elephant?" "Another elephant." "But what holds up *that* elephant?" "Don't ask: all the way down, nothing but elephants." All the way down, it was nothing but genres, plays generating other plays, other plays generating yet others, which in turn generated still more. From all of these plays certain common characteristics were distilled that constituted "the rules of the form," a concept that, if you were to take the word of our most respected literary historians, was as perfect and as self-sufficient as an egg in a void.

At Harvard as at Wellesley, yet another notion was conveyed, almost subliminally, and in paradoxical contradiction of the hours we spent sweating over volumes of Lit Crit for our generals. This was the notion that literature can't be taught: that there is some special quality called "sensitivity" that you either have or don't have, which needs no teaching, and which, being innate, can't be supplied where it is not. The literary-historical origins of the myth can be traced to the Romantic idea of artistic sensibility, which breeds similar notions about the reader's experience of literature. The artist is a Werther, privileged in his gifts, set above common humanity by them, beyond teaching.

The artist is conveyed by a writer like Hugo as a symbolic Christ on the mountaintop or in the olive grove—gifted, and also damned because of his gift. When I first read Hugo I remember having been charmed by this notion. The poetry seduced me into believing that I too was privileged, special, simply because I was able to read and understand what Hugo had written.

At Harvard the myth of sensibility lent style to the exercise of donnish privilege. The style involved a continual acting out of the charade: "I am a Harvard professor, and in truth, an artist, a rare sensibility, a connoisseur." This charade, a peculiarly "literary" dilettantism one observes in Harvard faculty in all their activities, is routinely enacted by faculty members and tutors in, say, the Common Rooms of Harvard houses. There one balances one's sherry glass nicely, is terribly witty, acts out one's favorite literary hero—Samuel Johnson, say, with all his tics and his "special sensitivity"—surrounded by one's clique (in other words, one's graduate-student protégés). This is literature as professorial ego-cult, literature as the property of the privileged. It sometimes produces fascinating lectures composed of anecdotes skillfully conveyed through the professor's own showmanship. But then Walter Bate just isn't Samuel Johnson (to cite an extreme example of the phenomenon). And the student hardly learns, but merely imitates the posturings of privilege, when she or he is put in the position of having to commit to memory the stagy insights the professor has had. Alas for those hours when I sat in that lecture hall watching sixty students look up breathlessly at Bate, pencils in hand, then feverishly down at their notebooks, where they scratched out posthaste the received doctrine: "The suffering of the heart was the result of a neurosis of self-doubt and what he felt was the treachery of imagination. As he said in a moment of irony to Mrs. Thrale . . ." And if you couldn't get all of that down, you wrote something like the following equation: "suffering of heart = treachery of imagination."

II. POLITICS AND LITERATURE

I took Bate's course on Johnson in 1963. At the time I felt disgusted at what I perceived as a patronizing form of teaching, and frustrated in the confines within which such teaching placed me. But I understood my reaction simply as "disenchantment," and understood only one cause for it—that the university was "irrelevant," a "womb" where learning infantilized us. Acknowledging that my own restlessness and dissatisfaction were real, that the cause lay outside myself, was an important first step. But it wasn't until I became involved in the left that I began properly to understand the *contradictoriness* of my disenchantment, and the fact that "irrelevance" was an incomplete term to describe the nature of university and much other work in this society. Such work was, more precisely, irrelevant because it was alienating in the full sense of that term for those who engaged in it. If I had to name the most important things we learned through movement activity, I would describe two. First, we discovered that what we called "personal hangups" manifested real contradictions in our experience. These were, in part, the contradictions between what we expected to find in learning and what we actually experienced once we got to college or graduate school. At Wellesley what I read moved me deeply; in so many words I was told that my feelings didn't matter, that it was "form" that did. What I read often moved me to reflect on my own experience; I was told essentially that literature was timeless, above the petty details of any one person's daily living. I loved literature; when I reached graduate school I was given to understand that loving literature had nothing to do with literary professionalism. I dimly felt that literature must give life exaltation, specific moral sense; I was told that Western civilization dictated the values of pure form, of "universality." In graduate school I began vaguely to realize that the gender of the critical mind (as a friend of mine has termed it) was masculine, and that to be a critic I would have to neuter my understanding.

Of course the reason our real intellectual experience in school differed from our expectations lay in the social uses to which our knowledge would be put. This was our second important lesson. I had expected, in some groping way, that I would be trained as an intellectual—though in 1958, when I was seventeen, I wouldn't have used that term. After all, that was what all the rhetoric was about—"broadening your mind, your experience, achieving a mastery of many areas of knowledge." Instead I was being trained to think bureaucratically. I was trained to think that way because my learning was preparing me to be an academic professional, and academic departments are not free space in which intellectuals may broadly work, but rather, are bureaucracies. Thus my work became an imposition; it dominated me, for I did not control it and did not understand its function. I was "alienated," not only from myself but from the results of my labor.

In the movement I and my sisters and brothers began to understand why these two things—our experience and our work—had been corrupted, made confusing. We began to envision what they might ideally be, and how we might begin to effect a future in which our understanding of social goals, our experience of society, and our work toward particular ends would be fused. For example, in 1968 I worked for the Resist office in Cambridge, putting out a newsletter every two weeks. It was routine work, sometimes equal in superficial dullness to the office jobs I had held during the two-year interval between my first and second years in graduate school. But the routine of the Resist job had a social function that I understood, in which I believed, and to which the work I was doing contributed.

Thus I began to learn that work didn't have fixed and universal laws but was a social product, with social uses. People could change the nature of their work by struggling to change its functions.

On the newsletter I learned about the war and its causes. At home and in school I had been given to understand that war (like art) was timeless, cyclically recurring, inevitable. If it was historical, it was then something imposed on the United States and other just civilizations by evil regimes that wanted to destroy timeless values, the greatest of which was American democracy. I now began to understand that the war in Vietnam was neither accident nor imposition, but simply the most recent in a century and a half of American wars of colonization and imperialism waged in the interests of economic hegemony.

To realize that events had real causes, and to know that our own lives were governed by real political and historical influences, was enormously liberating for the way we understood our own experience in relation to history and politics. The proposition that war was inevitable because "human nature *was* that way" was enslaving: if war was in the natural order of things, then all we could do was fold our hands and resign ourselves to the fact. It was shocking, enraging, to learn the real history of Vietnam, and to learn about America's long history of similar involvements. But we also became aware that there was something social and historical that we could take hold of. Against genetics, fate, or God, one could not struggle, but one could struggle against power.

For women like myself the most important development around 1967 was the rise of the women's liberation movement. A group of young women had broken away from SDS and SNCC and had begun taking stock of their treatment at the hands of their supposed comrades. The writing that appeared over the next few years reflected the attempt on the part of us all to put the circumstances of our own lives into historical, political, and economic perspective. This rational reassessment of facts we had earlier conceived to be personal, or biologically determined, permanently changed our lives. In my own case, it changed the way I regarded literature and culture. If my own life was subject to historical and political influences, so was literature; and if my deepest feelings and responses were not mere whims, idiosyncratic and negligible, then I might begin to accept them and examine their larger implications.

It was during this time that I began to consider the possible connections between my own experience, my political experience in particular, and literature.

The summer after I worked for Resist, I went to Yugoslavia. It happened that while I was there, Czechoslovakia was invaded. Groups of Czechs on vacation were also in Korčula, a small, beautiful island off the Yugoslav coast. These people could be seen sitting for hours, mutely, around radios, often weeping. They could not return home, and the reforms they had been hoping for, working for over the past year, had been blasted. Dubček's whereabouts became, during the time no one knew where he was, a primary concern in the life of the group of students with whom I was spending my time. We went out to dinner, always taking along a radio; in the middle of conversation we would turn it on to hear the news bulletins that poured in, many of them transmitted by the underground stations in Czechoslovakia. One evening at about eleven o'clock, we drove to a far and wild, lovely part of the island. We were on a hill overlooking the ocean, which pounded on the rocks below us. It was very dark and still. We turned on the radio; it cast a small circle of light around which we huddled, anxious, taut, in the dark. Through a buzz of static we heard that the Czech population as a whole had massed in a passive resistance effort. They were blocking out the names on street signs and the numbers on houses, so that the police couldn't track down the activists. We gazed at each other, extremely moved. All of us, though from different countries, were radicals; we were all feeling much the same thing: that in their place we would, if we could, do what the Czechs were doing. They were our sisters and brothers in a common revolutionary movement against state oppression; we did the work we did in a common spirit. I had read about "mass movements," but had thought about them abstractly until now. The term was quickly losing any abstract quality it still retained for me, and was being replaced by a feeling much like what I had usually felt for a single person. When it finally became clear that the invasion might be successful, I felt I was witnessing the death of an individual I felt strongly about. It wasn't "the death of an ideal"; it was nothing as abstract as that. It was there, strong, unique, and terrible: the defeat of efforts that involved in a whole population that compassionate view of human freedom we are taught is at once individual and ahistorical. It occurred to me that my feelings weren't only like the ones I had experienced in regard to people. They were also like my feelings about literature. This isn't to say that I viewed the invasion of Czechoslovakia as an aesthetic unity, nor did I view *King Lear* as such. For such "aesthetic" enjoyment of tragedy, or the corresponding self-stimulation in experiencing tragic events, seemed to me not sympathetic but sensationalistic. Suddenly it became clear that at the heart of any great piece of literature was some profound human truth; any great piece of literature told of complex, miraculous relationships among human beings in society. relationships that might move one to wonder, to laughter, to tears. It occurred to me, finally, that such feelings of sympathy were much the same as the feelings with which one engaged in political efforts. It also became clear to me that literature had been treated at Harvard—for example, at those perennial Common Room sherry parties—with arrogance. Discussions of literature were foppish, dilettantish, because they reduced literature to the cultural trappings of class privilege and of professionalism. What feeling and passion, what social content, what suffering might have informed the poetry of a Brecht was dispelled in an instant by some pallid fop in a three-piece suit who, swirling brandy in a glass, talked in the throaty accents peculiar to Harvard men about the latest edition of the *Hauspostille* as contrasted with the second edition. Thus did literature become the property of a professional elite—whereas Brecht had written for men and women like those who, in the summer of '68, were blacking out the signs in the streets of Prague. Thus was literature reduced to mummified constructs like Aristotle's definition of tragic flaw as conveyed by the $25,000-a-year professor at his podium: ". . . so one may trace the tragic flaw in *Lear* by examining the tragic rhythm of the drama. In your papers you should graph that . . ." Thus did literature serve, not to vivify and clarify the history of societies, not to strengthen and deepen feeling, but to keep up "academic standards."

What I was learning in Yugoslavia was how I might relate my literary to my political experience. By implication, I was also learning how I might relate my politics to my teaching. At that time I had had little teaching experience, and had as little notion of the difficulty of putting my theories into practice. What was important at this point in my education, however, was not the divergence between theory and practice, but the acquisition of the theory itself —and indeed, it was not so much a theory as a vision. This was most often a vision of what teaching after revolution might be—a natural extension of revolution, a continual process of learning in which both teacher and students might participate, in which education was coextensive with work and both were unalienated. At this time an important event, inasmuch as it contributed to my sense of what such wholeness might be, was the sanctuary that took place at MIT in November of 1968.[2] The sanctuary went on for two weeks. In a strange way it became a total context in which all one's waking experiences coalesced. You carried on your learning literally in the same physical surroundings as you led the rest of your life. A life in community with your companions developed, a life that had a daily rhythm moving around very real, workaday matters: collecting money at intervals for food, establishing places to sleep, places to eat. At night you relaxed, listened to a rock band, talked about the politics of the sanctuary and about the day's events; in the daytime a single large room housed in one corner a class on Proust, in another a class on symbolic logic, in another a discussion about community organizing; in another, people might just be sacked out. It was the absolute negation of academic life as we usually lived it, in which every part of our experience and every part of our intellectual lives was compartmentalized, fragmented. One of the points about having your class on Proust in such surroundings was that anyone passing by could drop in and listen; in the sheer physical proximity of a class on literature to one on philosophy or mathematics was the suggestion that in some sense, and probably the most significant one, there was no arbitrary division one could make between aspects of knowledge, a division such as, say, the holy triumvirate, Nat Sci, Soc Sci, Humanities. There was as well the immediate sense that one's deepest feelings, as one listened to the testimony of the GI who had left the army, were similar to those one sometimes had when studying Proust, cell biology, English social history; that one carried on all aspects of one's life within the clear, full light of political purpose. The conclusion, a gut one, was that indeed "politics" meant all actions and activities taken in pursuit of a social goal. "Politics" as defined by capitalism was a single, sterile, and compartmentalized act in which one was literally boxed in, isolated from others, rendered individual in the ultimate sense of the word.

Such a definition was as mechanical and asocial as similar definitions of knowledge and education.

Such a sense of integrated political and educational experience was valuable because it gave people like me the sense that there were educational alternatives to the fragmented education we ordinarily experienced. On the other hand, the sense of an integrated political and educational experience is achievable under capitalism only in a fabricated situation. If I am to stand apart from that event and judge it from a brutal distance, I might say that it was education as theater—a little mystical and utterly different from the real and frustrating struggle of socialist teachers to convey political truths in their classes at, say, a state college like the one in which I taught this year. On the other hand, to be kinder and even a little wiser, I must say that events like sanctuary are necessary, as is the experience of literature, in our everyday struggle; for they give to that frustrating and often dismaying effort the vision, the exaltation, the sense of ultimate purpose that we need if we are ever to be able to carry on.

III. What *Is* Literature?

"Feuerbach," writes Marx, "does not see that 'the religious sentiment' is itself a social product, and the abstract individual whom he analyzes belongs in reality to a particular form of society." Literature, said my teachers, is art, and as such it is free of the excrescences of daily living; beyond our lives and yours, it is timeless, classless, above society. My political experience freed me to understand that nothing of human design was separable from the historical moment in which it had been produced, or from the class that had given rise to it. With this realization it became natural for me to question the political and social assumptions embodied by the literature I read. In regard to certain poetry, stronger feelings than skepticism were involved. It was with something more like mourning that I turned, for example, to Yeats, whose poetry I had admired and loved, and found that I could no longer read him impartially.

> Hearts with one purpose alone
> Through summer and winter seem
> Enchanted to a stone
> To trouble the living stream.
>
> .   .   .   .
>
> Too long a sacrifice
> Can make a stone of the heart.
> O when may it suffice?
> That is Heaven's part, our part
> To murmur name upon name,
> As a mother names her child
> When sleep at last has come
> On limbs that had run wild.
> What is it but nightfall?
> No, no, not night but death;
> Was it needless death after all?
> For England may keep faith
> For all that is done and said.

> "Easter 1916"

It was shocking to read these lines in the light of my political experience; they had once stirred me profoundly. I realized, with a start, that the very stateliness of their cadence, the nearly hieratic, incantatory tone, the largeness of reference to high religious notions—heaven, sacrifice, maternal values as eternal ones—the spacious, mythic cast shed by allusions to generic notions ("sleep," "limbs," "nightfall"), allusions whose value inhered precisely in their lack of specificity, their strangely ahistorical quality in the supposedly historical poem—that all of these things were what had moved me. And all of these things bespoke

opposition to revolutionary activity; all of these things enshrined (embalmed, I might say) the values of the Irish
upper bourgeoisie, making them seem mythic, eternal, in
the same way as my teachers had conveyed all of Western
bourgeois literature as mythic, eternal. Yeats's sorrow, his
resignation, his fatalism, his nostalgia, were treacherous.
They were the patronizing sentiments of the pious bourgeois who bemoaned the falling away of misguided souls
from the light. I identified, not with the poet, but with
those people of whose revolutionary activity Yeats had
written only that it had turned their hearts to stone. Indeed, I understood that revolutionary activity might in
fact embitter one, turn one's heart to stone, but it was
surely not the resignation, the dreamy sorrow, the pious,
paternalistic lament of poetry like Yeats's that would turn
such bitterness to confidence. Another kind of art was
needed.[3]

It was not that I went in active search of a category—
"revolutionary art." It was that around this time, after I
had left graduate school in 1963, much of the reading I
did was in quest of historical roots for the movement.
It happened that certain historical accounts not generally
considered "art" moved me in the same ways that art did.
The more I read, the more questionable those divisions
I have already talked about became—divisions between
disciplines, between one sort of writing and another, between one sort of visual expression and another. To the
extent that any particular artifact, poem, historical document, mural, film, or statue might express the actions of
humanity at given moments, the balkings, the strivings,
the active reactions of men and women against the press
of social circumstances, to such an extent was it moving.
I stress the idea of activity; this was most important. For I
had always been taught to believe in the abstract realm of
pure ideas, in the "power" of thought divorced from human
activity and struggle; and now I realized that it was only

by means of the actions of whole populations that ideas
might arise, that art might be created.

I will explain in part what I mean by using a specific
example. Two summers ago I read a pamphlet put out
some thirty years ago by the CNT—the union of Spanish
anarchists that went into exile at the quelling of the revolution. The pamphlet, entitled *Collectivisations*, describes
simply, sometimes methodically, the business of setting up
workers' industries and communes during the brief period
in which anarchism might be said to have succeeded in
Spain. The accounts are rendered by individuals from the
rank and file who took part in what might have been the
great work of reconstructing Spain as a democratic, anar-
chosyndicalist society. In cumulative effect, *Collectivisations* contains a human greatness whose effect on the reader
is very like the effect of orthodox "Great Literature." Let
me quote the last paragraphs of the final essay, which concern a small town called Membrilla, a town at once poverty-
stricken and thoroughly anarchist.

> La commune possède 3.200.000 litres de vin, d'une valeur
> d'un million de pesetas, mais on manque d'étoffe pour les
> vêtements. Si on réussit à vendre le vin, on achetera des
> vêtements et des outils. . . . Le syndicat de la CNT a 900
> membres. Il n'y a pas de cotisations à payer puisque
> l'argent ne circule pas.
>
> Il n'y a pas de bibliothèque à Membrilla. Maintenant, le
> syndicat a acheté des livres pour 1.000 pesetas et installé
> une bibliothèque publique.
>
> Toute la population vit donc dans une grande famille,
> les fonctionnaires, délégués, secrétaire de syndicats, mem-
> bres du conseil municipal, élus, agissant comme des
> pères de famille. Mais des pères qui sont contrôlés, car on
> ne tolérerait pas la protection ou la corruption!
>
> Membrilla est peut-être la ville la plus pauvre d'Espagne,
> mais elle est la plus juste.
>
> (*Trans.*: The commune owns 3,200,000 liters of wine,
> amounting in value to a million pesetas; we lack, how-

ever, material for clothing. If we can sell the wine, we
will buy clothing and tools. . . . The CNT union has
900 members. There aren't any dues, because currency
isn't in circulation.

There is no library in Membrilla. Recently the union
bought some books for 1,000 pesetas and is in the process
of building a public library.

The whole population lives, then, as a large family; the
functionaries, the delegates, secretary of the unions,
members of the city council, are all elected and act as
fathers—but fathers upon whom restrictions are imposed.
For we would tolerate neither bribery nor corruption.

Membrilla is perhaps the poorest city in Spain, but it is
the most just.)

Alas for the fate of the poor and the small, the brilliant
struggles of anarchist Spain which were crushed by the
Communist Party in league with the capitalist powers. Alas
for the spirit of the great and finally tragic time so elo-
quently bodied forth in the simple writing of *Collectivisations*! When I first read this passage, I wept. I tried to think
of a poem, a story, that might parallel it. But such parallels
could be made only in terms of spirit, as one might be
made between the greatness of human spirit in *King Lear*
and that of the Czech resistance. Prebourgeois and bourgeois literary portrayals of the poor, except perhaps for a
writer like Brecht, are usually of their powerlessness; the
force of feeling conveyed by a "Ballade des Pendus" or a
Germinal is grief or anger at the society that causes the
plight of the people described. Bourgeois literature, moreover, celebrates individual exploits, individual sensibilities.
It puts forward the perfecting of individualism as the best
of social goals. But writing like the description of Membrilla gives you a sense of the dignity and the power of
collective effort, a power and a dignity that appear all the
greater for the fact that the effort described was carried on
by very poor, very "unimportant" people. Nor are there any
names, editorial or authorial, in *Collectivisations*; a fore-

word simply tells us that individual workers on the projects described in the pamphlet volunteered to do the writing for the CNT. There is thus no effort at personal aggrandizement; the spirit of a collective equality described in the passage is borne out in the form of the whole.

Such writing as this raises points that I think are important to raise, if one can, in one's teaching: the nature of collective work as opposed to individual competitiveness in American education and the general society; the nature of personality and individuality in such work; the notion of "individual initiative." Writing like *Collectivisations* could be introduced in a course, say, on work and art; American examples of such writing are the slave narratives and records of slave rebellions. Works like the ones mentioned above—by Brecht, by Zola, by Villon—works that raise questions about class and the nature of struggle, could be brought in to serve as contrast or substantiation.

But one teaches literature that represents collective effort because one has been moved, through one's own experience, by the dignity, the humaneness, and the power of such efforts. The question is whether one can translate that feeling in such a way that it will similarly move one's students. To answer very briefly, I don't believe that it is possible, in the confines of a classroom, to persuade students who have no experience of such struggles that they are desirable—let alone transforming.

This year I taught a book that is relatively unknown by people in the field of literature; certainly it isn't one of those books you would consider "literary" in the usual sense of the term. This book is Bill Haywood's autobiography; I taught it in my English composition course at the University of Massachusetts, Boston, where the students are petty-bourgeois and working-class. Bill Haywood was the founder of the Industrial Workers of the World, sometimes known as the Wobblies. The IWW, active in America near the beginning of this century, galvanized the energies of thousands of workers. It represented the only *movement* I would consider revolutionary at that time. The AF of L was explicitly an organization of compromise with capitalism.[4] The Socialist Party was frequently reformist. For the movement of the sixties, the IWW, in its actions and its declared goals, seems the only direct historical ancestor. Haywood's book moved me profoundly. For one thing, I had been greatly concerned with the question of the importance of national organization in radical politics; Haywood's book described, in relation to a historically significant movement, the details of organizational work. For another thing, I had been concerned with the notion of working-class culture. I had asked myself whether revolutionary art was possible in America. And by revolutionary art I meant art that responded primarily, not to the need for individual expression imposed on artists by bourgeois society, but to the need for collective expression called forth by collective struggle.[5] I meant, moreover, art that responded neither latently nor manifestly to the imperatives of the publishers' market, but instead responded to the imperatives of the movement out of which it arose.[6] Finally, I meant art whose style expressed the culture of the struggling class, not art that slavishly imitated the style of the class in power. Haywood's book was all of these. Its style was not literary in the bourgeois sense of the word. Yarn-spinning, discursive, associative, it came straight out of Western American agrarian and proletarian culture. It grew out of collective struggles; it was written for revolutionaries. (Otherwise, why the detailed descriptions of the work of setting up organization or IWW offices?) Moreover, although Haywood, a single person, had written it, the character that the writing bodied forth was collective. For surprisingly, one learns very little about Haywood's individual, personal progress in politics; what is related is related sparingly, drily, without egotism.

My students' reactions to the book were mixed. Nearly

all of them were shocked to learn that what their history books had told them about unions had simply ignored the struggles of the IWW. They were particularly surprised to find that Gompers, touted in their high school textbooks as a great hero, had been instrumental in smearing the IWW and had worked in collusion with the government to help destroy the union. Again, nearly all the students were confused by the style of the book. A remark made in both of my classes was that the book didn't "seem like literature." I interpreted the remark to mean that the book didn't have a story line, and in particular didn't present a continuous record of individual development and self-involvement. But finding this out for sure was difficult, since it was nearly impossible for my students to discuss the book directly.* I found that our discussions revolved around the questions raised by the book, but continually veered away from the book's specific content. Thus we spent several sessions in which some students heatedly debated the following questions: Should the miners own the mines? Should secretaries run offices? Should working people in general control and run their workplaces? What is the nature of work in the first place? Why is most work boring? What makes work different from your hobby? How could being on the job be like working at home on your hobby? I imagine it was a feat in the first place to have raised the issue of workers' control and to have continued discussion of the issue over several class sessions. On the other hand, it was impossible to discuss the content of Haywood's descriptions of IWW struggles, of particular instances described in the book in which miners *had* attempted to control their workplaces. A simple explanation for my students' inability to talk about these things was that some of them simply didn't read much of the book.

---

* It was difficult for them to discuss any reading directly, but I had better success with things they found more appropriate for discussion in a "real English class."

In conference with them I learned that many, in particular the women, had found the book boring. My private conclusion was that they found union struggles remote. Few of them had had any direct experience with unions. Those few whose parents belonged to unions said that their parents didn't attend union meetings. In the case of the women, I understood that union battles were even more abstract for them, practice in unions being as sexist, as exclusionary, as in other American institutions. But then again I received a few really impassioned papers the sentiments of which could not have been feigned. One student, born in Lawrence, wanted to go back to that town to talk with old people who might have been involved in the great strike of 1912, in which Haywood was a leader.

I can draw few conclusions for certain from my experience in teaching Haywood's book, but one thing was sure: Haywood's politics made my students very nervous, and this was predictable, given the rampant anticommunism of the neighborhoods in which they lived, the pervasiveness of cold-war ideas in their communities. The absence from the campus of radical activities that might arouse the sympathies of the mass of students and galvanize their energies ensured, moreover, that the left would continue to be remote from their experience.

IV. TEACHING AND THE PROFESSION

In a paradoxical way my political convictions and my desire to put them into practice have reinvigorated my interest in teaching, but at the same time they have sharpened the difficulties of teaching. Some idea of the sorts of difficulties involved may be conveyed if I describe a typical day in the life of radical junior faculty at the University of Massachusetts. In the morning I go to my mailbox, read a memorandum that tells me the chancellor has suggested that an additional college be added to the university, one that will "serve the community" by setting up vocational programs for the "underprivileged" into whose neighborhood U Mass will be moving in two years. (Translation: the Voc Tech college is a sop that will be thrown to the angry black residents of Columbia Point, a housing project the white state university has invaded. At the same time the Voc Tech program will be useful to the state; as it cools out popular discontent, it will channel the working- and subsistence-class blacks of Columbia Point right into the slots the economy cranks out as "appropriate" for them.) After reading my mail I go to teach my class. In it we discuss General Hershey's Channeling Memo; unlike my former students at Harvard, my present class hasn't yet had the news that those deferments they thought they were ripping off the system were planned by Hershey, when he headed the Selective Service, as being "in the national interest." "Why," says one indignant male student, "that's just like communism!" (Translation in terms of classroom success/failure scale: unparalleled initial success.) We then talk about Kafka's *Metamorphosis,* and the middle-class family under the pressure of work like Gregor's. Two students glower and say *their* lives are nothing like Gregor's, and their parents, unlike Gregor's, have worked hard; they have worked so that they, the children, may have the good things of life, part of which U Mass is. Two others warmly argue against the first; the rest sit mutely, in various attitudes of interest, humor, boredom, resentment. I keep my mouth closed, since in some sense— though perhaps a meager one U Mass may in fact repre- sent for some of them a step up. The students, of course, see no connection between the Channeling Memo and *The Metamorphosis.* Talking about the connections is a lay-on that may or may not spark in a week, a month, a year, several years. In order to make the notion of chan- neling immediate, some other device, a game, a bout of role-playing, or some such thing is needed, but for the moment I am stumped.

I have lunch with some other junior faculty. We bull-shit; our conversation is touched with accents of heavy irony about the precariousness of our position at the school, and about what we perceive as our failures in the classroom. (The undercurrent in all of our conversations is an intense seriousness about our teaching; indeed, a seriousness so intense, so pregnant with sometimes bitter concern, that irony becomes a refuge, a stay against ulti-mate discouragement.) At lunch on this particular day we make brief, wry speculations about the chances that we will be kept on for next year, given the current budget crisis. I talk with another friend about the women's studies course to be proposed for next semester to the curriculum committee, which is almost entirely male: "Literary Images of Women," because impeccably straight, may get through again for next year, as may two others equally conventional. We talk briefly about the idea of blasting part of the chancellor's tracking plans for "the under-privileged" by having welfare and working mothers get course credit at U Mass for learning how to set up and run community day-care centers without the intervention of the growing day-care franchise business. But we drop the subject: it seems "at this point," a phrase we continually use in such conversations, "unreal to think about."

I go to my next class, where I teach William Carlos Williams's "This Is Just to Say." I tell my students that I will show them how it is ordinarily taught. I run through the business about form and metaphor, ask a few questions about what makes it a poem; we spend a half-hour on that, have fun playing with it. I then ask, "Who's the poem written to?" We get into the issue of whether a man or a woman is talking. We talk about why it's assumed that the poem is addressed to a woman; we talk briefly about the notion of "woman's place"; since the class is predominantly male, there are many titters, gibes from the corner, and the girls shut up. I give a brief rap on the idea that all literature has social content. I reflect to myself on leaving the class that I should have given this lesson at the very beginning of the semester and built the whole course around it.

Such days as these raise the same questions. Am I a teacher of literature, or am I a woman revolutionary socialist using literature as a means of groping through the paradoxes, compromises, and occasional exhilarations that constitute radical political work in the university? Is there, ideally, no split between being the one thing—"a teacher of literature"—and the other—"a woman revolutionary socialist"? I should be able to say, "I teach literature because I am a socialist." But such an answer, though theoretically right, is too simple to describe the real circumstances. Again, what does political experience have to do with the experience of reading literature? I have already implied that I was unable fully to translate my own exhilaration about Bill Haywood's autobiography in a way that would make it meaningful for my students; indeed, in the absence of ongoing political work at U Mass, there was no way to do that; the task cannot be an individual one.

This last reflection raises an important problem— though many in the profession would consider it not a problem but a norm: that is, the nearly absolute isolation in which we all teach. In my department, team teaching by two of the junior faculty was attempted this year for the first time, and with success. But even in the atmosphere of a liberal department like this, it is hard to find that happy confluence of time, topic, and well-matched people which is necessary for team teaching. For the structure of the prevailing situation—in which this is only an experiment—fosters professional individualism, competition, mutual distrust, isolation.

During the year I was at U Mass, I often felt as though

I was in a glass tunnel: I could see the people on the outside, see their gestures, even see their lips move as they
talked; but there was no way of communicating with
them.[7] Thus in my glass tunnel I arrived at my office, was
shuttled off to my classes, and returned to my office, herme-
tically sealed. In talking to some of my colleagues, I found
that their experience, in degrees, was much the same. What
such isolation manifests, of course, is the power structure
of departments, thrown into high relief. It is, if you will,
the cultural manifestation of petty-bourgeois professionalism, in its finest distillation.

As I draw near the end of this essay, I am surprised to
find myself coming around to the very questions that oc-
casioned its original writing. In 1968 I had reached the
point I talked about earlier, where I was beginning in a
clear political way to understand the questions of work, of
my personal experience, and of professionalism. That fall
a friend of mine and I taught a course that came directly
out of our struggle with such issues. The course was about
the ways professionalism shapes the university curriculum.
It was an offshoot of two larger courses that received much
notice at the time. Soc Rel 148 and 149, as they were
popularly known, were a cluster of some fifty sections
more formally entitled "Radical Critiques of American
Society." During that year this set of courses, initiated and
taught by students, were the most popular at Harvard.
Total enrollment was over a thousand, and to the strike
against ROTC in the spring they contributed not a few
who had grown through them in radical conviction. In
our section we discussed with our students the nature of
professionalism, and the myths perpetuated by professional ideology—myths of "universality," of the falseness
of "ideologies," of pure form and pure ideas. To our
weekly seminars we invited representatives of various
disciplines; few of these were radicals. When we reached
the point at which it was logical to talk about the role

literary studies played in liberal-professional education at Harvard, I thought we should give our students something to read about why one might want to teach literature, and how it could be done. Because I found nothing to this point (a fact that itself bespeaks what literary-professional priorities are), I wrote the first version of this essay.

Our students liked what I had written. But I was talking in it not so much about why one should teach literature as about the similarities between literary and political sentiment. For that reason our students' question—How do you teach, rather than write about, such similarities?—was to the point.

The question was whether the course achieved at least part of what we set out to do. We had hoped that over the semester our students' attitudes about expertise would change; we would see them growing in strength and autonomy. We tried to convey the notion that the curriculum as it now existed turned students into passive recipients of predetermined professional and political values. Our basic text was *Education in a Free Society,* authored by Conant and other Harvard administrators, and for years the foremost exposition of the notion of "liberal education." A major premise in *Education in a Free Society* is that the United States is a country distinguished by the absence of class and racial differences and universally ready for the civilized urbanity the book peddles. A key concept is that "Western civilization" is universal—when in fact it includes only white, Greco-Roman, Anglo-Saxon, and European culture. In the history taught about that civilization, the masses are passive, grateful recipients of the discoveries, the productions, the acts of heroism, of individual men who, giantlike, all-powerful, masterfully stride forth to change whole epochs, whole civilizations. Literature as it is generally taught is used to present the same sort of notions. What do such notions serve to uphold? In my most immediate experience and in that of our students, they uphold the professional concept of expertise, a concept that gives one to understand that students are like children: passive, without valid ideas, they ought not to speak unless addressed.

I suppose that in the back of our minds there was some obscure notion that one of our students would stride forth into Walter Bate's lecture hall and, arms akimbo, call from the aisle, "Bullshit! What a lay-on! Now, you listen to us! What *we* want is . . ." Imagine how we felt when one evening, near the close of the semester, a student, astonished that we should suggest that he raise questions in a lecture course we were discussing, said, "But why should we ask questions? The professor asks our questions for us!" Thus did some of our fledglings cower in the nest, mouths agape, waiting for the next bit of intellectual grub.

Of course, in such expectations we were ignoring all our knowledge about the way political maturation takes place. We expected that what it had taken us years of long reflection and active work in the movement to understand, our students might comprehend through one semester of discussion in a classroom. Of the effect of the course on our students I should finally remark now, three years later, that it served at least to raise a few ideas in their minds. What "permanent effects" were wrought, I cannot say.

What the course meant for us who taught it was another matter. It came out of active social and historical processes in which we were involved.[8] Thus it was not so much a "course" as part of the active development of our knowledge about the need for and the forces of change, and it produced immediate effects on our lives. Earlier I began discussing certain ways in which I came experientially to understand the nature of professionalism. During the year I taught the course just described, I learned my first practical lesson in professionalism and in what its "standards" really represented. I am sure that the course I taught in the fall semester was not the immediate occasion of the incident I am about to recount, but it was part of a continuous process in which it was natural both that I teach about professionalism and that I have my run-ins with it.

A group of us in comparative literature had met for six weeks or so to discuss curriculum changes we might propose to the department chairman. The rumor circulated that we were going to present these as "demands." A countergroup composed of some of the chairman's student favorites called a meeting, one that became controversial through a story printed in the *Harvard Crimson*. The story alluded to the power issues involved in the conflicts apparent between the department chairman and us. The chairman was incensed by the story, and wrote a letter to the paper in which he named me as the instigator of trouble in what he felt was a happy departmental family. I rebutted with a letter of my own. Sometime during the ten days or so while this little storm raged, I went to see the chairman, accompanied by two other graduate students. The chairman spoke with some restraint with the three of us, making clear that he disapproved of my political activities and felt them incompatible with my professional interests. He then asked to see me alone. After the other two had left, he pulled what he obviously felt was his trump card. "Since you are so interested in teaching," he said, "I'd like to help you by showing you a letter that was written to me by Mr. W——, under whom you taught two years ago." He handed me the letter across his desk. The letter was in part a complaint about my teaching, relayed to the professor by a student; in greater part it was an evaluation of my teaching and of my personal qualities, by a man who had never bothered either to come to my class or to talk with me at the time about what he seemed to feel were my difficulties. It does to say that Mr. W—— had been bucking for a permanent job in the department while he was on a visiting professorship there. Reporting on his graduate assistants, it was clear, was one way of currying favor with the chairman; certainly he was scarcely interested in my difficulties and progress as a teacher, for had he been, he would have spoken with me and helped me while I was teaching in his course. On the chairman's part, the act of giving me the letter was simply a threat—indeed, a threat so thinly veiled that I was shocked at the crudeness of the gesture. I was given to know there was a dossier that might contain any number of notes and letters of the sort; in short, my chairman was reminding me of his power over me, and implying that I should toe the line.

V. Why Teach Literature?

The point of the preceding anecdote is that you can't say why you should teach literature until you have taken stock of the way it is used by men in power. Earlier, in talking about Bate's course and the Harvard Common Room ethos, I described the way what might be called "literary attitudes" are used to promote the style, in deportment, speech, and dress, of the academic elite. The anecdote about the Comp Lit department and my remarks about departmental professionalism at U Mass illustrate how literature becomes a means of preserving professional privilege, of justifying the bureaucratic procedures that ensure privilege.

Yet another, related use of literature is as a tool to impose on students the ideologies of classes in power. In academia, literature is made static: poems, novels, plays, are turned into so many museum pieces students acquire to paint an upper-middle-class patina on their lives.[9] The apology of liberal ideology is that literature "enriches" one's life. But this explanation turns literature into an adornment, an isolable unit that confirms the sterility of life under capitalism. The explanation presupposes a natural order in which only one kind of experience is "rich," existing solely to "enrich" all other experience, which is thin and poor. It is then possible to accept work, for example, as something that is naturally burdensome, onerous, or sterile, because there is always that other part of experience the given nature of which is to divert one from work.

The social uses of literature are illustrated by an interview reported several years ago in the *Harvard Crimson*. It seems that a Harvard senior was told by a GE recruiter who was interviewing him for a management position: "So you're majoring in English. Well, we like to have our men know something about literature; has a civilizing influence." In *The Village of Ben Suc*,[10] Jonathan Schell describes a Colonel Walker, an older officer responsible for carrying out missions in accordance with a strategy of 1968 that uprooted thousands of Vietnamese peasants and turned them into hopeless, demoralized refugees. This Colonel Walker, referred to deferentially by his staff officers as "the Old Man," "often listened to classical music on a tape recorder." Set apart from his staff by his reserve and his cultural attainments, Walker carried out atrocities with a bearing that conferred a special authoritativeness on his decisions.

The purposes to which it is generally put make literature, like music and art, at best ornamental in lives that serve the system relatively harmlessly. At worst it gives "tone" to the lives of those who carry out the power elite's most pernicious decisions, and rationalizes those decisions with notions like "fate" or "tragedy," notions taught with such apparent innocuousness in classrooms and through the critical literature.

Why, then, teach literature? Why not take to the streets, go underground, or form counterinstitutions? * Well, for

---

* I am proposing the alternatives the senior members of our departments are always assuming we "wild-eyed revolutionaries" will seriously consider.

one thing, those alternatives I have just facetiously suggested are incomplete as methods of change, or don't work. Even free schools, for example, simply isolate radicals in a way eminently convenient for the real universities, which can then proceed more smoothly in their normal functions. There are real, serious reasons for our continuing in academia as literary critics and as teachers. A hypothesis some people in the movement have put forward is that we are witnessing and participating in a preliminary or transitional stage in revolution. I myself believe this in some sense. Now, in all periods of revolutionary transition, or in prerevolutionary periods, it has been necessary that intellectuals criticize the ideologies of those in power. They propose new ways of viewing political relationships, culture, and historical causation. These new ideas diffuse outward, ultimately to be accepted and acted upon by larger masses of people.[11] An example of the way this process has taken place in recent years is in the diffusion and gradual acceptance by masses of Americans of the ideas of Noam Chomsky, Franz Schurmann, and other antiwar intellectuals.

To propose how a rewritten scholarship in literature might be connected with one's teaching, I suggest Edmund Spenser as an example of a writer one might prefer not to teach, in comparison, say, with Bill Haywood. On the other hand, Spenser, looked at with a political eye, might well be worth considering. The point is, far from rejecting Spenser, you now have several alternative ways of teaching him. You might teach *The Faerie Queene* as a web of Christian symbolism; as the culmination of a literary form exemplified earlier by the work of Ariosto; as the brightest gem in the literary tiara of the Elizabethan court (in which case you "locate Elizabethan attitudes" in the work and "relate" them to those exemplified by other pieces of writing). But this kind of teaching fails, I think, because it simply continues to project the religious, social, and economic notions of the Elizabethan aristocracy and the rising bourgeoisie as the only Elizabethan attitudes, and the members of the ruling classes as the only true Elizabethans. You might, instead, teach Spenser's work both as a particular kind of literary construct, and as a piece of writing that had a social function in Elizabethan society—more specifically, for the Elizabethan court. For example, a social function of *The Faerie Queene* is to substantiate and raise to the level of allegorical norm the standards of the Elizabethan aristocracy. I am fairly certain that students would find this topic more interesting than the question, What is allegory? For asking why Spenser wrote allegory, what it was used for, what class functions different allegories serve, is to pose a real problem with which the mind can grapple, a problem that can at once be placed in time and social circumstance, and that turns up real social answers as opposed to abstract, formal ones. It can also help illuminate the social functions of other efforts at mythmaking—the wastelands of Eliot or Fitzgerald, for example. The other problem—the meta-problem of "pure allegory"—is unreal; for one thing, there is no such thing as "pure form": all forms have social content and social origins. And not only is it false to talk about "allegory as genre," it is boring in the extreme.

I have used the terms "radical scholar," "radical scholarship," and "intellectual" rather self-consciously. In the socialist movement at present people tend to feel that "radical scholarship" is a bit of a cop-out; that people who practice "radical scholarship" are armchair revolutionaries, sitting by when the heat is on, or even joining with the forces that seek to repress the struggle against bourgeois and bureaucratic power. There is much historical truth in that. We have only to look, for example, at faculty "left" participants in university discipline committees. But there are other models, after all: Marx, Rosa Luxemburg, Alexander Herzen, for example, and in literary and cultural criticism, Christopher Caudwell and Raymond Williams. Their work suggests the legitimacy of, the need for, rewriting "literary" criticism as historical and cultural criticism. The process of learning about history, economics, politics, science, that this task involves in turn begins to transform us; for we are forced outside the confines of bureaucratically defined disciplines, and past the years of training I have reviewed. That transformation, the need to approach culture, history, economics with the compassion and the sense of real familiarity our new scholarship entails, takes place, my own experience suggests, only as we participate in struggle. After all, a major component of the radical movement of the sixties was shaped by intellectuals—university students and teachers —who, disillusioned with their class experience as professionals and as preprofessionals, went down South, or into the early SDS community organizing projects. In 1971 it is clear that dropping out is not a viable alternative, but that what is needed is the creation of an intelligentsia a large part of which engages in active political work.

This brings me finally to our most immediate political constituency: our students. Earlier I told the anecdote about teaching Bill Haywood's autobiography, and remarked that I could go just so far with that material in the classroom. I found that we were greatly limited by the absence of a student movement on campus. Now, I think that much can be done in the classroom with new approaches to traditional material (Spenser's *Faerie Queene*, for example). On the other hand, we cannot expect that what we have learned through theory and practice our students can learn exclusively through theory. When I taught my students about the suppression of revolutionary socialism in America, or when a friend of mine in the history department taught the basic Western civilization course from the perspective of the masses of peasantry and of common people, the response was, "O.K., that's terrible, but what can we do?" An honest response from the students: it made me aware that I was responsible not simply for raising critical questions but for working with some of my students and with others on campus to build a viable student movement. I could not accomplish this. First of all, I was not rehired. Second of all, building a campus movement, if indeed it is possible to do that at this point in history, takes not one person but groups of people, not one but two, three, four years. But for all the difficulty of such work, it must be done. For it is certain that revolutionary teaching, which aims at changing our students' experience and their conception of what they will do in life, becomes possible only in the context of an ongoing revolutionary movement. To be specific, in talking earlier about the uses of literature in rationalizing channeling, I implied that it was not only the teaching of literature but the channeling of students into various job slots that had to be attacked. Obviously, it can't be the task of this essay to lay out a strategy for doing so. But the student movement of the late sixties provides a recent historical example of the ways in which radical scholarship, teaching, and action mutually reinforce each other. While SDS developed as a national student movement, a body of radical scholarship was created on the sociology, the political and economic functions of the university. The dissemination of these ideas through a sophisticated, carefully documented literature created an informed population of radical students and young teachers who were able to shape and participate in courses like Soc Rel 148 and 149. It was around such knowledge that the many student strikes of 1968 were waged. And to show how curiously, how rapidly scholarship becomes part of the active knowledge of the general population, we have but to consider the majority of students entering elite schools today: for these students the ideas that the university isn't an ivory tower but is rather an industry, that it functions to channel students into class-related economic slots, that knowledge is a "product," are part of their intellectual equipment even as they enter their freshman year.[12]

Our responsibility as teachers of literature, then, in rebuilding scholarship, a new intelligentsia, an active socialist movement, is no different from the responsibility of our comrades in history, in economics, in biology. Our particular responsibility as teachers of literature is to act on the humanizing knowledge art can give us to construct with our students in class new, revolutionary ideas of culture, and to construct with them outside the classroom both an active socialist movement and culture. No doubt this is difficult. But if we falter at the threshold, we may wind up (to cite a prevalent example) in a closed circle of groovy classroom techniques. Sitting on the floor holding hands with our students, we will serve as living theater for the next swinging teaching manual of the Good Society, ten-dollar edition. And surely we want something other than that.

NOTES

1 More generally, that most of us came to college knowing there was such a writer as Wordsworth, and that we had grown up on the values manifest in bourgeois literature, is a fact that itself distinguished us from, for example, the students I taught this year at the University of Massachusetts in Boston—lower-middle-class and working-class young women and men.

2 "Sanctuary" was an important stage, at this time, in the development of the antiwar movement. To servicemen who went AWOL and wanted to make that act one of political protest, groups of people, affiliated usually with churches or universities, would extend the church or the campus as a "sanctuary." The importance of sanctuary was first and foremost that GIs who participated in it, and people who extended it, were willing by such an act of civil disobedience to implicate themselves in the swelling current of protest against the war.

3 Some readers will take from this that I am for something like socialist realism. This is not the case. I didn't reject writing like Yeats's; I came to a clearer understanding of it. It became more

valuable to me than it had been before precisely because I began to comprehend its social function. I was able to demystify it—which is surely something students don't usually learn to do in college, for example, in regard to Yeats's own mysticism, which is part and parcel of his conservatism. As for the notion of "another kind of art," I didn't mean an art that vaguely enshrined static notions of revolutionary activity in the way that socialist realism (which is neither socialist nor realistic) does. I meant, rather, an art that truthfully recorded revolutionary struggle and values in all their difficulties, as well as in their successes. An example of such art is Eisenstein's *Strike*, a film both the style and the content of which are revolutionary. The style preserves the best aspects of bourgeois Russian art—the best qualities of caricature and burlesque, and of lyricism. At the same time it exhibits the most daring job of cutting I have ever seen in film. A brutal, bloody strike scene, for example, is immediately followed by a shot of tiny, fluffy chicks toddling around in a barnyard; this vignette becomes the lyrical, symbolic representation of the lull and laziness, the sense of ease and playful exhilaration, that fill the strikers in the early part of the strike. Ultimately the film depicts the failure of prerevolutionary activity in Russia; it was banned, therefore, under Stalin. Our own sense of revolutionary activity, as we watch the film, is that it is necessary, inevitable; that it dares to strive toward justice. One realizes that it is the only just course to be taken toward preserving the compassionate, humane values of that ludicrous, sublime little vignette between the sequences about the bloody strike battles.

4   Gompers not only denounced the Wobblies; he facilitated, through his declarations and his alliances, the government's repression of them.

5   By the *imposed* need for individual expression, I merely mean the sort of thing Ian Watt writes about in *The Rise of the Novel* where, for example, he mentions the rise of private modes of living in response to the development of the bourgeoisie, and the development of the novel in response to the increased isolation of the artist. Watt speaks particularly compellingly in this vein about Richardson, who represents a neurotic extreme of the phenomenon of the bourgeois forced by urbanization into increasingly private, isolated modes of living. Richardson could hardly bear to carry on ordinary business conversations with his employees; he carried a handkerchief against his mouth as he walked through the city streets. In his critique of *Clarissa*, Watt does a masterful job of sociological analysis in relating the circumstances of Richardson's personal reactions to the social arrangements of his time, and to the form and content of his work.

Of course it is obvious that in invoking collective writing, or the expression by an individual author of collective efforts in which he or she is engaged, as *unimposed forms,* I posit the best kinds of revolutionary circumstances. The kind of collective expression imposed on writers under Stalin, with socialist realism, was a perversion, the grossest corruption, of what I have been talking about.

6 Significantly, *Collectivisations* is available only at the CNT office in Paris, a small, dusty, walk-up flat that it took me days to trace while I was in that city. The pamphlet itself is a paperback affair, printed on very cheap material. Bill Haywood's book is more readily available, but was published by International Publishers, an American Communist Party house.

7 The people from whom I was isolated were not only the senior members of the department, who habitually never spoke to me or, as far as I know, to other junior faculty. They were also my own peers, some of them radicals. Professional competition pitted us against each other in subtle ways. For example, when it came time to decide which of us would be kept on for next year and which not, which given full-time positions and which not, we tried our best to comfort each other in the anxiety and anger we all felt. But it had to get to one: the inevitable feelings one continually surprised in oneself were distrust, envy—the "Why did he get the job rather than me?" feeling.

8 At the time the course was given, the Columbia strike was but a few months past; so were the May strikes in France. A period was beginning to evolve in which we would develop the concept of education as a major industry, in which it was not only valid for radicals to work, but essential. For example, the radical curriculum at Harvard that year revealed possibilities we had barely considered earlier. It made clear to us that it was not only possible but desirable to work within the university to destroy its present values and construct humane, revolutionary ones.

9 Whether or not students themseves become self-conscious "collectors"—whether or not they ever read or quote Wordsworth once out of school—isn't the question. Many students at U Mass are in fact fairly cynical about literature courses: they see them as hoops they have to jump through if they are to get out and get what they really want—a job with good pay. On the other hand, the students accept the ruling-class definition of what constitutes legitimate culture and what doesn't. Their response to Bill Haywood's book—that it wasn't "real literature"—shows this. Thus the deeper and more pernicious effect of the academic teaching of literature—to preserve the cultural hegemony of the elite and to delegitimize working-class culture—is achieved.

10 Jonathan Schell, *The Village of Ben Suc* (New York: Random House, 1968), p. 96.

11 This is all somewhat schematic, I'll admit. I write it this way simply for clarity's sake, and because I can't devote a whole essay to it. Clearly the issue of how ideas get accepted by large numbers of people is a rich and complex one; certainly the diffusion of ideas into the general consciousness of a given class or classes in a population isn't a process to which one may give a universal formulation. Moreover, I certainly do not mean to imply that there is one element of the population whose task it is to contemplate while the other follows and acts. On the contrary, as I remark below, I feel that intellectuals must be activists. That they may beat a forward path in criticizing the ideologies of the power elite or in proposing more humane and truthful ways of viewing history, science, and culture does not make them a vanguard. Finally, a note about the idea that we are involved in a transitional revolutionary period: even if we *weren't* at that given historical point, it would still be the responsibility of intellectuals to forge a new and truthful body of scholarly material.

12 I refer to elite schools because they were the arenas of the movement in the sixties, and the movement's most immediate constituency was composed of middle- and upper-middle-class students. At petty-bourgeois and working-class colleges the notion of education-as-industry, of universities as channeling facilitators, is not current knowledge, either latent or manifest. On the other hand, my own students, and most students with whom I talked at U Mass, had absorbed the sentiments of the early antiwar movement. All were against the war; nearly all my students had participated in a demonstration. Then again, nearly none knew the history of the war; only one student in each of my sections, for example, had the vaguest idea of who Diem was. The implications for disseminating radical scholarship through one's teaching at such schools is clear; somewhat less clear is how those of us who teach at state and community colleges may help to build a student movement there.

THE TEACHING OF LITERATURE IN THE HIGHEST ACADEMIES OF THE EMPIRE

Bruce Franklin

> If you reproach the masses for their utilitarianism and yet for your own utility, or that of a narrow clique, force on the market and propagandize among the masses a work which pleases only the few but is useless or even harmful to the majority, then you are not only insulting the masses but also revealing your own lack of self-knowledge. A thing is good only when it brings real benefit to the masses of the people.
>
> Mao Tse-tung,
> *Talks at the Yenan Forum on Literature and Art*

He is white and he is male. When he works, he wears a tie and a jacket. He makes $14,000 a year for nine months' work. He is called "Sir" or "Doctor." He teaches one and a half hours a day. But he also attends meetings and gives advice. He reads books and articles and writes books and articles about books and articles. His books and articles are addressed to an audience of people like himself. He believes that he is one of the most intelligent people in the world. He believes that very few could possibly perform his work. He believes that his work is very important, because in every century there is a handful of men, and perhaps

one or two women, who have written great works that only
he and a few others can understand and explain. It is important to understand and explain these works, even if
only the "brightest" and the best-educated students can understand the explanation, because these works are supreme
human achievements. They stand above time and constitute the furthest advances of culture and civilization.
Nevertheless, even the great geniuses who wrote these
works had faults and weaknesses, and it is equally important for men like him to point these out. Thus he says even
more than the authors themselves. For he is the priest, and
his mute idols and unintelligible gods must speak through
him to the uninitiated. If it were not for him, practically
nobody could or would read them. And, alas, the vast majority can never hope even to get within earshot of him.
Nevertheless, he is a democrat and a liberal. He despises
the intolerant, particularly ruthless, avaricious businessmen and those materialistic, contented workers who make
his clothes, car, house, typewriter, books, and food. He is
for integration, and in fact, a black family has just recently
moved into his neighborhood. He is for peace, particularly
on the campus. He is for all freedoms, particularly academic freedom. He believes that he belongs to no particular social class, or at least that he has no particular class
interests. He believes that great literature, like himself,
stands outside social classes and their sordid struggles, commenting upon them with an Olympian overview. That is
why he is worth even more money than he gets. He is the
scholar–critic–professor of literature.

This ignorant, self-deceived parasite, perfect butt of the
satire he so admires, does indeed have an important role in
the twilight hour of the dictatorship of the bourgeoisie. He
is in charge of molding opinion as to what books are good
and bad, what books should be read or avoided, and what
we are to learn from the good books we ought to read. Now
no one, of course, would dream of making legislation to

force people to read certain books and to prevent them from reading others—which only proves that the spot quiz and final examination are more effective than laws. Only a totalitarian state would expect people to read Mao, who tells them that they are the real heroes of history, and that "it's right to rebel" because the earth belongs to the people. Only a highly civilized professor would compel people to read T. S. Eliot, who tells them that they are trash stuffed with straw, or Jonathan Swift, who tells them that they are shit-smeared monkeys.

The historic mission of the scholar–critic–professor of literature is none other than the shaping of values. At this point in the crisis of bourgeois ideology, these are the values he is to teach:

First, there is the over-all relationship between art and life. Great literary art transcends life. That is, literary achievements are more significant than social or political actions. Somehow it even follows from this that the *study* of great literary achievements is more significant than taking social or political action. In judging a professor, his colleagues should ask how many students he has won to the serious study of literature. If he has advised his students to do something else with what they have learned from literature, he might well be regarded as a traitor to the profession. How should great literary art be studied? Why, it should be studied on what is called "its own terms," that is, as a privately created world independent of the social and political context within which it developed. To complete the exaltation of the literary work, one must hold that its social, political, and moral effects have nothing whatsoever to do with its value. That is, either the work doesn't influence behavior at all, or if it does, that behavior casts no reflection back on the work itself. The effects are merely incidental. Whether they are good or bad has nothing to do with whether the work itself is good or bad. In fact, "the reaction to the work" usually refers to what re-

viewers and other critics *said* about it. To pay attention to
the social and political effects of the work would be to vul-
garize or degrade it "as literature." After all, the literary
critic has no credentials for making nonliterary judgments.

Then there is the relation between human "nature" and
art. The primary assumption here is that human "nature"
has always been, and will always remain, essentially the
same. It follows that literature is "timeless." The most essential quality of this human "nature" is that it's incor-
rigibly corrupt. The greatest works of literature are therefore hopeless, grotesque, tragic, or absurd. Hopeful works
are silly, naive, or, to use the most revealing term, sentimental. Good characters are often unbelievable, but no
character is too evil to believe. Desdemona is something of
an embarrassment; Iago is not only credible but fascinating. Only Dr. Pangloss or one of Pope's dunces could agree
with Mao that "the masses are the real heroes." We are to
join our view with that of Satan himself:

> . . .
> Mankind, created, and for him this World.
> So farewell hope, and with hope farewell fear,
> Farewell remorse: All good to me is lost;
> Evil be thou my Good . . .

The principal assumption about the audience of great
literary art is that it is generally an elite. This elite within
any particular society is the group most nearly resembling
the scholar–critic–professors of literature. It is the intellectual elite, not the people who wield real political and
economic power. No wonder that the greatest works, like
the professors who choose them, despise both the masses
and their rulers. Some great works are (or were) also popular, but that is quite incidental to their greatness. Popular
forms in general are "subliterary." Folk songs, mysteries,
Westerns, science fiction—all these are beyond the pale.

Since great literature is addressed to an intellectual elite, it follows that extraordinary intellectual preparation is necessary to teach literature. Further, the only relevant preparation is academic. Herman Melville was a consciously proletarian writer. He wrote about the life of working people on ships and in factories and offices. He never went to college, and he asserted in the face of the critics who sneered at him as a semi-illiterate that a whaleship was his "Harvard and Yale." But the qualifications to teach Herman Melville in a prestige American college or university are a B.A., a Ph.D., and, at the very minimum, an article or two in a learned journal. Who would have the nerve to suggest that anybody who had never done physical labor for a living was unqualified to teach Melville, and that working on a ship might be more to the point than publishing an article in *PMLA*?

The bias against women in the profession is open and explicit. Almost every major graduate school in the country gives strong preference to men in admission, arguing that statistics prove that women are a poor bet to finish and to become teachers of literature in colleges and universities. That is supposed to end the argument, because our graduate training is the only relevant preparation for this career. Yet most of the literature we teach has to do with the relations between men and women, and much of it concerns the experience of women. Because women drop out of graduate school to bear our children, they disqualify themselves from teaching that literature. After all, among the many questions asked by the qualifying examination, it would be preposterous to ask, "Have you ever borne or raised a child?" Such an experience is irrelevant to teaching *The White Devil, An American Tragedy, A Farewell to Arms, Tom Jones, Moll Flanders, The Scarlet Letter, Madame Bovary,* and *The Mother,* not to mention Anne Bradstreet or Ann Petry. And being a man or a woman has nothing whatsoever to do with one's understanding and evaluation of *The Rape of the Lock,* the poems of Swift or of Emily Dickinson, *Wuthering Heights, Middlemarch, The Taming of the Shrew, Pygmalion,* and *Lolita.* Only a graduate seminar could prepare one to teach the chapter "Eliot's Pulpit" of *The Blithedale Romance,* in which Hollingsworth declaims that woman's "place is at man's side," that "her office" is to be "the unreserved, unquestioning believer," and that "all the separate action of woman is, and ever has been, and always shall be, false, foolish, vain, destructive of her own best and holiest qualities, void of every good effect, and productive of intolerable mischiefs!" Hawthorne has his most ardent advocate of women's rights, Zenobia, tamely respond, "Let man be but manly and god-like, and woman is only too ready to become to him what you say!" The white men who pick their successors know deep down that Hollingsworth and Hawthorne are basically right. As Eldridge Cleaver beautifully shows in *Soul on Ice,* in our imagination the only fully rational beings are male and white. There are a few "exceptional" women and blacks in our profession, but wouldn't a truly rational woman or black be a bit of a freak?

But people and things are changing and being changed by each other. A male white professor of English and American literature at one of the most prestigious academies of the empire is writing this essay, aware of some of the curious contradictions in this fact. You are reading it, and you are almost certainly another literary professional. And as we found out in December of 1968 and 1969, you and I are not part of a tiny, impotent minority, even within the Modern Language Association. As the vast majority of the world's people begin to make history conform to their will, more and more people in our profession within our country join them. We reject the reactionary ghosts and monsters that have held our minds captive, and begin to see the world, including its culture, from the point of view of the oppressed rather than the oppressor or some supposed neutral arbiter.

To remold our ideas so that we can join the people and serve them, it is necessary to find out how we got to be what we are. We must practice self-criticism, and we must do this on the basis of objective analysis and a clear identification with the oppressed classes. What follows is a very primitive attempt on my own part to do just that. I believe that much of my own experience is common, and I offer it in the hope that it will clarify that of others.

I went to Amherst College, bastion of New Criticism, from 1951 to 1955. I majored in English, became an honors student, and received the appropriate honors from the English department and the college. It took me about a decade to recover from this experience, and I am only now beginning to understand what a grotesque exercise in a dying culture and class it was.

I was the first person in my family to go to college. Before I went to Amherst and during the summers, I worked in factories, large kitchens, and construction. I hated businessmen and people like them. Most of the other students at Amherst seemed to me perfect specimens to be groomed for their future business and professional careers. I despised them from the top of their crewcuts to the soles of their white bucks, mostly hating the smug tweediness in between. My wildest rebellion against the world of Amherst consisted of slouching around in a dirty, torn old leather jacket, not shaving, and not cleaning my room (the aptly named Dean Bacon sent me a letter admonishing me for living in a "pigpen"). I also fancied myself a brilliant, eccentric intellectual.

The point of our famous Amherst freshman English course was to convince us that the "real" world was merely perceptual, that being was merely consciousness, that symbols had a higher reality than objects, and that most people didn't have the faintest idea of the high truths we were privileged to learn from our extraordinarily brilliant professors, who lured us into knowledge with sly looks, bizarre

questions, and a thousand little suggestive ironies. My principal response to freshman English was to go back to my
room and throw things against the wall or kick the waste-
paper basket across the room, for which I became a noted
"character." But it didn't take too long for me to get sucked
into the game. By the end of the second year I was admitted
to the English honors program, sign of being among the
chosen few. Among some of the clever notes I took during
the junior seminar meetings, a few show some accurate perception—like a full page with BULLSHIT written in different sizes. Bit by bit, however, I began to lap it up. By the
end of that year, each of that small handful of select honors
students knew that we were the only ones at Amherst—and
among the very few in the entire world—who really understood the metaphysical poets, Alexander Pope, Matthew
Arnold, T. S. Eliot, and James Joyce. But most of the time
Amherst still seemed to me a fake world.

Senior year was different. I actually began to like the
place, something I now find hard to believe—and very embarrassing. I still wore my old leather jacket, even to those
thrilling but puzzling private conferences with the adviser
of my senior honors thesis, Benjamin DeMott, who now
seemed to accept it as just a little sign of eccentricity
(though he never seemed quite at his usual ease). I didn't
know quite what to write about, so DeMott guided me
into an attempt to develop evaluative criteria for distinguishing between "great" and "inferior" plays. This out-
landish project had the preposterous title "An Examination
and Evaluation of Changing Moral and Social Perspectives
in English Dramatic Literature." Its basic argument was
that in each historical period "great" plays present complex
views of human experience and avoid the "easy answers" of
"inferior" plays. It begins with a comparison of two Jaco-
bean tragedies, showing that the better play is the more
intellectually sophisticated and emotionally complex. The
next section proves that the greatness of Restoration

comedy lies in its "sophisticated complexity of attitude," whereas the drama that followed, written for the rising middle classes, was silly and sentimental. Then came the payoff—the final section, which proved that the proletarian drama of the 1930s was just crap, which we could understand by comparing it with Shaw's *Pygmalion*. What was so wonderful about Shaw? His understanding that "class terms are not the most important." I not only failed to see Shaw's own class bias, but even accepted his view of Liza's rise from the subhuman working class to real womanhood, i.e., becoming a cultured, civilized, refined bourgeois lady:

> The final significance of Liza's transformation is not merely that she has moved from one class to another, but that she has become someone who can no longer be referred to as either inanimate or nonhuman. No longer can terms such as "squashed cabbage leaf," "this baggage," "that thing," "this unfortunate animal," or "a lost umbrella" be used to describe Liza. Galatea, much to the surprise of Pygmalion, has come to life.

Shaw's greatness, according to my argument, lay precisely in his refusal to indulge in either "sentimental love talk" or "sentimental class talk."

How had I gotten to this point? Strangely enough, I still felt that in my heart I had more in common with working people, yet here I had written a monument to elitism and arrogance, consistently exalting antiproletarian culture and its values. After graduation, I got a job working on tugboats in New York harbor for about half a year. This restored some sense of reality, and occasionally I wondered about some of those brilliant ideas in my honors thesis. But it didn't seem that important, one way or the other.

I married a woman who had grown up on a tobacco farm in North Carolina, who had had a far less thorough and sophisticated brainwashing as an English major at Duke. I was in the air force for three years. There, as a navigator and intelligence officer in the Strategic Air Command, I began to get my first somewhat radical political ideas. We were refueling B-47 and B-52 bombers on their way to fly over the Soviet Union to spy, drop agents, and create provocations. Part of our job in SAC intelligence was to convince the American people that we were under imminent threat of a Soviet nuclear attack, while we knew (this was back in 1956–1958) that the Soviets didn't really have the means to deliver nuclear weapons on the United States. As I began to wonder what was going on here, certainly the idea never crossed my mind that there could be any possible relation between all this and my antiproletarian Amherst honors thesis.

We had two children, and the time came to start thinking about what to do after the air force. I was due out at the end of January 1959. Then I discovered that the air force was willing to let people out as much as thirty days early if they had been accepted by a college or graduate school whose term was starting. So I looked around to find a graduate school whose term opened at the very beginning of January, and found Stanford. There were still nights of agonized decision making, because I couldn't quite picture myself as a professor and was appalled by the idea of going back to school. Sometimes I would tell my wife that I wanted to go back to work on the tugboats; once I heatedly argued that I wanted to do something just to make a lot of money. But back to school I went, which meant that she became a graduate student's wife. Not once in all these discussions did either of us consider any options for her as an individual.

Stanford's English department was not elitist in the same way as Amherst's. Most of these well-off white gentlemen were more interested in writing books to be read by their peers than in indoctrinating students with the most sophisticated and up-to-date forms of antiproletarian values. The majority did "professional scholarship." A few made some pretense of dabbling in ideas. Not one was concerned with the major ideological questions of our century. Not one was familiar with the major ideas that attacked their own beliefs. They were universally ignorant of Marx, Engels, Lenin, Mao, and Marxist criticism. (This was before they hired, for two years as it turned out, that noted professional anticommunist Irving Howe.) The most active intelligence was that of the *isolato* Yvor Winters, who wrote an essay in which he characterized his archetypal colleague as Professor X, "a gentleman and a scholar":

> He conforms to established usages because he finds life pleasanter and easier for those who do so; and he is able to approve of Emerson because he has never for a moment realized that literature could be more than a charming amenity. He believes that we should not be too critical of literature; that we should appreciate as much literature as possible; and that such appreciation will cultivate us. Professor X once reproved me for what he considered my contentiousness by telling me that he himself had yet to see the book that he would be willing to quarrel over. Professor X, in so far as he may be said to have moral motion, moves in the direction indicated by Emerson, but only to the extent of indulging a kind of genteel sentimentality; he is restrained from going the limit by considerations that he cannot or will not formulate philosophically but by which he is willing to profit. His position is that of the dilettante: the nearest thing he has to a positive philosophy is something to which he would never dare commit himself; that which keeps him in order is a set of social proprieties which he neither understands nor approves. In a world of atomic bombs, power politics, and experts in international knavery, he has little to guide him and he offers extremely precarious guidance to others; yet by profession he is a searcher for truth and a guide to the young.[1]

Since the graduate program at Stanford was designed by Professor X and his colleagues, it was not necessary for a graduate student to know even one work by a black author, to read even one article by a Marxist critic, or to be aware of even one fact about proletarian culture. To the best of

my memory, not a single black or Marxist work was included in any course offered at that time. (I first heard the
name of Christopher Caudwell years later, in 1967, from a
fugitive black revolutionary in Paris. That black teacher
gave me my real basic education in critical theory. He had
had one year of high school. At that time, I was an associate
professor of English and American literature at Stanford.)
So my own total ignorance of the relations between literature and class struggle posed not the slightest obstacle to
my graduate work. At the end of graduate school in 1961,
Stanford hired me as an assistant professor.

This is not the place to describe my radicalization in political work, mostly for civil rights and against the Vietnam
war. The main relevant point is that this radicalization
took place almost entirely outside my professional work,
and an increasingly intense contradiction began to develop
between my political and my professional life. But by late
1966, this began to turn into its opposite, as my teaching
timidly started to make conscious relations to the actual social world in which we have our existence.

One night in the fall of 1967, about eight months after
I had begun to consider myself a Marxist-Leninist, a few
things fell into place. I was at the home of Tom Wilcox,
who had graduated from Amherst in 1940 and was now a
professor of English at the University of Connecticut. Each
of us tended to think of our own experience, both at Amherst and afterward in the profession, as individual and dis-
connected. But as we talked deep into the night, an important connection began to emerge. Growing up and going to
college in the 1930s, Tom had developed, like many others,
a fondness for proletarian literature. His senior honors essay was an attempt to arrive at some kind of literary evaluation of some proletarian works. He described his profound
disappointment when he "discovered" that the formal im-
perfection of this literature made it "inferior," not for
merely aesthetic reasons but because it displayed inade-

quate moral perception. He and I then saw the direct development from the ideology of his Amherst thesis to that
of mine. Here it was—the rise and triumph of formalism,
in a most subtle form. First it is necessary to raise form to a
higher principle than content by claiming that form is the
essence of content. Once this is accomplished, bourgeois
culture is proved superior to proletarian culture. Why? Because it has an older and fully developed set of traditions,
and its artists have an extremely high level of formal training, due in large part to their monopoly on education.
Once these bourgeois criteria are completely internalized,
it becomes "obvious" or even "intuitive" that the bourgeois
work, with its high degree of formal excellence and elegant
complexity, is superior to the crude, simple proletarian
work. Thus the weaknesses of dying bourgeois ideology,
its irresolvable contradictions and irrationalities, are magi-
cally turned into their opposite. The hallmarks of literary
greatness become complexity, irony, ambiguity. In the
present era, formalism is the use of aestheticism to blind us
to social and moral reality. It is the expression of the mentality of Mussolini's son, who was thrilled by the beauty of
the bursting bombs he dropped on the Ethiopian villages.

Modern New Criticism began as a conscious counter-
attack on rising proletarian culture. It was crude and
frankly reactionary formalism. We should continually remind ourselves of where and when the most influential
New Critics arose. Brooks, Warren, Ransom, and Tate all
developed within that citadel of reaction, Vanderbilt University, and then received further training in elitism at
Oxford. Remember the dates of their first influential
works? Allen Tate's honestly titled *Reactionary Essays*
came out in 1936, the same year as the first edition of
Cleanth Brooks and Robert Penn Warren's *Approach to
Literature*. In 1938 came John Crowe Ransom's *World's
Body* and the first edition of Brooks and Warren's *Understanding Poetry*. New Criticism, which emerged in the

1930s to halt the advance of proletarian culture, gained complete ascendancy in the early 1950s as part of the triumph of anticommunist ideology. Tom's 1940 thesis represented the ideology at an early stage. My 1955 thesis, written just after McCarthyism had swept the field, expressed the ideology of triumphant reaction.

The main thrust of the postwar anticommunist crusade was not, as it appears to the academic mind, an attack on a handful of leftish professors. It aimed first at smashing the radical wing of the labor movement, thus depriving every progressive struggle of its traditional leadership. We tend to forget that the years since Truman, Taft, Meany, and McCarthy did their job are the first period in twentieth-century American history when white workers in large numbers have been missing from the ranks of radical leadership. The second major aim was to expand the American empire, in which I played my minor role in the Strategic Air Command. The third major task of the anticommunist offensive was to develop and consolidate reactionary ideology. This job was also performed with immense success. It was only as a small part of this job that all professors with radically different views had to be driven out of higher education or made to shut up. And here was proved the success of the great brainwashing, for the attack on the left-wing professors was not the work of a few witch-hunting senators. The entire petty-bourgeois faculty—with precious few exceptions—eagerly agreed to purge themselves of any political deviations. The Assembly of the Academic Senate of the University of California, for example, passed the following resolution in 1950: "No person whose commitments or obligations to any organization, Communist or other, prejudice impartial scholarship and the free pursuit of truth will be employed by the university. Proved members of the Communist Party, by reason of such commitments to that party, are not acceptable as members of the faculty." Even the government was not as zealous as the professors, and this particular resolution was later declared unconstitutional by the United States Supreme Court. But the professors had an extralegal power and ability to force intellectual activity into irrelevant, supposedly apolitical channels. Ideology, after all, is more influential than laws. Imagine legislation forbidding professors of literature to get their noses out of their texts! It is no mere coincidence that New Criticism triumphed at exactly this moment.

This victory within higher education was of tremendous importance, for in the subsequent decade and a half, New Criticism, in various forms, was to pour down from the elite colleges and universities into the junior colleges and high schools. It is relatively easy for ideas promulgated in these few institutions of higher education to become dominant because of the rigidly hierarchical structure of the educational system. College teachers are drawn from the ranks of graduate students, who are trained at this handful of schools. All high school teachers are trained by college teachers. And the Advanced Placement Program, which placed high school teaching under even more direct control of the elite institutions, consciously enthroned formalism and fought against historical criticism (as I discovered when I became chairman of the National Conference on Advanced Placement in English in 1963).

But all this could not entirely sweep the field of literary study of any relevance to contemporary life. For one thing, high school and junior college students stolidly resist formalism and force teachers at least to pretend to deal with relevant material. And the objective conditions of life have a way of forcing themselves into the hallowed ground of the classroom, no matter how hard the door is closed.

So it was necessary to find less subtle vehicles of counter-revolutionary ideology. Alexander Pope and the metaphysical poets, Nathaniel Hawthorne and the Romantics, could hardly lure many students away from the contradictions of their own society or lead them into taking a reactionary view of them. Stronger medicine was needed, outright reactionary tracts written by contemporaries, works like *Lord of the Flies* and *Animal Farm*, which come right out and say in terms that everyone can understand: Man is a pig. (I just discovered that *Animal Farm* is the only book previously read by every freshman of the eighty-five in my Literature and Revolution course.) But this trash can't withstand the storms of rising revolution. For instance, how can you assert that revolutionary leaders are just pigs, as Orwell does, in the face of Malcolm X and Ho Chi Minh?

The big reversal began in 1963–1964. The first major black rebellions in urban centers (since 1943) broke out in the summer of 1964. The rise and development of the black liberation struggle has forced the universities, colleges, high schools, and even grade schools to open up not only to black teachers but to black literature. The house of cards of formalist criticism has of course collapsed. You can't teach *Soul on Ice, The Autobiography of Malcolm X, Native Son,* or even *Invisible Man* without talking about political content.

Then came the movement against the Vietnam war, a movement that more and more was forced to examine the ideologies of communism and anticommunism. The Vietnamese people, led by communists and striving toward socialism, brought Marxism-Leninism into the consciousness of the antiwar movement and strengthened it within the black liberation movement, thereby causing a radical shift of forces in American life. The heroic struggle of the revolutionary masses of Vietnam, Laos, and Cambodia throw the lie into the teeth of those who libel and degrade humanity. As they smash the machinery of the cynical men of power, they expose the hideousness of the apologists for cynicism, William Golding and Sidney Hook, George Orwell and Hayakawa, Nabokov and Daniel Bell. They are responsible for this book being produced, for my writing this essay, for your reading it.

So I was too harsh when I caricatured what Stanford English professors were like in 1959, for they, like myself, who certainly was no better, were produced by our social context. Today, some of these same professors are teaching courses in black literature while searching for black teachers to take their place, a few are reading a little Marx and Mao, and three or four have even removed their neckties. For there is a growing awareness among all of us that the revolutionary stirrings on campus are responses to the revolutionary masses who surround the academies of the empire.

[When *College English* published several of the essays written for this volume, Franklin's elicited the most voluminous, pained, and outraged response. Franklin's rebuttal, printed below, will allow readers to reconstruct some of the answers printed by *College English*. Even if they can't, we feel that the rebuttal makes significant additions to the original essay, and can stand independent of its targets.—EDITORS.]

Reply: On Hearing from Some Professors of the Amerikan Empire

. . . not criticism but revolution is the driving force of history, also of religion, of philosophy and all other types of theory.

Karl Marx, *The German Ideology*

This debate will not be settled in the pages of *College English*. Nor will these polemics persuade many readers either to join the worldwide proletarian revolution or to spend their lives appreciating bourgeois culture. But the debate will be settled, just as the debate between bourgeois and feudal theories of literature was settled. Imagine the consternation of medieval professors if some young upstarts had proposed that extended prose fiction detailing the most private thoughts and lives of a few ordinary citizens should not only be the dominant form of literature in society, but that students in the university should be given courses in how to read it. But it was not the rise of the novel, much less critical theories about it, that brought the bourgeoisie to power; quite the reverse was true.

In the dialectics of history, culture is primarily an expression of objective economic and social relations and only secondarily an influence upon these relations. Petty-bourgeois intellectuals cannot grasp this concept, for they believe that ideas come primarily from other ideas, so that a true intellectual must be a pure intellectual. They are therefore condemned to the delusion that they and their ideas are not the products of their class and historical experience.

The real reason to engage in arguments like this is for each side to arm its own partisans with ideological weapons, to raise their consciousness so that they can be more effective fighters. Each side is already fighting for particular class interests, though only one side recognizes that fact. Barbara Kessel, Kathy Ellis, myself, and a few hundred million others realize that we are putting forward ideas that serve the class interests of the oppressed and exploited masses of the Amerikan empire. Our opponents call this "propaganda," because they believe—characteristically for their class—that their ideas are classless, representing all that is humane and cultured, the finest flowers of Western civilization. In reality, their arguments represent the interests of their own tiny professional class, and, indirectly but significantly, of the imperialist class that comprises their various boards of trustees and regents. They literally cannot afford to recognize this fact, for to do so would undermine the ideological justification of their beautiful homes, gardens, lawns, lawn parties, and other class privileges.

Insofar as any of these replies admits that history has had

an impact on the teaching of literature, they take the attitude: "Ho hum, we had done with all this trashy Marxist propaganda in the thirties. Take Franklin and the rest out and shoot *The God That Failed* at them." Well, it's quite true that many of the American Marxist ideas of the 1930s failed, and many who held these ideas became disillusioned or even reactionary. But again, ideas are reflections of social reality. America in the 1930s was not in a revolutionary or prerevolutionary condition. The trouble with most of these primitive Marxists was not that they were "Stalinists," but rather that events had not yet prepared them to comprehend Stalin's analysis of the world revolution. Specifically, they did not understand that proletarian revolution in the imperialist countries would *follow* the national liberation struggles of the peasant masses of Asia, Africa, and Latin America, that it was necessary to establish liberated base areas surrounding the imperialist countries, and that within the United States proletarian revolution would be led by the liberation struggle of the black *nation*. Not being familiar with these ideas, these professors of literature can see neither that they are all coming true nor that their own lives are being directly affected by that historical truth.

The autobiographical section of my article was not, as these professors seem to believe, an attempt to re-create myself as some kind of hero. One would look in vain for any heroic acts in this narrative. Quite the opposite. Indeed it was painful and embarrassing to dredge up and publish an account of how I became a professor of English at one of the highest academies of the empire. I find it difficult not to be disgusted by this experience, and if my colleagues see in this account evidence that I am not intellectually suited to be in their club, that is some comfort. But neither was it my aim to engage in self-flagellation. This was merely an attempt to understand myself as a product of historical process and class experience, precisely because, despite the usual amount of unique details, my life is quite similar to that of many other people. If you fail to see that, fellow professors, you'll never know what happened at the 1968 MLA convention.

It's interesting that this little sketch should evoke such passionate replies and even lead to claims that I am lying about the facts of my education. My colleague David Levin offers the most direct challenge, one that may prove worth investigating.

Levin begins by misrepresenting my account of Stanford's English department. I did not say that it forced "innocent students into reactionary imitation of Allen Tate, Cleanth Brooks, and Donald Davidson," but almost exactly the opposite:

> Stanford's English department was not elitist in the same way as Amherst's. Most of these well-off white gentlemen were more interested in writing books to be read by their peers than in indoctrinating students with the most sophisticated and up-to-date forms of antiproletarian values.

That's one reason that, unlike at Amherst, very few (if any) professors taught freshman English, which wasn't considered a literature course. (Another reason, of course, was that there were graduate students to be exploited.) I indicated that most of these professors were in fact not New Critics, but rather did "professional scholarship."

I admitted that "A few made some pretense of dabbling in ideas," but said that "not one was concerned with the major ideological questions of our century," being, as they were, "universally ignorant of Marx, Engels, Lenin, Mao, and Marxist criticism." Levin triumphantly refutes this by indicating that freshmen once were required to study the trial of two anarchists. That he can think this a refutation proves my point, as does his claim that studying John Brown's raid, "the socialist [sic!] experiment of Brook

Farm," or the Salem witchcraft trials and *The Crucible* constitutes studying "serious social criticisms of the United States." He can cite only one occasion when a single brief narrative by a lone Marxist (John Reed) was assigned.

Levin next challenges my assertion that "to the best of my memory, not even a single black or Marxist work was included in any course offered while I was a graduate student." Part of his rebuttal is simply ridiculous: "And before his memory began to function so selectively, he was obliged in my own courses to read Thomas Paine, Benjamin Franklin, Thomas Jefferson, George Bancroft, and John Lothrop Motley. . . ." I still can't figure out which of these are supposed to be Marxists and which are black, and I have the same trouble with "Dreiser, Lewis, Dos Passos, Farrell, and Steinbeck," who, according to Levin, were "regularly assigned . . . throughout the 1950s." Apparently no Marxist author ever was assigned, though it's nice to know that a couple of black authors were "recommended" and one black novel was once actually assigned before I studied at Stanford. The course catalogues, however, challenge Levin's accuracy and reveal some significant historical facts about the teaching of literature in the period following World War II, at least at Stanford.

The first three courses designed specifically to study American prose fiction of the nineteenth and twentieth centuries began in 1946/47. In English 265, "American Novelists," students from 1946 to 1955 read "Cooper, Hawthorne, Melville, James, Wharton, and Glasgow." In 1955/56, Cooper, James, Wharton, and Glasgow were dropped from "American Novelists," which subsequently became known as "Hawthorne and Melville."

In 1946/47, the course description for English 269, "The Rise of Realism in American Fiction," read "Chief emphasis on Twain, Howells, Norris, Dreiser." The following year, Crane was substituted for Norris, and the same formula continued until 1960/61, when this course transmuted into "English 269. Twain, Howells, and James."

Then there's English 270, "Contemporary American Fiction." From 1946/47 through 1951/52, the course description read: "Sinclair Lewis, Ernest Hemingway, James T. Farrell, Thomas Wolfe, John Steinbeck." My article claimed that "New Criticism . . . gained complete ascendancy in the early 1950s as part of the triumph of anticommunist ideology." Well, lo and behold, in 1952/53, at the height of McCarthyism and the Korean War, the course description suddenly changes to "Intensive reading and analysis of the stories and novels of Gertrude Stein, Robert Penn Warren, Katherine Anne Porter, William Faulkner, and Thomas Wolfe." The added formula "intensive reading and analysis" reveals as much as the switch in authors. Here we see the essence of New Criticism: the ostrich sticks his head in the sand and admires the structural relationships among the grains. The description changes slightly three years later and then remains the same through 1964/65: "Intensive reading and analysis of the stories and novels of Theodore Dreiser, Willa Cather, Sinclair Lewis, Ernest Hemingway, and William Faulkner." The "big reversal" that I claimed "began in 1963–1964," with the civil rights movement, the antiwar movement, and the black rebellions, had radical effects on this course (and even produced a lone Marxist dissertation). Since then, I believe, black novels have been taught each year, and this past summer, when I taught it, a Chicano novel (Barrio's *The Plum Plum Pickers*) was assigned. Of course the catalogues don't tell the whole story. When I took English 270 from Stegner in the spring of 1959, we read one novel by Dreiser, Wharton, Lewis, Hemingway, Fitzgerald, Robert Penn Warren, and James Gould Cozzens, two by Faulkner, plus one from an optional list of thirty pure-white and non-Marxist authors.

In response to my claim that one could get a Ph.D. here without knowing a single work by a black author, a single article by a Marxist critic, or a single fact about proletarian culture, Levin maintains "that a student could have earned a Ph.D. here without having read a single New Critic." He also claims that I have "managed to forget . . . the questions about social issues on the Ph.D. comprehensive examination that he wrote in the summer of 1960." Even if both these statements were true, they would not refute a word I said. But in both these statements it is Professor Levin who has "falsified the academic history of the department." Here is every required and optional essay question on the comprehensive examination we took in the summer of 1960:

> Outline briefly the contents of Boethius's *De Consolatione Philosophiae* and indicate what you believe to be the nature and extent of the influence of this work on Old and Middle English literature. If possible, discuss specific passages of English literature exhibiting this influence.

> List several of the principal English translations of the Bible or parts thereof from Caedmon's paraphrases of about 670 to Tindale's Bible, about 1525. Discuss some of these works in terms of their value to us in understanding English literature.

> Trace the emergence of English prose style and prose literature from the earliest times through Malory's *Morte Darthur*. Include in your answer a fairly close analysis of one Old English and one Middle English work.

> Summarize three of the principal "digressions" in *Beowulf* and discuss the function of these passages in the work as a whole.

> Contrast Beowulf and Roland as epic heroes, with particular reference to pagan and Christian elements.

> Basing your discussion on four poems, discuss with reference to specific passages the "elegiac mood" of Old English poetry.

"Akin to the technique under discussion ('highly compressed dramatic expression') is the one in the ballad happily known as 'leaping and lingering.'" Explain this quotation with specific reference to several ballads.

"Read for the individual visions and scenes the poem (*Piers Plowman*) is genuinely absorbing, but it is the despair of anyone who seeks in it a completely orderly plan or logical development from episode to episode." Explain wherein recent studies of *Piers Plowman* tend to support or to refute this critical statement.

Discuss fully the problem raised by the epilogue in Chaucer's *Troilus and Criseyde*.

Discuss Shakespeare's *Richard III* or *Henry IV: Parts 1 and 2* as a dramatic representation of history.

Discuss the unique and the conventional elements in Spenser's *Amoretti* and *Epithalamion*.

Write a critique of the strengths and weaknesses of "Miltonic Style" in *Paradise Lost*.

Compare and contrast two of the following three passages as examples of Renaissance prose. Mention specific characteristics of the style of both selections.

Select any one of the following works and discuss in detail its content, method, purpose, and distinct contribution to literary criticism or scholarship. (Books by Hardin Craig, Glynne Wickham, Rosemond Tuve, Basil Willey, Madeleine Doran, Louis Martz, Hiram Haydn, Richard F. Jones, H. J. C. Grierson, Wylie Sypher.)

Discuss the development of the ode between 1660 and 1770, pointing out the ways in which techniques and subject matter changed during that period. Consider specific works of such poets as Dryden, Pope, Gray, Collins.

Discuss the effect on eighteenth-century poetry of the movement away from the classical story to the use of English materials.

Discuss the contributions of the Gothic novel to the literature of the so-called "Romantic movement."

Show as specifically as you can how the seventeenth-century theories of the epic influenced the drama of the Restoration and eighteenth century. Do these epic influences increase or decrease the literary value of particular dramas?

Discuss the attitude toward Puritanism of Trollope, Arnold, and Carlyle.

Discuss aestheticism, or art for art's sake, in Keats, Tennyson, and Rossetti.

Discuss the sonnet as practiced by Wordsworth, Elizabeth Barrett Browning, and Meredith.

Trace the decline toward naturalism and relativism in English criticism through Arnold, Pater, and Wilde.

Discuss the reform of the drama from Robertson through Shaw.

Write a comparative essay on social criticism in the fiction of Nathaniel Hawthorne and James Fenimore Cooper.

Write a comparative essay on regionalism in the fiction of Hawthorne and Twain.

Write a comparative essay on the literary influence of the New England ministry of 1640 and that of 1840.

Compare the portrayal of "national character" in Henry Adams's *History of the United States during the Administrations of Jefferson and Madison* and in a history by either John Lothrop Motley or Francis Parkman.

Discuss the chief examples of literary influence exerted by the following writers (through critical influence and practical aid) on their contemporaries: William Dean Howells, Edith Wharton, Gertrude Stein.

Discuss the influence of James Joyce on the fiction of two of the following: Faulkner, Wolfe, Dos Passos.

Discuss Henry James's theories regarding the nature of fiction, and his application of these theories in his criticism of two or three fictionists.

Discuss *The Mirror and the Lamp* with regard to the light it throws on the English backgrounds of twentieth-century American theories in the realm of criticsm.

Discuss the theory of the "romantic image" (cf. Frank Kermode)—that is, the impenetrable, inscrutable, or un-paraphrasable image or poem—as we encounter it in any two of the following writers: T. S. Eliot, Allen Tate, Cleanth Brooks, R. P. Blackmur, or any of the recent apologists for Yeats (American apologists).

The following poem ("Exhortation") is by Louise Bogan. Paraphrase the poem, discuss its meter, rhythm, and diction, and evaluate it.

To take this examination, you not only had to have read some New Critics; you had to be one most of the time. Where in the world are "the questions about social issues" that I have "managed to forget"? The closest we get to such a thing is the optional discussion of the "social criticism" of two nineteenth-century conservatives, Hawthorne and Cooper. In fact this examination magnificently documents each of the generalizations I made about the ideology of literary professors.

Levin's final charge, which he has made frequently in the past few years, explains the uncharacteristically pas-sionate tone of these other replies as well as the rage that has greeted our actions at the last few MLA conventions. When I repudiate my own false consciousness and see it as representative rather than unique, he says I'm wounding my colleagues' feelings. He's right. And they are quite correct, from their point of view, in being enraged. They understood, much sooner and more clearly than I did, that most of us in the New University Conference or similar groups are in fact class traitors to most of the gentlemen who teach literature in the empire's universities and col-leges. My article, like our behavior at the MLA conven-tions, is a treacherous betrayal of the ideas and values they depend upon in order to live. It's treacherous because you need a college education and have to be at least close to a Ph.D. in order to expose these ideas and values for what they are, at least in the MLA or *College English*. Proletarian people as yet rarely have the opportunity to study the ideas that are fucking them over. It's a betrayal because if working people realized that the titles "Doctor" and "Professor" merely mean that someone is an expert in anti-working-class values, and that for working people proletarian culture at this point in history is far more relevant than bourgeois culture, we'd all be out of jobs. We might even have to do some useful work.

That brings us to the heart of the matter, which is the split between body and mind, between being and consciousness, asserted in each of these replies. Why are most professors shocked when a few professors use their bodies to effect social change? Why do they find this not only nonintellectual but "mindless"? Because bourgeois values teach that there are two different kinds of activity—physical and mental. On one side, we have beings who work with their bodies. These are mindless, less than human. Then there are those who think, intellectuals, disembodied intelligences whose physical existence is essentially irrelevant to what they think.

This metaphysical dichotomy comes out strikingly in Professor Hendrickson's remarks on childbearing, physical labor, and Herman Melville. He thinks that bearing a child or working on a ship are *merely* physical activities. (Therefore he misinterprets my assertion that these experiences would be as good qualifications for a teacher as the opposite, that these experiences are unteachable.) In other words, he thinks that the thoughts of a woman having a baby and raising a child, or the thoughts of a worker undergoing physical exploitation and oppression, do not constitute intellectual activity. Conversely, if a worker reads and writes books, he is no longer proletarian. To these professors, a proletarian intellectual would be a contradiction in terms. And that is precisely why Professor Hendrickson personally is unqualified to teach Herman Melville.

Because in fact, workers do think. For one thing, they are conscious of being fucked over, and they wonder whether or not anything can be done about it. Herman Melville thought while he was working. One of the things he was thinking about was the fact that most of his fellow sailors were illiterate, so he could never hope to write books addressed to them. He also thought about the possibility of communicating their experience to the actual audience which read novels and romances, people with leisure and education, though he was never too hopeful about getting through to these petty-bourgeois ladies and professional gentlemen. That's why the very first paragraph of his very first romance ends like this:

> Oh! ye state-room sailors, who make so much ado about a fourteen-days' passage across the Atlantic; who so pathetically relate the privations and hardships of the seas, where, after a day of breakfasting, lunching, dining off five courses, chatting, playing whist, and drinking champaign-punch, it was your hard lot to be shut up in little cabinets of mahogany and maple, and sleep for ten hours, with nothing to disturb you but "those good-for-nothing tars, shouting and tramping over your head,"— what would ye say to our six months out of sight of land?

Within a year, Melville was forced by his publisher to delete this entire passage, so offensive to the delicate ears of his genteel audience, because as Chairman Mao points out, "All classes in all class societies invariably put the political criterion first and the artistic criterion second. The bourgeoisie always shuts out proletarian literature and art, however great their literary merit." So the bourgeois intellectuals of Melville's day, though amused by this "reading sailor spinning a yarn" with "nothing to indicate the student or the scholar," complained that "Mr.

Melville's mind, though vigorous enough, has not been trained in those studies which enable men to observe with profit" (*The Spectator,* February 28, 1846). Like Professor Hendrickson, they could not understand that it was precisely his experience as a "reading sailor" that enabled him to write *Moby-Dick,* the great philosophical romance whose highest achievement is demolishing the bourgeois mind-body dichotomy from a sailor's point of view. That is why they were so bewildered by the book's astonishing *physical* power. And so Melville was left to construct his verbal mantraps for the bourgeoisie, his fantastically brilliant displays of ante-bellum capitalist society: "Benito Cereno"; "Bartleby the Scrivener: A Story of Wall Street"; *The Confidence-Man*

In the final scene of his last completed novel, he prophetically displays the predicament of our professional gentlemen. In the "gentlemen's cabin" (hear the reverberation from that first paragraph of *Typee*) sits a "clean, comely," and "well-to-do" old man. He is left with only one activity before being led away into darkness: he must sit there studying a banknote to determine whether it is counterfeit. His best clue is a fleeting symbol: "the figure of a goose, very small, indeed, all but microscopic; and, for added precaution . . . not observable, even if magnified, unless the attention is directed to it." Unknown to this gentleman, the bank that issued the bill was part of the Mississippi Bubble, and had already gone bankrupt.

NOTES

This essay, in slightly different form, appeared in *College English,* Vol. 31 (March 1970), pp. 548–57.

1 Yvor Winters, *In Defense of Reason* (Chicago: Allan Swallow, 1947), pp. 601–2.

TEACHING AND STUDYING LITERATURE AT THE END OF IDEOLOGY

Richard Ohmann

I

Do we not have what we wanted, we professors of literature? Our classrooms filled up during the fifties and sixties as students left the sciences and sought wisdom in the arts. Teachers and even critics of literature acquired more prestige than they had had within living memory. With prestige came fast promotion, good salaries, low teaching loads, lots of graduate students, research factories, hundreds of new journals, computer-assisted bibliographies and concordances, fellowships, easy publication, textbooks, royalties, consultantships. Yet almost at the height of this prosperity the feeling spread that something had gone sour in the profession, some teachers came to suspect that literary culture might indeed be "irrelevant," and essays like the ones in this volume began to appear. How did professors of literature get into this fix? To help orient my discussion I shall allude at some length to an early expression of doubt, an essay by Lionel Trilling called "The Two Environments," written in 1965.[1]

When it appeared, it drew a good deal of interest, mainly, I imagine, because it cast doubt on some favorite premises of literary education, premises that Trilling himself has worked from, along with many of the rest of us. When we have had to justify the presence of literature in the curriculum, Trilling says, we have slipped easily into the vocabulary of the "whole-man theory" (p. 213). That is, we have held the study of literature "to have a unique effectiveness in opening the mind and illuminating it, in purging the mind of prejudices, and received ideas, in making the mind free and active." The result is "an improvement in the intelligence . . . as it touches the moral life" (p. 212). This argument has proved remarkably durable since Matthew Arnold gave it its best-remembered articulation, surviving innumerable challenges of the Auschwitz-commandants-read-Goethe variety. It has convinced not only teachers of literature, who after all need this kind of reassurance, but students in large numbers who want to read and live by modern literature, in particular. I think that Trilling is right in saying that for them "an involvement with modern literature goes with an insistent . . . concern with morality" (p. 220). This concern fixes on the sense of style, and of the cultural and moral values that inhere in style and are heightened in literature and by literary study. Literature really is criticism of life, and students and teachers of literature have been the conscience of the culture to an extent that might have satisfied even Arnold—whatever he might have thought of the concrete directives of that conscience.

But as Trilling rightly observes, the very success of literature has changed the terms of Arnold's plea. To oppose the philistines then, or even in Sinclair Lewis's time, was in effect to oppose *the* culture. That is no longer so. Now, Trilling says, "the student is at liberty to choose between two cultural environments" (pp. 226–27). One, still, is philistine culture, and the other defines itself by opposition to the philistines. But as we and our students find this second environment more peopled and more comfortable, the opposition to philistines itself becomes one of two established parties. These parties are now, even more than when Trilling wrote, in intellectual and stylistic opposition to one another—as is revealed by the continuing fuss about long hair, drugs, and sex, by the vogue of books like Reich's *The Greening of America* and Roszak's *The Making of a Counter Culture,* and by the voyeurism of timelifenewsweek. Yet both parties have eaten from the same board throughout their quarrel. That last is my observation, of which more later. Trilling's is that the second culture has lost some of its critical nip, that it carries in it a "trivializing force," which dissipates real cultural debate in "transcendent gossip." For this reason, he says, "those few teachers . . . who do not think that preparing students for entrance into the second environment is enough to do for them in the way of education, may one day have to question whether in our culture the study of literature is any longer a suitable means for developing and refining the intelligence" (p. 232).

A whole lot of history has happened to us since 1965. After our unpleasant awakening to the dissonance of external events, a rereading of Trilling's essay is a strange experience, punctuated with phantom exclamation points and asterisks not in the original.

But my subject is what happened before 1965, not after, and I have spread out the content of Trilling's essay at such length because it seems to me an extraordinarily telling account of trouble within academic literary culture. Telling, because the source of Trilling's malaise is the very success of our profession. Teachers of literature have had some part in creating a large, audible, sensitive, and highly moral adversary culture, which is what we meant to do, yet I imagine that even in 1965 Trilling was not alone in harboring doubts about this achievement. Needless to say, those who have looked at other indicators of professional health have been a good deal less equivocal than Trilling. Anyone can think of a dozen examples, straight off, of self-doubt or rage, directed at the management of academic literary culture: the MLA insurrection of 1968, Florence Howe's election to the second vice-presidency in 1970, the black studies movement, Don Cameron Allen's study of *The Ph.D. in English and American Literature,* the MLA panel called "Need Graduate Literary Education Be Obsolete?" the Anglo-American Seminar on the Teaching of English,[2] the rebellions of graduate students in many universities, the Commission on English, and so on. That the profession has been self-critical is not surprising, but that the critical mood set in precisely at the moment of amplitude and prestige bears comment.

In 1948 Stanley Edgar Hyman began his survey of contemporary criticism by judging it "qualitatively different" from—*better* than—any previous criticism. Looking ahead, he ventured that "the immediate future of criticism should be even greater, and a body of serious literary analysis turned out in English of a quality to distinguish our age." [3] The sense of vistas opening out was a common one. In 1948 I started college, and I recall the excitement communicated there by teachers of literature who would have agreed with Hyman's prognosis for criticism. And to be in graduate school in the fifties, even in the dim Eisenhower years, was to feel part of a fresh intellectual movement and a renewal of the vitality of literary study. We expected that the teaching of literature, too, would increase in quality and importance; Hyman saw "democratic possibilities for modern criticism," which, by making its method widely available, would train more people as capable critics, "in most cases not professionally, but in their private reading and their lives. And the vested interests *that* possibility menaces are much bigger game than the priesthood of literary criticism" (pp. 11–12). There it is:

we were confident then that we could challenge philistine culture and the hierarchical society by extending the influence of literature.

So the question I have been working up is, What happened to us—people who read and taught literature in universities—that in achieving pretty much what we set out to achieve we built a cultural situation that many of us find so distressing? How did we get to where we are? My way toward an answer will run first through a reconsideration of some things that New Criticism meant, taking full advantage of hindsight. For the New Criticism was the central intellectual force in our subculture during those years. Then I will quickly examine some of the counterforces, looking for the cultural foundation of the arguments brought against New Criticism. Finally I will try to relate this phase of our literary history to some wider cultural concepts. I hope it will be clear along the way that when I say "we" and "us" I intend no condescension to those whom I think benighted but hope to convert. I am, rather, making a crude effort to understand some of my own intellectual history, to let these past two decades teach me something now that I failed to learn at the time. This is no disinterested and scholarly attempt to discover new evidence about the past and to see what no one has seen before, but a close-in attempt to see the familiar landscape through a lens just slightly rotated.

II

At the outset of any retrospective on the New Criticism, it should be acknowledged that this school made its greatest impression on our day-to-day lives and work, not through the literary and cultural theory with which many of the chief figures occupied themselves, but through the style and method of close reading displayed in a relatively small number of essays, primarily by Cleanth Brooks,

William Empson, R. P. Blackmur, the I. A. Richards of *Practical Criticism,* and in the sacred textbook, *Understanding Poetry.* These taught us how to write papers as students, how to write articles later on, and what to say about a poem to *our* students in a fifty-minute hour. Surely we absorbed the cultural values inherent in close reading—exactness, sensitivity to shades of feeling, the need to see pattern and order, the effort to shut out from consciousness one's own life-situation while reading the poem, and to pry the words loose from their social origins —surely we absorbed these values as we imitated the models before us. But when we thought about what we were doing, especially when that was placed under attack, we would draw upon the rationale and the theory supplied by the New Critics. A theory becomes potent when called into play in defense of practice. So the theoretical talk of the New Critics is a convenient place to look for the ideas that support—that license—the work of students and teachers of literature. I want now to arrange some of those ideas in a convenient row (more convenient than is quite justified by their original development) leading from the poem itself out to the whole social and metaphysical context.

Start with the familiar notion that the poem is a self-contained whole, autonomous. This premise is often disparaged now, as it was twenty years ago, for seeming to absolve poetry of moral responsibility, for sponsoring a decadent aesthetic of art for art's sake. But that is much too simple a charge: the pages of the New Criticism are bound together with moral fiber, almost strident in urging a social mission for literature. To see what is really at stake in claiming the autonomy of the poem, it is best to consider what the New Critics themselves meant that proposition to deny.

They were denying, first, that poetic language has reference in the same way as prose, and that literature is in competition with science. The "heresy of paraphrase" is that you can take a message away from a poem, or mine the poem for its content, leaving form behind. Richards even allowed himself to say that "the greatest poets . . . refrain from assertion." [4] Second, the organic idea of poetry denies that the poem should be read as an avenue to the poet's intention, or as a part of his autobiography. And third, the New Critics meant to deny the "affective fallacy," that the poem is its psychological effects on the reader.

The intent of this ontological position is not to divorce literature from social and personal reality but to make the relationship an indirect one—of which more later. The New Critics know that poems are related to life, but they want to let the poem create its own mimetic life before seeing how it fits the world outside. And they know that the poem is not an object. As Wimsatt scrupulously says, "The poem conceived as a thing in between the poet and the audience is of course an abstraction. The poem is an act." [5] But for criticism, Wimsatt goes on, and for critical reading, the poem "must be hypostatized," detached from its origins and effects and from the stream of history. In brief, this is a point about how to experience and criticize literature. Wimsatt and the others ask us to relax our pragmatic and empirical muscles while reading a poem, to let the poem have its own way, to accept its world in a passive mood. Poetry is different from other uses of words, notably science, in the view of the New Critics, and requires a different state of consciousness.

It is a familiar observation that that state of consciousness excludes (willing suspension of disbelief) those modes of reality testing appropriate to scientific discourse, particularly looking for a one-to-one correspondence between propositions and parts of the external world. Less explicit but equally important is the separation of literary experience from action. In this the New Critics are with Auden:

"Poetry makes nothing happen." More sharply, in Richards's account of poetic experience the function of the poem is precisely to block any overbearing impulse to action, by bringing the "appetencies" into balance. Eliot would put it otherwise, but he and all the rest would agree that the sphere of a poem's operation is the sensibility, not the will.

Furthermore, although poems, as Wimsatt says, unquestionably are acts, both in their making and in their uttering, the New Critics make almost nothing of this. Wimsatt expresses the standard position, that "both speaker and dramatic audience are assimilated into the implicit structure of the poem's meaning," [6] so that action is only an artistic fiction rather than a dynamic in which the poem participates. By this account Yeats is not really, through "Easter 1916," taking sides in the rebellion, but putting forth an artistic hypothesis. Kenneth Burke, some way from the central group of New Critics, is the exception. He treats poems as "strategies" which, like all symbolic structures, produce "frames of acceptance." "Acceptance" here does not equate to passivity; rather, frames of acceptance "fix attitudes that prepare for combat"; they define a *we* and a *they*.[7] Burke allows some conflicts, at least, to be real, not fully containable by some arrangement of attitudes, and he sees poets and poems as participating in those conflicts. Given the wide currency of Burke's ideas, it is notable that the New Critics never built on this particular one. It accorded badly with their attempt to theorize a state of mind peculiar to literary experience.

The specialization of the mind is assumed by the aesthetics of New Criticism, too. Murray Krieger is right in holding that although the New Critics do not have an explicit theory of the unique aesthetic experience, they both need and imply one.[8] And Eliseo Vivas, much influenced by New Criticism, developed the appropriate one. The aesthetic experience, in his familiar phrase, is a state of "intransitive, rapt attention," [9] in which we feel all meanings and values to be in the art object rather than in the world beyond the object. Emotion and perception, as well as the intellect, need a separate set of rules for the right apprehension of literature.

I have been laying my stress on the fragmentation of self which is strongly implied by the New Critics. Yet their composite theorizing lays *its* explicit stress on a reconstruction of the whole person. Here is how that works. In return for the discipline of intransitive attention, of blocking interpretive instincts, setting action aside, and restraining all stock responses, the reader gets a total and unified experience. For Brooks the main task of the poet is to "unify experience," and so "return to us the unity of the experience itself as man knows it in his own experience." [10] Although the almost ritualistic iteration of the word "experience" shows where Brooks's wishes would lead him, the passage hardly explains why one would read a poem. What is so defective about the original, unmediated experience that we must resort to poetry to recapture it? Ransom, interpreting Eliot, gives a clear answer: "In action . . . the situation as a whole engages us too completely; . . . it is when this situation exists for imagination, not for action, that we are freed from its domination and can attend to its texture." [11] This is a crux. As I have already suggested, most of the New Critics would have agreed that action impedes the deeper flow of understanding and the refinement of emotion, and that wholeness of experience, paradoxically, is most available to us when we abstract ourselves from action and let consciousness have the field. Most comment on this special and intuitive knowledge of experience, held out as the main reward of poetry, has followed the New Critics' explicit distinction between poetry and science—poetry treats an "order of existence . . . which cannot be treated in scientific discourse." [12] But I think that the deeper message is in the continuation of Ransom's statement: poetry, he says, recovers the "denser and more refractory original world which we know loosely through our perceptions and memories." The "original world" can best be known by being out of it. The truest experience is abstract experience, well distanced by poetry.

Poetry lets us "realize the world" [13] for another reason as well. The world is infinitely complex, Brooks and several of the others insist. To see it clearly requires selection and ordering, both important activities of art, whatever theorist you read. But at this point one should ask why the selection and ordering that any of us performs just in the course of being awake, or that science offers, are inferior to the selection and ordering achieved by art. The answer is clear in the reasons the New Critics give for setting such extraordinary value as they do on irony, ambiguity, tension, and paradox, in critical practice: these devices are important for their "resolution of apparently antithetical attitudes," [14] which both daily life and science leave in dissonance. This idea has its origin, for the New Criticism, in Richards's *Principles of Literary Criticism,* where a "balanced poise" of the attitudes plays a central and almost therapeutic role. Richards supposes that our cultural sickness is a matter of attitudes and impulses in a state of imbalance, and that poetry can set us right by helping us achieve a state of equilibrium. The more discordant elements drawn into this unity, the more effective the poetry—for this reason Richards praises tragedy as "perhaps the most general, all accepting, all ordering experience known." [15] And Brooks says that the good poems manage a "unification of attitudes into a hierarchy subordinated to a total and governing attitude. In a unified poem the poet has 'come to terms' with his experience." [16] Now, putting together these suggestions with Eliot's famous diagnosis of a "dissociation of sensibility" in the modern world, I see a gestalt of this sort: The world is

complex, discordant, dazzling. We want urgently to know
it as unified and meaningful, but action out there in the
flux fails to reveal or bring about satisfying order. The
order we need *is* available in literature; therefore literature must be a better guide to truth than are experience
and action.[17]

But the specific content of the truth to be got from
literature is less clear than the desire for it; so are the
particular values that poetry advances nebulous. Not that
we can remain puzzled to know what values the *critics* are
for—these are plain enough, especially among those half-
dozen New Critics who are Anglicans or Catholics. But all
of them are surprisingly reluctant to ascribe their particular values to poetry. An obscurity sets in when they address
the subject; as when Richards looks to poetry for those
"most valuable" states of mind that "involve the widest
and most comprehensive co-ordination of activities and
the least curtailment, conflict, starvation and restriction,"
or when Wimsatt writes that "Poetry, by its concreteness
and dramatic presentation of value situations, whether it
inclines to a right answer or to a wrong answer . . . has the
meaning and being which makes it poetry. This is the
poetic value." [18] These formulations don't take us far. The
reason for the difficulty may be offered by another comment of Wimsatt's: that the Arnoldian view of poetry as
criticism of life is defective because "so much" of poetry
"is in one way or another immoral" that no one ethic can
accommodate all the great poems.[19] This is more helpful.
The value of poetry transcends the values of individual
poems and poets, and lies not in urging one or another
moral view but in embracing ("coming to terms with")
ethical complexities. A proper reading of poetry neutral-
izes and flattens out not only impulses toward action but
perhaps even those toward moral judgment. Poetry, capital P, can prefer no one value system or course of action,

but accepts and comprehends all values, all sections, and in fact everything that is the case.

Richard Foster, in a helpful book on the New Criticism, argues that most of these critics have a quasi-theological bent. They are the proper heirs of Matthew Arnold in substituting poetry for religion as man's "ever surer stay." [20] It seems to me that in spite of their talk about the decline of culture and sensibility, the "ever surer stay" they offer is the assurance that we *can*, after all, "come to terms with experience"—by containing it, by striking balanced attitudes, as a successful poet does, and emphatically not by acting to change the society which gives rise to our experience.[21]

Not only is this a passive solution. It is also, importantly, a personal one. The New Critics see poetry as serving the individual reader, and only very indirectly as amending the flawed society. In fact, many of the formulas they offer of desirable social goals are so abstract as to call into question the seriousness of their interest. When Richards says that our sickness is being cut off from the past and that myths and poetry will "remake our minds and with them our world," [22] when Tate says that the man of letters is "to attend to the health of society *not at large* but through literature—that is, he must be constantly aware of the condition of language in his age," [23] and that "the end of social man is communion through love"; when Eliot says in *After Strange Gods* that the function of literature is to combat liberalism; [24] when Ransom says that "the object of a proper society is to instruct its members how to transform instinctive experience into aesthetic experience" [25]—I find it easy to believe that they are thinking, not about the whole of any society, real or imagined, but about the style of life available to a man of letters within society. If so, it doesn't really matter how the society is organized, short of totalitarianism, since the man of letters can cope. "If modern man wishes to save himself as a human being in an abstractionist society, say all the New Critics, let him turn to literature and the arts."[26] But for "modern man" we had better substitute "the literary intellectual," for to whom else is this solution really available? Murray Krieger holds that the social mission of criticism, according to the New Critics, is "to affirm the uniqueness and indispensability of art's role in society."[27] This has to mean society *as it is;* for Krieger the issue is how we defend poetry within the status quo, and primarily *to* those who have any say about "art's role in society," the powerful classes.

Now, against any substantial analysis of society all of this is a parlor game, and the social pieties of the New Critics themselves are the sort of horn-tooting that you might try by way of asking the National Endowment for the Humanities to give you some money. Why are these generally sophisticated men so very inept when they discuss society? I think it is partly because everything in their ideology turns them away from politics. They see art as freeing man *from* politics by putting him above his circumstances, giving him inner control, affording a means of salvation, placing him beyond culture.[28]

III

It will be obvious that this is an angled shot of the New Criticism. I have deliberately tried to draw out those implications of the New Critics' work that will serve my present purpose, and my account has been critical. So I want to reiterate the perspective from which the criticism is leveled. I can myself understand if not accept Foster's labeling the New Criticism the "chief movement for literary humanism of this century." I think that these were sensitive and well-intentioned men, whose main effect on the academy was for the better. I do not hold them to blame for the present crisis of confidence in academic literary culture, much less for the viciousness of American culture at large. To go looking for the villain among critics and English teachers is, in my view, completely to misconceive the task of cultural analysis. Plainly the New Criticism, like its opponents, was a relatively minor cultural force. It did not create the academic literary scene of the fifties and sixties, but merely presented itself to us as a timely instrument to serve purposes of our own. A few words about that.

There were many aspects of the New Criticism that answered to our needs, but one worth singling out was its flight from politics. Trilling said of intellectuals today that "we all want politics not to exist." [29] That is particularly true in America, where social pressures that drive men to hard politics have rarely existed for long; for us "there has always seemed a way out." [30] Americans have generally been able to move on when a situation calling for politics arose—across the frontier, to a suburb, into technologically ensured privacy. What has increasingly governed American public life is what Philip Slater admirably calls the

> Toilet Assumption—the notion that unwanted matter, unwanted difficulties, unwanted complexities and obstacles will disappear if they are removed from our immediate field of vision. . . . Our approach to social problems is to decrease their visibility: out of sight, out of mind. This is the real foundation of racial segregation, especially in its most extreme case, the Indian "reservation." The result of our social efforts has been to remove the underlying problems of our society farther and farther from daily experience and daily consciousness, and hence to decrease, in the mass of the population, the knowledge, skill, resources, and motivation necessary to deal with them.[31]

In America we use technology and production to occlude social ills, and so to evade politics at whatever cost.

Academic humanists in the fifties had special reasons for wanting politics not to exist. McCarthy had made activism improvident for college teachers at the start of the decade, and in any case, the cold war had reduced ideology to seeming inevitabilities of free world and iron curtain, while drastically narrowing the range of domestic political positions available, and pretty much guaranteeing that support for Adlai Stevenson would seem the most daring political act within the bounds of realism. At the same time, technological advance and the rapid increase in production kept before us a vision of steady improvement, and made radical social change seem both remote and disturbing. What those of us who studied and taught literature particularly needed, therefore, was a rationale for our divorcing work from politics, for lying low in society.

Kenneth Burke wrote an analysis of such tranquil historical moments, back in 1937, that is worth quoting apropos the 1950s:

> The ideal conditions for thought arise when the world is deemed about as satisfactory as we can make it, and thinkers of all sorts collaborate in constructing a vast collective mythology whereby people can be at home in that world. Conflicts are bridged symbolically; one tries to mitigate conflict by the mediating devices of poetry and religion, rather than to accentuate the harshness.[32]

In such a period, ironic "frames of acceptance" are bound to be wanted. The New Criticism was such a frame, already built and ready for use by the end of the war.

Some homelier truths are also worth recalling. Academic salaries in this country touched bottom at the end of the forties, in terms of purchasing power. I well recall that as I came to graduate school in 1952, those leaving Harvard with Ph.D.'s counted $3,000 a good salary. Professors were poor; I thought of entering the profession as tantamount to taking vows of poverty. But economic conditions gradually improved for us through the decade, for demographic and political reasons (universities, recall, became an instrument in the cold war—the battle for men's minds). A new, distinctly less ragged style of life became possible, and with it an almost-earned upper-middle-class self-image. As we were switching from beer to booze and buying second cars, few felt any hard economic interest in politics. The social change that was carrying us along was quite satisfactory. And with this frame of mind, the New Criticism accorded well.

IV

So far I have virtually equated theory of literature in the postwar period with the New Criticism. In so doing I have of course hugely oversimplified the actual situation in universities, both by omitting the other schools and by slighting the polemical and contentious side of the New Criticism itself. I will not make up this deficiency. To do so would require roughly equal time for philologists, literary historians, Chicago critics, and so on.

Instead I will say just enough to suggest that in the terms I have outlined, the opponents of New Criticism offered no real alternative to it.

What kept the English department busy before New Criticism arrived was, of course, philology and literary history. Philology, whose territory was not deeply invaded, never really entered into battle with the New Critics, but literary history very much did. It could not help doing so, since the New Criticism challenged its right to control the curriculum and the budget. To be sure, the challenge came more in the form of physical presence than of doctrine, although Ransom did attack English faculties for being "mere historians," unable to recognize a good new poem when they saw one, much less deal with the texture of literature. In any case, the mere historians were embattled, and those of us who were in graduate school fifteen to twenty-five years ago will remember their grumblings and disparagings. Douglas Bush handed down the official indictment in a 1949 MLA talk. According to his bill of charges, the New Critics ignore historical context; they therefore make damaging errors; they glorify technical method and assume that "literature exists for the diversion of a few sophisticates"; they are "aesthetes" who "create a moral vacuum." Poetry deals with morality, and so should criticism.[33]

But in spite of the high feelings and the real antagonisms that split the profession for a while, the division was not deep. Bush would bring morality back into criticism —by siding with one or another ethic drawn from the past, as we know from his other writings and their championing of Christian humanism. Such free-swinging uses of the past do not bring criticism into closer touch with the concrete moral situation of the present than the New Critics were willing to do. The distance, with Bush, is simply of time rather than of abstraction. As I have said, the New Critics did not lack for moral sentiments.

As for the dispute about method, the scholars and the critics had after all a common intent: to get at the ethos of a work or a poet, to mediate his wisdom (his coming to terms), with empathy for all systems of thought, in the dispassionate way of the intellectual. The scholar would do this by coming at the work from outside, the critic by exploring its interior. Either method will suffice to withdraw the work from *our* history and politics. So scholar and critic have long since realized their community of interest, in a setting where differences of method—specializations—are a positive professional asset rather than a contradiction. It reduces anxiety if one can succeed as a scholar *or* as a critic, and leave half the "field" to another guild of experts with whom one is no longer in competition.

The other collective assault on the New Criticism came from Ronald Crane and the Chicago critics. They bore down on the New Critics' attempt to see all poems as importantly alike, and as distinct from prose or from science. The Chicago group would dwell more on the various genres and subgenres of literature, those traditional forms that shape individual works. In other words, for the criticism of a given poem it may be more helpful to say at the start that it is an elegy than that it is a poem. I reduce this doctrine to such a minimum, not to imply that no significant philosophical issues were at stake (there were some), but to show that the issues for teachers of literature were once again primarily of method. Almost everything I said about the ethos of New Criticism applies equally to the Aristotelian school. In fact, in the elaborate taxonomy of literary works that Chicago promised, in the prospect of a well-ordered and infinitely large body of practical criticism, and in Crane's plea for "much inductive theoretical research . . . into problems both of general poetics and of the specific poetics of literary forms," [34] the Chicago critics were even better equipped for the professional decade than the New Critics. And needless to say, their call for a "pluralistic" criticism, one that would take systems of thought as premises for inquiry rather than as competing doctrines, promised to reduce values to methodological preferences, and make an unthreatening place for them in the professional life.[35] My contemporaries in graduate school might recall maneuvering their way through first an Aristotelian paper on a narrative poem, then a myth-and-ritual job on a Restoration comedy, and on to a synthesis of Brooks and Lovejoy applied to several metaphysical lyrics. At most universities the graduate course in literary theory laid these methodological riches out before us, and left us free to make the choice appropriate to the critical occasion. If the Chicago critics had not come so much later onto the stage, and if they had offered more easily adaptable styles of practical criticism, they might well have stolen the scene, for their ideas met the same needs as did those of the New Critics.

Of the other attacks on the New Criticism, most were even less abrasive. Mark Spilka, in an article whose sub-title was "A New Critical Revision," praised the move-ment for "its promise of something like objective certainty about subjective truths," but accused it of partly losing this aim in a self-defeating formalism, succumbing to the methods of science in an effort to defeat science.[36] About the same time Roy Harvey Pearce, arguing that language itself embodies history, pled for a more historical under-standing of literature. Yet if I understand his rather com-plex essay, Pearce had no particular view of the meaning or direction of history such as to put us and our literature in dynamic relation to it; rather, he appropriated history as "an indefinite series of examples of what we would possibly have been were we not what we are." [37] Such a view preserves the New Critics' denial of our particular historical being, and their attempt to set us above history as "users" of the past. Probably Hyatt H. Waggoner ex-pressed the consensus of academic literary people at the end of the fifties when, in registering some complaints against the New Criticism, he nonetheless called it "the best criticism we have or are likely to have for a long time." [38] And studies like Krieger's and Foster's represent further stages in the domestication, adjustment, and as-similation of what was at the outset a rebellious body of criticism. The waters were fairly calm.

Moreover, those few who did frontally attack the New Criticism often did so on premises that would exclude almost *all* criticism. Very early Mark Van Doren set him-self in opposition to a criticism "obsessed with a desire to be scientific about poetry," and so destroying its beauties: "The poem is a bird that threatens to escape the net of analysis, so that the net grows ever wider, and tougher with interwoven analytic threads." [39] Although this was and is a common complaint, it can easily be recognized as an attack on thinking, not a call to a better mode of thought. And although Karl Shapiro, when he excoriated New Criticism twenty years later for being concept-ridden, dogmatic, and abstruse, avoided Van Doren's misty nostalgia in favor of a gritty plainness, he shared Van Doren's preference for intuition and a hegemony of taste. The critic's real job, he can only say, is "discriminating between" works of literature, without apparently employing any system of concepts.[40] These are aristocratic positions, rooted in the pride of the natural-born critic (and, usually, poet) who needs no shared ways of thinking, and whose advice to teachers would no doubt be "look into your guts and write—if you dare." It is not surprising that such views made little headway against the New Criticism, which at least aimed toward a democracy of critical ideas, available to all.

Meanwhile, there were a few explicitly political critiques of the New Criticism. The most influential, perhaps, was the argument offered in 1949 and 1959 by Robert Gorham Davis, and revived many times since, that the New Criticism implies a "reactionary position in politics and a dogmatic position in theology." [41] Although this is a bit closer to my own view, I hope it is clear that it won't hold up. There are indeed many remarks by Eliot, Tate, Ransom, and others praising monarchy, aristocracy, the ante-bellum South, etc.[42] But the criticism and literary theory, in sharp contrast to these political manifestos and asides, are square in the middle of the bourgeois liberal tradition.[43] The explicit politics of these men is a pseudo-politics. It constitutes an enabling mythology that ties their criticism to social yearnings and nostalgia, but not to any possibility of action or affiliation. And it has little or nothing to do with the implicit political content of their writings about literature. In implicit politics, all the competing criticisms of the fifties were pretty much the same. At the risk of vulgarization, I would say that the main political effect of our theorists was to help embed literary criticism, along with its producers, tightly and securely within the network of bourgeois institutions.

V

In the postwar period, as American universities underwent enormous growth, a much larger segment of the population came into these institutions than before. This meant that market conditions required a great increase in the professoriat. One consequence was the new academic prosperity to which I have already alluded. And along with the prosperity came unaccustomed prestige, as intellectuals and technocrats were brought into the making of national policy, not as in the past because of their social backgrounds, but for their expertise. In short, the university was a place where large numbers of people were cutting loose from their social origins and joining an intellectual elite. And a new elite of this sort needs a set of myths that justify its status to itself and to the larger society.

Here a broad principle of ideology is helpful: A privileged social group will generalize its own interests so that they appear to be universal social goals ("What's good for General Motors . . ."). In America in the fifties the bourgeois intellectual needed assurance that his privileges were for the general good. For example, a critic and teacher of literature whose work is fun and respectable, but who sees little evidence that he is helping to ameliorate social ills, or indeed serving any but those destined to assume their own positions in the ruling class—a teacher in this dubious spot will welcome a system of ideas and values which tells him that politics and ideology are at an end, that a pluralistic society is best for all, that individual freedom is the proper social goal for rich and poor alike, and that the perfection of self can best be attained through humanistic intellectual endeavor. And this is what the New Criticism and its competitors had to offer. Their tacit ideology has its proper place in bourgeois culture; its main features are practically inevitable because necessary to sustain class privilege in a capitalist society that depends heavily on knowledge and hence on university people.

Bourgeois culture rests on the idea of freedom.[44] In our society people interact mainly through the market, and this medium tends to obscure all social ties except those mediated by commodities, the cash nexus. An example: the patent law is our way of dealing with useful knowledge. It regularizes and makes legal the private ownership of ideas and emphasizes their cash value, but ignores the social origin of all inventions—the shared knowledge that underlies them—and also the sometimes devastating social consequences of their use.

It is easy in a free-enterprise system to ignore one's total dependence on other people, and especially easy for the affluent. Their relationship to other people is indirect, transmitted through money. Possession of means gives them frictionless control over other people's labor, and such control feels like freedom. The affluent can do as they please, up to a point, and it is natural enough for them to conclude that their well-being *derives* from freedom. It is but a short step for them to elevate freedom into a universal social goal, not seeing that the kind of freedom they enjoy can't be made universal because it depends on the slavery of others: on the other side of the cash nexus is someone whose choices are fewer and who does not feel free.

Though bourgeois culture declares its allegiance to freedom, the security of the well-to-do demands that there be close limits (law and order) to freedom of action by the powerless. Hence the ideologue settles on freedom of *thought* as fundamental, and he is willing to allow everyone that freedom so long as it does not lead to "disruption." The university perfectly embodies this notion. Our dogma is academic freedom, which in practice means that you can think and write what you like, but as your speech approaches to political action you are more and more likely to find yourself without a job. Universities are supposed to remain neutral, stay politically pure.

The literary wing of the academy wholly subscribed to these doctrines through the fifties, as I hope I have sufficiently shown, and developed its own local version of them. Literature was divorced from particular ideologies and identified with a pluralism that would help preserve individual freedom. The doctrine of diversity is often advanced, even in the midst of doctrinal wars ("I disagree with what you say but I will defend to the death your right to say it"), by the Chicago critics and by their opponents. Even an often dogmatic man like Tate finds it natural to say in the midst of controversy, "nobody knows what criticism is relevant to a democratic society. I like a lot of free play. I think that people ought to find out the truth wherever they can." [45] It is easy to translate this into the implied language of the powerful: "You are entitled to your opinion, and it won't affect me one whit."

As a corollary of this stress on freedom, the bourgeois intellectual sees art and aesthetic values as independent of social process. Caudwell points out that beauty can only be a construct generated by culture, a "specific social product." [46] But since the bourgeoisie relies for its comfort on the discomfort of others, it has good reasons for cloaking or ignoring the realities of social process and it looks away from labor and economic activity to find beauty. Art is, in brief, a means of freedom from society. And that seems to me the best explanation for the way our criticism has justified literature: as freeing man by setting him above his circumstances, by letting him "come to terms" intellectually, but taking him out of the present and making him one with "the tradition." All the schools of criticism agree that literature is a very special and separate thing, whose privileged cultural position needs defending—against science, against politics, against commercialization, against vulgarity, against nearly the whole social process.[47]

The other cardinal principle of bourgeois culture is that we must prefer thought to action—in fact, abstain from all social action except the pursuit of our individual economic goals in the market, and voting for candidates for public office. I have pointed to the distancing of action by the New Criticism. In part, the preference for contemplation owes to a natural wish for security from social upheaval. But it is also surely the case that we prefer thinking to action because thinking is the mark of our separation from and economic superiority to those who do physical labor. As Caudwell says, thought is "favored socially to the extent to which it separates itself from action, because it is just this separation which has generated its superior status as the mark of the ruling, 'cunning,' or administrative class." [48] In our technological time, the university is built on precisely this distinction. That is why the cliché used by its enemies is "ivory tower." It is where the administrative class learns to think, where the scientific foundations of technology are laid, and where ideology is built to sanction the distribution of power and wealth in capitalist society. In this last task the literary profession has cooperated, in part by insisting that the means to personal well-being and wholeness is through withdrawal from social action and the achievement of all-embracing states of mind. That is where the New Criticism pointed us, and where most of us, under the banner of humanism and the advancement of knowledge, gladly went.

Where else we might have gone, under different historical circumstances, it is profitless to guess. Marxist criticism did, of course, offer a logical alternative. It could con-

nect literature and goals for action, thus rebuilding somewhat the whole person. It could bridge the seeming gulf
between high culture and the lives of ordinary people.
And it could use literature as an agent of liberation, rather
than of the bourgeois freedom which depends on exploitation. But that is another story. All that need be said here is
that, given how American academic intellectuals were functioning in the forties and fifties, Marxist criticism was
bound to be excluded from among the possibilities for respectable discourse about literature.

VI

A few words of recapitulation. After the war, the academic literary profession in this country set an exciting
course for itself: to revive literary culture and disseminate
it widely and democratically, to the general benefit of
society. This project was, as Richard Foster said of the New
Criticism, "perhaps the most extraordinarily successful of
all consciously waged literary revolutions." [49] And its legacy
has been in many ways admirable. To quote Foster again,
education in English departments trains students to be
"more alive and catholic" than an earlier generation. They
and we constitute a "coherent and meaningful literary culture," which has advanced a "religiously felt resurgent
humanism." In all this the socioliterary history of the last
twenty-five years has indeed nearly fulfilled Arnold's wish-
ful prophecy. Yet many of us are deeply dissatisfied with
where we have arrived, with the professionalism, the
vestigial disdain for the unwashed, the "second environment" of which Trilling spoke.

I think that in retrospect we can see the origins of our
present malaise in the core of our earlier beliefs. We
wanted to move out of social action; we wished politics
out of existence. But as Georg Lukacs says, "everything is
politics"; every human thought and act is "bound up with

the life and struggles of the community." [50] The denial of politics could not hold out forever. For one thing, external events caught up with us and disturbed the great bourgeois peace of the fifties—the war, the uprising of oppressed peoples here and abroad, the destruction of the biosphere through unchecked forces of the free-market economy. No walls built around the free play of intellect could exclude these world historical events.

But also, the very humanism we learned and taught was capable, finally, of turning its moral and critical powers on itself. Not directly. First, the humanism saw the inhumanity of the society outside the university—and credit to it for doing so. No one can tell exactly how much the values and perceptions of literary culture, as diffused among the young, helped make *visible* the war on Vietnam and, at home, racism and poverty. But there can be no doubt that those living in the "second environment" were among the first to wake from two decades of political sleep. From the burning of draft cards to the perception of humanism's role in maintaining class privilege and the insane, exploitative consumerism that is destroying this country is not, perhaps, very far. I would like to think not, because I take seriously Caudwell's prediction, made thirty-five years ago: "Humanism, the creation of bourgeois culture, finally separates from it." [51] It "must either pass into the ranks of the proletariat or, going quietly into a corner, cut its throat."

NOTES

1 In Lionel Trilling, *Beyond Culture: Essays on Literature and Learning* (New York: Viking Press, Compass Books, 1968), pp. 209–33.

2 A highly critical discussion of English in the schools, held at Dartmouth in 1966 and reported informally in Herbert J. Muller, *The Uses of English* (New York: Holt, Rinehart & Winston, 1967).

3 Stanley Edgar Hyman, *The Armed Vision: A Study in the Meth-*

ods of Modern Literary Criticism, rev. ed. (New York: Random House, Vintage Books, 1955), p. 5.

4 Ivor A. Richards, *Principles of Literary Criticism* (New York: Harcourt, Brace & World, Harvest Books, n.d.), p. 276.

5 William K. Wimsatt, *The Verbal Icon: Studies in the Meaning of Poetry* (New York: Farrar, Straus & Giroux, Noonday Press, 1958), p. xvii.

6 *Ibid.,* p. xvi.

7 Kenneth Burke, *Attitudes Toward History.* I quote from an excerpt in Kenneth Burke, *Terms for Order: Studies in Evaluation,* ed. Stanley Edgar Hyman (Bloomington: Indiana University Press, 1964), p. 70.

8 Murray Krieger, *The New Apologists for Poetry* (Minneapolis: University of Minnesota Press, 1956), p. 129.

9 Eliseo Vivas, "Problems of Aesthetics," in *Creation and Discovery: Essays in Criticism and Aesthetics* (Chicago: Henry Regnery Co., 1955), p. 146.

10 Cleanth Brooks, *The Well Wrought Urn: Studies in the Structure of Poetry* (New York: Harcourt, Brace & World, Harvest Books, n.d.), pp. 212–13.

11 John Crowe Ransom, *The New Criticism* (Norfolk, Conn.: New Directions, 1941), p. 156.

12 *Ibid.,* p. 281.

13 John Crowe Ransom, *The World's Body* (New York: Charles Scribner's Sons, 1938), p. x.

14 Brooks, *Well Wrought Urn,* p. 157.

15 Richards, *Principles of Literary Criticism,* p. 247. It is worthwhile speculating if this is not one of the reasons for the extraordinarily high value our culture sets on tragedy. Georg Lukacs points out that bourgeois theories of tragedy see this mode as arising from "the terrible side of life" (Schopenhauer), and so degrade specific historical tragedies into occasions for the "universal human tragedy" (*The Historical Novel,* trans. Hannah and Stanley Mitchell [Boston: Beacon Press, 1963], p. 122). But I don't think that Lukacs is right in crediting this fondness for tragedy to belief in the "futility of life in general," although that phrase no doubt does justice to Schopenhauer. More recent bourgeois ideas of tragedy stress its integrative force, its ability to reconcile and bring about acceptance. The New Critics' theory of poetic structure may explain why—and why we have so many books with titles like *The Tragic Vision* and *The Tragic Sense of Life.*

16 Brooks, *Well Wrought Urn,* p. 207.

17 In an essay called "Art for Art's Sake," E. M. Forster said quite

openly what I take the New Critics to be saying more confusedly
or obliquely:

> . . . order in daily life and in history, order in the social and
> political category, is unattainable under our present psychol-
> ogy. Where is it attainable? . . . The work of art stands up by
> itself, and nothing else does. . . . It is the one orderly product
> which our muddling race has produced. (*Two Cheers for De-
> mocracy* [New York: Harcourt, Brace & World, Harvest Books,
> 1951], pp. 91–92.)

The parallels between Bloomsbury and the New Criticism are
often close.

18 Richards, *Principles of Literary Criticism,* p. 59; Wimsatt, *Verbal
Icon,* p. 98.

19 Wimsatt, *Verbal Icon,* p. 89.

20 Richard J. Foster, *The New Romantics* (Bloomington: Indiana
University Press, 1962), esp. Chap. 2. That the New Critics do so
is undoubtedly one cause of the cultural situation Trilling describes in "The Two Environments." By the time Trilling wrote,
a generation of college teachers trained to New Criticism had
acted as missionaries for literature, not as the attainment of a
gentleman, but as an alternative to the religious life.

21 It is interesting to note that Richards, probably the most influential founder of the movement, tied his work to a number of social
causes: improving international communication, spreading literacy, creating basic English, improving university teaching, and so
on. But the social aims yielded, among his followers, to the other
side of Richards's intentions, the subjective and therapeutic.

22 Ivor A. Richards, *Coleridge on Imagination* (New York: Harcourt,
Brace & Co., 1935), p. 229.

23 This in defending his vote for Ezra Pound to receive the Bollin-
gen Prize; *The Man of Letters in the Modern World: Selected
Essays, 1928–1955* (New York: Meridian Books, 1955), p. 266. The
quotation that follows is on p. 22 of the same book.

24 T. S. Eliot, *After Strange Gods* (London: Faber & Faber, 1934).

25 Ransom, *World's Body,* p. 42.

26 Foster, *New Romantics,* p. 44.

27 Krieger, *New Apologists,* p. 5.

28 I have not mentioned R. P. Blackmur in this essay, partly because
of the difficulty I have in understanding his later essays, but it is
at least clear that those later essays urge the transcendental uses
of literature I am stressing.

29 Trilling, *Beyond Culture,* p. 164.

30 Irving Howe, *Politics and the Novel* (New York: Fawcett World

Library, 1967), p. 164. Howe is explaining why political ideas have never shaped up so clearly here as in Europe, and why the tradition of the political novel is correspondingly thinner.

31 Philip Slater, *The Pursuit of Loneliness: American Culture at the Breaking Point* (Boston: Beacon Press, 1970), p. 15.

32 From Burke, *Attitudes Toward History,* quoted in Hyman, ed., *Terms for Order,* p. 77.

33 Douglas Bush, "The New Criticism: Some Old-fashioned Queries," *PMLA,* Vol. 64 (Supplement, Part 2, March 1949), pp. 19–21.

34 Ronald S. Crane et al., eds., *Critics and Criticism: Ancient and Modern* (Chicago: University of Chicago Press, 1952), p. 19.

35 On this matter of values, the case of Yvor Winters is instructive: Winters relentlessly kept his values out in the open, and partly as a result of this has had less influence than any of the other major New Critics—except among his own students, who tend to remain fervently loyal. Values were to be kept in their place.

36 Mark Spilka, "The Necessary Stylist: A New Critical Revision," *Modern Fiction Studies,* Vol. 6 (Winter 1960–61), pp. 284, 297.

37 Roy Harvey Pearce, "Historicism Once More," *Kenyon Review,* Vol. 20 (Autumn 1958), p. 588.

38 Hyatt H. Waggoner, "The Current Revolt Against the New Criticism," *Criticism,* Vol. 1 (Summer 1959), p. 224.

39 Mark Van Doren, *The Private Reader: Selected Articles and Reviews* (New York: Henry Holt & Co., 1942), p. xiv.

40 Karl Shapiro, *In Defense of Ignorance* (New York: Random House, Vintage Books, 1960), p. 12.

41 Robert Gorham Davis, "The New Criticism and the Democratic Tradition," *American Scholar,* Vol. 19 (Winter 1949–50), pp. 9–19, and American Scholar Forum, "The New Criticism," Vol. 20 (Winter 1950–51 and Spring 1951), pp. 86–104, 218–31.

42 To conduct the assault on this level quite properly invites the kind of response Tate offered to Davis: that Eliot voted Labor, that an American New Critic voted for Norman Thomas, that Tate himself voted for FDR, etc. (*American Scholar, Vol. 20,* p. 87.)

43 As is, after all, appropriate to their social origins. Read the first chapter of Louise Cowan's *The Fugitive Group: A Literary History* (Baton Rouge: Louisiana State University Press, 1959), for an account. Myths of the Old South don't apply well to this amiable collection of middle-class college boys, the liberal heirs of nineteenth-century capitalism.

44 Through this part of the discussion I am drawing on Christopher Caudwell's *Studies in a Dying Culture* (London: John Lane, The

Bodley Head, 1938) and *Further Studies in a Dying Culture* (London: John Lane, The Bodley Head, 1949).

45 Allen Tate, in American Scholar Forum, "The New Criticism," p. 87.

46 Caudwell, *Further Studies,* p. 87.

47 Stated at this level of generality, the goal of postwar criticism is much the same as that of most English criticism since the spread of literacy through the industrial revolution. This was Arnold's aim and that of his contemporaries, with partial exceptions like Morris and Ruskin who sought the interpenetration of art and the reality of daily labor. But to hope for a vital literary culture among the working class was to hope against the economic stream, for reasons made clear enough by Martha Vicinus's article in this book and by Q. D. Leavis's *Fiction and the Reading Public* (1932; reprint ed., New York: Russell & Russell, 1965).

48 Caudwell, *Further Studies,* p. 117.

49 Foster, *New Romantics,* p. 22. The quotation that follows is on p. 28 of the same book.

50. Georg Lukacs, *Studies in European Realism* (New York: Grosset & Dunlap, 1964), p. 9.

51 Caudwell, *Further Studies,* p. 72.

ARNOLD'S OTHER AXIOM

Katherine Ellis

Two years ago, as I sat in a Broadway theater reading my souvenir program and waiting for the curtain to go up on Howard Sackler's *The Great White Hope,* I came across a passage that had a hauntingly familiar ring to it:

> Sackler's Jack Jefferson, though inspired by [heavyweight champion Jack] Johnson, is in a sense an Everyman, one who is thrust into a position he did not seek, did not want and could not overcome. He could easily have been white, as easily been butcher, baker or candlestick maker. He represents men who have existed since the beginning of time and who will continue to be with us to the end. For, unfortunately, there will always be those who are ready to take advantage of the more vulnerable, and the vulnerable will always be there.

Whence this sense of familiarity? It came from the fact that I am an English major who is about to conclude twelve years of expensive education and begin to transmit what I have learned to succeeding generations of students. During these twelve years I have taken scores of literature courses, in each of which the point was made that great literature is timeless and that its heroes are Everyman.

What made this passage interesting to me, though, was not simply its familiarity, but rather the context in which it was placed; it occurred, that is, after three or four pages of historical background that included the following piece of information:

> Fevers ran so high that when a former white champion returned from retirement only to be defeated by the black man, race riots erupted across the country, twenty-six persons were killed, and the Federal Government banned the interstate shipment of fight films to avoid further bloodshed.

Nevertheless, according to the author of these remarks, the play is not about racism, but about a man who could have been any color, who could have lived at any time, and who can therefore be considered a "tragic hero."

What I was reading is an example of the way in which ideas of "culture" developed by academics are reinterpreted at the popular level. What the anonymous critic is telling his readers is that the proper way to approach a work of art is to strip it of its historical "background," the better to extract from it the message that there will always be oppressors and victims of oppression, those who are "more vulnerable" and those who—with the full force of the law behind them—"are ready to take advantage" of others; that class differences are really temperamental differences, which "have existed since the beginning of time and . . . will continue to be with us to the end."

It seems to me that it is not at all accidental that this particular perspective on literature should be one of the mainstays of a "liberal education" in this country. Such an education has two complementary functions. On the one hand, it rationalizes the hierarchical social and economic relations necessary to a capitalist economy, much like the writer of our souvenir program. After all, it was traditionally intended, we should remember, for those destined to occupy positions of power in that society. At the same time, it is a means for propagating the egalitarian sentiment that informs the myth of equal opportunity. In their self-proclaimed role as defenders of "culture," our elite universities fulfill both these class functions. Thus, when we speak of class bias in liberal education, we are speaking not just of the universities' admissions policies and overt channeling procedures, but of assumptions or attitudes so pervasive, so essential to every phase of academic life, that they pass almost unnoticed. These attitudes are especially rooted, and unnoticed, in departments of literature, in part because of the close relationship that exists between the material that is taught and the leisure class for whose consumption culture has traditionally been produced.

The rationale that underlies the canon around which English departments are organized is based on a distinction between "high" and "popular" culture, a distinction that sets the leisure of the masses (and the "entertainment" created to fill it) over against the leisure of the great, without which the monuments of our Western heritage could not have been patronized or written. We have a vocabulary to talk about high culture, and anything that is obscured by this particular perspective is not great art but trash. An educated person deplores the mass media, and, more important, he looks down upon those for whom "Bright Promise" and "Dark Shadows" are rituals answering a daily need.

When a liberal education was restricted to a select group whose level of culture could be assumed to be fairly uniform and fairly high, there was less need of a system to distinguish the qualified from the unqualified, the worthy from the "hopeless cases." Since students and their teachers came from the same class, subjective judgments did not carry the same impact, nor were grades the measure of personal worth that they have become, since the present worth and potential success of the members of this class

were determined not by their work but by their membership in the class itself.

The transformation of literary scholarship from a pas-
time into a profession was accompanied—indeed made possible—by a shift in emphasis from "responses" to "techniques," by a substitution of "scientific methods" for what
had been the sole constituent of literary criticism up to the
nineteen-thirties: the sensibility of cultured gentlemen. By
demonstrating so conclusively the dependence of this sensibility upon knowing who a particular author is in order
to assign him to his due place in "the emancipated and
humane community of culture," I. A. Richards literally
launched a revolution in the field of criticism.

This revolution did not put an end to elitism among
literary critics, however. It simply reclothed it in the irre-
proachable garments of science. Now the presence of science in any subject, as Northrop Frye will tell us, "changes
its character from the casual to the causal, from the random
and intuitive to the systematic, as well as safeguarding the
integrity of the subject from external invasions." [1] If one
applies the scientific method rigorously, as Frye professes
to do, one can dispense with chronology and leap from
Homer to Hakluyt, from Eliot to the prose Edda, at a single bound.

Ironically, "scientific" criticism arose as part of an anti-
materialist ideology, one concerned with defending "culture" from the majority of the population that has no concern beyond making money. The most influential apologist
for this view of the critical enterprise is Matthew Arnold,
who saw an antidote to nineteenth-century materialism and
unbelief in the search for "a perfection which consists in
becoming something rather than in having something, in
an inward condition of the mind and spirit, not in an outward set of circumstances." [2] This definition of culture has
since become the *raison d'être* of liberal education, whose

chief value, so the argument goes, lies not in the money it brings you when you graduate, but in what it does to the inner you. Northrop Frye puts it this way:

> Revolutionary action, of whatever kind, leads to the dictatorship of one class, and the record of history seems clear that there is no quicker way of destroying the benefits of culture. If we attach our vision of culture to the conception of ruler-morality, we get [Matthew Arnold's] culture of barbarians; if we attach our vision of culture to the conception of a proletariat, we get [Arnold's] culture of the populace; if we attach it to any kind of bourgeois Utopia, we get the culture of philistinism. . . .
>
> It seems better to try to get clear of all such conflicts, attaching ourselves to Arnold's other axiom that "culture seeks to do away with classes." The ethical purpose of a liberal education is to liberate, which can only mean to make one capable of conceiving society as free, classless, and urbane. No such society exists, which is one reason why a liberal education must be deeply concerned with works of imagination. The imaginative element in works of art, again, lifts them clear of the bondage of history. Anything that emerges from the total experience of criticism to form part of a liberal education becomes, by virtue of that fact, part of the emancipated and humane community of culture, whatever its original reference.[3]

Most English departments have been rather more cautious than Frye's critical theory and practice would suggest. They continue to divide literature up into chronological periods and to identify the monuments, great and small, that exist within them. What remain outside, separated absolutely from the realm of culture, are the realities of politics, economics, and everyday life. It is this material history from whose bondage academic criticism frees cultural works, so that they may be arranged and discussed purely with reference to one another. This is what Eliot had in mind when he said that "the existing monuments form an ideal order among themselves which is modified by the introduction of the new (the really new) work of art among them." [4]

What that ideal order looks like is anybody's guess, and perhaps this is why the idea is so popular among scholars, whose hypotheses find infinite scope in journals and the publication lists of university presses. Graduate school catalogues offer only the simplest possibility in arranging major authors chronologically. In his *Anatomy of Criticism*, Frye offers four other possibilities, each one different and none of them chronological. His theory of modes, for example, posits a descending order from mythic to ironic, from god-like freedom to total human bondage. But what follows irony is not revolution, since "revolutionary action, of whatever kind . . . destroy[s] the benefits of culture," but a return to mythical modes of thought and imagination. His conception of order is totally circular, and thus cannot be modified by the introduction of the new, "the really new," work of art into it. It is no wonder that the new— "the really new"—works of literature are considered by many of the leading scholars in our field to be inappropriate objects of serious academic concern, or that, whatever our views, we have no critical or pedagogical methods for understanding those aspects of our present culture to which we cannot respond with critical detachment. If each time one of these "really new" works is to be admitted to the now established order of "monuments" the entire order must be modified, if a different *Arcadia* can be created by a reading of *Soul on Ice,* how can we speak of a "body of knowledge" that a degree candidate is supposed to "know" in order to measure up to a set of objectively verifiable standards? Of what value is the presence of "science" if the very idea of an ideal order in any field, and beyond that an ideal order in the field as a whole, is as much an illusion as the idea of a constant, unchanging, perceiving self in a novel by Proust?

A corollary to the assumption that an ideal order exists is that until one is acquainted with this ideal order in its overwhelming entirety, one is not really qualified to speak with authority on any part of it. For undergraduates, this myth serves to instill into them an awe (expressed as a fear of appearing stupid) of their professors, who are supposed to carry within them "the whole of literature of Europe from Homer, and within it the whole of the literature of their own country." Since this kind of knowledge is not expected of students, they, as amateurs, fall automatically into a different class from their teachers, the pros.

In graduate school, the fear of appearing stupid becomes a disease—a virulent pathology—which can be relieved only by massive doses of approval by some member of the pantheon in one's department. The cure clearly does not bring about a state of health, but rather an intense desire to be in turn regarded with awe (expressed as a fear of appearing stupid) by one's own students. Graduate students are supposed to be measuring themselves by "professional standards." This means that they must be constantly faking, constantly trying to give the impression that they do, in fact, carry the whole of the literature of Europe within them (and a lot of the criticism of that literature besides), or else they must adopt an apologetic attitude toward whatever they do know, offering their observations rarely and with great misgiving in seminars and conferences and confessing that they can't really talk in an intelligent (i.e. "professional") way about, say, Dickens, because that energetic author wrote upwards of twenty novels, while they, poor slobs, have read only those that everyone *likes*.

All this pretense culminates in the writing of a dissertation, since this is where you are supposed to show the "big people" that you can talk their language. The "big people" are those white male professors who greet each other with jocular camaraderie in the halls, and who talk shop from time to time over a few drinks at the faculty clubs of the highest academies of the empire. The thesis, now cynically referred to as a "union card," once opened the door to an exclusive men's club, outfitted in traditional "masculine" decor with leather chairs, Oriental rugs, Chinese urns, and the rest. It has not lost this aura, despite the current over-production of Ph.D.'s, as any doctoral candidate at an elite school can tell you. It is not writing itself that is harmful, only the kind of ventriloquism through which aspiring scholars are required to transform themselves into "one of the boys" by addressing their professors as peers.

This sounds very jolly, very egalitarian, very "emanci-pated and humane" even. It is not. Rather, it reminds me of the Indian petty officials in one of Orwell's stories of Burma, imitating the officious manners, the locutions and gestures, of their British superiors, striving even to outdo them in polished eloquence as they attempt to deny the humiliating reality of their own class position through scrupulous imitation of the "cultured" diction of their masters.

As I have intimated, the process of thus "acculturating" students begins with undergraduate education. As univer-sity education ceased to become the exclusive property of our "future leaders," the notion arose that an enthusiasm for "monuments" and a disdain for mass culture could be within the reach of most who entered a university. To sort out those incapable of cultivation and to begin shaping the sensibilities of those who were capable, a set of initiation rituals was developed, a series of required courses in "Con-temporary Civilization," in art, in music, and of course, in literature. Those who do not respond appropriately to this prescribed and piecemeal exposure to all that is best in our heritage from Homer to the present are apprised of their deficiencies early, so that they may have the greatest possi-ble opportunity to pull themselves up by their bootstraps. But the fact is that there will always be some students who will never be capable of conceiving society as free, classless, and urbane no matter what is done for them.

The first responsibility of those who teach this introduc-tory gamut is to find out who these people are. In courses consisting of facts to be memorized, this can be done in a reasonably objective way. But in literature and composition, a judgment on what a student does is inevitably a judgment on a person. It is a judgment of a level of culture. In internalizing the picture of himself reflected from above, the student makes an important step in the direction of imitating the masters. Later on, the initiate, through an understanding of the benefits of culture, will come to deplore "revolutionary action, of whatever kind." A while ago, I mentioned to one of my former teachers that I was writing something on the subject of class bias and the teaching of literature. "I don't know what you mean," she said. "I have never been aware of the class of any of my students"—the implication being that perhaps I was not treating my students equally, that my own class bias was undermining my impartiality as a dispenser of grades. Of course, obliviousness to class is a particularly American habit of mind, a response to the myth of equal opportunity. It is especially important for sustaining the self-importance of teachers, and this seems to me to offer the most reasonable explanation of why it is that for my teacher, and for most people's teachers, "the emancipated and humane community of culture" already exists. One has only to be initiated into it.

At the university, the obliteration of classes through culture—Arnold's other axiom—embraces the whole realm of taste. "The man who likes what you like," John Ruskin observed, "belongs in the same class with you." [5] Then if it is the function of a liberal education, and within that the function of criticism, to make culture available to all who are capable of appreciating it, classes will be done away with once all members of a given society like the same "existing monuments," those they have been taught to regard as "good."

In the long passage I have cited, Frye presents three visions of an aesthetic "good," each corresponding to one of Arnold's three classes. His wording suggests that culture itself is unrelated to class, but can be *attached* to any one of the three. It seems better, to me, to steer clear of such hypotheses, and to admit that the works of imagination at the core of a liberal education are attached already to a morality that justifies the values of those holding power in the society that produced the works, and the liberal education. For, if one does away with the ahistorical community in which Frye has placed our culture and allows it a role in the historical process, it must be admitted that literature does not help us to conceive society as free, classless, and urbane. Rather, it makes us capable of accepting as "eternal truth" a view of human nature that makes, if not inconceivable, at least highly impracticable a society that might be defined by those characteristics.

I am not talking about the experience of creation, which very well may lift the writer for a moment clear of the bondage of history, but rather, how the fruits of those moments are conceived, taught, and written about in our universities. There Frye's approach represents a still widely accepted solution to a problem that is common to critics and teachers: the relationship between the "fit audience" for whom the author of a given work was writing, and the academic audience to whom the critic or teacher is speaking. I would refer to this solution as simply "New Criticism," were it not that this school is now considered out of date, while the practices I am speaking about are still alive and well, especially in the English departments of the elite universities.

The solution lies in treating a work as a self-contained totality whose ideology (or morality) is absorbed into, and thus inseparable from, its structure. This dissolution into "form" of the didactic element in literature accomplishes two things: it avoids the kind of "moral" criticism of literature that Wayne Booth and others are trying to revive, and it admits academics (actual and potential) of all persuasions into the compass of the "fit audience" for any major author. But it does these things at a price: by proscribing, as inappropriate to a scholarly discussion of literature, those beliefs and experiences which prevent a reader from suspending his disbelief in, let us say, the Greek view of Fate.

The rationale behind this silence is clear, whether or not it is ever spelled out: If one accepts a work as "good," one does not quarrel with its ideology. This acceptance by default would not be problematic if such ideas as the Greek view of Fate could be immersed in "the total experience of criticism" and come out as the ideology of a society that is free, classless, and urbane. This is obviously impossible. The real question is, Why should it seem necessary to Arnold and Frye?

To answer this, one must first go back and ask a question that is as old as literature itself: In what sense do poets "speak true"? If the remarks of the chorus in a play by Sophocles are "true," not only for the citizens of Thebes but for the citizens of Chicago as well, is this because they speak to an eternal struggle of the human heart that is experienced by all men irrespective of the society in which they live? Or are they true precisely because they are part of the "ruler morality" of a particular society that was neither free nor classless, achieving urbanity only by executive fiat? Historically, culture has been consumed in people's leisure hours. Its morality, therefore, has tended to be one that "explained" the continuing power of whatever class controlled the allotment of leisure: the oligarchs and warrior kings in pre-industrial times and the captains of industry in our own. Frye maintains that the benefits of culture are destroyed when the culture of one class dominates. Yet after several thousand years of "ruler morality" a gradual shift took place in the pattern of literary heroes, and the warrior was transformed into an "outsider" without any perceptible diminution in the benefits of culture for those who have traditionally received them, that is, the ruling class. What remained unaltered was the critics' acceptance of inflexible social hierarchies based on "eternal truths" of human nature.

I think it would be better to rephrase Arnold's axiom to say that culture seeks to do away with the awareness of class. To do so is to pursue a line of thought that opposes unequivocally Arnold's separation of culture and politics:

> The ideas of the ruling class are in every epoch the ruling ideas: i.e. the class which is the ruling material force of society, is at the same time its ruling intellectual force. . . . The ruling ideas are nothing more than the ideal expression of the dominant material relationships, the dominant material relationships grasped as ideas; hence of the relationships that make the one class the ruling one, therefore the ideas of its dominance.[6]

What Marx is suggesting here is that culture is not politically neutral, that it cannot be attached at will to whichever of the three classes one prefers. Rather, acceptance by critics and teachers of that conception of neutrality and institutional promulgation of that doctrine help keep control over mental as well as material production safe in the hands of a small number of people.

Our protected academic discipline, as well as the university's larger social role, bears out Marx's view of the connection between material and intellectual forces. The university, for instance, reflects the pattern of increased urbanization in the "outside" world. But the pattern itself reflects a contradiction. People come together to compete, and to discover their worth on the free and open market. Here, however, the competition becomes so intense, so potentially explosive, that without a controlling power transmitted from above, the group is in danger of destroying itself. So while we are improving the product through competition, we require a large measure of distancing in order to survive. Distancing is a conservative force in both senses of the word. It serves, so to speak, as our invisible protective shield.

The effect of overcrowding on the "emancipated and humane community of culture" has been a displaced materialism, but one where time is still money as long as it is spent in the pursuit not of pleasure but of virtue—otherwise known as professional competence. We cannot begin to talk about free inquiry in a "value-free institution" whose very existence depends upon an acceptance, by its members, of a set of values which in turn shape the vocabulary of scholarly discourse. Instead one simply learns this vocabulary—learns to speak of Great Chains of Being, of the Realm of Nature and the Realm of Grace, of Decadence and Discontinuous Time—without ever asking unscholarly questions about the values—or the cash value—embedded in those handy phrases.

If we take this matter of values a bit further, it becomes clear that the function of criticism, as a classroom commodity, is to create a demand for culture. The mounting bulk of scholarly articles is an example of a demand that is artificially created at the top and then forced upon students as a prerequisite of professional status. Yet while the problem of "keeping up" in one's field increasingly discourages all but the most compulsive and conflicts with the simultaneous edict to "publish or perish," the stultifying effects of such a market orientation are viewed in the faculty clubs in more or less the same light as inhabitants of large cities view the problem of what to do with solid waste.

Although Arnold saw his idea of culture as an alternative to the vulgar aspects of capitalism, enshrinement of that idea has hardly created the humanist counterculture he set out to define. Rather, it exhibits what Tocqueville called "a kind of virtuous materialism" that "would not corrupt, but enervate the soul, and noiselessly unbend the springs of action." [7] The alternative to this—and it is one that no liberal education will ever make us capable of conceiving—is not a classlessness of and in the mind, but rather a set of economic and political relationships that will define culture in accordance with a new set of social needs.

NOTES

This essay, in slightly different form, appeared under the title "The Function of Northrop Frye at the Present Time" in *College English,* Vol. 31 (March 1970), pp. 541–47.

1 Northrop Frye, *Anatomy of Criticism: Four Essays* (Princeton, N.J.: Princeton University Press, 1957), p. 7.

2 Matthew Arnold, "Culture and Anarchy," in *Poetry and Criticism of Matthew Arnold,* ed. A. D. Culler (Boston: Houghton Mifflin Co., Riverside Editions, 1969), p. 412.

3 Frye, *Anatomy,* pp. 347–48.

4 T. S. Eliot, "Tradition and the Individual Talent," in *Selected Essays of T. S. Eliot* (New York: Harcourt, Brace, & World, 1932), p. 5.

5 John Ruskin, "Traffic," in *The Genius of John Ruskin,* ed. John D. Rosenberg (Boston: Houghton Mifflin Co., Riverside Editions, 1963), p. 276.

6 Karl Marx and Frederick Engels, *The German Ideology* (New York: International Publishers Co., 1963), p. 39.

7 Quoted in Richard Hoggart, *The Uses of Literacy* (Boston: Beacon Press, 1961), p. 141.

II

THE LAYING OFF OF "CULTURE"

OR, "AIN'T NO BLACK GOD THAT'S DOIN' THAT BULLSHIT"

FREE, CLASSLESS, AND URBANE?

Barbara Bailey Kessel

I

Once upon a time I realized that the word "liberal" in the phrase "liberal education" was related to the political designation "liberal." A "liberal" American values justice, equal opportunity, and freedom, and he also believes that these social qualities are built into the structure of things so that if all men act rationally, with good will, and with energetic concern, the result will be liberty and justice for all. Since we have obviously not arrived at this result, the fault must be in the irrationality, bad faith, and apathy of you and me. An educator in the liberal tradition starts from this premise to work on the irrationality and mis-anthrophy of Man—embodied concretely in his unregen-erate students. He does this by pointing to the "self-evident truths" of his subject matter, be it English, history, art, or biology. These truths appear to him as objective, ethically neutral, and given. His articulation of them to a younger generation seems to be pure public service. Any alterna-tives, such as teaching dialects in place of standard English or Cuban poetry under Contemporary Literature, appear

to him highly partisan and political, while his own acquies-
cence to a tradition appears to be an act of reason.

The selection of the monuments of the literary tradition
is a very mysterious process. It obviously does not operate
by popular acclaim, since *Gone with the Wind* and *Uncle
Tom's Cabin* (a monument in another field) are not making
it. We do not have boards which designate the classics, and
prizes are often wide of the mark. Northrop Frye describes
it as a magical process, wherein works that liberate the
mind are liberated into the culture by the minds they
liberated:

> The ethical purpose of a liberal education is to liberate,
> which can only mean to make one capable of conceiving
> society as free, classless, and urbane. No such society
> exists, which is one reason why a liberal education must
> be deeply concerned with works of imagination. The
> imaginative element in works of art, again, lifts them
> clear of the bondage of history. Anything that emerges
> from the total experience of criticism to form part of a
> liberal education becomes, by virtue of that fact, part of
> the emancipated and humane community of culture,
> whatever its original reference. Thus liberal education
> liberates the works of culture themselves as well as the
> mind they educate.[1]

Notice how the works *emerge* and float upward—leaving
history and classes down below—to join the "free, classless,
urbane world" which exists only in the minds of the truly
educated. Although the vocabulary is anthropomorphic
and the human agent is obscured, it is there: "the total
experience of criticism" is the originator, and that means
critics, or men and women. In America that means liberals.
How do they know when they meet a great work of art?
When it is ironic, ambiguous, and humane—which means
filled with the nobility of freedom, justice, compassion, as
well as the tragedy of Man's irrationality and misanthropy.
This may seem a peculiar kit with which to greet the

working-class, nonelite students that most English teachers teach, but these values are the "critical tools" that were laid on us in graduate school or before, where alternatives were alluded to as minor heresies of one kind or another.

As I have implied, the true liberal has a lot to do to make the system work: his task is nothing less than humanizing and civilizing people who would otherwise remain irrational and misanthropic. This means that he must have in his mind some model of a humane, civilized person. From Northrop Frye, one of the most admired critics in American graduate schools, I learn that the civilized man spends most of his mental energy in a "free, classless, urbane society." At the same time, he must transcend by scorn, like Camus's Sisyphus, the fact that he doesn't actually live in such a world, which means that irony becomes an important strategy for survival. If only the blacks, the students, and the workers could be persuaded to adopt this superior mode of being, society might be peaceful, and the powerful might be free of "social problems."

My first years of teaching, though joyful at times, were filled with a general frustration. My students were not being humanized by contact with *Huckleberry Finn* or *The Scarlet Letter*. They had a stubborn literal-mindedness that steadily refused my invitation to take flight into societies and lives of the imagination. They insisted on looking at things from their point of view: they did not see any rivers to boat down or houses in the woods to retreat to with embroidery. One student told me he was "very disappointed in me" for my professed desire to live by a Walden Pond. They were not moved by Huck Finn's lack of racism to feel guilt over their own racism, partly because there is plenty in the book to confirm their racism. Above all else, they were offended by Huckleberry Finn's *shiftlessness*. Nobody had ever allowed them to be shiftless and nobody, it appeared, ever would. Why, here they were, for example, sweating away in English class learning to talk proper and Huck Finn didn't even give a damn that he sounded ignorant.

As for Sisyphus, or one version of civilized man, the students, be they black or white, cannot agree less with the dictum that "there is no fate that cannot be surmounted by scorn." Many teachers who live with themselves as failures surmount it by scorn of their students, if not the whole human race—a common fruit of the liberal world-view. But nonelite students are seldom liberals and they face rocks to push that are not mental or psychological, but physical, and the confrontation between them and the possibility of futility in their labors cannot be transcended. ("Do you mean that my parents spent their lives in those crummy jobs and saved their money so that I could go to college, and I am still not going to do any better? Do you mean that people can try as hard as they can and still not make it in America?") A life of alienated labor is not transcendible by scorn, because there is no way of feeling superior to that fate—only intellectuals can feel superior to a condition of powerlessness and manipulation. Sometimes that strategy breaks down for them, too.

There are three basic responses to the discovery, gradual or swift, that one is not getting ahead of most people in a society where everyone worth anything is supposed to get ahead of everyone else. First, an internal sense of failure and inadequacy, known as self-hatred. Second, a sense of oppression due to a partial understanding that failure doesn't come simply from one's own inadequacy; what follows is a shifting of blame to someone else, usually socially fostered targets: black people, Jews, communist "conspirators," and women (usually one's wife or mother), who become objects of deep resentment. Third, a sense of anger and outrage, not at the victims, but at those responsible for perpetuating a system in which human potentiality is either crushed or channeled into the building of empire

at home and abroad, and in which the only way to get
ahead is to climb on bodies. This third possible response
is the most rational, the least self-destructive, the most socially constructive, and the rarest—not because people are
basically irrational and prone to hate others, but because
everything possible has been done, through the media, the
textbooks, the school discipline, the military, and the organization of the work force, to socialize people toward the
first two modes of being. This is neither conspiratorial nor
unnatural, for social systems develop according to principles of preservation. What may be reasonable for the survival of a particular social system may have little to do,
however, with the survival of the people in it. Teachers
face daily the contradiction that to serve the school and the
curriculum is to hurt the students. As an English teacher,
I came to realize that my particular curriculum—when it
"takes"—tends toward the production of alienated, anxious, phony people, thoroughly mystified about themselves
and their society, who are thus manipulable all their working lives long, just like the professors who are the prototypes of this kind of intellectual socialization.

Seeing this, the radical teacher, at the strong risk of short
tenure, must attempt to provide analyses that will help
locate the sources of power and responsibility in this society. Or his attempt to turn people on to themselves (à la
Holt, Kohl, and Herndon) will be the hundred flowers
blossoming, but withering the same day. For example, students need to learn that language is a social and political
tool, constantly being changed for social purposes. If all the
people who say "he ain't" and "he be" changed miracu-
lously tomorrow to saying "he isn't," there would be just
as miraculous a compensatory change up higher in the
social scale, so that the lower people could never catch up.
One Eliza Doolittle is O.K., but her cousins and her uncles
and her aunts are definitely too many. Most English teachers don't know that themselves, and liberals are teaching

that all dialects are groovy, but we must use each one only where appropriate—"separate but equal," each to its rightful place, is what the students can hear. This is some more of that "free, classless, urbane society" that we don't live in.

II

From the beginning of teaching, I could hear my students—whether white or black, in high school or college— saying, "English stinks." Until America radicalized me, I could not understand that their gutsy rejection was not in childish rebellion against what was good for them, but out of some awareness of who they were. Of course, there are students who are completely niggerized and come to the teacher for treatment so they will be acceptable. ("I'll do anything you say; just tell me how, so I can get an A.") But I am happy to report that there are millions of kids out here, *One Dimensional Man* to the contrary, who are insistent: "English stinks—even more than History, Biology, and PE. They mess over your mind in this place, man!" Since the best way to understand someone else's oppression is to understand your own, it was my own similar suspicion in graduate school that taught me to respect such a conclusion, and to embark on "learning from the people" what was wrong with my teachers. While this revolutionary slogan may ring dead to most people in the United States, it has rich tones of meaning to a radical in a profession, who realizes that his skills will serve only the powerful unless he can learn to see through eyes other than his own middle-class ones. This is not to suggest the romanticism that all wisdom lies in the working class. It is only to say that my working-class students provided me with some essential wisdom, with a fresh perspective on the limits and deficiencies of currently accepted literary and "liberal" values of irony, ambiguity, and humanity.

In a community college class on Third World Literature, composed of twelve black and two white students, we
read "The Prisoner," a story by a black South African in
African Writing Today.[2] The story concerns the switching
of roles between the white boss, George, and his black
servant, Mulela. The narration is in the first person by
Mulela, who informs us that George is in jail in the basement but that he receives the best of care despite rumors
about whippings and electric shock. Mulela lives upstairs
with George's wife and they both cry over "poor George"
while lolling in bed together. The end suggests strongly
that just as George lost his position of power by lusting
after a black servant-woman, so Mulela, too, may fall because of his weakness for the white wife. Before class discussion, students wrote three type of papers. From the
whites came an outraged sympathy for Poor George who
was being so cruelly persecuted. To them he was "the
Fixer." From most of the blacks came exultant praise of
Mulela, who was clever enough to escape being a slave and
yet generous enough not to treat his former master with
cruelty. From one light-skinned and rather bourgeois young
black man came a discourse on man's inhumanity to man
in this "dog-eat-dog world." I carefully demonstrated the
irony of the story, which made both straight views of
George and Mulela incomplete or false and pointed out
that the lone student had "gotten" the irony, but if that
was the conclusion to be drawn from it, I'd have to think
again about the story, which I had "instinctively" liked
because of its irony. The students were depressed—they
had all liked the story very much, precisely because they
had read it as very straightforward, a sort of "Under the
Lion's Paw" in black and white, or white and black. Coming
to the story from our individual perspectives of black oppression, white oppression, middle-class upward mobility,
and literary learning, we had collided in the middle and

the story had slipped out from under us all. There was a feeling of betrayal—as if we had all come home from an inspiring rally to find that the main speaker was really an agent.

What happened next appears in retrospect to have been a series of attempts to recoup the loss. The students discussed role-playing the story as it had first appeared to various people. This proved to be too scary, but each re-asserted his vision of the story while discussing the projected role-playing. I asked them, "Why *should* the author, who was black himself, treat it as ironic that Mulela oppresses and tortures George? That kind of revenge-oppression is perfectly understandable in terms of psychology or of Old Testament justice. Did Nat Turner need to have interesting sexual fantasies in order to desire the death of his masters?" They didn't have any answers for me, and none were necessary, for it was my hangup, not theirs. The lesson that emerged for me in time was the one which forms the basis of this paper: oppression is not amusing or ironic to those who are actually oppressed. It is an aesthetic mode most appropriate to the ruling class. One of Northrop Frye's definitions of irony is helpful here. (His definitions are ordinarily useful because, unlike New Critical definitions, they are given, at least, in social terms.)

> If inferior in power or intelligence to ourselves, so that we have the sense of looking down on a scene of bondage, frustration, or absurdity, the hero belongs to the *ironic* mode. This is still true when the reader feels that he is or might be in the same situation, as the situation is being judged by the norms of a greater freedom. . . . During the last hundred years, most serious fiction has tended increasingly to be ironic in mode.[3]

This explains to me why ironic literature is so very appealing to those on the way down in the social scale (the norms of greater freedom) and so unappealing or incomprehensible to those who are struggling upward or who are permanently down—that is, to most everyone.

III

The English professor tends to portray as a model his own ironic, faintly self-mocking life-style. It is his defense against having gone to an elite institution and ending up on the frontier—at State U or Community College teaching the Barbarians. If he takes his irony far enough, he simply finds all convictions naive and rather amusing. If he does not have the fortitude and alienation to be so extreme, he may employ another defense and use his cultivated capacity to create or find ambiguity where things would seem to be simple. He feels confident that such perceptions are the mark of superior intellect, and they give him the grounds for moderate, balanced stands (a little evil in all positions) on all matters political or poetical. This use of ambiguity has its dangers, for most people do not consider ambiguity a comfortable resting place. A classroom where ambiguity has filtered into students' minds becomes electric; no one can sit still for the restlessness of it.

Of necessity, people act continually, so that doubt cast upon the validity of anything previously accepted demands immediate attention lest we become "hung up"—unable to act in any way convincing to ourselves. Artists generally are human beings who deal, through some medium, with this agonizing transition from one way of perception to another. Their works can be an invitation to an audience to participate in that process as they have structured it. However, this is an embarrassingly dynamic and moral situation, and the New Criticism provides a poetic ideology that can get around it by treating the poem as a monument, cut off from author and audience. Thus ambiguity becomes a technical matter, internal to the literary work alone. The professor can then interpret any work exhaustively without question of his own moral values, for these supposedly do not touch on his authority to interpret, which springs from his technical expertise. The student then becomes the apprentice to the master metaphor analyst, and the classroom settles down to a cemetery atmosphere appropriate to monuments.

This is the general ambience of graduate schools of English—and if you don't like it, you can leave. But of course, high schools are filled with captives, not apprentices. Adolescents are naive, that is to say, they take themselves rather seriously, so when they "take" a work of art, they take it seriously, as something addressed to them. (They take it if they can see it as addressed to them; otherwise, nothing happens but "teacher talk.")

In my first year of teaching, I had assigned American plays to be read in small groups within a class. Typical of a first-year teacher, I had no particular purpose in mind: we were "covering" American literature. Electricity began crackling in one group of five as they discussed *The Glass Menagerie*. When Laura, the crippled sister, blows out her candles at the end of the play, it is not apparent whether she is blowing away illusion or life itself. Interpretation depends upon the meaning constructed around the gentleman caller who decided to treat Laura as though she were a healthy girl, who talked with her, danced with her, and kissed her good night. The breaking of her glass unicorn, a symbol of her fantasy life, may be seen then as a moment of entry into reality or as the smashing of her only possible world. The tone of the whole play tends to put weight upon the latter construction, but the question is open enough artistically that one acting company spent a week arguing about whether the ending ought to be played for hope or despair. The five students felt so strongly about their different interpretations that they wanted to present their cases to the rest of the class, each side feeling that they could convince the others. As it turned out, the two boys who felt that the gentleman caller had done something good for Laura found the whole class in opposition, which amazed but did not discourage them.

Now what difference did it all make? We were all aware that the issue was deeper than "What did Williams intend?" The play was enticing us, it seemed, to clarify what we each thought about the way life is. The play touched an area crucial to adolescents: almost every adolescent has in his own secret estimation some crippling feature; to be adolescent is to need legitimization, from your peers especially, and as male or female in particular. The girls in the class had a lot to say about the tricky gentleman caller, who, most importantly, did not intend to call again and was therefore "leading her on." The culture says that a girl is not a real woman until she has obtained a marriage contract from some man; hence, what good was this brief encounter, no matter how lovely or transforming? Most of the boys agreed—it was "plain common sense." The two rebels without constituency were handsome All-American types, but far from boorish, and in their view the gentleman caller had performed a service of unselfish compassion by treating Laura nicely, letting her see what she could be, letting her know that the power to be a person as well as a woman was inside her and nowhere else. He had gotten nothing out of it, in the conventional trade of sex for security. In fact, he was not to be condemned for not offering her security, but applauded for getting away from the whole dishonest game. He was kind, self-confident, a loving guy. Laura was a healthier person for his passing through.

I understand more clearly now than then. The girls were angered, and even threatened, because they heard only another masculine "line." The culture, which offers little hope, either social or economic, to an unmarriageable girl, requires of women both strategy and suspicion with regard to "gentlemen callers."

When the debate had exhausted itself, there was no left-over urge either to write to Tennessee Williams or ask the teacher to arbitrate the matter. Nor was there a feeling that the majority ruled. The ambiguity in that play was *in* the play, also in them; thus it spoke to them powerfully, and each person who so heard it had to deal with it as something real. In short, this was no academic matter: it was serious. Ambiguities that matter are always serious business. That is why it is an insult to trivialize both life and art by dealing with ambiguity as a strictly internal matter, between one image and another, as New Critics usually do.

IV

I would like to conclude by comparing working-class students as literary critics with a recognized critic of liberal vision, Murray Krieger. The work of art that occupied the Third World Literature class was *Man's Fate* by André Malraux, a novel of China in 1927, during a phase of the Chinese Revolution that ended in failure. It concerns psychology and history, the relation of the personal and the political, human subjectivity and will as they interact with objective forces. Krieger starts a discussion of the work in *The Tragic Vision* by using a quotation from Berdyaev:

> It is worthy of note that the slavery of a man may be the result alike of his being exclusively engulfed by his own ego and concentrated upon his own condition without taking note of the world and other people; and of his being ejected exclusively into the external, into the objectivity of the world and losing the consciousness of his own ego. Both the one and the other are the result of a breach between the subjective and the objective.[4]

In other words, what we call human freedom cannot exist outside of the tension between self and other. Neither side of this tension can be reduced into the other without total distortion.

In *The Tragic Vision*, Krieger maintains that tragedy is no longer a cathartic vision which restores to harmony a challenged moral order, but an ironic vision which challenges moral order radically without restoration of transcendence. This framework helps Krieger to illuminate most of the modern novels he describes, but not *Man's Fate*, a book about one phase in the most massive and profound revolution in world history. A revolution challenges the past moral order and transcends that challenge with the assertion of a new moral order. Necessarily, to apply "the tragic vision" to *Man's Fate*, Krieger must find that the human beings who participated in the Revolution did so as slaves, not as people who chose to involve themselves. He must also view the Revolution itself as a stage-managed affair, controlled from above and having little to do with the desires of multitudes. Krieger proceeds to analyze the characters against the melodramatic *backdrop* of a revolution, while my students analyzed the characters in relation to the process of revolution.

There is one character on whom Krieger's analysis works, because for him the Revolution *is* merely backdrop. That is Ch'en, a terrorist who has a great drive to suicide which he transforms into a need to die for the Revolution, to "die on the highest possible plane." The students were very much interested in him, a couple of them admiring him greatly as the perfect revolutionary, totally dedicated, ready to "die for his people." But other students talked them out of this view, pointing out as part of their persuasion that, as he did not wish to *live* for the Revolution, he did not die for it either, but merely used the Revolution for his own psychological needs. "If everyone were that way, you'd never accomplish a revolution." They felt that the tension between the normal desire to live in a revolutionary new society and the willingness to die to make that society real was desirable.

This tension is present in Kyo, the tactical leader of the Shanghai revolt. Because of his intimate relationships with his wife, his father, and his comrades in the struggle, Kyo's life is dear to him and the imminence of his death is pain-ful. The students decided unanimously, after discussion with each other, that Kyo was the perfect revolutionary leader. For them, his death was not tragic because, even though he shrank from death personally, part of him—sym-bolized by his recorded voice—reached out to objective reality, and that part of him had always known that to will his actions in that situation would probably mean death. It did not come to him through his own flaws or errors, or with his own complicity or desire. Death to revolution-ary leaders is a normal part of a process, as black students, at least, are only too well aware. To call it tragic is to see only the personal side of the tension between subjective and objective.

For Krieger, Kyo, analyzed against the Revolution as backdrop, simply becomes another Ch'en, driven and com-pulsive—though to do this, Krieger must first convict Malraux of losing control over his book, of being unable to project what he clearly intends as a contrast.

Krieger also makes a Ch'en of Hemmelrich, someone, on the other hand, the students felt they had all known, a guy out of whom all revolutions really come. He is an utterly wretched member of the Shanghai poor, who helps the rev-olutionary leaders hide their matériel during the time of secret planning, but feels a sense of rage and helplessness because he cannot help them fight since his crippled wife and diseased child would die without his work. Hemmel-rich says, "I am a lamppost in the street that everything free in the world pisses on." When his wife and child are killed by the enemy, he is delivered into a state of frenzy that sends him out to kill with joy. At the end we are told that he has escaped to Russia, where he works in peace and happiness. The students, including two whose families con-tain ten children each, were delighted with Hemmelrich. They said that his feelings as he killed were much more understandable than the psychotic Ch'en's. Instead of becoming sick with self-hate and frustration as Ch'en did, it was better to kill your real enemy, your oppressor. This was a liberating act, both psychologically and virtually, so that one might become for the first time peaceful; whereas Ch'en had to go on killing till he died. He could never treat the enemy as truly external because his enemy was so firmly within himself. Once again, the students' careful sense of the relations between subjective and objective is admirable. Here is Krieger on Hemmelrich:

> While all this goes on within him, the blood of his wife and child, splattered everywhere, has been bewitching him, by smell and touch, under his feet on the floor, under his fist as it madly pounds the counter. And as we read of his "frightful intoxication" and of the mixture in him of "horror and satisfaction," we must recall Ch'en's description of his own opiumlike ecstasy and his confession to Gisors that at the sight of his victim's blood he felt "not *only* horror." The later description of Hemmelrich engaged in combat leaves no doubt that he has not restrained the violent impulses that have now been freed to act.
>
> I have had to treat Hemmelrich at this length in order to establish how completely we can use the terms of Ch'en to explain him. Considered this way, Hemmelrich can be shown to point to the split in Malraux between artist and ideologue. The aesthetic imperfections this split leads him into in *Man's Fate* allow the novel its continuing interest because it develops a metapolitical interest. The Ch'en-like temperament, which I hope will be now conceded to include Hemmelrich, can of course not be contained by Marxist doctrine, cannot be satisfied or even appeased by the Communist version of revolution. The "need" that characterizes it is not one that social-political conditions alone create or that a change in these conditions can dissipate, all of which suggests we are dealing with an ontological affair rather than a political one.[5]

Why is it that Krieger cannot realize that the killing of Hemmelrich's wife and child by the military police was a political act, and that his rage is an appropriate human response to naked injustice, rather than an "opium high" on the smell and feel of human blood? In the liberal imagination of such critics, called "liberated, civilized, and humane" by Northrop Frye, a revolutionary cannot conceivably be other than demonically possessed and suffering broken connections between his own subjective will and the objective reality of history. A mass revolution becomes, for such minds, a horde of schizophrenic puppets being manipulated by a Party. Why is it impossible for liberal critics to conceive of miserable, oppressed people freely choosing to struggle against their own oppression? A liberal education should *enlarge* the imagination. What was wrong with *Man's Fate* for Krieger was *not,* as he wishes to insist, a matter internal to the work, but a political-philosophical disagreement with Malraux—or, perhaps, a fundamental failure to understand the political realities Malraux portrays.

The academic system, no less than any other sector of American society, has rewards and sanctions that shape the product; since the cold war began, the mainstream of scholarly effort in every field displays this same attempt to divorce values and ideology from the field and to define the advanced study of anything as a body of value-free techniques. The result, of course, is that we are taught capitalist and imperialist ideology disguised as technology. The most important effect of this training is to shape human beings into manipulable objects rather than determiners of meaning and sources of power. Meaning falls outside the realm of education into the private realm or flies upward to be determined by the programmers of your computer tape. The students and the teachers merely learn *how to*—carry out a field study, calculate the GNP, translate a poem into prose, or develop a germ culture that would destroy the world.

The liberal at this point would say, "So what else is new?

Very few people can really think for themselves (beyond terms set for them) anyhow. That is not capitalism, but human nature."

And I would reply, "If that's your view of human nature, then you are quite right to be an ardent capitalist. Like the Grand Inquisitor, you do us all a great good turn by thinking for us. But, of course, you aren't an ardent *ist* of any sort; you're much too ironic. Do be careful to maintain the delicate balance which irony requires, or you might find yourself feeling moral, humane, and rational while performing your pacification services upon the restless, powerless populace."

NOTES

This essay appeared, in slightly different form, in *College English*, Vol. 31 (March 1970), pp. 531–40.

1 Northrop Frye, *Anatomy of Criticism: Four Essays* (Princeton, N.J.: Princeton University Press, 1957), pp. 347–48.

2 Lewis Nkosi, "The Prisoner," in Ezekiel Mphahlele, ed., *African Writing Today* (Harmondsworth: Penguin Books 1967), pp. 294–307.

3 Frye, *Anatomy of Criticism*, pp. 34–35.

4 Nicolas Berdyaev, *Slavery and Freedom*, quoted in Murray Krieger, *The Tragic Vision* (Chicago: University of Chicago Press, Phoenix Books, 1966), p. 50.

5 Krieger, *Tragic Vision*, p. 58.

THE LOGIC OF
NONSTANDARD ENGLISH

William Labov

In the past decade, a great deal of federally sponsored research has been devoted to the educational problems of children in ghetto schools. In order to account for the poor performance of children in these schools, educational psychologists have attempted to discover what kind of disadvantage or defect the children are suffering from. The viewpoint which has been widely accepted, and used as the basis for large-scale intervention programs, is that the children show a cultural deficit as a result of an impoverished environment in their early years. Considerable attention has been given to language. In this area, the deficit theory appears as the concept of "verbal deprivation": according to this concept, black children in the urban ghettos receive little verbal stimulation, hear very little well-formed language, and as a result are impoverished in their means of verbal expression: they cannot speak complete sentences, do not know the names of common objects, cannot form concepts or convey logical thoughts.

Unfortunately, these notions are based upon the work of educational psychologists who know very little about language and even less about black children. The concept of verbal deprivation has no basis in social reality: in fact, black children in the urban ghettos receive a great deal of verbal stimulation, hear more well-formed sentences than middle-class children, and participate fully in a highly verbal culture; they have the same basic vocabulary, possess the same capacity for conceptual learning, and use the same logic as anyone else who learns to speak and understand English.

The notion of verbal deprivation is a part of the most modern mythology of educational psychology, typical of the unfounded notions which tend to expand rapidly in our educational system. In past decades linguists have been as guilty as others in promoting such intellectual fashions at the expense of both teachers and children. But the myth of verbal deprivation is particularly dangerous, because it diverts the attention from real defects of our educational system to imaginary defects of the child; and as we shall see, it leads its sponsors inevitably to the hypothesis of the genetic inferiority of black children which it was originally designed to avoid.

The most useful service which linguists can perform today is to clear away the illusion of "verbal deprivation" and provide a more adequate notion of the relations between standard and nonstandard dialects. In the writings of many prominent educational psychologists, we find a very poor understanding of the nature of language. Children are treated as if they have no language of their own in the preschool programs put forward by Bereiter and Engelmann.[1] The linguistic behavior of ghetto children in test situations is the principal evidence for their genetic inferiority in the view of Arthur Jensen.[2] In this essay, I will examine critically both of these approaches to the language and intelligence of the populations labeled "verbally" and "culturally deprived."[3] I will attempt to explain how the myth of verbal deprivation has arisen, bringing to bear the methodological findings of sociolinguistic work, and some substantive facts about language which are known to all linguists. I will be particularly concerned with the relation between concept formation on the one hand and dialect differences on the other, since it is in this area that the most dangerous misunderstandings have arisen.

I. VERBALITY

The general setting in which the deficit theory has arisen consists of a number of facts which are known to all of us: that black children in the central urban ghettos do badly on all school subjects, including arithmetic and reading. In reading, they average more than two years behind the national norm.[4] Furthermore, this lag is cumulative, so that they do worse comparatively in the fifth grade than in the first grade. Reports in the literature show that this bad performance is correlated most closely with socioeconomic status. Segregrated ethnic groups, however, seem to do worse than others: in particular, Indian, Mexican Americans, and black children.[5]

The term "lower-class" is frequently used to describe children of the urban ghetto. But in the several sociolinguistic studies we have carried out, and in many parallel studies, we have found it useful to distinguish "lower-class" from "working-class" groups. Lower-class families are typically female-based, or "matrifocal," with no father present to provide steady economic support; whereas in the working class there is typically an intact nuclear family with the father holding a semiskilled or skilled job. The educational problems of ghetto areas run across this important class distinction; there is no evidence, for example, that the father's presence or absence is closely correlated with educational achievement.[6] The peer groups we have studied in south central Harlem, representing the basic vernacular culture, include members from both family types. The attack against "cultural deprivation" in the ghetto is overtly directed at family structures typical of lower-class families, but the educational "failure" we have been discussing is characteristic of both working-class and lower-class children.

In the balance of this essay, I will therefore refer to "children from urban ghetto areas," rather than "lower-class children": the population we are concerned with are those who participate fully in the vernacular culture of the street and who have been alienated from the school sys-tem.[7] We are obviously dealing with the effects of the caste system of American society—essentially a "color-marking" system. Everyone recognizes this. The question is, By what mechanism does the color bar prevent children from learn-ing to read? One answer is the notion of "cultural depriva-tion" put forward by Martin Deutsch and others: black children are said to lack the favorable factors in their home environment which enable middle-class children to do well in school.[8] These factors involve the development, through verbal interaction with adults, of various cognitive skills, including the ability to reason abstractly, to speak fluently, and to focus upon long-range goals. In their publications, these psychologists also recognize broader social factors.[9] However, the deficit theory does not focus upon the inter-action of the black child with white society so much as on his failure to interact with his mother at home. In the lit-erature we find very little direct observation of verbal in-teraction in the black home; most typically, the investiga-tors ask the child if he has dinner with his parents, and if he engages in dinner-table conversation with them. He is also asked whether his family takes him on trips to mu-seums and other cultural activities. This slender thread of evidence is used to explain and interpret the large body of tests carried out in the laboratory and in the school.

The most extreme view which proceeds from this orien-tation—and one that is now being widely accepted—is that lower-class black children have no language at all. Some educational psychologists first draw from Basil Bernstein's writings that "much of lower-class language consists of a kind of incidental 'emotional accompaniment' to action here and now." [10] Bernstein's views are filtered through a strong bias against all forms of working-class behavior, so that he sees middle-class language as superior in every respect—as "more abstract, and necessarily somewhat more flexible, detailed and subtle." One can proceed through a range of such views until one comes to the practical program of Carl Bereiter, Siegfried Engelmann, and their associates.[11] Bereiter's program for an academically oriented preschool is based upon their premise that black children must have a language which they can learn, and their empirical findings that these children come to school without such a language. In his work with four-year-old black children from Urbana, Illinois, Bereiter reports that their communication was by gestures, "single words," and "a series of badly connected words or phrases," such as *They mine* and *Me got juice.* He reports that Negro children could not ask questions, that "without exaggerating . . . these four-year-olds could make no statements of any kind." Furthermore, when these children were asked "Where is the book?" they did not know enough to look at the table where the book was lying in order to answer. Thus Bereiter concludes that the children's speech forms are nothing more than a series of emotional cries, and he decides to treat them "as if the children had no language at all." He identifies their speech with his interpretation of Bernstein's restricted code: "The language of culturally deprived children . . . is not merely an underdeveloped version of standard English, but is a basically non-logical mode of expressive behavior." [12] The basic program of his preschool is to teach them a new language devised by Engelmann, which consists of a limited series of questions

and answers such as *Where is the squirrel?* / *The squirrel is
in the tree*. The children will not be punished if they use
their vernacular speech on the playground, but they will
not be allowed to use it in the schoolroom. If they should
answer the question "Where is the squirrel?" with the illogical vernacular form "In the tree," they will be repre-
hended by various means and made to say, "The squirrel
is in the tree."

Linguists and psycholinguists who have worked with
black children are apt to dismiss this view of their langauge
as utter nonsense. Yet there is no reason to reject Bereiter's observations as spurious: they were certainly not
made up. On the contrary, they give us a very clear view of
the behavior of student and teacher which can be dupli-
cated in any classroom. In our own work outside the adult-
dominated environments of school and home,[13] we do not
observe black children behaving like this, but on many occasions we have been asked to help analyze the results of
research into verbal deprivation in such test situations.

Here, for example, is a complete interview with a black
boy, one of hundreds carried out in a New York City
school. The boy enters a room where there is a large,
friendly white interviewer, who puts on the table in front
of him a block or a fire engine, and says, "Tell me everything you can about this!" (The interviewer's further remarks are in parentheses.)

[*12 seconds of silence*]
(What would you say it looks like?)
        [*8 seconds of silence*]
A space ship.
(Hmmmmm.)
        [*13 seconds of silence*]
Like a je-et.
        [*12 seconds of silence*]
Like a plane.

[20 seconds of silence]

(What color is it?)

Orange. [2 seconds]. An' whi-ite. [2 seconds].
An' green.

[6 seconds of silence]

(An' what could you use it for?)

[8 seconds of silence]

A je-et.

[6 seconds of silence]

(If you had two of them, what would you do with
   them?)

[6 seconds of silence]

Give one to some-body.

(Hmmm. Who do you think would like to have it?)

[10 seconds of silence]

Cla-rence.

(Mm. Where do you think we could get another one
   of these?)

At the store.

(Oh-ka-ay!)

We have here the same kind of defensive, monosyllabic
behavior which is reported in Bereiter's work. What is the
situation that produces it? The child is in an asymmetrical
situation where anything he says can literally be held
against him. He has learned a number of devices to *avoid*
saying anything in this situation, and he works very hard to
achieve this end. One may observe the intonation patterns of

$$I \quad a \quad know \quad \text{and} \quad a \quad space \quad shi^{p}$$

which black children
often use when they are asked a question to which the answer is obvious. The answer may be read as "Will this sat-
isfy you?"

If one takes this interview as a measure of the verbal
capacity of the child, it must be as his capacity to defend
himself in a hostile and threatening situation. But unfortunately, thousands of such interviews are used as evidence

of the child's total verbal capacity, or more simply his verbality: it is argued that this lack of "verbality" *explains* his poor performance in school. Operation Headstart and other such intervention programs have largely been based upon the "deficit theory"—the notion that such interviews give us a measure of the child's verbal capacity and that the verbal stimulation which he has been missing can be supplied in a preschool environment.

The verbal behavior which is shown by the child in the test situation quoted above is not the result of ineptness of the interviewer. It is rather the result of regular sociolinguistic factors operating upon adult and child in this asymmetrical situation. In our work in urban ghetto areas, we have often encountered such behavior. Ordinarily we worked with boys ten to seventeen years old, and whenever we extended our approach downward to eight- or nine-year-olds, we began to see the need for different techniques to explore the verbal capacity of the child. At one point we began a series of interviews with younger brothers of the Thunderbirds at 1390 Fifth Avenue. Clarence Robins returned from an interview with eight-year-old Leon L. with the following minimal responses to topics which had aroused intense interest in interviews with older boys:

CR: What if you saw somebody kickin' somebody else on the ground, or was using a stick, what would you do if you saw that?

LEON: Mmmm.

CR: If it was supposed to be a fair fight—

LEON: I don' know.

CR: You don' know? Would you do anything? . . . huh? I can't hear you.

LEON: No.

CR: Did you ever see somebody got beat up real bad?

LEON: . . . Nope ? ? ?

CR: Well—uh—did you ever get into a fight with a guy?

LEON: Nope.
CR: That was bigger than you?
LEON: Nope.
CR: You never been in a fight?
LEON: Nope.
CR: Nobody ever pick on you?
LEON: Nope.
CR: Nobody ever hit you?
LEON: Nope.
CR: How come?
LEON: Ah 'on' know.
CR: Didn't you ever hit somebody?
LEON: Nope.
CR: [*incredulous*] You never hit nobody?
LEON: Mhm.
CR: Aww, ba-a-a-be, you ain't gonna tell me that.

It may be that Leon is here defending himself against accusations of wrongdoing, since Clarence knows that Leon has been in fights, that he has been taking pencils away from little boys. But if we turn to a more neutral subject, we find the same pattern:

CR: You watch—you like to watch television? . . .
       Hey, Leon . . . you like to watch television?
       [*Leon nods*] What's your favorite program?
LEON: Uhhmmm . . . I look at cartoons.
CR: Well, what's your favorite one? What's your
       favorite program?
LEON: Superman . . .
CR: Yeah? Did you see Superman—ah—yesterday,
       or day before yesterday: when's the last time
       you saw Superman?
LEON: Sa-aturday.
CR: You rem—you saw it Saturday? What was the
       story all about? You remember the story?
LEON: M-m.
CR: You don't remember the story of what—that
       you saw of Superman?

LEON: Nope.

CR: You don't remember what happened, huh?

LEON: Hm-m.

CR: I see—ah—what other stories do you like to watch on TV?

LEON: Mmmm ? ? ? ? .... umm ... [*glottalization*]

CR: Hmm? [*four seconds*]

LEON: Hh?

CR: What's th'other stories that you like to watch?

LEON: Mi-ighty Mouse ...

CR: And what else?

LEON: Ummmm ... ahm ...

This nonverbal behavior occurs in a relatively *favorable* context for adult-child interaction, since the adult is a black man raised in Harlem, who knows this particular neighborhood and these boys very well. He is a skilled interviewer who has obtained a very high level of verbal response with techniques developed for a different age level, and has an extraordinary advantage over most teachers or experimenters in these respects. But even his skills and personality are ineffective in breaking down the social constraints that prevail here.

When we reviewed the record of this interview with Leon, we decided to use it as a test of our own knowledge of the sociolinguistic factors which control speech. We made the following changes in the social situation: in the next interview with Leon, Clarence

1. Brought along a supply of potato chips, changing the "interview" into something more in the nature of a party.

2. Brought along Leon's best friend, eight-year-old Gregory.

3. Reduced the height imbalance. When Clarence got down on the floor of Leon's room, he dropped from 6 feet, 2 inches to 3 feet, 6 inches.

4. Introduced taboo words and taboo topics, and proved to Leon's surprise that one can say anything into our microphone without any fear of retaliation. It did not hit or bite back. The result of these changes is a striking difference in the volume and style of speech.

[*The tape is punctuated throughout by the sound of potato chips.*]

CR: Is there anybody who says "your momma drink pee"?

{ LEON: [*rapidly and breathlessly*] Yee-ah!
{ GREG: Yup.

LEON: And your father eat doo-doo for breakfas'!

CR: Ohhh! [*laughs*]

LEON: And they say your father—your father eat doo-doo for dinner!

GREG: When they sound on me, I say "C.B.M."

CR: What that mean?

{ LEON: Congo booger-snatch! [*laughs*]
{ GREG: Congo booger-snatcher! [*laughs*]

GREG: And sometimes I'll curse with "B.B."

CR: What that?

GREG: Black boy. [*Leon crunching on potato chips*] Oh that's a "M.B.B."

CR: M.B.B. What's that?

GREG: 'Merican Black Boy.

CR: Oh.

GREG: Anyway, 'Mericans is same like white people, right?

LEON: And they talk about Allah.

CR: Oh yeah?

GREG: Yeah.

CR: What they say about Allah?

{ LEON: Allah—Allah is God.
{ GREG: Allah—

CR: And what else?

LEON: I don' know the res'.

GREG: Allah i—Allah is God, Allah is the only God, Allah—

LEON: Allah is the *son* of God.

GREG: But can he make magic?

LEON: Nope.

GREG: I know who can make magic?

CR: Who can?

LEON: The God, the real one.

CR: Who can make magic?

GREG: The son of po'—(CR: Hm?) I'm sayin' the po'k chop God! He only a po'k chop God! [14] [*Leon chuckles*]

The "nonverbal" Leon is now competing actively for the floor; Gregory and Leon talk to each other as much as they do to the interviewer.

One can make a more direct comparison of the two interviews by examining the section on fighting. Leon persists in denying that he fights, but he can no longer use monosyllabic answers, and Gregory cuts through his façade in a way that Clarence Robins alone was unable to do.

CR: Now, you said you had this fight, now, but I wanted you to tell me about the fight that you had.

LEON: I ain't had no fight.

GREG: Yes you did!   He said Barry,

CR: You said you had one! you had a fight with Butchie,

GREG: An' he say Garland! . . . an' Michael!

CR: an' Barry . . .

LEON: I di'n'; you said that, Gregory!

GREG: You did!

LEON: You know you said that!

GREG: You said Garland, remember that?

GREG: You said Garland!   Yes you did!

CR: You said Garland, that's right.

GREG: He said Mich—an' I say Michael.

{ CR: Did you have a fight with Garland?

  LEON: Uh-uh. }

CR: You had one, and he beat you up, too!

GREG: Yes he did!

LEON: No, I di—I never had a fight with Butch! . . .

The same pattern can be seen on other local topics, where the interviewer brings neighborhood gossip to bear on Leon, and Gregory acts as a witness.

CR: . . . Hey Gregory! I heard that around here . . . and I'm 'on' tell you who said it, too . . .

LEON: Who?

{ CR: about you . . .

  LEON: Who?

  GREG: I'd say it! }

CR: They said that—they say that the only person you play with is David Gilbert.

{ LEON: Yee-ah! yee-ah! yee-ah! . . .

  GREG: That's who you play with! }

{ LEON: I 'on' play with him no more!

  GREG: Yes you do! }

LEON: I 'on' play with him no more!

GREG: But remember, about me and Robbie?

LEON: So that's not—

GREG: and you went to Petey and Gilbert's house, 'member? Ah haaah!!

LEON: So that's—so—but I would—I had came back out, an' I ain't go to his house no more . . .

The observer must now draw a very different conclusion about the verbal capacity of Leon. The monosyllabic speaker who had nothing to say about anything and could not remember what he did yesterday has disappeared. Instead, we have two boys who have so much to say they keep interrupting each other, who seem to have no difficulty in using the English language to express themselves. And we in turn obtain the volume of speech and the rich array of grammatical devices which we need for analyzing the structure of black English (BE): negative concord [*I 'on' play with him no more*], the pluperfect [*had came back out*], negative perfect [*I ain't had*], the negative preterit [*I ain't go*], and so on.

One can now transfer this demonstration of the sociolinguistic control of speech to other test situations—including IQ and reading tests in school. It should be immediately apparent that none of the standard tests will come anywhere near measuring Leon's verbal capacity. On these tests he will show up as very much the monosyllabic, inept, ignorant, bumbling child of our first interview. The teacher has far less ability than Clarence Robins to elicit speech from this child; Clarence knows the community, the things that Leon has been doing, and the things that Leon would like to talk about. But the power relationships in a one-to-one confrontation between adult and child are too asymmetrical. This does not mean that some black children will not talk a great deal when alone with an adult, or that an adult cannot get close to any child. It means that the social situation is the most powerful determinant of verbal behavior and that an adult must enter into the right social relation with a child if he wants to find out what a child can do. This is just what many teachers cannot do.

The view of the black speech community which we obtain from our work in the ghetto areas is precisely the opposite from that reported by Deutsch, Engelmann, and Bereiter. We see a child bathed in verbal stimulation from morning to night. We see many speech events which depend upon the competitive exhibitions of verbal skills: singing, sounding, toasts, rifting, louding—a whole range of activities in which the individual gains status through his use of language.[15] We see the younger child trying to acquire these skills from older children—hanging around on the outskirts of the older peer groups, and imitating this behavior. We see, however, no connection between verbal

skill at the speech events characteristic of the street culture
and success in the schoolroom; which says something about
classrooms rather than about a child's language.

II. VERBOSITY

There are undoubtedly many verbal skills which children from ghetto areas must learn in order to do well in
school, and some of these are indeed characteristic of
middle-class verbal behavior. Precision in spelling, practice in handling abstract symbols, the ability to state explicitly the meaning of words, and a richer knowledge of
the Latinate vocabulary may all be useful acquisitions.
But is it true that *all* of the middle-class verbal habits are
functional and desirable in school? Before we impose
middle-class verbal style upon children from other cultural
groups, we should find out how much of it is useful for the
main work of analyzing and generalizing, and how much
is merely stylistic—or even dysfunctional. In high school
and college, middle-class children spontaneously compli-
cate their syntax to the point that instructors despair of
getting them to make their language simpler and clearer.
In every learned journal one can find examples of jargon
and empty elaboration—and complaints about it. Is the
"elaborated code" of Bernstein really so "flexible, detailed,
and subtle" as some psychologists believe? [16] Isn't it also
turgid, redundant, bombastic, and empty? Is it not simply
an elaborated style, rather than a superior code or system? [17]
Our work in the speech community makes it painfully
obvious that in many ways working-class speakers are more
effective narrators, reasoners, and debaters than many
middle-class speakers, who temporize, qualify, and lose
their argument in a mass of irrelevant detail. Many academic writers try to rid themselves of the part of middle-
class style that is empty pretension, and keep the part
necessary for precision. But the average middle-class

speaker that we encounter makes no such effort; he is en-
meshed in verbiage, the victim of sociolinguistic factors
beyond his control.

I will not attempt to support this argument here with
systematic quantitative evidence, although it is possible to
develop measures which show how far middle-class speakers
can wander from the point. I would like to contrast two
speakers dealing with roughly the same topic: matters of
belief. The first is Larry H., a fifteen-year-old core member
of the Jets, being interviewed by John Lewis. Larry is one
of the loudest and roughest members of the Jets, one who
gives the least recognition to the conventional rules of
politeness.[18] For most readers, first contact with Larry
would produce some fairly negative reactions on both
sides: it is probable that you would not *like* him any more
than his teachers do. Larry causes trouble in and out of
school; he was put back from the eleventh grade to the
ninth, and has been threatened with further action by the
school authorities.

JL: What happens to you after you die? Do you
       know?
LARRY H: Yeah, I know. (What?) After they put you
       in the ground, your body turns into—ah
       —bones, an' shit.
JL: What happens to your spirit?
LARRY: Your spirit—soon as you die, your spirit
       leaves you. (And where does the spirit go?)
       Well, it all depends. (On what?) You know,
       like some people say if you're good an' shit,
       your spirit goin' t'heaven . . . 'n' if you bad,
       your spirit goin' to hell. Well, bullshit!
       Your spirit goin' to hell anyway, good or
       bad.
JL: Why?
LARRY: Why? I'll tell you why. 'Cause, you see,
       doesn' nobody really know that it's a God,
       y'know, 'cause, I mean I have seen black

> gods, pink gods, white gods, all color gods,
> and don't nobody know it's really a God.
> An' when they be sayin' if you good, you
> goin' t'heaven, tha's bullshit, 'cause you
> ain't goin' to no heaven, 'cause it ain't no
> heaven for you to go to.

Larry is a paradigmatic speaker of black English (BE) as opposed to standard English (SE). His grammar shows a high concentration of such characteristic BE forms as negative inversion [*don't nobody know*], negative concord [*you ain't goin' to no heaven*], invariant *be* [when they *be sayin'*], dummy *it* for SE *there* [*it ain't no heaven*], optional copula deletion [*if you're good . . . if you bad*], and full forms of auxiliaries [*I have seen*]. The only SE influence in this passage is the one case of *doesn't* instead of the invariant *don't* of BE. Larry also provides a paradigmatic example of the rhetorical style of BE: he can sum up a complex argument in a few words, and the full force of his opinions comes through without qualification or reservation. He is eminently quotable, and his interviews give us a great many concise statements of the BE point of view. One can almost say that Larry speaks the BE culture.[19]

It is the logical form of this passage which is of particular interest here. Larry presents a complex set of interdependent propositions which can be explicated by setting out the SE equivalents in linear order. The basic argument is to deny the twin propositions:

(A)   If you are good,   (B) then your spirit will go to heaven.

(~A) If you are bad,   (C) then your spirit will go to hell.

Larry denies (B), and asserts that if *(A) or (~A), then (C)*. His argument may be outlined as follows:

(1) Everyone has a different idea of what God is like.

(2) Therefore nobody really knows that God exists.

(3) If there is a heaven, it was made by God.

(4) If God doesn't exist, he couldn't have made heaven.

(5) Therefore heaven does not exist.

(6) You can't go somewhere that doesn't exist.

(~B) Therefore you can't go to heaven.

(C) Therefore you are going to hell.

The argument is presented in the order: (C), because (2) because (1), therefore (2), therefore (~B) because (5) and (6). Part of the argument is implicit: the connection (2) therefore (~B) leaves unstated the connecting links (3) and (4), and in this interval Larry strengthens the propositions from the form (2) *Nobody knows if there is* to (5) *There is no*. Otherwise, the case is presented explicitly as well as economically. The complex argument is summed up in Larry's last sentence, which shows formally the dependence of (~B) on (5) and (6):

> An' when they be sayin' if you good, you goin' t'heaven,
> [The proposition, if A, then B]
>
> tha's bullshit,
> [is absurd]
>
> 'cause you ain't goin' to no heaven
> [because ~B]
>
> 'cause it ain't no heaven for you to go to.
> [because (5) and (6)].

This hypothetical argument is not carried on at a high level of seriousness. It is a game played with ideas as counters, in which opponents use a wide variety of verbal devices to win. There is no personal commitment to any of these propositions, and no reluctance to strengthen one's argument by bending the rules of logic as in the (2, 5) sequence. But if the opponent invokes the rules of logic, they hold. In John Lewis's interviews, he often makes this move, and the force of his argument is always acknowledged and countered within the rules of logic. In this case, he pointed out the fallacy that the argument (2-3-4-5-6) leads to ($\sim$C) as well as ($\sim$B), so it cannot be used to support Larry's assertion (C):

JL: Well, if there's no heaven, how could there be a hell?

LARRY: I mean—ye-eah. Well, let me tell you, it ain't no hell, 'cause this is hell right here, y'know! (This is hell?) Yeah, this is hell right here!

Larry's answer is quick, ingenious, and decisive. The application of the (3-4-5) argument to hell is denied, since hell is here, and therefore conclusion ($\sim$B) stands. These are not ready-made or preconceived opinions, but new propositions devised to win the logical argument in the game being played. The reader will note the speed and precision of Larry's mental operations. He does not wander, or insert meaningless verbiage. The only repetition is (2), placed before and after (1) in his original statement. It is often said that the nonstandard vernacular is not suited for dealing with abstract or hypothetical questions, but in fact speakers from the BE community take great delight in exercising their wit and logic on the most improbable and problematical matters. Despite the fact that Larry H. does not believe in God, and has just denied all knowledge of him, John Lewis advances the following hypothetical question:

JL: . . . But, just say that there is a God, what color is he? White or black?

LARRY: Well, if it is a God . . . I wouldn' know what color, I couldn' say—couldn' nobody say what color he is or really *would* be.

JL: But now, jus' suppose there was a God—

LARRY: Unless'n they say . . .

JL: No, I was jus' sayin' jus' suppose there is a God, would he be white or black?

LARRY: . . . He'd be white, man.

JL: Why?

LARRY: Why? I'll tell you why. 'Cause the average whitey out here got everything, you dig? And the nigger ain't got shit, y'know? Y'unnerstan'? So—um—for—in order for *that* to happen, you know it ain't no black God that's doin' that bullshit.

No one can hear Larry's answer to this question without being convinced that they are in the presence of a skilled speaker with great "verbal presence of mind," who can use the English language expertly for many purposes. Larry's answer to John Lewis is again a complex argument. The formulation is not SE, but it is clear and effective even for those not familiar with the vernacular. The nearest SE equivalent might be: "So you know that God isn't black, because if he was, he wouldn't have arranged things like that."

The reader will have noted that this analysis is being carried out in standard English, and the inevitable challenge is: Why not write in BE, then, or in your own nonstandard dialect? The fundamental reason is, of course, one of firmly fixed social conventions. All communities agree that SE is the "proper" medium for formal writing and public communication. Furthermore, it seems likely that SE has an advantage over BE in explicit analysis of surface forms, which is what we are doing here. We will return to this opposition between explicitness and logical statement in sections III and IV. First, however, it will be helpful to examine SE in its primary natural setting, as the medium for informal spoken communication of middle-class speakers.

Let us now turn to the second speaker, an upper-middle-class, college-educated black man being interviewed by Clarence Robins in our survey of adults in central Harlem.

CR: Do you know of anything that someone can do, to have someone who has passed on visit him in a dream?

CHAS. M.:   Well, I even heard my parents say that there is such a thing as something in dreams, some things like that, and sometimes dreams do come true. I have personally never had a dream come true. I've never dreamt that somebody was dying and they actually died, (Mhm) or that I was going to have ten dollars the next day and somehow I got ten dollars in my pocket. (Mhm.) I don't particularly believe in that, I don't think it's true. I do feel, though, that there is such a thing as—ah—witchcraft. I do feel that in certain cultures there is such a thing as witchcraft, or some sort of *science* of witchcraft; I don't think that it's just a matter of believing hard enough that there is such a thing as witchcraft. I do believe that there is such a thing that a person can put himself in a state of *mind* (Mhm), or that—er—something could be given them to intoxicate them in a certain—to a certain frame of mind—that—that could actually be considered witchcraft.

Charles M. is obviously a "good speaker" who strikes the listener as well-educated, intelligent, and sincere. He is a likable and attractive person—the kind of person that middle-class listeners rate very high on a scale of "job suitability" and equally high as a potential friend.[20] His language is more moderate and tempered than Larry's; he makes every effort to qualify his opinions, and seems anxious to avoid any misstatements or overstatements.

From these qualities emerges the primary characteristic of this passage—its *verbosity*. Words multiply, some modifying and qualifying, others repeating or padding the main argument. The first half of this extract is a response to the initial question on dreams, basically:

(1) Some people say that dreams sometimes come true.

(2) I have never had a dream come true.

(3) Therefore I don't believe (1).

Some characteristic filler phrases appear here: *such a thing as, some things like that, particularly*. Two examples of dreams given after (2) are afterthoughts, that might have been given after (1). Proposition (3) is stated twice for no obvious reason. Nevertheless, this much of Charles M.'s response is well directed to the point of the question. He then volunteers a statement of his beliefs about witchcraft which shows the difficulty of middle-class speakers who (*a*) want to express a belief in something but (*b*) want to show themselves as judicious, rational, and free from superstitions. The basic proposition can be stated simply in five words:

But I believe in witchcraft.

However, the idea is enlarged to exactly one hundred words, and it is difficult to see what else is being said. In the following quotations, padding which can be removed without change in meaning is shown in brackets.

(1) "I [do] feel, though, that there is [such a thing as] witchcraft." *Feel* seems to be a euphemism for "believe."

(2) "[I do feel that] in certain cultures [there is such a thing as witchcraft]." This repetition seems designed only to introduce the word *culture*, which lets us know that the speaker knows about anthropology.

Does *certain cultures* mean "not in ours" or "not in all"?

(3) "[or some sort of *science* of witchcraft.]" This addition seems to have no clear meaning at all. What is a "science" of witchcraft as opposed to just plain witchcraft? [21] The main function is to introduce the word *science*, though it seems to have no connection to what follows.

(4) "I don't think that it's just [a matter of] believing hard enough that there is [such a thing as] witchcraft." The speaker argues that witchcraft is not merely a belief; there is more to it.

(5) "I [do] believe that [there is such a thing that] a person can put himself in a state of *mind* . . . that [could actually be considered] witchcraft." Is witchcraft as a state of mind different from the state of belief denied in (4)?

(6) "or that something could be given them to intoxicate them [to a certain frame of mind] . . ." The third learned word, *intoxicate*, is introduced by this addition. The vacuity of this passage becomes more evident if we remove repetitions, fashionable words, and stylistic decorations:

> But I believe in witchcraft.
> I don't think witchcraft is just a belief.
> A person can put himself or be put in a state
>   of mind that is witchcraft.

Without the extra verbiage and the O.K. words like *science, culture,* and *intoxicate,* Charles M. appears as something less than a first-rate thinker. The initial impression of him as a good speaker is simply our long-conditioned reaction to middle-class verbosity: we know that people who use these stylistic devices are educated people, and we are inclined to credit them with saying something intelligent. Our reactions are accurate in one sense: Charles M. is more

educated than Larry. But is he more rational, more logical, or more intelligent? Is he any better at thinking out a
problem to its solution? Does he deal more easily with abstractions? There is no reason to think so. Charles M. succeeds in letting us know that he is educated, but in the end
we do not know what he is trying to say, and neither
does he.

In the previous section I attempted to explain the origin
of the myth that lower-class black children are nonverbal.
The examples just given may help to account for the corresponding myth that middle-class language is in itself
better suited for dealing with abstract, logically complex,
and hypothetical questions. These examples are intended
to have a certain negative force. They are not controlled
experiments; on the contrary, this and the preceding section are designed to convince the reader that the controlled
experiments that have been offered in evidence are misleading. The only thing that is "controlled" is the superficial form of the stimulus: all children are asked, "What do
you think of capital punishment?" or, "Tell me anything
you can about this." But the speaker's interpretation of
these requests and the action he believes is appropriate in
response are completely uncontrolled. One can view these
test stimuli as requests for information, as commands for
action, as threats of punishment, or as meaningless sequences of words. They are probably intended as something altogether different: as requests for display,[22] but in
any case the experimenter is normally unaware of the problem of interpretation. The methods of educational psychologists like Deutsch, Jensen, and Bereiter follow the
pattern designed for animal experiments where motivation
is controlled by such simple methods as withholding food
until a certain weight reduction is reached. With human
subjects, it is absurd to believe that an identical "stimulus"
is obtained by asking everyone the "same question." Since
the crucial intervening variables of interpretation and mo-

tivation are uncontrolled, most of the literature on verbal deprivation tells us nothing about the capacities of children. They are only the trappings of science: an approach which substitutes the formal procedures of the scientific method for the activity itself. With our present limited grasp of these problems, the best we can do to understand the verbal capacities of children is to study them within the cultural context where they were developed.

It is not only the BE vernacular which should be studied in this way, but also the language of middle-class children. The explicitness and precision which we hope to gain from copying middle-class forms are often the product of the test situation, and limited to it. For example, in the first part of this paper I stated that working-class children hear more well-formed sentences than middle-class children. This statement may seem extraordinary in the light of the current belief of many linguists that most people do not speak in well-formed sentences, and that their actual speech production or "performance" is ungrammatical.[23] But those who have worked with any body of natural speech know that this is not the case. Our own studies of the "grammaticality of everyday speech" show that the great majority of utterances in all contexts are complete sentences, and most of the rest can be reduced to grammatical form by a small set of "editing rules."[24] The proportions of grammatical sentences vary with class backgrounds and styles. The highest percentage of well-formed sentences are found in casual speech, and working-class speakers use more well-formed sentences than middle-class speakers. The widespread myth that most speech is ungrammatical is no doubt based upon tapes made at learned conferences, where we obtain the maximum number of irreducibly ungrammatical sequences. All too often, "standard English" is represented by a style that is simultaneously overparticular and vague. The accumulating flow of words buries rather than strikes the target. It is this verbosity which is most easily taught and most easily learned, so that words take the place of thought and nothing can be found behind them.

When Bernstein describes his "elaborated code" in general terms, it emerges as a subtle and sophisticated mode of planning utterances, achieving structural variety, taking the other person's knowledge into account, and so on. But when it comes to describing the actual difference between middle-class and working-class speakers, we are presented with a proliferation of "I think," of the passive, of modals and auxiliaries, of the first-person pronoun, of uncommon words—these are the benchmarks of hemming and hawing, backing and filling, that are used by Charles M.—the devices which so often obscure whatever positive contribution education can make to our use of language. When we have discovered how much of middle-class style is a matter of fashion and how much actually helps us express ideas clearly, we will have done ourselves a great service; we will then be in a position to say what standard grammatical rules must be taught to nonstandard speakers in the early grades.

III. GRAMMATICALITY

Let us now examine Bereiter's own data on the verbal behavior of the children he dealt with. The expressions *They mine* and *Me got juice* are cited as examples of a language which lacks the means for expressing logical relations—in this case characterized as "a series of badly connected words." [25] In the case of *They mine*, it is apparent that Bereiter confuses the notions of logic and explicitness. We know that there are many languages of the world which do not have a present copula, and which conjoin subject and predicate complement without a verb. Russian, Hungarian, and Arabic may be foreign, but they are not by the same token illogical. In the case of black English we are

not dealing with even this superficial grammatical difference, but rather with a low-level rule which carries contraction one step further to delete single consonants representing the verbs *is, have,* or *will.*[26] We have yet to find
any children who do not sometimes use the full forms of
is and *will,* even though they may frequently delete it. Our
recent studies with black children four to seven years old
indicate that they use the full form of the copula *is* more
often than preadolescents ten to twelve years old, or adolescents fourteen to seventeen years old.[27]

Furthermore, the deletion of the *is* or *are* in black English is not the result of erratic or illogical behavior: it follows the same regular rules as standard English contraction.
Wherever standard English can contract, black children
use either the contracted form or (more commonly) the
deleted zero form. Thus *They mine* corresponds to standard English *They're mine,* not to the full form *They are
mine.* On the other hand, no such deletion is possible in
positions where standard English cannot contract: just as
one cannot say *That's what they're* in standard English,
That's what they is equally impossible in the vernacular
we are considering. The internal constraints upon both of
these rules show that we are dealing with a phonological
process like contraction, sensitive to such phonetic conditions as whether or not the next word begins with a vowel
or a consonant. The appropriate use of the deletion rule,
like the contraction rule, requires a deep and intimate
knowledge of English grammar and phonology. Such
knowledge is not available for conscious inspection by
native speakers: the rules we have recently worked out for
standard contraction [28] have never appeared in any grammar, and are certainly not a part of the conscious knowledge of any standard English speakers. Nevertheless, the
adult or child who uses these rules must have formed at
some level of psychological organization clear concepts of

"tense marker," "verb phrase," "rule ordering," "sentence embedding," "pronoun," and many other grammatical categories which are essential parts of any logical system.

Bereiter's reaction to the sentence *Me got juice* is even more puzzling. If Bereiter believes that *Me got juice* is not a logical expression, it can only be that he interprets the use of the objective pronoun *me* as representing a difference in logical relationship to the verb; that the child is in fact saying that "the juice got him" rather than "he got the juice"! If on the other hand the child means "I got juice," then this sentence form shows only that he has not learned the formal rules for the use of the subjective form *I* and oblique form *me*. We have in fact encountered many children who do not have these formal rules in order at the ages of four, five, six, or even eight.[29] It is extremely difficult to construct a minimal pair to show that the difference between *he* and *him* or *she* and *her* carries cognitive meaning. In almost every case, it is the context which tells us who is the agent and who is acted upon. We must then ask: What differences in cognitive, structural orientation are signaled by the fact that the child has not learned this formal rule? From the tests carried out by Jane Torrey, it is evident that the children concerned do understand the difference in meaning between *she* and *her* when another person uses the forms; all that remains is that the children themselves do not use the two forms. Our knowledge of the cognitive correlates of grammatical differences is certainly in its infancy, for this is one of the very many questions which we simply cannot answer. At the moment we do not know how to construct any kind of experiment which would lead to an answer; we do not even know what type of cognitive correlate we would be looking for.

Bereiter shows even more profound ignorance of the rules of discourse and of syntax when he rejects "In the tree" as an illogical or badly formed answer to "Where is the squirrel?" Such elliptical answers are of course used by everyone, and they show the appropriate deletion of subject and main verb, leaving the locative which is questioned by *wh + there*. The reply *In the tree* demonstrates that the listener has been attentive to and apprehended the syntax of the speaker.[30] Whatever formal structure we wish to write for expressions such as *Yes* or *Home* or *In the tree*, it is obvious that they cannot be interpreted without knowing the structure of the question which preceded them, and that they presuppose an understanding of the syntax of the question. Thus if you ask me, "Where is the squirrel?" it is necessary for me to understand the processes of *wh*-attachment, *wh*-attraction to the front of the sentence, and flip-flop of auxiliary and subject to produce this sentence from an underlying form which would otherwise have produced *The squirrel is there*. If the child had answered *The tree*, or *Squirrel the tree*, or *The in tree*, we would then assume that he did not understand the syntax of the full form, *The squirrel is in the tree*. Given the data that Bereiter presents, we cannot conclude that the child has no grammar, but only that the investigator does not understand the rules of grammar. It does not necessarily do any harm to use the full form *The squirrel is in the tree*, if one wants to make fully explicit the rules of grammar which the child has internalized. Much of logical analysis consists of making explicit just that kind of internalized rule. But it is hard to believe that any good can come from a program which begins with so many misconceptions about the input data. Bereiter and Engelmann believe that in teaching the child to say *The squirrel is in the tree* or *This is a box* and *This is not a box,* they are teaching him an entirely new language, whereas in fact they are only teaching him to produce slightly different forms of the language he already has.

IV. Logic

For many generations, American schoolteachers have devoted themselves to correcting a small number of nonstandard English rules to their standard equivalents, under the impression that they were teaching logic. This view has been reinforced and given theoretical justification by the claim that black English lacks the means for the expression of logical thought.

Let us consider for a moment the possibility that black children do not operate with the same logic that middle-class adults display. This would inevitably mean that sentences of a certain grammatical form would have different truth values for the two types of speakers. One of the most obvious places to look for such a difference is in the handling of the negative, since we encounter here one of the nonstandard items which has been stigmatized as illogical by schoolteachers: the double negative, or as we term it, negative concord. A child who says *He don't know nothing* is often said to be making an illogical statement without knowing it. According to the teacher, the child wants to say *He knows nothing* but puts in an extra negative without realizing it, and so conveys the opposite meaning, "He does not know nothing," which reduces to "He knows something." I need not emphasize that this is an absurd interpretation: if a nonstandard speaker wishes to say that "He does *not* know *nothing*," he does so by simply placing contrastive stress on both negatives, as I have done here, "He *don't* know *nothing*," indicating that they are derived from two underlying negatives in the deep structure. But note that the middle-class speaker does exactly the same thing when he wants to signal the existence of two underlying negatives: "He *doesn't* know *nothing*." In the standard form *He doesn't know anything,* the indefinite *any-thing* contains the same superficial reference to a single preceding negative in the surface structure that the non-standard *nothing* does. In the corresponding positive sentences, the indefinite *something* is used. The dialect difference, like most of the differences between the standard and nonstandard forms, is one of surface form, and has nothing to do with the underlying logic of the sentence. The Anglo-Saxon authors of the Peterborough Chronicle were surely not illogical when they wrote *For ne waeren nan martyrs swa pined alse he waeron:* literally, "For never weren't no martyrs so tortured as these were." The "logical" forms of current standard English are simply the accepted conventions of our present-day formal style.

Negative concord is more firmly established in black English than in other nonstandard dialects. The white nonstandard speaker shows variation in this rule, saying at one time *Nobody ever goes there* and the next time *Nobody never goes there*; core speakers of the BE vernacular consistently use the latter form. In the repetition tests which we conducted with adolescent black boys,[31] standard forms were repeated back instantly with negative concord. Here, for example, are three trials by two thirteen-year-old members of the Thunderbirds:

MODEL: *Nobody ever sat at any of those desks, any-how.*

BOOT–1; Nobody never sa—No[whitey] never sat at any o' tho' dess, anyhow.

 –2: Nobody never sat any any o' tho' dess, anyhow.

 –3: Nobody [əs·] ever sat at no desses, anyhow.

DAVID–1: Nobody ever sat in-in-in-in- none o'—say it again?

 –2: Nobody never sat in none o' tho' desses any-how.

 –3: Nobody—aww! Nobody never ex— Dawg!

It can certainly be said that Boot and David failed the test; they have not repeated the sentence back "correctly"— that is, word for word. But have they failed because they could not grasp the meaning of the sentence? The situation is in fact just the opposite: they failed because they perceived only the meaning and not the superficial form. Boot and David are typical of many speakers who do not perceive the surface details of the utterance so much as the underlying semantic structure, which they unhesitatingly translate into the vernacular form. Thus they have an asymmetrical system:

PERCEPTION	Standard	Nonstandard
PRODUCTION	Nonstandard	

This tendency to process the semantic components directly can be seen even more dramatically in responses to sentences with embedded questions:

MODEL:	*I asked Alvin if he knows how to play basketball.*
BOOT:	I ax Alvin do he know how to play basketball.
MONEY:	I ax Alvin if—do he know how to play basketball.
MODEL:	*I asked Alvin whether he knows how to play basketball.*
LARRY F.–1:	I axt Alvin does he know how to play basketball.
2:	I axt Alvin does he know how to play basketball.

Here the difference between the words used in the model sentence and in the repetition is striking. Again, the boys "fail" to pass the test. But it is also true that these boys understand the standard sentence, and translate it with extraordinary speed into the BE form—which is the regular Southern colloquial form. This form retains the inverted order to signal the underlying meaning of the question, instead of the complementizer *if* or *whether*, which standard English uses for this purpose. Thus Boot, Money, and Larry perceive the underlying structure of the model sentence:

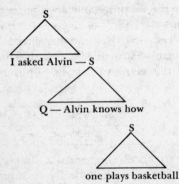

The complementizers *if* or *whether* are not required to express this underlying meaning; they are merely two of the formal options which one dialect selects to signal the embedded question. The colloquial Southern form utilizes a different device: preserving the order of the direct question. To say that this dialect lacks the means for logical expression is to confuse logic with surface detail.

To pass the repetition test, Boot and the others have to learn to listen to surface detail. They do not need a new logic; they need practice in paying attention to the explicit form of an utterance rather than its meaning. Nothing more than this is involved in the language training in the Bereiter and Engelmann program, or in most methods of "teaching English." There is of course nothing wrong with learning to be explicit—as we have seen, that is one of the main advantages of standard English at its best. But it is important that we recognize what is actually taking place, and what teachers are in fact trying to do.

I doubt if we can teach people to be logical, though we

can teach them to recognize the logic that they use. Piaget has shown us that in middle-class children logic develops much more slowly than grammar, and that we cannot expect four-year-olds to have mastered the conservation of quantity, let alone syllogistic reasoning. Whatever problems working-class children may have in handling logical operations are not to be blamed on the structure of their language. There is nothing in the vernacular which will interfere with the development of logical thought, for the logic of standard English cannot be distinguished from the logic of any other dialect of English by any test that we can find.

V. What's Wrong with Being Wrong?

If there is a failure of logic involved here, it is surely in the approach of the verbal deprivation theorists, rather than in the mental abilities of the children concerned. We can isolate six distinct steps in the reasoning which has led to programs such as those of Deutsch, Bereiter, and Engelmann:

(1) The lower-class child's verbal response to a formal and threatening situation is used to demonstrate his lack of verbal capacity, or verbal deficit.

(2) This verbal deficit is declared to be a major cause of the lower-class child's poor performance in school.

(3) Since middle-class children do better in school, middle-class speech habits are said to be necessary for learning.

(4) Class and ethnic differences in grammatical form are equated with differences in the capacity for logical analysis.

(5) Teaching the child to mimic certain formal speech patterns used by middle-class teachers is seen as teaching him to think logically.

(6) Children who learn these formal speech patterns are then said to be thinking logically, and it is predicated that they will do much better in reading and arithmetic in the years to follow.

In sections I–IV, I have tried to show that these propositions are wrong, concentrating on (1) (4) and (5). Proposition (3) is the primary logical fallacy which illicitly identifies a form of speech as the *cause* of middle-class achievement in school. Proposition (6) is the one which is most easily shown to be wrong in fact, as we will note below.

However, it is not too naive to ask, What is wrong with being wrong? There is no competing educational theory being dismantled by the Bereiter-Engelmann program, and there does not seem to be any great harm in having children repeat "This is not a box" for twenty minutes a day. We have already conceded that BE children need help in analyzing language into its surface components, and in being more explicit. But there are, in fact, serious and damaging consequences of the verbal deprivation theory. These may be considered under two headings: (1) the theoretical bias and (2) the consequences of failure.

It is widely recognized that the teacher's attitude toward the child is an important factor in the latter's success or failure. The work of Robert Rosenthal on "self-fulfilling prophecies" shows that the progress of children in the early grades can be dramatically affected by a single random labeling of certain children as "intellectual bloomers." [32] When the everyday language of black children is stigmatized as "not a language at all" and "not possessing the means for logical thought," the effect of such a labeling is repeated many times during each day of the school year. Every time that a child uses a form of BE without the copula or with negative concord, he will be labeling himself for the teacher's benefit as "illogical," as a "noncon-

ceptual thinker." Bereiter and Engelmann, Deutsch, and
Jensen are giving teachers a ready-made, theoretical basis
for the prejudice they already feel against the lower-class
black child and his language. When they hear him say
I don't want none or *They mine*, they will be hearing,
through the bias provided by the verbal deprivation theory, not an English dialect different from theirs, but the
primitive mentality of the savage mind.

But what if the teacher succeeds in training the child to
use the new language consistently? The verbal deprivation
theory holds that this will lead to a whole chain of successes in school, and that the child will be drawn away from
the vernacular culture into the middle-class world. Undoubtedly this will happen with a few isolated individuals,
just as it happens in every school system today for a few
children. But we are concerned not with the few but the
many, and for the majority of black children the distance
between them and the school is bound to widen under this
approach.

Proponents of the deficit theory have a strange view of
social organization outside the classroom: they see the attraction of the peer group as a *substitute* for success and
gratification normally provided by the school. For example,
Whiteman and Deutsch introduce their account of the
deprivation hypothesis with an eye-witness account of a
child who accidentally dropped his school notebook into a
puddle of water and walked away without picking it up.

> A policeman who had been standing nearby walked over
> to the puddle and stared at the notebook with some
> degree of disbelief.[33]

The child's alienation from school is explained as the result of his coming to school without the "verbal, conceptual, attentional and learning skills requisite to school
success." The authors see the child as "suffering from feel-

ings of inferiority because he is failing. . . . he withdraws or becomes hostile, finding gratification elsewhere, such as in his peer group."

To view the peer group as a mere substitute for school shows an extraordinary lack of knowledge of adolescent culture. In our studies in south central Harlem we have seen the reverse situation—the children who are rejected by the peer group are most likely to succeed in school. In middle-class suburban areas, many children do fail in school because of their personal deficiencies; in ghetto areas, it is the healthy, vigorous, popular child with normal intelligence who cannot read and fails all along the line. It is not necessary for me to document here the influence of the peer group upon the behavior of youth in our society, but we may note that somewhere between the time that children first learn to talk and puberty, their language is restructured to fit the rules used by their peer group. From a linguistic viewpoint, the peer group is certainly a more powerful influence than the family. Less directly, the pressures of peer-group activity are also felt within the school. Many children, particularly those who are not doing well in school, show a sudden sharp down-turn in the fourth and fifth grades, and children in the ghetto schools are no exception. It is at the same age, at nine or ten years old, that the influence of the vernacular peer group becomes predominant.[34] Instead of dealing with isolated individuals, the school is then dealing with children who are integrated into groups of their own, with rewards and value systems which oppose those of the school. Those who know the sociolinguistic situation cannot doubt that reaction against the Bereiter-Engelmann approach in later years will be even more violent on the part of the students involved, and the rejection of the school system will be even more categorical.

The essential fallacy of the verbal deprivation theory lies in tracing the educational failure of the child to his per-

sonal deficiencies. At present, these deficiencies are said to
be caused by his home environment. It is traditional to explain a child's failure in school by his inadequacy; but
when failure reaches such massive proportions, it seems
necessary to look at the social and cultural obstacles to
learning and the inability of the school to adjust to the
social situation. Operation Headstart is designed to repair
the child rather than the school; to the extent that it is
based upon this inverted logic, it is bound to fail.

The second area in which the verbal deprivation theory
is doing serious harm to our educational system is in the
consequences of this failure and the reaction to it. As
Operation Headstart fails, the interpretations which we receive will be from the same educational psychologists who
designed this program. The fault will be found, not in the
data, the theory, or the methods used, but rather in the
children who have failed to respond to the opportunities
offered them. When black children fail to show the significant advance which the deprivation theory predicts, it will
be further proof of the profound gulf which separates
their mental processes from those of civilized, middle-class
mankind.

A sense of the failure of Operation Headstart is already
commonplace. Some prominent figures in the program
have reacted to this situation by saying that intervention
did not take place early enough. Bettye M. Caldwell notes
that

> the research literature of the last decade dealing with
> social-class differences has made abundantly clear that all
> parents are not qualified to provide even the basic essen-
> tials of physical and psychological care to their children.[35]

The deficit theory now begins to focus on the "long-stand-
ing patterns of parental deficit" which fill the literature.
"There is, perhaps unfortunately," writes Caldwell, "no
literacy test for motherhood." Failing such eugenic mea-

sures, she has proposed "educationally oriented day care for culturally deprived children between six months and three years of age." The children are returned home each evening to "maintain primary emotional relationships with their own families," but during the day they are removed to "hopefully prevent the deceleration in rate of development which seems to occur in many deprived children around the age of two to three years." [36]

There are others who feel that even the best of the intervention programs, such as those of Bereiter and Engelmann, will not help the black child no matter when they are applied—that we are faced once again with the "inevitable hypothesis" of the genetic inferiority of the black people. Many readers of this paper are undoubtedly familiar with the paper of Arthur Jensen in the *Harvard Educational Review* (1969), which received early and widespread publicity. Jensen begins with the following quotation from the United States Commission on Civil Rights as evidence of the failure of compensatory education.

> The fact remains, however, that none of the programs appear to have raised significantly the achievement of participating pupils, as a group, within the period evaluated by the Commission.

Jensen believes that the verbal deprivation theorists with whom he has been associated—Deutsch, Whiteman, Katz, Bereiter—have been given every opportunity to prove their case and have failed. This opinion forms part of the argument leading to his over-all conclusion that the "preponderance of the evidence is . . . less consistent with a strictly environmental hypothesis than with the genetic hypothesis": that racism, or the belief in the genetic inferiority of blacks, is a correct view in the light of the present evidence.

Jensen argues that the middle-class white population is differentiated from the working-class white and black pop-

ulation in the ability for "cognitive or conceptual learning," which Jensen calls Level II intelligence as against
mere "associative learning," or Level I intelligence:

> Certain neural structures must also be available for Level
> II abilities to develop, and these are conceived of as being
> different from the neural structures underlying Level I.
> The genetic factors involved in each of these types of
> ability are presumed to have become differentially dis-
> tributed in the population as a function of social class,
> since Level II has been most important for scholastic per-
> formance under the traditional methods of instruction.

Thus Jensen found that one group of middle-class children
were helped by their concept-forming ability to recall
twenty familiar objects that could be classified into four
categories: animals, furniture, clothing, or foods. Lower-
class black children did just as well as middle-class children
with a miscellaneous set, but showed no improvement with
objects that could be so categorized.

The notion that large numbers of children have no
capacity for conceptual thinking would inevitably mean
that they speak a primitive language, for even the simplest
linguistic rules we discussed above involve conceptual
operations more complex than those used in the experiment cited by Jensen. Let us consider what is involved in
the use of the general English rule that incorporates the
negative with the first indefinite. To learn and use this
rule, one must first identify the class of indefinites involved, *any, one, ever,* which are formally quite diverse.
How is this done? These indefinites share a number of
common properties which can be expressed as the concepts "indefinite," "hypothetical," and "nonpartitive." One
might argue that these indefinites are learned as a simple
list by "association" learning. But this is only one of the
many syntactic rules involving indefinites—rules known to
every speaker of English, which could not be learned
except by an understanding of their common, abstract

properties. For example, everyone "knows" unconsciously that *anyone* cannot be used with preterit verbs or progressives. One does not say *Anyone went to the party* or *Anyone is going to the party.* The rule which operates here is sensitive to the hypothetical property of the indefinites: "*if* you choose one, no matter which. . . ." Whenever the proposition is not inconsistent with this feature, *anyone* can be used. Everyone "knows," therefore, that one can say *Anyone who was anyone went to the party,* or *If anyone went to the party,* or *Before anyone went to the party.* There is another property of *anyone* which is grasped unconsciously by all native speakers of English: it is "distributive." Thus if we need one more man for a game of bridge or basketball, and there is a crowd outside, we ask, "Do any of you want to play?" not "Do some of you want to play?" In both cases, we are considering a plurality, but with *any* we consider them one at a time, or distributively.

What are we then to make of Jensen's contention that Level I thinkers cannot make use of the concept "animal" to group together a miscellaneous set of toy animals? It is one thing to say that someone is not in the habit of using a certain skill. But to say that his failure to use it is genetically determined implies dramatic consequences for other forms of behavior, which are not found in experience; the knowledge of what people must do in order to learn language makes Jensen's theories seem more and more distant from the realities of human behavior. Like Bereiter and Engelmann, Jensen is handicapped by his ignorance of the most basic facts about human language and the people who speak it.

The research of the educational psychologists cited here is presented in formal and objective style, and is widely received as impartial scientific evidence. Jensen's paper was instantaneously reported by Joseph Alsop and William F. Buckley, Jr., as "massive, apparently authoritative" in the *New York Post,* March 20, 1969. It is not my intention to examine these materials in detail, but it is important to realize that we are dealing with special pleading by those who have a strong personal commitment. Jensen is concerned with class differences in cognitive style and verbal learning. His earlier papers incorporated the cultural deprivation theory which he now rejects as a basic explanation.[37] He classified the black children who fail in school as "slow learners" and "mentally retarded," and urged that we find out how much their retardation is due to environmental factors and how much to "more basic biological factors." [38] His conviction that the problems must be located in the child leads him to accept and reprint some truly extraordinary data. To support the genetic hypothesis, he cites the following table of Rick Heber for the racial distribution of mental retardation: [39]

ESTIMATED PREVALENCE OF CHILDREN
WITH IQs BELOW 75

SES	White	Negro
1	0.5	3.1
2	0.8	14.5
3	2.1	22.8
4	3.1	37.8
5	7.8	42.9

This report, that almost half of lower-class black children are mentally retarded, could be accepted only by someone who has no knowledge of the children or the community. If he had wished to, Jensen could easily have checked this against the records of any school in any urban ghetto area. Taking IQ tests at their face value, there is no correspondence between these figures and the communities we know. For example, among 75 boys we worked with in central Harlem, who would fall into Heber's SES 4 or 5, there were only three with IQs below 75: one spoke very little English, one could barely see, and the third was emotionally disturbed. When the second was retested, he scored 91, and the third retested at 87.[40] There are of course hundreds of realistic reports available to Jensen; he simply selected one which would strengthen his case for the genetic inferiority of black children.

Jensen's evidence for the genetic limitations on the intelligence of black children is based entirely on IQ tests. He acknowledges the fact that IQ tests are essentially predictors of scholastic performance, and notes the circularity of the view that intelligence is what IQ tests measure. Nevertheless, he accepts this kind of "intelligence" as the only kind we can deal with and IQ data as the only objective way we have of measuring it. The elaborations of his further discussions of psychometrics and experimental evidence disguise the fact that this original decision discards the search for more valid indices of intelligence in favor of a reliable, practical, and convenient measurement—that is, one that fits the investigator's way of thinking and working rather than any basic characteristics of his subjects.

The frequent use of tables and statistics by educational psychologists serves to give outside readers the impression that this field is a science, and that the opinions of the authors should be given the same attention and respect that we give to the conclusions of physicists or chemists. But careful examination of the input data will often show that there is no direct relationship between the conclusions and the evidence (in Jensen's case, between IQ tests in a specially selected district of Milwaukee and the intelligence of lower-class black children). Furthermore, the operations performed upon the data frequently carry us very far from the common-sense experience which is our only safeguard against conclusions heavily weighted by the author's theory. As another example, we may take some of the evidence presented by Whiteman and Deutsch for the cultural deprivation hypothesis.

The core of Martin Deutsch's environmental explanation of poor performance in school is the Deprivation Index, a numerical scale based on six dichotomized variables. One variable is "the educational aspirational level of the parent for the child." Most people would agree that a parent who did not care if a child finished high school would be a disadvantageous factor in the child's educational career. In dichotomizing this variable, Deutsch was faced with the fact that the educational aspiration of black parents is in fact very high—higher than for the white population, as he shows in other papers.[41] In order to fit this data into the Deprivation Index, he sets the cutting point for the deprived group as "college or less." [42] Thus if a black child's father says that he wants his son to go all the way through college, the child will fall into the "deprived" class on this variable. In order to receive the two points given to the "less deprived" on the index, it would be necessary for the child's parent to insist on graduate school or medical school! This decision is never discussed by the authors: it simply stands as a *fait accompli* in the tables. Readers of this literature who are not committed to one point of view would be wise to look as carefully as possible at the original data which lie behind each statement, and check the conclusions against their own knowledge of the people and community being described.

No one can doubt that the inadequacy of Operation Headstart and of the verbal deprivation hypothesis has now become a crucial issue in our society.[43] The controversy over Jensen's article has often taken as a given that programs such as Bereiter and Engelmann's have tested and measured the verbal capacity of the ghetto child.[44] The cultural, sociolinguistic obstacles to this intervention program are not considered, and the argument proceeds upon the data provided by the large, friendly interviewers that we have seen at work in the extracts given above.

VI. The Linguistic View

Linguists are in an excellent position to demonstrate the fallacies of the verbal deprivation theory. All linguists agree that nonstandard dialects are highly structured systems; they do not see these dialects as accumulations of errors caused by the failure of their speakers to master standard English. When linguists hear black children saying *He crazy* or *Her my friend* they do not hear a "primitive language." Nor do they believe that the speech of working-class people is merely a form of emotional expression, incapable of relating logical thought.[45] Linguists therefore condemn with a single voice Bereiter's view that the vernacular can be disregarded.

There is no reason to believe that any nonstandard vernacular is in itself an obstacle to learning. The chief problem is ignorance of language on the part of all concerned. Our job as linguists is to remedy this ignorance: Bereiter and Engelmann want to reinforce it and justify it. Teachers are now being told to ignore the language of black children as unworthy of attention and useless for learning. They are being taught to hear every natural utterance of the child as evidence of his mental inferiority. As linguists we are unanimous in condemning this view as bad observation, bad theory, and bad practice.

That educational psychology should be strongly influenced by a theory so false to the facts of language is unfortunate; but that children should be the victims of this ignorance is intolerable. It may seem that the fallacies of the verbal deprivation theory are so obvious that they are hardly worth exposing; I have tried to show that it is an important job for us to undertake. If linguists can contribute some of their available knowledge and energy toward this end, we will have done a great deal to justify the support that society has given to basic research in our field.

NOTES

This essay originally appeared in James E. Alatis, ed., *Linguistics and the Teaching of Standard English to Speakers of Other Languages or Dialects,* Monograph Series on Languages and Linguistics, No. 22 (Washington, D.C.: Georgetown University Press, 1969), pp. 1–43. The essay as it appears above has been slightly abridged.

1 Carl Bereiter and Siegfried Engelmann, *Teaching Disadvantaged Children in the Preschool* (Englewood Cliffs, N.J.: Prentice-Hall, 1966).

2 Arthur Jensen, "How Much Can We Boost IQ and Scholastic Achievement?" *Harvard Educational Review,* Vol. 39 (Winter 1969), pp. 1–123.

3 I am indebted to Rosalind Weiner, of the Early Childhood Education group of Operation Headstart in New York City, and to Joan Baratz, of the Education Study Center, Washington, D.C., for pointing out to me the scope and seriousness of the educational issues involved here, and the ways in which the cultural deprivation theory has affected federal intervention programs in recent years.

4 A report of average reading-comprehension scores in New York City was published in the *New York Times* on December 3, 1968. The schools attended by most of the peer-group members we have studied showed the following scores:

SCHOOL	GRADE	READING SCORE	NATIONAL NORM
J.H.S. 13	7	5.6	7.7
	9	7.6	9.7
J.H.S. 120	7	5.6	7.7
	9	7.0	9.7
I.S. 88	6	5.3	6.7
	8	7.2	8.7

The average is, then, more than two full years behind grade in the ninth grade.

5 Our own work in New York City confirms the fact that most black children read very poorly; however, our studies in the speech community show that the situation is even worse than has been reported. If one separates the isolated and peripheral individuals

from the members of the central peer groups, the peer-group members show even worse reading records and to all intents and purposes are not learning to read at all during the time they spend in school. See William Labov and Clarence Robins, "A Note on the Relation of Reading Failure to Peer-Group Status in Urban Ghettos," *Teachers College Records*, Vol. 79 (1969), pp. 395–405.

6 There are a number of studies reported recently which show no relation between school achievement and the presence of a father in the nuclear family. Preliminary findings to this effect are cited from a study by Bernard Mackler of the Center for Urban Education in Thomas S. Langner and Stanley T. Michaels, *Life Stress and Mental Health* (New York: Free Press, 1963), Chap. 8. Jensen, "How Much Can We Boost IQ?" cites James Coleman's study *Equality of Educational Opportunity* (Washington, D.C.: Office of Education, 1966), p. 506, and others to illustrate the same point.

7 The concept of "black English" (BE), or "nonstandard Negro English," and the vernacular culture in which it is embedded is presented in detail in William Labov, Paul Cohen, Clarence Robins, and John Lewis, *A Study of the Non-Standard English of Negro and Puerto Rican Speakers in New York City*, Final Report, Cooperative Research Project No. 3288 (Washington, D.C.: Office of Education, 1968), Vols. 1 and 2, sections 1, 2, 3, and 4.1. See Vol. 2, section 4.3, for the linguistic traits which distinguish speakers who participate fully in the BE culture from marginal and isolated individuals.

8 Martin Deutsch et al., *The Disadvantaged Child: Studies of the Social Environment and the Learning Process* (New York: Basic Books, 1967); Martin Deutsch, Irwin Katz, and Arthur Jensen, eds., *Social Class, Race, and Psychological Development* (New York: Holt Rinehart & Winston, 1968).

9 For example, in Deutsch, Katz, and Jensen, *Social Class*, there is a section on "Social and Psychological Perspectives," which includes a chapter by Proshansky and Newton on "The Nature and Meaning of Negro Self-Identity" and one by Robert Rosenthal and Lenore Jacobson on "Self-fulfilling Prophecies in the Classroom" (pp. 178–218 and pp. 219–53, respectively).

10 Arthur Jensen, "Social Class and Verbal Learning," in Deutsch, Katz, and Jensen, *Social Class*, p. 118.

11 Carl Bereiter et al., "An Academically Oriented Pre-School for Culturally Deprived Children," in Fred M. Hechinger, ed., *Pre-School Education Today* (New York: Doubleday & Co., 1966), pp. 105–137; Bereiter and Engelmann, *Teaching Disadvantaged Children*.

12 Bereiter et al., "An Academically Oriented Pre-School," p. 113.

13 The research cited here was carried out in south central Harlem and other ghetto areas in 1965–1968 to describe structural and functional differences between black English and standard English of the classroom. It was supported by the Office of Education as Cooperative Research Projects 3091 and 3288. Detailed reports are given in Labov, Cohen, Robins, and Lewis, *Non-Standard English;* William Labov, Paul Cohen, and Clarence Robins, *A Preliminary Study of the Structure of English Used by Negro and Puerto Rican Speakers in New York City,* Final Report, Cooperative Research Project No. 3091 (Washington, D.C.: Office of Education, 1968), Vols. 1 and 2; and William Labov, "Some Sources of Reading Problems for Negro Speakers of Non-Standard English" in Alexander Frazier, ed., *New Directions in Elementary English* (Champaign, Ill.: National Council of Teachers of English, 1967), pp. 140–67.

14 The reference to the "pork chop God" condenses several concepts of black nationalism current in the Harlem community. A "pork chop" is a Negro who has not lost the traditional subservient ideology of the South, who has no knowledge of himself in Muslim terms, and the "pork chop God" would be the traditional God of the Southern Baptists. He and his followers may be pork chops, but he still holds the power in Leon and Gregory's world.

15 For detailed accounts of these speech events, see Labov, Cohen, Robins, and Lewis, *Non-Standard English,* section 4.2.

16 Jensen, "Social Class and Verbal Learning," p. 119.

17 The term "code" is central in Bernstein's description of the differences between working-class and middle-class styles of speech. The restrictions and elaborations of speech observed are labeled "codes" to indicate the principles governing selection from the range of possible English sentences. No rules or detailed descriptions of the operation of such codes are provided as yet, so that this central concept remains to be specified.

18 A direct view of Larry's verbal style in a hostile encounter is given in Labov, Cohen, Robins, and Lewis, *Non-Standard English,* Vol. 2, pp. 39–43. Gray's Oral Reading Test was being given to a group of Jets on the steps of a brownstone house in Harlem, and the landlord tried unsuccessfully to make the Jets move. Larry's verbal style in this encounter matches the reports he gives of himself in a number of narratives cited in section 4.8.

19 See Labov, Cohen, Robins, and Lewis, *Non-Standard English,* Vol. 2, pp. 38, 71–73, 291–92.

20 See *ibid.,* section 4.6, for a description of subjective reaction tests which utilize these evaluative dimensions.

21 Several middle-class readers of this passage have suggested that *science* here refers to some form of control as opposed to belief; the "science of witchcraft" would then be a kind of engineering of mental states; other interpretations can of course be provided. The fact remains that no such difficulties of interpretation are needed to understand Larry's remarks.

22 The concept of a "request for verbal display" is here drawn from Alan Blum's treatment of the therapeutic interview in "The Sociology of Mental Illness," mimeographed.

23 In a number of presentations, Noam Chomsky has asserted that the great majority of the sentences which a child hears are ungrammatical ("95 percent"). In *Aspects of the Theory of Syntax* (Cambridge, Mass.: M.I.T. Press, 1965), p. 58, he presents this notion as one of the arguments in his general statement of the "nativist" position: "A consideration of the character of the grammar that is acquired, *the degenerate quality and narrowly limited extent of the available data* [my emphasis], the striking uniformity of the resulting grammars, and their independence of intelligence, motivation, and emotional state, over wide ranges of variation, leave little hope that much of the structure of the language can be learned. . . ."

24 The editing rules are presented in William Labov, "On the Grammaticality of Everyday Speech," paper given at the annual meeting of the Linguistic Society of America, New York City, December 1966.

25 Bereiter, et al., "An Academically Oriented Pre-School," pp. 113ff.

26 Labov, Cohen, Robins, and Lewis, *Non-Standard English*, section 3.4.

27 From work on the grammar and comprehension of black children four to eight years old being carried out by Professor Jane Torrey of Connecticut College in extension of the research cited above in Labov, Cohen, Robins, and Lewis.

28 Labov, Cohen, Robins, and Lewis, *Non-Standard English*, section 3.4.

29 From the research of Jane Torrey cited in note 27.

30 The attention to the speaker's syntax required of the listener is analyzed in detail by Harvey Sacks in his unpublished 1968 lectures at the University of California, Irvine.

31 More complete data on these memory tests is given in Labov, Cohen, Robins, and Lewis, *Non-Standard English*, section 3.9.

32 Robert Rosenthal and Lenore Jacobson, "Self-fulfilling Prophecies in the Classroom: Teachers' Expectations as Unintended Determinants of Pupils' Intellectual Competence," in Deutsch, Katz, and Jensen, *Social Class*, pp. 219–53.

33 Martin Whiteman and Martin Deutsch, "Social Disadvantage as Related to Intellective and Language Development," in Deutsch, Katz, and Jensen, *Social Class*, pp. 86–87.

34 For the relationship between age and membership in peer groups, see Peter Willmott, *Adolescent Boys of East London* (New York: Humanities Press, 1966).

35 Bettye M. Caldwell, "What Is the Optimal Learning Environment for the Young Child?" *American Journal of Orthopsychiatry*, Vol. 37 (Winter 1967), p. 16.

36 *Ibid.*, p. 17.

37 In "Social Class and Verbal Learning," Jensen expounds the verbal deprivation theory in considerable detail. For example: "During this 'labeling' period . . . some very important social-class differences may exert their effects on verbal learning. Lower-class parents engage in relatively little of this naming or 'labeling' play with their children. . . . That words are discrete labels for things seems to be better known by the middle-class child entering first grade than by the lower-class child. Much of this knowledge is gained in the parent-child interaction, as when the parent looks at a picture book with the child. . . ." (p. 119).

38 *Ibid.*, p. 167.

39 Heber's studies of 88 black mothers in Milwaukee are cited frequently throughout Jensen, "How Much Can We Boost IQ?" The estimates in this table are not given in relation to a particular Milwaukee sample but for the general population. Heber's study was specifically designed to cover an area of Milwaukee which was known to contain a large concentration of retarded children, black and white, and he has stated that his findings are "grossly misinterpreted" by Jensen *(Milwaukee Sentinel,* June 11, 1969).

40 The IQ scores given here are from group rather than individual tests and must therefore not be weighted heavily: the scores are from the Pintner-Cunningham Test, usually given in the first grade in New York City schools in the 1950s.

41 Table 15-1 in Deutsch et al., "An Academically Oriented Pre-School," p. 312, section C, shows that some degree of college training was desired by 96, 97, and 100 percent of black parents in Class Levels I, II, and III respectively. The corresponding figures for whites were 79, 95, and 97 percent.

42 Whiteman and Deutsch, "Social Disadvantage as Related to Intellective and Language Development," p. 100. In an earlier version of this essay, this discussion could be interpreted as implying that Whiteman and Deutsch had used data in the same way as Jensen: to rate the black group as low as possible. As they point out (personal communication), the inclusion of this item in the Depriva-

tion Index had the opposite effect, and it could easily have been omitted if that had been their intention. They also argue that they had sound statistical grounds for dichotomizing as they did. The criticism I intended to make is that there is something drastically wrong with operations which produce definitions of deprivation such as the one cited here. It should of course be noted that Whiteman and Deutsch have strongly opposed Jensen's genetic hypothesis and vigorously criticized his logic and data.

43 The negative report of the Westinghouse Learning Corporation and Ohio University on Operation Headstart was published in the *New York Times* on April 13, 1969. The evidence of the failure of the program is apparently decisive, and it seems likely that the discouraging conclusions will be used by conservative congressmen as a weapon against any kind of expenditure for disadvantaged children, especially blacks. The two hypotheses mentioned to account for this failure are that the impact of Headstart is lost through poor teaching later on, and more recently, that poor children have been so badly damaged in infancy by their lower-class environment that Headstart cannot make much difference. The third, "inevitable" hypothesis of Arthur Jensen is not reported here.

44 Such assumptions are carefully exposed in Joan and Stephen Baratz, "Early Childhood Intervention: The Social Science Base of Institutional Racism," *Harvard Educational Review*, Vol. 40 (Winter 1970), pp. 29–50, among other articles.

45 Differences in analysis by various linguists in recent years are the inevitable products of differing theoretical approaches and perspectives as we explore these dialect patterns by different routes—differences which are rapidly diminishing as we exchange our findings. For example, William Stewart differs with me on how deeply the invariant *be* of *She be always messin' around* is integrated into the semantics of the copula system with *am, is, are,* etc. The position and meaning of *have . . . ed* in BE is very unclear, and there are a variety of positions on this point. But the grammatical features involved are not the fundamental predicators of the logical system. They are optional ways of contrasting, foregrounding, emphasizing, or deleting elements of the underlying sentence. There are a few semantic features of BE grammar which may be unique to this system. But the semantic features we are talking about here are items such as "habitual," "general," "intensive." These linguistic markers are essentially points of view—different ways of looking at the same events—and they do not determine the truth values of propositions upon which all speakers of English agree.

THE POLITICS OF BIDIALECTALISM

Wayne O'Neil

Bidialectalism or biloquialism (Jim Sledd has suggested that the expression "double-speak" is more in keeping with the genius of the language) refers to a movement in education to systematically render lower-class students able to speak both their native dialect and standard English. It is a less vague and haphazard continuation of earlier attempts, as old as popular education, to eradicate dialect. And it offers the lower class a traditional choice: convert so that it can progress in the ongoing social game. There is no offer to change the rules of the game or its name. Bidialectalism also differs in that it is meant mostly for lower-class blacks and not for the lower class in general. It comes at a time when many blacks are piecing together their identity, saving it from powerful attempts to fragment and destroy it. It is therefore controversial and widely discussed.[1] But it has not been discussed in a clear enough political context, so it is my purpose to do that in the following pages, thus to indicate why this ill-advised attempt to change people should be rejected, eradicated.

Let me begin with what I understand to be some facts and some pretty good hunches about language and language learning. It is, for example, an assumption subject to empirical support that language differences intuitively understood as dialect differences are relatively superficial. That is, they amount to rule differences (in the terminology of the linguistic theory of Noam Chomsky) which fall quite low in the ordered set of rules that constitutes a grammar of a language, the internalized knowledge of a language that speakers possess. We do not expect dialects of a language to differ in any important ways: in their underlying constituents or their order, in their major transformations, in their underlying phonological segments. And in fact, work on transformational dialectology has borne this working assumption out. When we look at different languages we do expect rule differences to be more radical, which is also in fact true. Yet in no sense is there any empirical evidence to support such notions as that language A is "impoverished" vis-à-vis language B, or that dialect x of language C is impoverished with respect to dialect y of language C, i.e., that the grammar and vocabulary of x are some diminished subset of the grammar and vocabulary of y. Such notions are meaningless, for the grammars of x and y are simply equal sets that intersect in vast and important ways.

Now it is because of these intersections that speakers of the several dialects of any language can generally understand each other. Presumably understanding what someone has said to you entails your being able to employ perceptual strategies that get you from the surface noises through to deep structure clues and on to the underlying relationships of words and meaning. Unless there is significant overlap of grammar and vocabulary between speaker (writer) and hearer (reader), the process of understanding will break down immediately. There are, however, dialect relationships that involve patience and time on both sides for mutual intelligibility. Charles Hockett somewhere discusses natives in a village talking about the dialects in nearby villages being two-day languages or seven-day languages; they mean that you have to sit around with the folks over there a couple of days before the noises clear up enough for you to get on with your business. There are also instances of one-way intelligibility: objective ones, between Faroe Islanders and Icelanders, for example; subjective ones, mostly between teachers and lower-class students.

Finally, some hunches. It is reasonable and logical to assume that when the speakers of the several dialects of a language have relatively little difficulty understanding one another, it will be extremely difficult (because it serves no purpose) for the speakers of one dialect to learn to produce rather than simply understand one of the other dialects. The dialect differences may of course be quite obvious and plain and even interesting, but if no real problem of understanding hangs on them, to learn to mimic one of the other dialects is to work away at a task that has nothing to do with language and communication. Indeed, if we were to set up an experiment whose goal was to get speakers of one dialect to learn to speak another dialect, the subjects would be bewildered by any arguments that, contrary to the observable facts, claimed there to be a problem of intelligibility.

There are, however, ways of attacking and breaking down and displacing bewilderment. Let us imagine the following experiment: Say that there was a dialect of English that employed forms of the verb *be* in a number of vacuous ways. For example, instead of expressing predicate adjectives, predicate locatives, and the progressive aspect of a verb by a simple, direct, and economical subject/predicate word structure, i.e., instead of saying "He big," "He here," "He eating supper," this dialect would in its uneconomical way say "He is big," "He is here," "He is eating supper." Say also that it had a high-front/mid-front vowel distinction before nasals, such that rather than having homonymous *pin* for the thing that a tailor hems up a garment with and for the enclosure one keeps animals in, this dialect distinguished phonologically (what any but the most impoverished context—say a rhyme-word drill— would normally distinguish) *pin* for the tailor's tool and *pen* for the animal enclosure. Say also that speakers of this dialect used imprecise, counterfactual, and confusing words and expressions like *Vietnamization, protective reaction, unarmed reconnaissance flights,* etc. We could of course imagine a whole set of such differences at various levels in the grammar of a language. But these few will suffice for the purposes of illustration.

How could we then persuade the speaker of this dialect to cease speaking his way and start speaking ours? There are several tacks to follow. First off we could simply tell him that his way of doing it is wrong. The problem with this method is that the subject will probably suffer severe depression and loss of identity, the more so if his family and friends (who do not have the benefit of this particular experiment) turn up on this score to be wrong too. Second, we might tell him that it's not exactly wrong, but that for him to persist in saying "He is eating supper," "He is out by the pigpen," etc. is a grave social error, at least in the context of the experiment and in any similar and vaguely defined situations. And since those situations aren't about to change, he had better—if he wants to be a good subject and succeed. The consequences of this method (especially if the subject is young) would be very little different from those of the first method discussed. Finally, we could mod- ify the experiment slightly by telling the subject that if he could learn this new way of speaking he would then be richer than people who know only one way—like being told that there are two ways to get from here to the Amer- icana: you can walk or you can hop and you're the richer for that, but you'd best hop if anyone you don't know is watching. Again the consequences of this method, which by the way defines bidialectalism, would seem to be very little different from those of the other two. For hopping is a tough, self-conscious way of going through life and would have to be justified to oneself. We could of course add that his getting and keeping a job depends upon his hopping.

There are certainly several other methods that an alert experimenter could devise, but all would be extremely time-consuming and none could avoid the severe psychological consequences to the subject mentioned above—not to speak of frustration, since the chances of the experiment's succeeding are quite low, a point to which I return below.

Ludicrous as it may seem, such experiments, badly and casually formulated ones as well as neatly and tightly designed ones, are a regular and extensive part of American school curricula and of school curricula in general. From the very beginning of popular education in America—from the time that New England schoolteachers began to move west with their three Mary's (*marry*'s or *merry*'s)—there has been a sustained attempt to eradicate dialect, to replace it with preferred, standard speech. For various reasons these attempts have not succeeded, to the same extent and for the same reasons that very little of what goes on at the surface in schools has taken hold, which failure—as I shall indicate later—is not without its purpose. Systematized attempts to eradicate dialect are of very recent vintage and follow from the rapid, postwar development of the social pseudo-sciences. For it was during and following World War II that simplistic social and behavioral scientific explanations of complex aspects of individual and collective human behavior held sway. After all, hadn't the army enlisted the linguists who knew how language was learned and hadn't the critical languages of the world been learned by our warriors? America's very successful World War II hard technology lent credence to the false claim that out of that same war there came a soft technology ready also to fight the cold war and solve bothersome problems at home, in particular educational ones. It is also these pseudo-scientists who have changed the name of the game from "eradication" to "duplication," i.e., to "bidialectalism" or "double-speak."

At this point we can well ask why all the bother, since the task is unnecessary and difficult (if not impossible), consumes an inordinate amount of time out of the formal educational life of a child to no success, and successfully entails severe psychological disorientation. The reasons, complex, mixed, and confusing, need to be sorted out.

But first it is best to point out what should be common knowledge: though dialects are from the point of view of their grammars partially separate but equal, they do exist in social, cultural, political, and economic settings that wash away their linguistic equality, replacing it with value judgments that follow from the power and control that speakers of one dialect have over speakers of other dialects and from the low regard in which speakers of one dialect will hold speakers of others. Furthermore, in this connection we must distinguish why individuals want to change or "enrich" the language of lower-class children from what motivates institutions. I will not argue that individuals necessarily have well-thought-out, formulated positions—though this may in some instances be the case. But it is certainly the case that institutional, governmental motivation is well formulated and quite exactly intentioned.

There are, then, a variety of reasons or arguments that individuals will give and that can be ascribed to them in justification of their persisting in the business of dialect eradication or duplication. Let me list some of them:

(1) Cultural elitism: "The permissive linguists urge speaking and writing the dialectic [sic] language of the region and the racial and economic group; some un-schooled areas have considerable raciness of diction. It is not intellectually precise, however, and its jargon takes on strong emotional and constantly warped meanings. It

deserves observation, but not inclusion in standard English until its floating (and possibly ephemeral) meanings have settled. 'I gottcha' and 'Yeah, sure, man' are slurring our speech and 'Do like I say,' 'Tell it like it is' are at a dangerous work of erosion. Respect for and decent craftsmanship in the use of language may seem secondary in a world of struggle for survival or for social justice, but if we relax the rear-guard defense of these dignities, whatever survives the assaults of ruthlessness and blind idealism that resorts to anarchic violence will be debased and rudderless." [2] Or read any issue of Mortimer Smith's *Bulletin, Council for Basic Education.*

(2) Pragmatism: Holders of this position argue that given the social and economic class structure of American society, bidialectalism is the only way out or part of a way out of lower-class-ness, or more narrowly, lower-class blackness. For if you hold to the standards of those in power all the good things of life will follow: a college education, a good job, the respect of those in power, etc.

(3) Racism: These people are simply somewhere in their heads bent on putting down blacks. (Bidialectalism or dialect eradication is in this case reserved for a particular segment of the lower class and not meant, as in (2), for the lower class in general or, as in (1), for everyone who hasn't graduated from an Ivy League school.) They may of course resort to (2) in their own justification of what they do, but in fact (3) can be fairly clearly seen in their statements and work. For example, in talking about Northern blacks, Charles W. Ferguson has said, "We have to face a rather difficult question as to whether we want to *make* these people bi-dialectal . . . or whether to *impose* some kind of standard English on these people and *eradicate* the kind of sub-standard English they speak" (emphasis added).[3] By what right?

Now certainly there are other motivations (e.g., government and foundation dollars) that guide individuals in their pursuit of bidialectalism; yet let's not hang on them. For I think it more important to look at institutional motivations, governmental motivations: i.e., political forces guiding educational systems that are far more important for our understanding of educational problems. I believe that except for the dollars, we can dismiss right off the motivations that I have argued guide individuals. These forces are important, certainly, for the proper functioning of individuals in the schools, but they are not what guides educational systems.

A not unrelated digression can clarify this point: When a few short years ago there was rioting and confrontation at Columbia University, one of the charges leveled against the university was that it was pursuing a racist expansion policy. On the other hand, MIT has successfully (and without confrontation) pursued exactly the same policies in constructing its Tech Square complex and enticing NASA to Cambridge, but this at the expense of the small industry of Cambridge and the white working class.[4] Now either we must argue that Columbia and MIT were (and are) pursuing fundamentally different expansion policies—an argument that is quite difficult to sustain—or that the racist charge against Columbia is superficial and that Columbia and MIT were, in fact, simply expanding their power the way (nonprofit) corporations like government are wont to do, that the only difference between the two universities was the color of the skin of lower-class people living at their perimeters. This latter interpretation is—I believe—the correct one. By a related argument I would then dismiss the racist charge (insofar as he means this to apply to government and educational systems) in Jim Sledd's essay previously cited. So also would I dismiss (1) and (2) above—though the government's rhetoric (e.g., for Upward Bound) is lodged in (2).

For educational systems serve a quite clear and well-understood political-economic purpose, and serve it quite well. American education is effective in a way that the government and the ruling class want it to be—not at all in a way that I or most of us want it to be. It ensures the status quo; it ensures that workers will be alienated from their labor, that the managers' sons will be managers, the laborers' sons laborers, etc. It puts people in their place. This quite correct analysis is best presented at length in an admirable book by eight Italian schoolchildren, *Letter to a Teacher*.[5]

How then does language education—without, remember, worrying about the motivations of individual teachers, school administrators, or textbook makers—fit into this analysis? The analysis suggests that the enterprise of making lower-class speakers over into middle-class speakers was never meant to be successful except insofar as it has been necessary from time to time to recruit some few of them into the middle class. The main purpose was indeed part of the main purpose of popular education, i.e., to render schoolchildren skilled enough to be exploited but finally uneducated, used to failure, and alienated enough to oppose their exploitation; thus, for them to continue to agree that they had had their chances to succeed in a free and open society but that they had failed. No one's fault but their own.

So much for the past, which of course continues into the present—except that the present concern to render blacks bidialectal is an attempt at the most obvious kind of political co-optation and a cruel joke to boot. For what it means is that education is offering a particularly vocal and angry segment of the lower class a special but foredoomed chance to succeed inside the system. It is a crumb, a symbol that finally something of moment is being done for them. But in fact, it remains a symbolic gesture only, nothing more—no matter how well it is gotten up in scientistic garb. For the rules of the game are unchanged; there is no new social, political, or economic justice. To their credit, many blacks reject the gesture and insist on the primacy of their own cultural identity and dialect, on their right to change American society in fundamental ways: properly so, for decisions about education belong to the people they affect.

Educational and social reform is ever such gesture. For it is the nature of reform to tinker with the surface in order to secure the underpinnings. At MIT for example—related digression number two—we have just finished spending who knows how many tens of thousands of dollars on a study of MIT education (*Creative Renewal in a Time of Crisis*) which seeks to answer, not how can science and technology serve the people, but rather how can MIT engage its freshmen so that they come out the way they are supposed to: good technical servants to the American corporate interests. Indeed all of the educational reform currently about is simply responding to signals that human alienation is not deep enough, to a desire to better control people, their heads, and their lives. Thomas Szasz's work on the role of psychiatry in defending the social and political status quo simply underscores the point.[6]

It is in this general context that we should understand bidialectalism: it is a modern, fancy, but false promise to help black people get into the good life while putting them on and keeping them down. It does not move one bit toward facing the injustices of American political and economic life. Nor is it intended for that. For this reason *it* should be put down—and for this reason alone. It is uninteresting to me to know (because these are not *basic* counterarguments) that it can't work, that the knowledge for making it work doesn't exist, that the money for making it work if the knowledge existed isn't available. It is enough to understand that double-speak is a response *meant* to keep things as they are.

Educators ought to do better. For, we like to say, our real job implies opposing efforts to maintain the status quo. Education should move people to an exultation in and understanding of human differences, to the realization that they can control their own destinies, to a realization that stupid, pointless, destructive work is not what life or society is about, and to organizing and fighting for a life of peace, health, and meaning. Bidialectalism relates to none of these ideals—except as part of the social and political machinery meant to destroy them.

NOTES

The present essay is a slightly revised and expanded version of a paper presented at the annual meetings of the Modern Language Association of America, December 29, 1970, at the New York Hilton Hotel. It is printed in slightly different form in *College English,* Vol. 33 (January 1972), pp. 433–38.

1 See, for example, Olivia Mellan, "Black English: Why Try to Eradicate It?" *New Republic,* November 29, 1970, pp. 15–17.

2 "A Teacher's Plea for Certain Values," *Boston Globe,* November 26, 1970.

3 Cited in James Sledd, "Bi-Dialectalism: The Linguistics of White Supremacy," *English Journal,* Vol. 58 (December 1969), pp. 1307–15, 1329.

4 All of this is well documented in S. Shalom and B. Shapiro, *Two, Three, Many Tech Squares: M.I.T.'s Role in the Transformation of Cambridge* (Boston: New England Free Press, 1969).

5 Schoolboys of Barbiana, *Letter to a Teacher* (New York: Random House, 1970). See my reviews of this book: *New Republic,* July 18, 1970, pp. 25–26, and *Harvard Educational Review,* Vol. 40 (November 1970), pp. 657–74. For a more particular discussion of the American scene, see Paul Lauter and Florence Howe, *The Conspiracy of the Young* (New York and Cleveland: World Publishing Co., 1970), especially Chaps. 8 and 9.

6 See, e.g., his "The Psychiatrist: A Policeman in the Schools," in Satu Repo, ed., *This Book Is About Schools* (New York: Pantheon Books, 1970), pp. 405–27.

III

"BUT ALL THIS IS SO—SO UNPOETICAL"

Charles Kingsley

OR, TOWARD NEW LITERARY PRACTICE

WHY TEACH POETRY?—
AN EXPERIMENT

Florence Howe

(with the help of Carol Ahlum,
Mary Kai Howard, and others) [1]

Damn, my whole life I've been told poetry was this or
that. That you have to be somebody—an artist—to write
poetry. And here I was writing a poem, and I wasn't
going to be afraid to show it to a teacher.

Wendy Lasser

Poetry is people—that's what I've learned. The kids
taught that to me. I don't think I ever looked at it that
way before—I was too busy being analytical and searching for meaning. But I have learned that poetry is what
I am, if I place my experiences before me as I read the
poem.

Miriam Brown

"Man, ya' gotta' have confidence in yourself. What dya'
mean, you can't write a poem?"

High School Student

I

Beginning in 1968, twice a week a dozen Goucher undergraduates and I invaded one or more Baltimore city
high schools with mimeographed sheets of contemporary
poems.[2] We were testing several different but related ideas:
that the youth, energy, and interests of college students

equipped them for innovation and flexible teaching, and that such teaching might be educational for them; that the high school English classroom could become a place for creative, organized discussion—about feelings, ideas, language, poetry; that small-group instruction (using non-authoritarian teaching techniques) was a useful step in the classroom preparation of teachers; and finally, that contemporary poetry might provide good curricular materials for the high school English class. In other essays, I have emphasized the teaching aspect of the experiment, and in particular, the delight of the high school students, their poetry, and their positive evaluation of the experience.[3] In this essay, I shall try to do the same for the undergraduates. It is clear enough that they enjoyed themselves; the questions to be answered are Why? and How was the experience of use to them? How, beyond the typical study of poetry in the college classroom, has the experiment contributed to their futures as writers, graduate students, teachers of literature, or as people? What, if anything, can be learned about poetry through teaching it to average tenth-grade students? What can be learned about why literature should be studied at all?

When the 1968 "pilot project" became an "experimental" English course at Goucher in 1969, its title was "The Study of Poetry Through the Teaching of Poetry." Early in 1970, the following description was posted for students:

ENGLISH 210

Though this course has not yet appeared in the catalogue, it has functioned for the past two years as the poetry project," and last year experimentally for credit. Experiment is still its mode of being. One central idea of the course is that teaching is a useful way of learning, especially for the teacher. Another is that participatory forms of learning—that is, relatively "open" discussions—are particularly useful for the study of poetry. A third, that reading and writing poems are both integral to the study of poetry.

Undergraduates will spend two hours a week teaching small groups of high school students during regular class periods in selected inner-city schools. Poetry readings and the visits of poets to the classroom are additional features. The curriculum is a continuing experiment, since one aim of the course is to identify poems that interest high school students. (We work closely with teachers and supervisory personnel in the Baltimore City Public Schools.) Undergraduates will keep detailed journals of each teaching hour: these contribute to their development as teachers, and at least as significantly, allow them to record their developing understanding of poetry. Undergraduates will also attend weekly workshops about the curriculum and the teaching styles they are developing. The course is open to sophomores, juniors, and seniors, whether or not you conceive of yourself as a future teacher. It is essential that you enjoy poetry and highly desirable that you enjoy writing.

This was a four-year experiment that involved thirty-nine undergraduates [4] and approximately four hundred high school students who were members of thirteen English classes, taught by twelve different high school teachers, in five different high schools.[5] Chiefly, though not exclusively, the high school students were working-class, in lower (or non-college-bound) "tracks" or "ability groups." [6] In the high school, each undergraduate worked with a small group of six to thirteen high school students who knew that they were, for two hours, released from their regular English class to participate in an experiment. They were told that they would not be graded for their participation, and that we were interested in whether they might want to read poetry and whether they might help to find poems suitable for high school students. For those students, the initial, and often the continuing, reaction was mixed: it was fun to be out of the regular classroom and in a small group with a "teacher" only three to six years your senior; it was not always fun to be handed a page of poetry. "Why poetry?" many of them groaned.

For the undergraduates, the poetry was central: either they were "poets" interested in discovering whether they might encourage high school students to read and write poetry, or they were prospective "critics" (English majors) —especially fond of poetry—interested in seeing whether they might be effectively different from most teachers. In any case, all of the early participants were part of an informal poetry workshop that had met on Monday nights through the fall of 1967. By winter, when plans for the experiment were under way, twelve undergraduates had volunteered to take the project on in the spring as an extra-curricular activity for which they expected to receive no credit. There was general agreement about the method: in the open manner of poetry workshops we were going to read and write poems. There was general agreement also about our preference for an inner-city school and for alleg-edly "unteachable" students, those for whom poetry was traditionally regarded as "unnecessary" or "impossible." Perhaps we made the second decision somewhat roman-tically: we were using my experiences and those of several of the Goucher undergraduates in the Baltimore tutorial program and in summer projects; we were also attracted by the writing of Sylvia Ashton-Warner and David Hol-brook, an early essay by Herbert Kohl, and John Holt's first book. We held workshops through the first winter of 1967–1968 to discuss our goals and perspectives: Were we "missionaries," bringing to the "deprived" some culture in the form of poetry? [7]

A number of considerations—chiefly common sense— saved us from such zeal. The undergraduates, in the first and all the following years, were attracted to the experi-ment because it took them out of the college classroom and into an activity that might be considered socially useful. At least they would be "doing" something, as opposed to the customary reading, writing papers, and listening to lectures. Why should they, then, impose yet another classroom on other students? How could they justify "doing" to high school students what they were escaping from at Goucher?

Most of the undergraduates, moreover, were critical of (if not hostile to) their own high school experience and to schools generally. They were anti-authoritarian in their attitudes and consciously anti-teacher as well.[8] They were intent upon whatever would allow people "to think for themselves." To that end, they valued the experience of the poetry workshop, or of small groups, generally, as promoting an atmosphere in which learning was a communal activity, the discussion not the responsibility of one person but of a group. Even the "teacher" or "discussion leader" was ultimately responsible to the group rather than an authority in it. Finally, since we didn't know what poems to teach—there was no established curriculum!—we were once again saved from the missionary's role. In fact, we were usually clear about the deliberate reversal of role here: we handed poems to the high school students which they were free to reject. And when one group of high school students "accepted" a poem, we simply noted that other groups ought to see whether the poem worked for them too. The success or failure of the poem was gauged by the quantity and quality of discussion evoked. The undergraduates knew that there were endless poems to be "tried out," but that their students were there to stay.

Opening days established the experiment's tone and some of its ground rules. Usually, we were able to make arrangements in schools so that groups could meet separately or at least in opposite corners of very large rooms. Two opening journal entries suggest the variety of undergraduate styles: [9]

I was a little frightened when I first walked in. I sat down, introduced myself as Miss Kusnitz and apologized for being late. Seven of nine students were there —we went around the circle introducing ourselves, and I repeated each name after the student. I told the students a little about the experiment; that is, I asked them to help choose which poems they liked and didn't like; I said we were interested in finding out their reasons why too—it would be helpful for the curriculum. They agreed to help—and then I said we would begin by reading a page of poems silently and then discussing the ones they liked.

Marcia Kusnitz, 1969

. . . we shuffled into the library (too noisy, traffic outside, bad acoustics). I asked for their names, giving mine as "Ida." They looked at the poems I handed out. SILENCE. Glances up and quickly back down to hide under the pages. I hear whisperings to my right —A. is arguing with P. They are pointing to poems so I feel free to ask what's up with those poems? . . . I go back to A.'s statement that she doesn't understand "Separation" and ask if anybody can help her out with that. An attempt by P., but very soft and unsure: "A boy and girl go apart and she misses him all the time." Nobody picks this up. Silence. . . . A. still doesn't see. . . . I decide to give my opinion. I figured, well, it might ease her mind to give her an idea, and plus I was pretty excited about the image forming in my mind. Good time to talk about pictures and how poems paint them in your mind. I tried to get as much eye contact as possible and went on to describe myself, or the others, as a needle and the feeling of missing someone as the thread and how from there it follows P.'s earlier description. That thread goes through everything. A few sparkles in the eyes. Me: "You know what I mean, missing somebody?" Knowing smiles; they look together in something.

Ida Little, 1971

On most opening days, the discussion flourished at once, to the surprise and joy of the undergraduates. Here is Fay

Lewis, striking neither the formality of Marcia nor the easy style of Ida, but somewhere in between:

> So we sat down, after arranging chairs and tables in an oval. I introduced myself—adding the Fay or Miss Lewis, which was probably not necessary due to the informality of the tone already. . . . There were no real silences during this introductory time—pretty much side-talk and discussions. I repeated the aims of the project: no grades, your teacher doesn't see anything you do, doesn't count for anything in school, you can say anything you want. . . . So we began: I passed out sheet one, asked them to look it over, and see which one they'd like to discuss. . . . "Eating Poetry" . . . was read by six people, beginning with the silent three on my left and moving around the circle.

EATING POETRY

Ink runs from the corners of my mouth.
There is no happiness like mine.
I have been eating poetry.

The librarian does not believe what she sees.
Her eyes are sad
and she walks with her hands in her dress.

The poems are gone.
The light is dim.
The dogs are on the basement stairs and coming up.

Their eyeballs roll,
their blond legs burn like brush.
The poor librarian begins to stamp her feet and weep.

She does not understand.
When I get on my knees and lick her hand,
she screams.

I am a new man.
I snarl at her and bark.
I romp with joy in the bookish dark.

Mark Strand

There were mixed reactions to the initial reading.
Some of the girls seemed amused, most were a little
puzzled. *And so the rest of the period was spent sorting out what really was going on in the poem.* . . .
For the longest time "eating" in line 3 was just assumed to mean "reading," and when I pointed out
the poet's choice of words, everyone took a new look
at what the poem was saying. I asked who the dogs
were, and why the librarian was afraid of them. . . .
They said that . . . since "their blond legs burn like
brush," the librarian was afraid that they would burn
up the books. I asked if these were real dogs in the
library. D. began a very careful interpretation of the
whole poem. She said that this man has not literally
been eating poetry—he had been reading it, and it
had made him feel like a dog, who might romp and
play. She described how it felt sometimes when you
read something and really got into it. This was happiness that this man was deriving from his poetry. I
asked why the librarian was stamping her feet and
weeping. "She does not understand"—she probably
never has read poetry. . . . There was a split in the
class between those who really knew and felt this idea
about getting a real happiness out of reading something and those who were still puzzling over the dogs
and what relation they had to the man, the librarian,
and the idea of poetry in general. The argument continued. . . . [Italics added.]

                                    Fay Lewis, 1970

How to continue the detailed interest and enthusiasm
and debate of the first day through many days? What makes
a good hour? Fay suggested one answer in her first journal:
"mixed reactions" from the group, and hence the possibility of debate and conflict. Some were "amused," some "puzzled": or in other words, the poem was entertaining at least
in its immediate impact, and while not obvious (so as to
preclude discussion), not entirely obscure either. The hour

became, then, a "sorting out of the poem." In other journals, Fay continued to wrestle with the problems of purpose. She mentioned several, one of which is the most obvious and the easiest to accomplish: interaction among students. But what of the poetry itself? Should she not try "to show that some interpretations are better than others, since there is more evidence for some than for others"? Again and again, Fay urges herself to try harder to "clarify meaning" and "to move deeper into the poem."

One of the frustrations of the project for the undergraduate teachers is that "deep" discussions may come unannounced, and occasionally in opening hours, and often as a part of the general development of the high school students into a functioning—which means listening and talking—group. It isn't simply, as some new teachers think, that first you must get the group to become a group; and that only afterward can they really discuss poetry. In fact, the two processes are typically simultaneous ones.

Because the small group is fundamentally different from other classroom experiences, both teachers and students need to learn about its processes and possibilities.[10] It is closest to some casual occasions—a small, informal gathering at home, perhaps lingering in serious conversation after dinner, or an informal rap session late at night in a dormitory or after a party. But we rarely think about such discussions as learning groups, and only more rarely still do they become continuing groups. Public school officials, quite understandably, react to the idea of small groups by claiming they are too expensive to be possible. But of course, the small group need not—indeed should not—meet constantly; three or four hours a week would be sufficient.

Two factors are especially important to small groups: the intimacy and the continuity. The intimacy is important for several reasons. From the participants' point of view, a group is small enough for people to note other people's reactions as they occur. In fact, reactions become part of the content of the group's learning. Normally a class watches a teacher: she is the focal point for instruction or entertainment. To make the teacher uncomfortable may be the aim of the class that sits in rows before her. But the small group democratizes the relationship, at least in theory, since all—say, eight students and a teacher—sit in a circle facing each other. All are equally visible to each other, though of course the teacher may still be more "visible" *qua* teacher than any of the students.

Let us acknowledge her visibility for a moment. Students may learn from watching the teacher (as well as other students) relate to the poetry and to each other. The teacher's interest in a student's response may be contagious. The small group allows everyone to see what a face looks like when it reads something that is sad. Or how a face begins to crinkle when a poem's comedy catches it unawares. A teacher in the small group cannot talk to a mass, hoping that a level of relative silence means that she has engaged a listening audience in *her* thoughts and words. A teacher in the small group can read the faces and bodies of the students around her and know at once whether they are listening or absent, hostile or friendly, frightened or at ease. What's more, students can note a teacher's feelings— that she has feelings—her fears and confusions, her confidence and laughter. The poems she brings with her become something she offers to them as a friend might offer an idea for honest judgment.

As in most arrangements for learning, the continuity is important. People in a small group need time to learn to trust that they will not be ridiculed for a frank response or a personal anecdote. There is special value in the spaces between meetings, when bits of conversation float back into your head and you wish you had said something else or plan what you will try to say the next time.

What does the teacher do in a small group? She learns to

be silent and listen; rather than respond to every comment with a comment of her own, she encourages students to respond to each other. She may even, from time to time, assume the role of moderator. She learns to relax enough to look interested, to be receptive to students' comments, to encourage the expression of differences, to keep calm when strong feelings emerge. And yet she must be willing, when queried by students, to say what she feels or thinks, and to be honest. She is not playing games with the students, leading them into traps which she will then expose. She is interested in the students' responses to the poems, at least in part because she expects to learn something from those responses. She expects that the students will learn, even as she has, from speaking what they think and feel. The teacher, who has been in other small groups, knows that the group exerts a silent pressure to speak that few can withstand; and that the necessity to speak forces people to think about what they feel and to grow conscious of their feelings.

"How does the poem make you feel?" is a question that the undergraduates have responded to in their own training workshops with me.[11] Often, the teacher in the small group will choose to be silent because she expects that someone else in the group will respond somewhat as she herself might have. But even if that doesn't happen, the teacher may decide that the group does not need to hear her views that day. After all, she is not the focus of the lesson. The poem is—and the students' responses to that poem: "How does the poem make you feel?" "Why does it make you feel sad or angry or pleasant?" What matters is that the students see and hear and feel the poem and their own responses to it (and all the possibilities therein, given the complexity of poems and the variety of students in any group). What matters is for the students to see the language and rhythm functioning, deciding and controlling ideas, thoughts, feelings.

So here is a group, and the silence is to be broken by a few poems on mimeographed sheets. Why poems? Later I will describe a number of reasons for choosing poems as curriculum. Here it is useful to mention only those that have to do with small groups. Many poems are personal, even private, just as people are. Yet, in the sense that the poet is writing to be read by others, the poem is an offering to a public. And people in a group eventually begin to share some of their personal and private thoughts and feelings. The poem, moreover, serves as a model for the group's discussion. If the poet can express her feelings and thoughts in words—can get them out in a coherent, satisfying whole—maybe people in groups can manage that too. I don't mean writing poems, though that may also begin to happen. I mean that the personal poem or the poem on a topic that is somewhat taboo—abortion, drugs, or race relations, for example—invites intimate, honest conversation. Conversely, for meaningful discussion of poems, intimacy and honesty are essential.

Sometimes it is easier for a small group to argue about rationally contradictory ideas than about contradictory feelings. An early hour on a little poem by Gregory Corso may illustrate the connection between a group's development and a literary discussion of a poem. Because I had reported that "Thought" had been a favorite of all groups during the first and second years of the project, Tobie Sperry included it on a sheet of four poems she prepared for her third meeting. Her diary records more than a thousand words of an hour's discussion in which the eleven members of her group participated. First the poem, and then the climax of the group's discussion:

THOUGHT

Death is but is not lasting.
To pass a dead bird,
The notice of it is,

Yet walking on
Is gone.
The thought remains
And thought is all I know of death.

Gregory Corso

Suddenly P. announced that people were explaining things to V. *wrong*: "You're all talking about this poem as if the subject of the poem is death, but it isn't *death*, it's *thought*." And as soon as P. said this, it was like a cue for everyone to explode. Suddenly there were voices coming from everywhere, which was great except that I wanted to hear all of them. So every once in a while I would say, "Wait—let her finish, and then you can disagree," to various people, but the entire thing was a direct interchange among the girls, talking to each other, no waiting to be called on, no formality. I loved it and they did too. . . . I let P. completely explain her position. . . .

N.: This is a poem about death, and the bird in the poem is an example of death.

P.: This is a poem about thinking and thoughts, and death is an example of one kind of thought.

Things were getting too noisy. I took a poll. Four people agreed with N. and five people with P.

E. (who agreed with N. that the poem is about death) must have wanted a rational discussion of which side was right, and she thought she could initiate it by switching to the form of the poem, which we had talked about at the beginning, but without much enthusiasm. And so E. explained to V. that the dead bird was in the poem just to make the poem easier to understand and see, because an example always helps you to understand. . . .

Though more than a dozen classroom hours followed this early one, and though longer and more complex poems were discussed, few caught fire in precisely this way. For one thing, the littleness of the Corso poem allowed students to hold it as they could not, at least at first, hold a longer poem. They could see that the poem contained three elements—"thought," "death," and "a dead bird." Their hour-long activity, the establishment of relationships or hierarchies, is, indeed, a function of criticism. At the same time, the dispute evoked by the attempt to establish the organization of the poem was interesting to the participants and to the undergraduate teacher for its own sake, since public school classrooms (and college classrooms) do not usually allow, much less promote, conflict and explosions. Of course, Tobie could have "settled" the dispute, but she chose not to do so, since that was not the role she wanted to establish for herself as discussion leader.

II. "LISTENING TO YOUR EMOTIONS"

In 1970, one undergraduate, Mary Kai Howard, organized her curriculum to change a group's skepticism about communication. She began accidentally when a student on the first day chose Langston Hughes's "Impasse" in response to Kai's direction: "Look for a poem on this sheet you particularly like, for whatever reason."

IMPASSE

I could tell you,
If I wanted to,
What makes me
What I am.

But I don't
Really want to—
And you don't
Give a damn.

Langston Hughes

Kai asked why the student liked it: "Because it is a truth," she replied. The dialogue that followed, Kai recalls, was "slow and stiff."

I prodded and eleven skeptical faces coughed up answers. In my journal that night I wrote: "Do they think no one really cares about another person? Tomorrow I think I will start over at this point. . . . It might be saying something about their own unresponsiveness. I want them to know their opinion counts!"

Kai realized, in the course of writing her first journal, that "Impasse" was ironically appropriate as a description· of the group's first meeting:

The dialogue had met impasse after impasse. I was not at ease as teacher, and the girls were insecure about revealing themselves to the other members of the group. The irony was compounded by the second choice of the girls, a little Merwin poem.

SEPARATION

Your absence has gone through me
Like thread through a needle.
Everything I do is stitched with its color.

W. S. Merwin

A student chose the poem, she said, "because it is about love." Kai recalls that the discussion "centered around the way the poet felt and the way the poem made the girls feel."

KAI: How do you think the poet feels about separation?
J.: He feels pain.
SH.: He is aware of her. Her absence affects everything he does. It *is* painful.

Once again, the title was appropriate to the discussion: the students responded separately to Kai's questions, directing their answers to her, the teacher, for approval. In her journal, she wrote:

What about "Impasse"? They all seem to think no one cares anyway, period. Yet "Separation" "moved" them. This is their own vocabulary. They understand the poet's pain. Why? Tomorrow I will say, "Do you think it was worth it for Merwin to write his feelings in a poem? Is poetry only good to the person who wrote the poem? Who is listening to the poet anyway? Do we always listen to one another? Should we?"

Before many more hours had passed, Kai understood that her students' cynicism was ambivalent or "contradictory." "On the one hand," she wrote, "they had said, 'NO ONE CARES,' and on the other, 'WE CAN SHARE FEELING.'" The contradiction provided a goal for Kai's work in the project: "that developing community would lead to good dialogue, to better reading, to good writing, to *better* community, and so on in this cyclical progress of expanding confidence." She concluded from the early meetings that her group "would move away from 'impasse' because, in the girls' own vocabulary, communication was possible. It had begun between them and the poet, and I promised myself it would happen between themselves and myself soon."

How to accomplish her goal: to encourage "cooperation among the girls themselves to build an interpretation of the poem which we could all feel"? As Kai began, she was aware of the obvious differences among her students—at least their skin color told her that seven were black, four white—but she had to learn for herself the importance of *working from differences.*

The first breakthrough came in the fifth meeting, during a second hour spent discussing Nikki Giovanni's "Nikki-Rosa":

NIKKI-ROSA

childhood remembrances are always a drag
if you're Black
you always remember things like living in Woodlawn
with no inside toilet

and if you become famous or something
they never talk about how happy you were to have your mother
all to yourself and
how good the water felt when you got your bath
from one of those
big tubs that folk in chicago barbecue in
and somehow when you talk about home
it never gets across how much you
understood their feelings
as the whole family attended meetings about Hollydale
and even though you remember
your biographers never understand
your father's pain as he sells his stock
and another dream goes
and though you're poor it isn't poverty that
concerns you
and though they fought a lot
it isn't your father's drinking that makes any difference
but only that everybody is together and you
and your sister have happy birthdays and very good
christmasses
and I really hope no white person ever has cause
to write about me
because they never understand
Black love is Black wealth and they'll
probably talk about my hard childhood
and never understand that
all the while I was quite happy

                                        Nikki Giovanni

At first, several black students were, Kai recalls, "offended
by the exclusive 'blackness' of Giovanni's poem." The
white students remained silent throughout, and discussion
was not easy in general. When Kai asked whether people
thought the poet was black, two black students who responded affirmatively changed the course of the discussion:

    sh.: I think she is because she says, "Black love is
        Black wealth." No one else could know this.

JU.: She must have experienced it . . . because she
says that if you haven't experienced it, you
wouldn't understand it. . . . It's in the poem.

From this point on, students noted and commented on the
details of black life in the poem with some feelings of
pride, and perhaps a bit of self-conscious embarrassment
rather than shame. In fact, as Kai notes, before the hour
had ended, it had become important—at least to the black
students—that "Giovanni really be black to make the poem
live."

But Kai was not satisfied with the discussion, since it
had been one only for her and the black students, with the
four poker-faced white women observing. She wanted, in
the next hours, "to talk about pride and shame—about the
transition they had made yesterday. About transitions I've
made in my lifetime. Some in theirs." Also, she had not
been satisfied with the aspect of the discussion that had
assumed economic poverty as the poem's center. And so
she began with the line that had been key, "Black love is
Black wealth," and the question, "Is all love wealth?" For
some reason, perhaps because I was present as a strange
observer, several students agreed that you didn't have to
be black to have experienced Giovanni's childhood, but
you did have to be poor. Kai asked, "Is love wealth only
for poor people? Do you have to be poor to recognize this?"

AN.: Yes. Rich people are independent. They don't
need each other. They can do what they want.
. . . They have enough money to get away from
each other. Poor people have to stay together.

But Kai pressed: "Why then emphasize blackness as well
as poverty?"

AL.: Because—maybe that's where it's centered.
KAI: Where love's centered?
AL.: Yes.

After a minute of silence, Kai asked again, How can the love be centered in blackness? Sh. murmured that she thought that love was wealth even for rich people. And then the student who had earlier insisted on the independence of rich people shifted her view:

> AN.: If you're rich and black and the only black family in the neighborhood and nobody'll have anything to do with you, it holds the family together. They only associate with each other.

For the students in the group, this was a fresh thought: that black need not be equated with poverty, nor wealth with exemption from racism. And though the white students had still not participated, they had witnessed the shifting interpretations of and feelings about the poem. Kai had wanted students to get more deeply into the poem, "to talk about what makes being black different from being white other than economics," and she had accomplished that goal. Finally, she turned to her second aim, and asked the group "about their own transition from offense to pride the last time." No one had noticed or remembered that shift, and so Kai asked more generally whether anyone "remembered being ashamed of something which they were later proud of." The discussion veered away from blackness and an emphasis on the uniqueness of that experience to allow white and black students to share several similar memories. One student remembered her brown oxfords when everyone else had loafers. Later she learned to be proud of being different, she said, "After my mother drummed it into me." Another student "remembered being studious and 'good' in the fifth and sixth grades—and being ashamed of being different. But when she got recommendations and good remarks from teachers later she was proud." Kai chose that moment to talk about her own experience, about "being on scholarship and thinking, at first, that it was something to be ashamed of. Learning to be proud of it." Kai's remarks evoked laughter and skepticism, especially from several of the students, black and white, who were often silent. Kai's good-humored response in the next moments was important, probably more than she realized, since this was the first time that she and the group had moved so far away from the poems to talk of themselves. She notes in her journal: "The girls all laughed with Ju. Smiled for me and opened up, about Goucher being all white and rich. It isn't, not quite. . . ."

The few moments that I regard as a breakthrough established a new intimacy for the group, a new honesty. They had been nearly hostile to Kai, and she had managed those moments with dignity and yet without rancor toward the students. She had established the tone needed for serious conversation: a willingness to hear anything, even skepticism about oneself.

The moments were also an interlude before the discussion moved on to Ellen Bass's "I Am in the Back Room." This time most students, black and white, participated, and with special pleasure on the question of the poet's identity. Giovanni's poem had established for them the primacy of the writer's experience, and they liked the idea that you could try to tell something about the poet from the poem. If a poem seemed to be about poverty or suffering, could the poet have been describing her own life? Could a *poet* have been poor? And why write about poverty?

The atmosphere during this last half of the hour, moreover, had perceptibly shifted. As Kai notes in her journal, "the girls took over—they answered each other's questions and listened carefully without waiting for my direction." First, the poem, then an excerpt from the journal:

I AM IN THE BACK ROOM

I am in the back room of our liquor store
crying among the cases of Cliquot Club
     and pints of Tiger Rose

looking at the floor where the boards close the stairs
       at my puffed face in the peeling mirror above the
              yellow sink and yellow soap.
My grandmother is lying on a couch
saying tomorrow
     when she's stronger
     she'll put on her rings.
My father is in the front of the store
     waiting on a customer
     asking fifths or quarts
My father says she should be in a home
     until she's finished dying.

                              Ellen Bass

KAI: Do you like the poem?
D.:   No, it doesn't say anything. There's no action.
JA.: It doesn't make sense. What happens? Why is
      she crying?

  A. explains that she is crying because she is sad that
her father is going to send her grandmother away.
She reads the lines of the poem in defense of her
statement.

SH.: Perhaps she is sad because she has to see her
      grandmother dying slowly.

  They talk about her father: Is he mean? Maybe he
thinks he is doing the best thing? Maybe a home will
be better for the grandmother. Nobody likes the way
the last line is written. Ja. says the father shouldn't
have put it that way. . . . Others that the girl loves
her grandmother and that is the way she feels about it.
  Al. thinks the poet must be a boy. De. says that even
though the poet is a girl she might be pretending to
be someone else. Ga. thinks this is possible. Sh. does
not. They talk about experience vs. fiction again. Ga.
explains that you can walk down a street and get a
feeling about living in a place without actually living
there. Everyone listens carefully when Ga. speaks be-

cause it is not often, and because she is very serious if she speaks at all.

Al. gets back to the idea that the speaker is a boy, because of the liquor store and noise and "fifths" and "quarts." Also because of the language—the bluntness. Others say a boy would not cry. Al. says, "Yes, men cry." But not boys? someone asks. The conversation moves into the meaning of "crying." Al. says we sometimes cry inside. Su. says this is ridiculous "because crying is crying." Sh. says Al. is wrong, too, because "her face is puffy."

Al. says the speaker is poor. Why? someone else asks. Because of the yellow sink, Al. replies. An. thinks of yellow as bright and gay. In this scene? Al. queries a bit tartly. Al. associates yellow with dinginess and poorness and oldness. I ask if the person in the poem is very young. Someone: she could be anyone—even our age—and very attached to her grandmother. . . . Su. thinks this could be a childhood remembrance—about childhood from the perspective of an older person—as in the poem above it.

I asked if the poet here is proud or ashamed of remembrance.

su.: She is ashamed of her father—of the whole situation.

Just before the close of the period, Kai asks if they think the person in the poem is black. One of the black students says yes, that is the way she "pictures" it. Others say that she might be black or white, that "there is no evidence in the poem." When Kai tells them who Ellen Bass is—one of the initial members of the poetry project, and white—no one is really surprised, not even the black student who had offered her "picture" of the poem.

Kai followed this hour with others in which students wrote and discussed their own "poems of experience." Then, bringing in two Merwin poems, she turned deliberately to another area of (poetic) communication. "Fable" and "Sea Monster," mimeographed on a single sheet, Kai reports, "were popular, but they didn't meet our first criterion of valid communication, experience."

KAI: Do you think Merwin experienced this event (described in "Sea Monster")?

AL.: No, because he doesn't tell it good enough. . . .

JU.: And he doesn't tell us how they felt.

KAI: He says they were not surprised.

JU.: He tells us how they didn't feel, but he does not tell us how they did feel. They might not have been surprised, but they might have been afraid at the time.

SU.: It sounds like a story that was told to him by somebody else. But it didn't really happen to him.

But if it didn't "happen to him" in reality, could it have happened in another way? The discussion moved on into such matters as illusion and delusion, into using your imagination for some purpose, known or unknown to you beforehand. "The girls," Kai writes, "were excited by Merwin's imagination, and then excited by their own." In the next hour, the students wrote "poems from our imagination" and in spite of the fact that they had moved into an area more private even than experience, there was in the last ten minutes of the period, Kai writes, "a general and very friendly exchange of poems among all of us. We walked around the room to read each other's work or to discuss a problem. . . ."

In the last portion of her time, Kai moved on to poems "about things we feel strongly." This, in the spring of the Cambodian invasion, proved to be war. And after the group had read several professional poems, Kai once again asked the group to write. "The assignment," Kai notes, "required a recognition of poetry as communication. It also assumed a kind of confidence in the group feeling established to that point. In order to write a poem about strong feeling, the girls needed to trust each other to care."

At the very end, in the manner of an inventive experimenter, Kai searched for an idea that might demonstrate something that her group had learned and at the same time help make the last hour an especially memorable one. She decided to ask the students to write, during the first fifteen minutes of the period, a poem in the style of a note, using as model William Carlos Williams's "This Is Just to Say." Thus the poem was to contain most obviously "the properties of communication" that the group had been "investigating for seven weeks." Kai was not disappointed: the hour and the experiment concluded with her reading the poems aloud so that the students might guess the author. Even with three strange visitors and me present, the students laughed unembarrassedly at themselves as they guessed incorrectly most of the time. As Kai explained in her journal, the poems were revealing of significant changes in the attitudes of several students. G., who had been one of the most skeptical and least attentive members of the group to begin with, called her experience "beautiful," and, in a corner of her paper, drew a small peace sign, saying, "peace and love forever." Ju., the group's loner, who used to sit outside the circle, wrote:

> This is Just to Say
> That people don't always have
> To voice their opinions to make
> Known what they feel but
> It is better that way.

Ja. wrote that she has "learned to respect other/people/ for their ideas and thoughts." The two longest poems, written by Al. and Sh., bring us back to the beginning. Al. writes that poetry is a "means of expressing myself," but that "Poems are written not to be just praised or criticized but for/each man's opinions." That is, this student manages to separate, in terms of function, the poet from the reader. She concludes with a memorable sentence: "Poetry has filled an empty/space within." Sh. sums up all that Kai had hoped for in a poem that is, except for a memorable phrase, prosier than most:

> This is to say to the group:
> That being in this group has brought us
> closer to each other than being in the
> same class all year. I enjoyed reading
> your poetry and listening to your emotions.

The originality and consistency with which Kai approached her group led to the development of a coherent curricular plan, a virtually singular accomplishment for an experienced teacher, let alone an undergraduate. There is evidence in her journal and in two essays she wrote afterwards [12] that her curriculum developed from her experience dynamically as she proceeded. At the same time, it is clear enough that she continued throughout to test her primary (and essential) intuition: that the development of the group would occur simultaneously with the students' developing abilities to read poems. There was, she has made clear, an organic relationship between the two processes.

> If dialogue is deep and exciting the group is probably relating sensitively. A student will only try to say what is on her mind if she is assured that people are listening and care about what she says. If a sensitive group feeling develops, the girls will talk about things that are important to them. Otherwise, they are limited to saying things which others cannot use against them.

Is poetry then useful as curriculum because it facilitates the group's development? Does dividing one's attention between the group and the poetry ultimately distract from the poetry? For teachers like Kai, the students are prime, if one has to make choices. Her own view of poetry changed in the process of teaching, and this change, too, reflects her priorities. She had begun, in the manner of her students, to test poems for the "life in them." She now preferred "experience" to "art"—the reality caught roughly in a poem rather than the exquisitely empty shell.

Kai represents those undergraduates who never questioned the value of using poetry. Rather, they used it— for pleasure and for teaching people how to care about each other. Perhaps they could do so, in part, because they had fastened, explicitly, on a purpose. Kai had glimpsed the dynamics even as the process was beginning.

But from the beginning, there was another tension in the project. After all, we were English teachers. If we were not missionaries of high culture, bringing poetry to those who would not ordinarily read it, what were we? Explorers of unknown sensibilities? Discoverers of "improbable" poets? Curriculum developers? Teachers of language? If we were none of these, if we were chiefly facilitators of discussions, why then were we not working with prose? Did we not value *poetry* or merely its utility? Why were we teaching poetry?

III. WHY POETRY?

Why teach poetry at all—and especially to high school students like the ones we wanted and were assigned to teach? That is a fundamental question, not only for this essay, but one that I continued to press on myself and the undergraduates throughout the four years. The same question, moreover, was pressed on them by the high school students. On opening day of the first year, for example, in a vocational school, a tenth-grader commented: "I guess they are trying to make gentlemen out of auto mechanics, or as we drop the oil pan on a car we are supposed to recite poetry." The young man assumed, quite correctly, that poetry belongs (in the United States) to a certain class of people, and that it is ornamental rather than functional in relation to most people's lives—even those people who "possess" it. These are the assumptions of most classrooms, and when I began, in 1967, I could not (and did not) argue any other view. Nowhere in the early conception of the experiment was there an explicit statement about the elitist nature of poetry or about the desirability that poetry *belong* to masses of people rather than to a group of intellectuals who call themselves poets, critics, or professors. It was not only that I was, in 1967, incapable of abstracting such ideology; it was, rather, that I came to the experiment more aware of pedagogical problems than ideological ones.

The idea for the experiment came from a series of experiences in Mississippi Freedom Schools and from other inner-city projects, in which black and white students who were nominally poor readers enjoyed poetry. Even in the midst of Mississippi Summer's political activity that led students out of and back into the classroom, poetry became important. The poems of Langston Hughes caught many of their feelings, and the style of William Carlos Williams and E. E. Cummings illustrated new freedoms with language and punctuation. Black students took what they wanted from the "white" or "majority" culture and made poetry out of their own lives. Such attempts at writing, moreover, seemed to contribute to the students' desire or ability to read.[13]

When I began in 1967, there were several reasons in my head for using poetry as curriculum—and that was the word I wrote, "using." First, I argued, poems were brief bits of writing, and thus could be examined in the space of a classroom hour, as though one had a raindrop under a high-power microscope, or a delicate cameo in the palm of one's hand. No homework was necessary, no reading of lengthy fictions, and whatever the reading levels of the students, all could manage the relatively few words on the page. Moreover, given the idiosyncratic forms of contemporary poetry—as exemplified in the "little" poems of

William Carlos Williams—students would learn quickly to invent their own versions of these forms. In both these respects, I was not disappointed: high school students and undergraduates learned the power of *making* a poem. Implicit, of course, was the assumption that whether you were a vocational high student or a college English major, poetry could be yours.

I argued also that just as contemporary poetry reflected in its diction and syntax the language we speak today, so did its (rebellious) themes reflect the interests of young students. If this was true, if the language of poems allowed relatively easy access, and if the subjects and themes were interesting, then would the students not *want* to read and discuss poems? There would be no need, I speculated, for forcing students to pay attention or for using punitive devices—tests, grades, and so forth. Using poetry as curriculum was a device for ensuring that even the most "turned-off" students would cooperate. Again, I was generally correct in my assumptions, though it is impossible to assess this aspect of the experiment without at least mentioning the attraction to high school students of the chief pedagogical device: small groups run by undergraduates. Nor did I anticipate several problems with respect to curriculum: the sensitivity of high school officials to the use of "bad" language and "controversial" themes, and the narrowness of interests among certain groups of high school students.

Finally, I speculated in 1967 about two other functions of poetry as curriculum. Just as poets attempted to express the connection between thoughts and feelings, so would the proper teaching of poetry help students to understand the connections between their own thoughts and feelings. Poetry is, I was fond of quoting Wordsworth on the subject, "feeling intellect." That is, a poem catches feeling and thought in a form as symbolic as language itself. The poem is never abstract! The feeling takes shape in images and rhythms. I was not totally incorrect here, though I was vague and excessively ambitious. What mattered was that students and undergraduates both learned that poems expressed feelings as well as thoughts. How to talk about feelings and how to make connections between feelings and thoughts were, in fact, major tasks of undergraduates.

More significant still is an associated function: the patterns of language and rhythm are enjoyable. The poem is not only linguistically accessible; not only are its subject and theme interesting; its rhythms are pleasing to the ears and even to other senses once students begin to read poems (confidently) aloud. People might read poems, even in classrooms, for pleasure! But as a pedagogue, I could not refrain from pursuing this point to its obvious end. I argued that pleasure was pedagogically useful, for students who enjoyed poems would not only want to read them and discuss them, they would also *want* to learn grammar, syntax, spelling, etc. It was not that I was incorrect: students who enjoy reading obviously are better readers—for a number of reasons—than those who do not enjoy it; and it is true that students who are curious and eager to learn are receptive even to correction, and may ask for training in skills with some sense of their usefulness. It was, rather, that I could not value the pleasure for its own sake. I could not do so, at least in part, because, like the young man who was learning to become an auto mechanic, I could not perceive any function for poetry beyond the narrowly utilitarian, for him or for the undergraduates. I might add, however, that there was a distinction in my mind between the young man and the undergraduates, since they were middle-class women whose futures included, I assumed, leisure time to fill with such ornamental pleasures as poems.

In short, the reasons I offered to the Baltimore City Public Schools, to Goucher College, and to Teachers and Writers Collaborative were, and still are, sound pedagogical reasons for introducing contemporary poetry into the high school curriculum (and we have accomplished that much in several Baltimore classrooms). But the question of its *value* continued to plague the experiment, at least in part, because, as I now surmise, the reasons I offered to begin with were incomplete. I assumed that the high school students would have had no experience with poetry, that they would in fact be hostile to it, and that their hostility would be a functionally useful place to begin. Students could freely express their views that a poem was "stupid," and then attempt to explain why. In the explanation was, typically, the seed of a useful discussion of the poem. Obviously, many critics work most effectively from negative reactions! But I did not account for the undergraduates who would continue to press me with my own question: Why teach poetry to students whose futures lay either in the rice paddies of Vietnam or on the assembly line? Or later, when we were teaching only women students, Why, or even how, teach poetry to women who were likely to be store clerks or typists until they could escape to the kitchen stove?

In the second year of the experiment, Carol Ahlum, who was teaching a group of boys studying auto mechanics, questioned, often in despair, the value of her work. Why, she asked, am I teaching these guys to read and write poetry? They hate school; they cut all their classes some days and then sneak back into school for the poetry group. And they are writing poems. But what good will it do them? Most of them will be off to Vietnam in a year or two—that's what they're writing about, and that's where they even want to go. And none of my reasons satisfied Carol in 1969. She left the experiment at the end of her sophomore year, questioning its value and that of schools generally.

The reasons I offered to Carol and other undergraduates for using poetry were not incorrect but insufficient. They did not explain even my own pleasure in reading poetry nor theirs. Mostly, we assumed that pleasure; rarely did we admit to it or discuss its significance for the teaching project. Had we pursued the subjects of pleasure and of our own initiation into poetry, or of our own sense of its function in our lives, I expect that we might have reached more quickly toward the conclusions I will offer here. For several of us were of working-class origins. We had not been "born" to poetry, at least not to the poetry of Shakespeare and Milton, nor of Eliot and Pound. Some of the students were even closer than I to the excitement of "discovering" poetry that was "ours," Plath, Levertov, Rich, and Sexton, for example. But all of us had become *un*-thinking members of the middle class; as college people, we assumed that poetry was our property. For utilitarian reasons, it was to be on loan to the nonprivileged.

Several students' journals trace the frustrations associated with such class-bound views. Carol Ahlum's journal records fifteen hours of working with six eleventh-grade boys in a vocational track, most of them intending to be auto mechanics. They met behind glass walls in a library seminar room, open to the stares of the curious. Soberly, and for the most part quietly, they examined Carol's offerings. The patterns of single hours were rarely neat curves of organized discussion. Rather, they flashed brilliance even as the bits that follow. The students went at the language of a poem as though they were inspecting an engine. In an early lesson, for example, they read Karl Shapiro's "Man on Wheels":

MAN ON WHEELS

Cars are wicked, poets think.
Wrong as usual. Cars are part of man.
Cars are biological.
A man without a car is like a clam without a shell.
Granted, machinery is hell,

> But carless man is careless and defenseless.
> Ford is skin of present animal.
> Automobile is shell.
> You get yourself a shell or else.

Karl Shapiro

After "they all said it was a stupid poem which they didn't understand," Carol records that B. asked "Why does he say 'machinery is hell'? And what does he mean, 'Get yourself a shell or else'? Or else what?" In the process of dealing with those questions, the discussion focused on the word "Ford."

D.: He could have used Dodge because a Dodge is better than a Ford.

T.: But he isn't saying that a Ford is good. He's criticizing the Ford because it's "skin of present animal."

After a discussion which extended to Chevrolets and Plymouths, Carol records "they broke into trying out foreign-car names in the line of poetry." Finally, they agreed that a single syllable sounded better than anything else.

They also looked carefully at the placement of words on the page. In a discussion of David Henderson's "Documentary on Airplane Glue," D. asked, "Why does he put 'soaring' on a separate line and over to this side? There has to be a meaning of why he put it this way. There's always a meaning for what poets do. They just don't do anything." Carol agreed and asked what he thought:

D.: Maybe he wants you to get a feeling of flying and that's what you feel when you read "soaring."

B.: It also makes you feel as if the flying is moving downward. [*He moves his hands in a back-and-forth downward motion, illustrating the words on the page.*]

CAROL: Do you think he wants you to think of falling down?

B.:   Yes.

CAROL: Why?

D.:   Because the effect wears off. . . .

In other discussions, students were critical of language they didn't understand. Here, too, they went at the poem empirically, as craftsmen. Why, for example, did a poet use expressions like "blank monkeys of the hierarchy" and "zinc gripped steel" instead of writing "what he means." On the other hand, they admired Langston Hughes's "Impasse" because, as one student quipped, "It's a smart remark that I might make." They told Carol again and again that though they didn't like poetry in general (at least in part because it was not an obviously masculine preoccupation), they did "like poetry that [they] can understand."

Conscious that she had been probing for what her students liked, Carol fastened on the word "understand" in a journal entry about midway through her teaching hours.

> But now, understanding that they like what they understand, what do I do when I know that some poems aren't understandable for them? Hopefully, "Auto Wreck" might be a way into this blank wall. It's a hard poem but they like the subject. Maybe both together will help us to get into other hard poems.

Carol's assumption was an intelligent one: that to enlarge understanding means, in part, to broaden vocabulary, to get students into complex language and thought. And she chose subjects of poems she expected would interest her students—autos, chewed-off squirrels' necks, accidents, death, and finally, war. And indeed she did interest them, and they continued to look carefully at the words of poems and to feel free about criticizing the poems offered to them. Here they are on Shapiro's "Auto Wreck":

After the reading, B. began speaking without questions from me.

B.:   Seems like he's writing two different poems. Another part begins after "Empty husks of locusts, to iron poles." I don't understand this second part.

CAROL: How is it different from the first part?

B.:   Well, see, he starts talking about an accident and the ambulance comes to pick up the victims and then the people and cops are standing around and even this third part is O.K. But then he starts talking about guns and war. And this part asks questions about death and starts talking of death. He's started talking about a whole other idea and that shouldn't be. I think the poem should end after the third part. . . .

C.:   [*Shaking his head—he has spoken before only twice, though he sometimes volunteers to read*]: The questions do fit because they're asking who shall die and who is innocent— and someone has probably just died and the poet wants to know, probably, who is to blame.

B.:   But the poet uses words I don't understand: like what does "denouement" mean? [*Carol explains.*] OK, but in the line "One hangs lanterns on the wrecks that cling,/Empty husks of locusts, to iron poles," What does he mean—"Empty husks of locusts"—do the lanterns look like empty husks of locusts?

Understanding, however, is not enough, especially if it is reserved for cognition. In the hours that follow, Carol asked more directly about feeling and got some responses (to Henderson's "Documentary"):

CAROL: But how does the poem make you feel? Is it a happy or sad poem?

D.:   There's a part which really touched me. Let's see, this part around "unless they return to Puerto Rico flying from poverty to poverty above the clouds/. . . and *not* back to Africa?"

CAROL: What do you mean by "touched"?

D.:   It makes me think about these little kids who sniff glue. They probably don't have anything else to do and no playgrounds and stuff to use in their spare time. I feel glad that I'm not poor. I feel sad for them.

I finally realized that Denny was answering my question about feeling.

Robert Frost's "Out! Out!" evoked the most open expression of feeling thus far, though at first it was buried in mock sobs and laughter. The students quarreled about whether the boy's hand "dies" or whether he does, refusing at first to accept the death. They argued also about the doctor's complicity in death, returning again and again to the poem's words for "evidence." In this hour more than in others, side conversations distracted from and then took over the group's discussion. Just before the bell, for example, a side conversation silenced the group:

D.:   Well, you have to die sometimes. And then you mourn a little and then have to forget it.

DE.: But they didn't even *cry*.

T.:   They don't do anything. They just go about "their affairs," as if they didn't care.

Carol named this hour as "probably the best so far."

I didn't constantly question in order to lead. The group questioned and challenged each other. . . . I also felt I worked more with the guys' comments— even more than before, even though there was lots of talking and chaos. Today I was able to get their attention by asking another question and they responded through the chaos. I was able to say, for instance, "O.K., now, let's get back to D.'s question," and they would follow. We were able to work with the chaos.

When the students turned their attention to their own poems, in the following hours, the intensity and energy rose further. In response to a poem that described the ocean "As a world without any sin," B. challenged: "Your line is a lie because the world isn't without sin and neither is the ocean. I know two people who have drowned. If you had a girlfriend or son or daughter who drowned, you couldn't say that the ocean was without sin."

Most of the poems were immediately bound to the students' daily lives and expectations—girlfriends, autos, cutting grass and shoveling snow, patriotism, the war, and hippies. The following poem, for example, was written by a student who had declared himself for the war:

> Soldierboy, Soldierboy
> That gun isn't a toy.
> It's used to destroy.
> Soldierboy, Soldierboy
> With it you kill.
> Soldierboy, Soldierboy
> Doesn't that make you feel ill?
> For one day it might be you,
> Who the enemy will kill
> Soldierboy, Soldierboy
>
> Bill Nusz

When asked why he chose to use "Soldierboy" rather than "Soldier" throughout, the poet said, "It sounds better" (as he wrote it). When pursued, he read it aloud both ways, and then another student commented, "It's not the same." The discussion circled around the effect of the word "boy" without ever naming it. Boys shouldn't have to kill and yet they have to, was one student's way of putting it.

BILL: We can vote and choose our president, but if the nut starts a war, we have to fight.

During the next hour, in the midst of a discussion of other poems, Bill asked for time to speak:

BILL: Now I'll explain what the poet meant to say. He talked about "boy" and "toy" and how together they mocked the idea of fighting. He said that "boy" talks about the fact that little boys play with guns and play "killing," and that they can't realize until they are older that some day they might really die by a gun.

The explanation evoked still another discussion, summarized finally by T., who questioned Carol first about whether a poem can have two meanings at the same time. Assured that this was possible, he explained: "About the little boys playing war and not realizing that some day they might really die; and then, also, the guys who fight really *are* boys, not men. So you can have this other meaning."

As I summarized and organized some of the moments of Carol's fifteen teaching hours (that emerge in two hundred typed pages of journals), I wondered why her conclusions were not joyful ones. Had she not managed to engage six young men in a dozen complex poems? and in writing and discussing their own? Why did she not feel purely "successful"? Instead, she records her own enjoyment and her "mixed feelings about parts of the project." Her pleasure has to do with "teaching":

The project was playtime for me, in the best sense of this phrase. . . . I found I could certainly direct the group and get the guys to work on the problems of poetry. For me this was the project, the actual teaching, the discussion of the group. . . . All this made me again find that teaching is a frame of mind with which I react with children or students; it's *enjoying life* and wanting to help others enjoy it also. [Italics added.]

About poetry, she records and apologizes by labeling as "Nothing new" her realization "that poetry is feeling, something I've known but haven't felt, really. I mean, I actually saw that this is true. And that it's a form of conversation."

But the "mixed feelings"—they come out when she tries to talk about the group of boys:

> My group, I don't think, came to get involved in the poetry. It was merely something they had to do and which was better than most classes. Except for this Monday's group when we worked with Betsy's pictures. Something different happened that day. Three of the guys, the ones who talked, were out of their usual selves. They were acting, not just speaking. Poetry should take you out of your self, to something beyond the ordinary, even if it speaks about the ordinary. The guys never came to feel beyond their normal emotions. Damn, I don't know any of this to be true.

Carol's reference is to her penultimate hour when she brought a friend's photography in, hoping her students would want to write poems suggested by the pictures. The pictures did stimulate discussion, which led Carol to suggest that the students write down just what they were saying. Maybe their words—written down—would be poetry. They refused, but smartly suggested that Carol could do the writing if she wanted to. The results are lengthy; here is a bit based on a photo of an automobile crash:

> what would you say hit it?
> a one hundred and ninety-five pound kid on a tricycle
> a fire plug
> definitely not a pole
> because the top would have been pushed in
>
> Mr. Boyer, you do have a point there
> according to the impact and the distance of the outrun
> and the reaction time . . .

At the end of her journal, Carol records:

> They didn't want to write down what they were saying, although they were obviously feeling and thinking and therefore had stuff to say. . . . It seemed that writing was foreign to them; why should they write when they could talk? . . .

On the following day, Carol asked her students to write about our customary "T sheet," a page of poems we use at the end of the experiment chiefly to gauge whether we've taught anything to the relatively quiet participants. "Write anything you want," Carol told them. "Can I draw a picture of my feelings?" T. quipped. The results were not extraordinary, by any standards. Yet they shocked Carol, who wrote:

> Today, after reading my group's essays, I could have cried. I am assuming, I realize, that everyone should know how to read and write and that these guys don't. Maybe they're happy and will be happy, but I, from my own little world, can't imagine these kids finding a world in which they are happy. . . . Today I saw the guys as pitiful. Perhaps I look too optimistically at myself, but I do feel free to live as I want, and I have the freedom and knowledge, ability to create my own life. Do these guys? Do most kids?

Carol's response was also not surprising. Only four years older than her students, Carol felt worlds apart from them. Why? What world had she hold of that she wanted them to have too? It is hard to talk about the world of literature or even literacy. What Carol emphasizes elsewhere in her entry is the discrepancy between "forcing kids to sit through eight hours of school for twelve years" and the results: illiteracy for one thing, but beyond that, since Carol equates pleasure and the written word, the denial of "happiness and enjoyment" to these same students. And of course, she assumes that the project can hardly be said to compensate. On the contrary, it can only point up the loss.

For Carol, freedom meant the ability (and desire) to choose the intellectual's life, and like others of her generation she valued wholeness: "her work life and private self would be a whole, consisting of literature, poetry, writing, language." Teaching auto mechanics to read poetry was, in her view, "useless" because "they would be doing manual work, unrelated to poetry and language." Even if she conceived of her students reading poetry in their spare time, for pleasure, she would regard that as insufficient. And she expected that her students would not, as a result of the sessions with her, turn to reading poetry.

Carol's views—nearly three years ago—were class-bound. Though she had *chosen* teaching, she never assumed that her students might have *chosen* auto mechanics. Teaching meant, as she wrote, "enjoying life and wanting to help others enjoy it too." It was inconceivable to her that some people might enjoy playing around with cars and engines, that physical work might be pleasureful. Similarly, playing around with language orally, merely for fun—not for grades, papers, degrees, publications, promotions—was also outside the experience of a middle-class student, taught early in her school life that the written word is more valuable than speech, the revised and polished poem preferable to improvisation. Songs and ballads, folk tales, even epics, after all, become literary and literature only when they have been written down. Then they become the possession of English teachers, poets, and critics.

Carol pitied her students, she said afterward, because "they were not going to be able to choose or control their work lives." Even if they liked playing around with cars to begin with, their lives were likely to become dreary, routinized. Manipulated by others, the worker would live without intellect or passion—in short, without poetry. This may seem a cartoon, but it is not an unrealistic portrait of working-class life as drawn by middle-class students and others older than they. From Carol's point of view, the gulf between the classes was unbridgeable. Education had failed her students in general, and the poetry project was in no manner able to compensate for that failure. Since a missionary's zeal was unacceptable, what function had poetry for those who were not intellectuals, teachers, poets, or critics?

I could not answer Carol's questions; I could not provide the bridges she was searching for, in part simply because I didn't know enough then and had not thought deeply about her questions, but in part also because there were other pressures on the project, more immediate questions to be answered.

In the project's third year, we were assigned to Western, a women's high school. This was 1970, the spring not only of Cambodia but of the stirrings on campuses across the country of the women's movement. We were struck early in the project by the request from students for poems about "love," as well as by their rejection as morbid, unpleasant, or boring of poems that had interested the male students we had been teaching. We began to scramble for new curriculum, and Carol's question was mostly forgotten.

And yet, Carol's question came to be answered a year later, easily and without much formal discussion. Suddenly, there it was, not only in my head, but taken for granted by many of the fourth-year participants. As one black undergraduate stated the purpose of her curriculum, she wanted to choose poems about blackness and about being a woman, since she and her students were black women. That's what she knew about and what she thought they might want to (and ought to want to) think about. Suddenly, almost inexplicably, Carol's question about the function of poetry for those who were not likely to become intellectuals had its own response. Poems had been written about the feelings of women, about how it is to be black, and others remained still to be written. If students were black (or white) and women, there was no question about the function of poetry in their lives. Poems might be liberating personally, as individual expressions. And because poems are also communal, they might function to express the culture of a class or a group of people.

Class differences had not vanished. We were still mainly middle-class people teaching working-class (or lower-middle-class) students, and there were problems still about how to talk, therefore, about such matters as marriage 'or abortion. How could we complain about the empty lives of middle-class suburban housewives to the daughters of welfare mothers? Marge Piercy's satire on the secretary's life, "Metamorphosis of a Bureaucrat," was not a laughing matter to women headed for the typing pool. Nor were we as teachers self-conscious about being part of a revolutionary social movement, and hence, in the tradition of other periods of poetic vitality. The few black undergraduates, I should add, assumed a connection between the social upheaval of their people nationally and internationally and its expression in contemporary black poetry. But most of the white undergraduates had not yet reached that level of consciousness. And yet, something new had begun to happen to all of us.

The conception of wholeness which Carol Ahlum had posed in terms of reading and writing poetry as a total (professional) absorption was not at issue. The wholeness now lay in the connection between one's self, one's life, and the poem. Poetry might be integral with your life, not in the sense of being the stuff you work on as an intellectual, but being the record of your feelings as a woman, a worker. And the bridge that Carol was searching for is not one that connects with ease the middle-class teacher to the working-class student; nor is it the bridge that leads the working-class student into the middle-class world. Rather, if the idea of bridges is viable at all, it is in the sense that Hart Crane's bridge functions to connect his sensibility with the world he would like to create. Poems, in school or outside, might function, we began to see, in the lives of many men and women, not as decorations or commercial artifacts, but as expressions of individual and communal feelings, experiences, thoughts, hopes. They needed no other excuse for being.

It may be inappropriate to compare our work with that of Paulo Freire:[14] we were notably less rigorous and systematic; we had no coherent ideological perspective; we were not working with illiterate Brazilian peasants. And yet, we arrived at similar conclusions. For Freire, the words "work," "word," and "world" are, if not actual equivalents, then most closely related. Words have "transforming power," Freire believes, in that the consciousness of language transforms a person's view of himself in relation to the world. If he has power over the naming process, if he can name the world, he can change its name. And so, for Freire, literacy is a political and humanizing necessity if there is to be a changed world of the future. As Freire puts it, "To exist, humanly, is to *name* the world, to change it. Once named, the world in its turn reappears to the namers as a problem and requires of them a new *naming*." Such naming, he continues, such work, "is not the privilege of some few men, but the right of every man." Such naming is not a matter of "cultural invasion," but rather of "cultural revolution." As they learn to read, peasants discover, according to Freire, that they are creators of culture: "I work and working I transform the world."

Though there are several connections between Freire's work and ours, his belief in a *people's* culture (rather than an elitist one) is of most significance here. The notion that the fulfillment of life is possible only in art, and that art means "high culture," is a relatively recent idea in the history of the world as well as an elitist one. The genuine pity that Carol Ahlum felt for her working-class students who were not able to live the life of art actually demeaned the possibilities of fulfillment they had as artisans. And

here is the full horror of modern alienation and dissociation: that one class can find its wholeness (through art)
only by negating the very way of life of another class—and
with the very best of intentions. Thus, if "high" art and
poetry are not to be destructive, we must develop different
functions for them.

Such functions begin with demystification. Ordinarily,
the tradition of poetry blocks the allegedly "uncultured"
from the experience of poetry. But recent poetry, in the
language of the reader, opens doors. Once encouraged to
do so, average high school students can make poetry theirs,
claim what of it they want and reject the rest. With such
activity comes the possibility of producing their own
poetry. What are the cultural implications of classrooms in
which students—working class or not—write poetry that is
taken seriously by their peers and teachers? Miriam Brown
writes of one possibility:

> I found that if you (as a teacher) learn to value their
> ideas and thoughts, they learn to value them. The
> chain is virtually endless, for once they value their
> thoughts, they begin to gain self-confidence, which is
> part of what learning is all about. The best example
> of this that I can find is P. On the day we wrote, P.
> threw her poem away. I talked and talked and finally
> she retrieved it from the trash can. I read it and asked
> questions about it. Was she talking about an addict
> who was dying from an OD? She was pleased that I
> had found a *meaning* in it. Later, when I talked
> about the anthology we were going to print, P. said
> "Don't put my name on mine." But then A. said, "Is
> this your poem?" P. nodded and A. added, "I think
> it's a nice poem." After that P. said it was okay to
> put her name on her work.

(Freire quotes a similar process among peasants: "The
peasant begins to get courage to overcome his dependence
when he realizes that he is dependent. Until then, he goes

along with the boss and says, 'What can I do? I'm only a peasant.' ") The high school students' shyness about writing did not prevent them, generally, from treating their "work," as Miriam Brown notes, "with a great deal of respect." "I suppose the greatest reason why the discussion of the students' poetry," she continues, "was so successful was that it came out of their own lives, but they had found a new and interesting way of expressing their experience." The "but" in Miriam's sentence is revealing: of course people are interested in their lives, *but* only certain people know that poems may express their feelings in ways that move them and others. What if everyone wrote poems? What if it were possible to demystify poetry for masses of people usually deprived of such forms of expression, celebration, and prophecy?

Recently, I witnessed a poetry reading by a group of black Danforth fellows replete with costume, dance, "found" musical instruments, and song. Only one of them was a poet, but the poems belonged to the group. The six had practiced for two hours that afternoon; five of them had never seen the poems before. The dozen poems were good, but the performance was extraordinary. "How can they do that on two hours of preparation?" an observer blurted. A white male, also a Danforth fellow and a poet, responded without envy, with admiration for the dazzling power of the black students: "When you have so much inside, it's easy."

NOTES

1 I could not have written this essay without the journals kept by the undergraduates, in particular those of Mary Kai Howard (Kai) and Carol Ahlum. Both women graduated from Goucher College in 1971. Kai Howard is traveling; Carol Ahlum is a graduate student in education at the University of Massachusetts, Amherst. I wish to express my special gratitude here to them and to the

other undergraduates without whom there would not have been "the poetry project."

2 From the beginning, the project functioned under the joint co-operation of Goucher College, the Baltimore City Public Schools, and Teachers and Writers Collaborative—who supplied funds, during the first two years, which we used to support the visits of poets to the high schools.

3 An unpublished monograph is available in Xeroxed form from the author: "Report on a Pilot Project," 1968. A very brief version of this report appeared as "Untaught Teachers and Improbable Poets," *Saturday Review*, March 15, 1969, pp. 60–82. "Experiment in the Inner City," a lecture prepared (with Barbara Danish) for the Lehigh University Poetry Festival, spring 1969, appears in Nancy Larrick, ed., *Someone Turned A Tap On . . .* (New York: Delacorte Press, 1971). In these essays, I relied chiefly on the journals and experiences of 1968. Here, I will draw on the years 1969, 1970, and 1971.

4 Four of the undergraduates were able to participate twice, since no college credit was given to students for the first year. More than half the participants were sophomores, the rest juniors and seniors. It is my impression that, as often as not, the sophomores were as successful as the older students. Carol Ahlum was a sophomore, Mary Kai Howard a junior during their respective years in the project.

5 There were, in all, more than fifty small groups, each of which met for from twelve to twenty hours. In the second year, teachers participated as small-group leaders rather than as observers. The project has amassed more than seven hundred journal entries, the length of each approximately five pages or one thousand words. This written body of material forms the basis of my remarks, though I have also collected tapes and notes of the hundred workshops held in the course of four years. Some of the small groups taught by the undergraduates were all male, nearly half were all female, and some were mixed; some were all white, some all Black, and others integrated.

6 Teachers and high school classes were selected by officials of the Baltimore City Public Schools (chiefly by L. Earl Wellemeyer, Supervisor of English) on the basis of interest and availability. A class that met during the last period of the day, for example, was convenient for the schedules of undergraduates who were also attending other courses. After the first year, teachers were selected with an eye to their interest in poetry as well as in experimentation. From the beginning, I had asked for classes that were considered relatively "unteachable," and for the most part we taught students who were not college-bound. The first year we were

assigned to a vocational-technical high school, to a class of future auto mechanics and another of boys studying industrial electronics.

I will not return, in this essay, to the subject of project workshops. Once the teaching began, we met once or twice a week, some of the time with teachers and school officials, for workshops focused either on methods or curriculum or on special topics like introducing writing or revising poems. Before the teaching had begun, I worked with the undergraduates to raise their awareness of what I did as I taught them. Undergraduates also attempted bits of teaching in these early workshops. But little of this was as valuable as workshops that followed the actual contact with high school students.

In the main, we held three different types of workshops, though they were usually not as distinctive as the following description suggests. First, the methods workshops: how to open a discussion on a poem; how to "hook on" to a response from a student and so continue the discussion; how to keep such discussions open and yet focused; how to conclude or to resist conclusions. Typically, such discussions focused on questions. What kind of questions to use? This is most difficult for undergraduates trained traditionally to answer only "safe" questions, those that the teacher "wants."

Second, the curriculum workshop: which poems should be used and in what order; how to arrange a page of poems. We used, from the beginning, a device that I fell upon in Mississippi, where I had no books and so mimeographed a page of poems each night for the next lesson. Because I also had a small supply of paper, I crammed as many poems on a single page as I could. Thus it was possible to offer students a choice from a limited selection of poems, four or five, on a single page. At the same time, the device offered the possibility not only of variety but of unity: four different poems about death, for example, or four "skinny" poems on different subjects.

Third, the writing workshop: how to get students into writing poems, and once there, how to get them to discuss their poems. We developed certain guidelines and gambits: if the teacher was "easy" about writing, her students would be too—whatever the device she used. And so some teachers said simply, "Today we will write," and explained that spelling didn't count, that she was going to write too, and that they didn't have to hand anything in if they didn't want to. If poems were handed in, the teacher explained that she was going to mimeograph them and hand them out the next hour for discussion. Students decided whether or not they wanted their names to appear. Teachers corrected spelling but left dialect and unique devices untouched.

During discussion, poets could refrain from identifying themselves or even from speaking if they chose to: the poem spoke for them. And students were usually willing to discuss the poems of their group with seriousness, even reverence.

8 There was an unpleasant, though mild, clash with school authorities at the end of the initial year, particularly on the question of the undergraduates' attitude toward the cooperating teachers and school officials. During that year and the next, there was also some concern about the appearance of the undergraduates, the length of their hair and the brevity of their skirts. Such concerns disappeared in 1970 and 1971 either because of other anxieties or because we were then in a women's high school. There were also problems of censorship: after all, public schools are not accustomed to the use of such language as "shit," "pees," and "ass"— all out of poems we were using—nor to frank focus on such topics as race, drugs, and war. We solved these problems in rational ways worked out over a period of time. Those poems denied immediate acceptance into the curriculum by school officials were named "workshop poems." In the workshop, we discussed the poems thoroughly, and often the undergraduates were able— because of their skills as readers and their general maturity—to persuade school officials to change their minds. Of course, there were occasions when such workshops concluded differently, but those occasions were also useful for undergraduates considering a future of public school teaching. One final matter: the attitude of undergraduates toward cooperating teachers was directly related to the intellectual capacity, strength, flexibility, openness, and honesty of the teachers.

9 The undergraduates were responsible for teaching, for choosing their curriculum, and for writing a journal describing each teaching hour and attempting some analysis of its pattern. The journal functioned in lieu of a lesson plan. Its value lay in the student's conscious reliving of the hour and in the self-critical modes of thinking thus developed. The style of teaching necessary to small-group discussion depends, not on the typical rigidities of a lesson plan, but on the development of alternative routes of entry into poems and out of discussions, or out of discussions and into poems. For each undergraduate, the journal became a distinctive mode of reporting her development.

10 I owe the discussion of small-group process that follows to the insistence of Ellen Bass, one of the early undergraduate participants, who read an early draft of this essay. Ellen Bass is a poet who lives in Cambridge and teaches nondirective counseling techniques to people connected with Project Place. She is of the opinion that she learned more about teaching than poetry from the project.

11 I have written at some length about the use of open questions in the essay called "Experiment in the Inner City" (see note 3). Briefly, the characteristics of an open question include the following: (1) the teacher does not know *the* answer to her question, but she wants *an* answer because she is really interested in what her students think or feel; (2) the open question opens discussion or leads to another question, rather than leading to a particular answer that the teacher is searching for, the finding of which usually ends all possibility of discussion; (3) the open question should encourage students to respond emotionally or intuitively, and then, followed by a "why" from the teacher (or another student), should lead to thoughtful, even analytical, reflection upon those responses. Thus the open question follows the pattern that most creative writers do—from feeling to consciousness. It fosters independent thinking, rather than second-guessing or pleasing the teacher.

12 At the end of each project, undergraduates wrote essays evaluating the course. At the invitation of the *Goucher Quarterly*, Kai Howard also wrote a narrative essay about her experience in the project: a new editor then rejected the essay as allegedly of limited interest to Goucher alumnae. I have, of course, drawn heavily on it here.

13 See my essay "Mississippi's Freedom Schools: The Politics of Education," *Harvard Educational Review*, Vol. 35 (Spring 1965), pp. 144–60.

14 Paulo Freire, *Pedagogy for the Oppressed*, trans. Myra Bergman Ramos (New York: Herder & Herder, 1970). Carol Ahlum coincidentally brought me Freire's book after I had written the first draft of this essay and was checking with her that I had not misrepresented her views.

UP AGAINST THE
GREAT TRADITION

Sheila Delany

He is a man who thinks
He sits in a tiny corner of the rain.

He is what he is not thinking of.
He is a large part of Japan.

He is closed, like a small business.
An illustration of the snow.

> John Morris, "Shh! the Professor
> Is Sleeping"

If you teach English literature, you may find it more difficult to relate left political convictions to teaching than do your friends in the social sciences, for your job is to disseminate the monuments of a culture many of whose central values you reject. You don't generally give courses designed to accommodate a critical point of view: courses on, say, the economic basis of slavery, the authoritarian personality, the modern urban community. You may teach Chaucer, who praises submission to one's lot:

> For, sith a womman was so pacient
> Unto a mortal man, wel moore us oghte

> Receyven al in gree that God us sent;
> For greet skile is, he preeve that he wroghte.

> "The Clerk's Tale"

You may specialize in Spenser, whose *Faerie Queene* articulates both the neo-Platonic idealism fashionable among Elizabethan literati and the ruling-class political aims which that idealism supported:

> Most sacred vertue she [Justice] of all the rest,
> Resembling God in his imperiall might;
> Whose soveraigne powre is herein most exprest,
> That both to good and bad he dealeth right,
> And all his workes with Justice hath bedight.
> That powre he also doth to Princes lend,
> And makes them like himself in glorious sight,
> To sit in his owne seate, his cause to end,
> And rule his people right, as he doth recommend.

> Book V

Or perhaps you teach Yeats, who in many of his poems expresses his ambivalence toward the Irish revolutionary movement in which his friends participated:

> I know not what the younger dreams—
> Some vague Utopia—and she seems,
> When withered old and skeleton-gaunt,
> An image of such politics. . . .
> Dear shadows, now you know it all,
> All the folly of a fight
> With a common wrong or right.
> The innocent and the beautiful
> Have no enemy but time . . .

> "In Memory of Eva Gore-Booth and
> Con Markiewicz"

When one of Yeats's editors warns us that the political poems "must not be read as a record of historical events or of Yeats's political opinions," poetry is not absolved of its service to the ruling class. On the contrary, criticism is implicated in the attempt to mystify experience by disguising class relations as eternal truths.

Nor does the teaching of composition always provide a solution to the conflict between political conviction and professional obligation, for the classic essays used to illustrate the art of writing are also conservative in ideology. One thinks, for example, of T. S. Eliot, John Henry Newman, Thomas Carlyle, Alfred North Whitehead, Samuel Johnson, John Donne, Sir Francis Bacon. The preface to the *New University Reader,* an anthology used widely in composition courses, explains quite clearly the contemporary uses of literary tradition:

> During the last decade or so, American education at all levels has been undergoing a critical reassessment, brought about largely by the ideological struggle between Communism and the free world. Perhaps the most significant consequence of this reassessment is that Americans are coming to recognize and acknowledge the unique significance of intelligence in preserving our ideals and in enabling us to compete successfully against totalitarian societies.

Plainly the author of this passage uses "intelligence" to mean "literary propaganda." To use communism as a synonym for totalitarianism; to imply that the American way is intrinsically nontotalitarian; to suggest that the goal of intelligence should be successful competition against socialist societies—all this is a perversion of intelligence, in the service of capitalism and cold-war ideology. But the premise—that a literary training can help create conservative consciousness—is not mistaken, for the masterpieces of English and American literature have usually supported conservative values: the sanctity of private property, the inevitability of social classes, woman's natural inferiority, and an other-worldly rationale for the way things are. The lines quoted earlier from Chaucer, Spenser, and Yeats obviously can't convey the full complexity of their authors' attitudes, but they do represent a cultural norm: the loyalty of most literature to ruling-class values of its time.

By way of illustration I want to explore some ramifications of a literary myth that is central to our own tradition: hierarchy. It is not, of course, myth only but a structural reality in many institutions—church, army, most universities—and in society at large. My concern here is not, however, hierarchy itself—which may or may not be democratic, may or may not be repressive—but the class interests served by the hierarchic structure of our institutions and the hierarchic myths of our culture. When hierarchy is abstracted from class structure and made an abstract model—when it becomes myth—it operates in fact as ruling-class ideology. It permits those in power and, more important, those who are controlled to think of exploitation as inevitable, in the natural order of things.

For relations based on power often pass for something else, pasted over with labels that automatically generate sentiment: "my maternal duty," "your filial obligation," "love of one's country," "reasonable discourse." That students have begun to perceive the mechanics of power in some of their roles makes those roles more difficult to sustain:

> Satan prefers to suffer in hell where he is the ruler, rather than serve in heaven. In this way he was a hero. Like today, it's the same thing the black man is saying— we rather make and live in our own hell than keep being slaves for the rest of society.
>
> From a black student's paper on
> *Paradise Lost*

This is the classic mistake about Satan, and it leads to a classic political mistake, for hell remains hell even if made by fallen angels. But in the poem, as in the experience that illuminates and is illuminated by it, power is the issue. How much of what teachers do, or are expected to do,

sustains a relation of power? Some routines establish personal power over students: taking attendance, penalizing
for late papers, rejecting unorthodox opinions. Some acknowledge the university's power over teacher and students alike: rigid adherence to prescribed syllabi and
curricula, resistance to structural reform. Some reinforce
society's power over all three: insisting on "objectivity" as
a prime critical virtue, teaching literature mainly as
techne, defining politics as irrelevant to literature or to
the academy.

Much of what is amusing, tragic, or interesting in Western literature is concerned with someone's attempt to
break out of a vertically ordered system. That notion of
vertical arrangement, or degree, is essential: it is as if we
cannot conceive of "the great chain of being" on its side.

> Behold also the order that god hath put generally in all
> His creatures, beginning at the most inferior or base, and
> ascending upward . . . so that everything is order, and
> without order may be nothing stable or permanent;
> and it may not be called order, except it contain in it
> degrees, high and base, according to the merit or estima-
> tion of the thing that is ordered. . . . Where all thing is
> common there lacketh order, and where order lacketh
> there all thing is odious and uncomely.

> Sir Thomas Elyot, *The Book of the Governor*

Shakespeare casts the theory into poetic form in his *Troilus
and Cressida* when Ulysses, describing the hierarchic structure of nature and of human institutions, asserts the dis-
astrous results of denying that structure.

> O, when degree is shak'd,
> Which is the ladder to all high designs,
> Then enterprise is sick! How could communities,
> Degrees in schools, and brotherhoods in cities,
> Peaceful commerce from dividable shores,
> The primogenitive and due of birth,
> Prerogative of age, crowns, sceptres, laurels,

But by degree, stand in authentic place?
Take but degree away, untune that string,
And hark what discord follows! Each thing meets
In mere oppugnancy. The bounded waters
Should lift their bosoms higher than the shores
And make a sop of all this solid globe.
Strength should be lord of imbecility,
And the rude son should strike his father dead.
Force should be right; or rather, right and wrong,
Between whose endless jar justice resides, . .
Should lose their names, and so should justice too.

This ideology has an important function within the play,
for the Greeks face a crisis of factionalism in their long
war against the Trojans. That the war has not yet been
won is due, according to Ulysses, precisely to "neglection
of degree": insubordination. Nor is it coincidental that
property relations—civil corporations, guilds, commercial
agreements, inheritance laws—figure so prominently in
the speech, for behind the question of degree lies the
question of which class shall control relations of property.
What better person than Elizabeth herself to unveil the
perspective of ruling-class power behind the literary
myth? Intervening in a quarrel between the gentleman Sir
Philip Sidney and the earl of Oxford, the queen reminds
Sidney of his class duty; she

> lays before him the difference in degree between earls
> and gentlemen, the respect inferiors owed to their su-
> periors, and the necessity in princes to maintain their own
> creations as degrees descending between the people's
> licentiousness and the anointed sovereignty of crowns:
> how the gentleman's neglect of the nobility taught the
> peasant to insult both.

> Fulke Greville, *Life of Sir Philip Sidney*

Dante's hell is hierarchic, so is Milton's heaven; and
though their spiritual geography is irrelevant now, we
have internalized the map. Articulating our myths and

dream-journeys as Dante did for the Middle Ages, Freud
offers a structure of mind that combines psychic, moral,
and political hierarchies. Personality is fragmented into
id, ego, and superego; upon the proper ranking of these
fragments rests the health of individuals and civilization.
Such an analogy between psychic and social structure is
not new. It was stated in Plato's *Republic,* where virtue in
the state and virtue in the individual are defined as the
correct distribution of power among three component
parts. For the aristocratic Plato, as for the bourgeois
Freud, hierarchic psychology functions as ruling-class
politics. In Freud's political vision, as in Plato's, the ruling
class is a kind of cultural superego, while the masses correspond to the disorderly id:

> It is just as impossible to do without government of the
> masses by a minority as it is to dispense with coercion
> in the work of civilization, for the masses are lazy and
> unintelligent, they have no love for instinctual renuncia-
> tion, they are not to be convinced of its inevitability by
> argument, and the individuals support each other in
> giving full play to their unruliness.

> *The Future of an Illusion*

So much for working-class solidarity. In this context it
cannot surprise us that Freud's theories of female sexuality
lend full support to another hierarchic and repressive
social myth: male supremacy.

Our vocabulary of praise and blame is full of words
which dissolve class distinctions into moral categories.
"Gentle," "noble," "churl," and "villain" all originally
designated social class, and only gradually came to represent the stereotyped moral character which the ruling class
associated with various strata. We can be sure that neither
the laudatory connotations of "nobility" nor the pejorative
sense of "villainous" reflected the point of view of the
villein: the tenant farmer owing substantial agricultural
services to his lord.

A remark by the late critic C. S. Lewis will perhaps help to illustrate the interdependence of literature, myth, and social behavior. Discussing the moral of *Paradise Lost* ("that obedience to the will of God makes men happy, and that disobedience makes them miserable"), Lewis asks:

> Has this not the desolating clarity and concreteness of certain classic utterances we remember from the morning of our own lives; "Bend over"—"Go to bed"— "Write out *I must do as I am told* a hundred times"— "Do not speak with your mouth full."

Desolating indeed, to imagine the life whose morning has been so obscured by blatant displays of power. By showing that very similar feelings are generated by a normative childhood experience and by the reading of a masterpiece, Lewis prompts one to wonder whether this is the best that Western literary culture can do for its children.

So that, given the class content of our literary tradition, it is possible to see why teachers often become petty tyrants behind the desk; why they consider "unprofessional" the idea of organizing for protest or bargaining; why they refuse to consider themselves employees; why they decline to defend colleagues who have been fired for political reasons. They have absorbed the myths of bourgeois society and are daily engaged in perpetuating them. To reject those myths—that is, to oppose the real relations of power they represent—necessarily changes your role in the university, your relation to students, and your analysis of literature. I want to focus mainly on the last two with respect to teaching.

Like yourself, students are the victims of an economic order which sanctions certain kinds of behavior and certain concepts of self in its members so that the order may survive. It is always unnerving to hear a nineteen-year-old say, "When I grow up . . ." or "If I were an adult . . . " or

"I must be crazy but I think that . . . " Like yourself, students can learn to identify and resist a system which aims to keep them uncertain and unaware. That many students will resist a new consciousness is the condition the radical teacher has most urgently to address. How can you do it in a semester's novel survey, medieval survey, or composition course?

A beginning would be to desanctify literature itself by showing that it is a means of persuasion, in the service of a vision controlled by political as well as aesthetic values. You can show how the work of art embodies social values and expresses social conditions. (The love-debate in Chaucer's *Parliament of Fowls* is more than a traditional rhetorical device. As Chaucer uses it, it reflects felt ambivalence that had a real social model in the late medieval breakdown of authorities.) Instead of providing a checklist of great works, you might demonstrate a critical method that relates means to ends, techniques to values. No deprecation of craft is implied here; on the contrary, style offers an entrance to the created world of art. (The logical tension created by zeugma, antithesis, and chiasma in Pope's *Rape of the Lock* duplicates on a small scale the sexual tension in his heroine and the moral tensions in the society she inhabits.) Like philosophy, religion, and the plastic arts, literature grows from a particular historical environment. (The subversive individualism of Roland, hero of the eleventh-century *Chanson de Roland,* defines heroism in a way which validates the ambitions and alliances of a particular group of aristocrats of the period.) So that a Marxist view finds in literature attitudes that history may not be able directly to reveal. In this it resembles the Renaissance idea that poetic invention combines the best of philosophy and history, presenting events and judgments together.

The way such general ideas will influence a syllabus or a classroom hour must vary, for the radical teacher, like anyone else, may be a performer, a group therapist, or a bore. Priorities matter: you might offer a course on Renaissance concepts of justice (e.g., More, Spenser, Shakespeare) instead of one on variations in the sonnet form. You can teach the American revolutionary tradition (Tom Paine and Patrick Henry, John Brown, Eugene V. Debs, Malcolm X) instead of the Boston Brahmins, though you will have to operate outside the traditional elitist definition of what constitutes "literature."

In composition you work with students' writing and any other material that offers insight into the techniques of communication. I have worked with types of rhetoric: political (Lincoln's Second Inaugural Address, an essay on history by John Kennedy, a speech by Lyndon Johnson), scientific (a standard psychology text, an army field manual), and literary (a speech by William Faulkner, Mark Twain's parody of Victorian prose). All of them manipulate the reader through language. Students can consider the devices through which politicians try to achieve a consensus: the plain-man persona, "we," the image of history as an organism governed by eternal laws and unresponsive to human intervention. You might show how, for the social scientist, polysyllabic Latinate jargon dignifies a trivial subject, while for the propagandist it creates the feeling of detachment ("objectivity") in his reader, who would otherwise be revolted:

> Antipersonnel biological agents accomplish their effects on targets with little or no physical destruction. This constitutes an advantage in combat operations, where it may be essential to save facilities for future use by friendly forces.
>
> U.S. Army Field Manual, FM 3–10

You can examine in detail the political implications of Faulkner's comparison of unassimilated minorities to a herd of wild horses loose in a small town.

Such analysis is often relevant to the forms of manipulation students practice, for although students usually consider themselves innocent of rhetoric, they have learned the art of self-presentation. A student's irony or fantasy may help him to evade a painful subject or simplify a complex one. Gentility of diction may sterilize "unacceptable" feelings. (Once I assigned a short paper called "A Person I Dislike." One boy insisted violently he could think of no one, then handed in a paper in which "hate" was substituted for "dislike": the paper was about his mother.) The vacuous sentimentality of some female students' writing has a great deal to do with the sex roles imposed upon them in society and in the classroom. And if some students are already too skilled in the art of manipulation, others have yet to learn it. "The way it really happened" is not always the most interesting or persuasive way to narrate an incident; the person called "I" on paper need not correspond exactly to the writer. When students experience writing as purposeful, then the critical formalism which discourages the serious examination of values can be analyzed as itself a political stance. (It is not coincidental that when a well-known Canadian scholar at a recent professional meeting gave a lecture entitled "The Message Does Not Matter," his examples of irrelevant message included the films of Leni Riefenstahl, Hitler's movie maker.)

In a traditional poetry course, perhaps a teacher's most meaningful effort is to help students understand why poetry is often inaccessible to them, why its vocabulary and images are not part of their world—and to see that this is not necessarily a bad thing. From a traditional point of view the modern student is handicapped. He does not fear hell, observe nature closely, go to church or to prostitutes, listen to people die or be born, die of love or consumption or the pox, venerate old men—the experiences from which much of our poetry is made. What was experience has become scholarship. But students do sometimes possess a new consciousness which literature hasn't caught up with. It isn't necessarily a political consciousness, but its unsentimental pragmatism can be the basis for a political consciousness.

> She's a twentieth century fox:
> No tears, no fears,
> No ruined years,
> No clocks;
> She's a twentieth century fox.

> She's the queen of cool,
> And she's the lady who waits,
> Since her mind left school
> It never hesitates;
> She won't waste time
> On elementary talk;
> She's a twentieth century fox.

The Doors

Once I assigned William Ernest Henley's short poem "Madame Life." The poem, an allegory, presents Madame Life as a prostitute (though without explicitly saying so), death as her pimp exacting the price of enjoyment, and "you" as the customer deceived in the lady's intentions. Only a few students saw that the central figure was a prostitute. When this was explained, many found it difficult to understand why a man should go to a prostitute at all (sex being so easily available among themselves), and why, if he did, he would be so simple-minded as to misunderstand the relationship. Only a discussion of Victorian sexual mores and their own could clarify the poem.

Experimental or innovative work can supplement critical analysis: rock lyrics, poems composed by students or their friends, classes run by students on what interests them in the work. Such assignments are usually carried out with enthusiasm, but they don't always change stu-

dents' ideas about poetry as much as you would like, or
their ideas about themselves as much as you would hope,
for many are as alienated from their own feelings as they
are from those of John Donne. At the very least, though,
students need not think that their lack of comprehension
is due to stupidity, or that their own modes of feeling and
expression can't develop beyond what they ordinarily observe about them. Attitudes like these, of self-contempt
and incompetence, are of course political attitudes which,
in creating docile passivity, will affect students far beyond
the years they spend in college.

It is an occupational hazard that teachers spend most of
their time manipulating ideas. The danger is that people
in the profession, from force of habit, mistake intellectual
activity for an ideal condition; in reality it is only an
instrument. Substituting the process of ratiocination for
its goal—the apprehension of relations among material
facts—too many academics consider that they have performed well in finding a hundred reasons why we cannot
expect to understand history, government, literature, or
ourselves: reasons why intellectuals ought not to commit
themselves to ideology or action. Truth, they complain, is
so complicated that no one can hope to make a correct
choice. The complexity of truth no one will deny. But the
existence of complexity does not relieve us of choice, for
in refraining from choice we acquiesce in the exercise of
power. When an intellectual proudly professes his independence of ideology, on the grounds that every ideology
intrudes as a screen between oneself and reality, at that
moment he declares himself the victim of ideology: the
ideology of cynicism, passivity, and indecision which is
the best support a moribund society can hope for from its
intelligentsia.

Most radical teachers, however, aware that there is no
freedom from ideology, resemble the type described by

Fidel Castro: "the artist or intellectual who does not have a revolutionary attitude toward life but who is an honest person." Such a teacher can sympathize with those who do have a revolutionary perspective, can give them material and financial help, can try through his teaching to prepare his students to accept revolutionary ideology and action.

Late medieval philosophers found faith and reason irreconcilable. Some of them resolved the conflict by providing two answers to any given question, a logical answer and a doctrinal one. As long as they believed in God at all, they could do nothing else. I don't propose that we as teachers give double answers. But for the radical teacher who is not himself a communist, that sort of split consciousness will be necessary until a revolutionary (that is, a communist) literary tradition exists. It is a split which can, I believe, be healed in the commitment to communist ideology and action, but it will continue to be felt by those who retain the illusion that capitalist society can fulfill their radical aims. As long as our greatest aesthetic achievements convey nonprogressive moral and political values, it will be impossible to gratify aesthetic and political convictions at once. We lack contemporary mythic models for radical convictions, and such models cannot convincingly be developed in the arts until history again provides the prototypes, as it always has done. Nothing short of that can generate a literature in which the radical teacher will feel at home, or a tradition that will not require him to be "what he is not thinking of."

THE STUDY OF NINETEENTH-CENTURY BRITISH WORKING-CLASS POETRY

Martha Vicinus

The attack on New Criticism and traditional historical research in recent years has led many American academics in English and history to revaluate their teaching and research, and to reconsider the "canon" of their respective fields. For many this has led to a widening of the definition of acceptable evidence for study; oral traditions, folk customs, music, film, and the mass media are now receiving attention from both historians and literary critics. The study of racial minorities and submerged cultures, such as those of the working class, women, religious groups, and millennial movements, has also opened new perspectives. Nevertheless, much more could be done. Journals still mainly publish textual studies or accounts of parliamentary and administrative quarrels. Annually countless critical analyses of the novels of Faulkner, Conrad, or Henry James issue forth from our university presses, and we are already inundated with surveys of consensus-making history. In the meantime, we have left unexplored the lesser-known cultures which contribute to Anglo-American society. These areas of study deserve serious attention both for themselves and for the insights they give into better-known writers and movements. Black studies programs across the country have proved invaluable for ethnic minorities and white students who daily grow more aware of the large areas of American culture left unexamined and unread. The same potential for teaching and study exists in working-class studies, women's studies, and Euro-American studies, not to mention the domains now considered more appropriate for the folklorist and anthropologist.

The following essay is a case study in the analysis of nineteenth-century working-class poetry, which it is hoped will provide a guide for research into similar literature in America, the Commonwealth, and other English-speaking countries.[1] While such working-class institutions as trade unions, the cooperative movement, religious groups, and musical organizations have all been studied to a greater or lesser extent, working-class literature has been almost completely ignored, except by folklorists usually looking for rural throwbacks rather than industrial characteristics.[2]

Yet, in the nineteenth century the printed word as a source of information, pleasure, and propaganda enjoyed a primacy it had never had before nor has had since. Literacy was growing, and reading matter had few competitors for leisure time beyond the new team sports (which became popular only at the end of the century) and music. Many poems and songs written by working people reflected continuing values and traditions in times of great social change, thus giving us evidence of how earlier cultures survived in a dynamic society. At the same time, literature was receptive to new ideas and customs; the immense popularity, for example, of a hit song gives us information as to how contemporary attitudes and beliefs were absorbed. Thus, working-class literature functioned both as a reminder of a traditional heritage and as a socializing force within the new industrial society. In this latter capacity literary works are valuable evidence as to why and how the English worker, thought to be close to revolution through the 1840s, came to accept industrial life as inevitable and to emulate many of the values and characteristics of the dominant middle class.

There are a number of problems in studying working-class literature. Much of what remains is fragmentary, and information on writers, publishers, and sellers is scanty; yet this kind of information is particularly necessary if we are to estimate the importance of literature in the daily lives of working people. Religious organizations distributed millions of tracts, but, if *Bleak House* is any indication, they were probably little read. While some working men pooled their money to buy copies of Tom Paine, William Godwin, and Mrs. Gaskell, most could ill afford even a few pence for leisure-time reading.[3] Newspapers were considered more essential, and there was a long tradition of sharing the costs of the heavily taxed newspapers published in the early part of the century.[4] Since the level of literacy varied enormously, penny broadsides with songs or poems intended for oral recitation were the most widely sold form of recreational literature.

In addition to the problems of the money and time a worker could spend on reading matter, we must consider how different types of literature functioned in the lives of individuals. We all know that "working classes" would be a more accurate term than the singular; a pub habitué, a Methodist lay reader, and a Mechanics' Institute member, to mention only three obvious types, would each prefer a different kind of literature. A rowdy music-hall song, a pious hymn, and an imitation of Tennyson were written by and for different members of the working class, and each served a different function (although, to be sure, tastes sometimes overlapped). Some poems were purely escapist, others reflected current values, and others spoke of individual aspirations for improvement. But I believe, different as they were in intention and subject matter, all these types shared common characteristics that help define the

literary culture of the working class. To reach this definition the key questions are, What kinds of literature were
emerging with the consolidation of the new urban proletariat, and how did they reflect the attitudes of this class?

I

I have chosen four poems, two about courting and two
about hard times, from the cotton districts of Lancashire as
most representative of the cultural changes a people and an
area underwent during the years 1800–1865. Cotton was
the first major commercial enterprise to alter radically
through industrialization; the change from self-sufficient
families weaving and spinning at home to the employment of hundreds under one roof to man the new power-
driven machinery caused severe cultural and economic
dislocations.[5] These were caused by the movement of
families from villages to the growing cities, the change in
working conditions that made women and children more
employable than men, the continued existence of older
working methods alongside the new, and the very economic instability of the period. Factory workers found
themselves alternating periods of overemployment and
underemployment, with little control of their working
hours or conditions.[6] Stories about those suffering in the
"dark Satanic mills" were all set in Lancashire and the
adjoining West Riding—and yet the county's long and
respected weaving traditions continued in spite of these
enormous changes. The poems and songs dating from
the sixteenth century about handloom weavers and their
lasses were replaced by factory songs, but the habit of
making and singing songs and poems continued.[7] On the
one hand, we have the first and most severe process of
industrialization, and on the other, the continuation of a
rich and powerful literature and customs.

The French Wars from 1790 to approximately 1810

created an artificially high demand for woven cloth; handloom weaving prospered throughout Lancashire. Recent
inventions, such as the spinning jenny and the flying
shuttle, made the various stages of turning raw cotton
into finished cloth less arduous. While the soil was generally too poor for full-time farming, most families worked
small allotments which provided them with fresh vegeta-
bles and added variety to their daily work. Near starvation
could still threaten the remoter areas of the county after
a bad harvest, but families lived a frugal and respected
life in the many villages dotting the countryside. The time
was remembered throughout the century as the Golden
Age of handloom weaving, when workers did not have to
"stand at *their* command," but were free to work their
own hours at their own pace.[8]

Even during this period, however, the importance of
the middleman, or "putter-out," was growing rapidly, and
with it, self-sufficiency was diminishing. An increasing
number of weavers rented their looms and obtained prepared warps from him. He also inspected their finished
cloth, and had absolute authority in bating (fining) them
for errors, and for the piecework rate which he paid them.
As competition from power-loom cloth grew, these rates
fell ruinously. In 1835 the Select Committee on Handloom Weavers reported that for the period 1797–1804 the
average weekly income for a weaver's family was 26s. 8d.,
which could buy 281 pounds of flour, oatmeal, potatoes,
and butcher's meat. By 1825–1832 wages had declined to
6s. 4d., which bought only 83 pounds of produce.[9] There
is a story told by one raconteur of how a weaver in the
1820s was charged sixpence apiece for two small holes; he
asked the putter-out if the charge was per hole, and was
told yes. He promptly tore the two holes together, making
one large gash, and thereby saved himself sixpence.[10]

During the Golden Age the new Dobbie looms per-
mitted the weaving of elaborate patterns but needed fre-

quent and skillful attention. An itinerant joiner was usually called upon to "square," or fix, these looms when he passed through town. Like so many earlier picaresque figures, he was soon characterized as a free-and-easy blade who attracted the village women. One of the most popular poems celebrating the life of a joiner was "The Bury New Loom," first published as a broadside in 1804:

As I walked between Bolton and Bury, 'twas on a moonshiny
    night,
I met with a buxom young weaver whose company gave me
    delight.
She says: Young fellow, come tell me if your level and rule
    are in tune.
Come, give me an answer correct, can you get up and square
    my new loom?

I said: My dear lassie, believe me, I am a good joiner by trade,
And many a good loom and shuttle before me in my time
    I have made.
Your short lams and jacks and long lams [a] I quickly can put
    in tune,
My rule is in good order to get up and square a new loom.

She took me and showed me her loom, the down on her warp
    did appear.
The lams, jacks and healds [b] put in motion, I levelled her
    loom to a hair.
My shuttle run well in her lathe,[c] my treadle it worked up
    and down,
My level stood close to her breast-bone, the time I was reiving [d]
    her loom.

The cords of my lams, jacks and treadles at length they began
    to give way.

   [a] lams] foot treadles that operate the jacks. jacks] levers on the Dobbie machine that raise the harness controlling the warp thread.
   [b] healds] a loop of cord or wire through which the warp threads pass; a number of these make up a harness.
   [c] lathe] supporting stand on the loom
   [d] reiving] to rob or raid

The bobbin I had in my shuttle, the weft in it no longer
 would stay.
Her lathe it went bang to and fro, my main treadle still kept
 in tune.
My pickers[e] went nicketty-nack all the time I was squaring
 her loom.

My shuttle is still kept in motion, her lams she worked well
 up and down.
The weights in her rods they did tremble; she said she would
 weave a new gown.
My strength now began for to fail me. I said: It's now right
 to a hair.
She turned up her eyes and said: Tommy, my loom you have
 got pretty square.

But when her foreloom-post[f] she let go, it flew out of order
 amain.
She cried: Bring your rule and your level and help me to
 square it again.
I said: My dear lassie, I'm sorry, at Bolton I must be by noon,
But when that I come back this way, I will square up your
 jerry hand-loom.[11]

We have here the familiar form of sexualizing the imple-
ments of one's craft, yet with a new emphasis on its tech-
nicalities.[12] The special knowledge needed to understand
the poem must have been relished by the Lancashire
weaving community. The vocabulary is an amusing combination of technical terms with overtly sexual images,
such as "reiving her loom," "the down on her warp," and
"nicketty-nack," which is not only onomatopoeic for the
motion of the loom, but is also slang for the female sexual
organs.

"The Bury New Loom" combines highly specific details with complete impersonality, partly because it deals

  [e] pickers] attachments to the upper end of the picking stick which
impels the shuttle through the warp threads during the weaving
  [f] foreloom post] the overhanging front portion of a loom

with sexual intercourse and not individuals, but also because the writer speaks in complete confidence that his audience will understand the world he describes and the nature of the symbols used. There is no distance between them and the poem, since it is based on their knowledge of the harmonious movement of an intricate machine, which comes to represent the most important human actions. The richness of the weaving community life can be seen in its contribution to the creative imagination of both poet and reader; only a deeply felt and understood vocation can become symbolic of basic human needs and desires—and be within the reach of the good humor and comedy implicit in this poem. The weaver and joiner are part of a society where they can draw both their identity and actions from the machinery which is central to their respective vocations. Their energy does not go into acquiring each other, or material goods, but into enjoying each other. The competitive pace of power-loom weaving and factory work was reflected in later poems by the acquisitive, materially oriented nature of the verse, but this poem is based on mutual harmony and good will. Not only are we given a clear sense of the sexual pleasure enjoyed by the couple, but we can also feel the cultural strength of a vital community.

The symbolism of this poem would not be possible at a later date when factory work left the operative with less knowledge of the machinery he worked, and responsibility for only one part of the process of production. Although skill and understanding were needed to work such imperfect machinery as power looms, the weaver worked under conditions that often divided him or her from the family, or from close association with all parts of the cloth-making trade. Inevitably poetry turned away from using actions related to a specific vocation as meaningful symbols of human life; few persons would feel the necessary intimacy with their work and its tools to identify with them. Actions which occurred during work, rather than the work itself, became topics for working-class verse; for example, the problems of illicit courting during factory hours became a popular subject for broadsides. But the factory itself could not be symbolic of courting. In this process poetry became more personalized, since more emphasis was placed on characterization, but it concomitantly lost in symbolic richness and variety.

"The Bury New Loom" was frequently reprinted as a penny broadside and sold well in all the weaving districts of Lancashire. Poems of a similar type about faithless soldiers, handsome rakes, and aristocratic strangers remained popular throughout the century. The old tale of the prince marrying the beautiful and virtuous peasant maid became the tale of the factory girl marrying the rich stranger. The reverse story of the wealthy damsel in love with the factory boy also existed. In this case the angry father has the boy impressed into the navy, but the lady buys his freedom; they marry and live happily ever after. The general impression these poems create is one of inexplicable fate ruling the characters' lives. Their personal virtue, good fortune, or probable future are all guided by chance. The theme of "virtue rewarded," particularly active, earned virtue, is quite rare. Narratives about "the fortunate factory girl" and the like were purely escapist, and appealed most to those many operatives, men and women, who found their lives uneventful and unnoticed. Such tales often seemed within the realm of probability because they were built upon realistic details, even when the action was improbable. Readers could identify with the hero or heroine and escape to love or adventure, and find the satisfaction that was missing from their personal lives.

While escapist literature remained in demand, narrative poems were increasingly concerned with the processes of courting and marriage. The leisure time of the working class became the emotional center of life, rather than the work itself, or even the adventures of sailors or soldiers—or joiners. While the monotonous and disciplined life of the factory is a partial explanation for this shift in interest, a more important reason, I believe, is the increased acceptance of middle-class values and customs. Regularity of personal habits, a close family life, and a romantic courtship leading to a blissful marriage were all part of the better life espoused by the advocates of self-help. With this change in personal values came a demand for a different type of reading matter. Literature was turned to not only to escape a dull job, but also to find a reflection of one's own life and its values. Poems that mirrored the best qualities of home life and courting became immensely popular from about 1850. There were, of course, many intervening stages before domesticity replaced eroticism, and many different types of poems coexisted for years. Nevertheless, the dominant tone changed; overtly sexual poems became pornographic, and poetry came to describe ideal types of working-class men and women.

This change was reflected in the manner of selling literature and the type of works preferred. Old village characters, singers of local satires, and itinerant performers died out and no one rose to take their places.[13] Lancashire mill hands after 1850 earned enough to support a variety of full-time professional entertainers quite different in quality and temperament from those earlier characters. They looked to lecturers, readers, and singers who could provide education, uplift, and pleasure for the family at a reasonable price. Songs and poetry remained throughout the century the most popular genres, but short stories and dramatic dialogues suitable for home and public recitation grew in variety and sales. In the meantime, broadside sellers became increasingly disreputable and fewer in number, while the cheap literature market was taken over by the penny press and local sellers of pamphlets and magazines. By the 1860s most broadsides were either propaganda for religious, temperance, or political organizations, or they were copyrighted songs and poems written by local entertainers to further their fame and income. These were sold in reputable shops, at evening entertainments, and at the regularly held bazaars, soirées, and other fund-raising occasions.

The demand for specifically local literature, filled earlier by such poems as "The Bury New Loom," continued. Nineteenth-century Lancashire literature was characterized by the persistence of handloom-weaving and village customs, descriptions, and images. This older way of life, usually idealized but sometimes condemned,[14] continued to hold the imagination of readers and writers, but with the superimposition of the newer self-help and family-oriented values. For example, a particularly popular poem was R .R. Bealey's "My Piece is o bu' Woven Eawt" (1865), a handloom weaver's evaluation of his life in terms of weaving for his "Mester" in heaven. The most significant change from earlier poetry is the shift to a self-conscious use of Lancashire dialect; previously Lancashire phrases and words had crept into various reprinted versions of poems, but now working-class writers strove to imitate their own and their readers' language.[15] These writers knew that they limited their potential audience by writing in a local dialect, but they preferred to write about and for their own class, rather than risk the national market or try unfamiliar subject matter.

The best-known Lancashire poet of this new type was Edwin Waugh (1817–1890), the son of a Rochdale shoemaker. Waugh held a variety of jobs, including journeyman printer, stationery shop clerk, traveling secretary for the Lancashire Secular Education Association, and unskilled factory worker, until the success of his *Lancashire Songs* in 1859 freed him to become a full-time writer and public reader. The local literary circles lionized him as a poet who seemed to reflect traditional Lancashire ways. Influential friends invited him to join the board of the English Dialect Society, and in 1886 were able to place him on the Civil List to receive a pension of ninety pounds a year. When he died the local and national press praised him as the Burns of Lancashire, who had written immortal verse for the factory folk of the county. Although Waugh spent most of his adult life in Manchester, he wrote primarily about the village weaving customs and daily life which he remembered from his youth. His works were enthusiastically received by city mill hands who knew the country only from Sunday outings or through family reminiscences and traditions.[16]

One of Waugh's most popular courting poems was "Come, Mary, Link Thi Arm i' Mine," written about 1855:

> Come, Mary, link thi arm i' mine,
>   An' lilt away wi' me;
>   An' dry that little drop o' brine,
>   Fro' th' corner o' thi e'e;
> Th' mornin' dew, i'th heather-bell's
>   A bonny bit o' weet;
> That tear a different story tells,—
>   It pains my heart to see't.
>   So, Mary, link thi arm i' mine.
>
> No lordly ho',[a] o'th country side's
>   So pleasant to my view,
> As th' little corner where abides
>   My bonny lass an' true;
> But there's a nook beside yon spring,—
>   An' if theaw'll shar't wi' me;
> Aw'll buy tho th' bonny'st gowden ring
>   That ever theaw did see!
>   So, Mary, link thi arm i' mine.

<hr>

[a] ho'] house

My feyther's gan mo forty peawnd,[b]
   I' silver an' i' gowd;
An' a pratty bit o' garden greawned,
   O' th' mornin' side o'th' fowd; [c]
An' a honsome bible, clen an' new,
   To read for days to come;—
There's leaves for writin' names in, too,
   Like th' owd un 'at's awhoam.[d]
     So, Mary, link thi arm i' mine.

Eawr Jenny's bin a-buyin' in,
   An' every day hoo brings
Knives an' forks, an' pots; an' irons
   For smoothin' caps an' things;
My gronny's sent a kist [e] o' drawers,
   Sunday clooas [f] to keep.
An' little Fanny's bought a glass
   Where thee an' me can peep.
     So, Mary, link thi arm i' mine.

Eawr Tum has sent a bacon-flitch;
   Eawr Jem a load o' coals;
Eawr Charlie's bought some pickters, an'
   He's hanged 'em upo' th' woles; [g]
Owd Posy's white-weshed th' cottage through;
   Eawr Matty's made it sweet;
An' Jack's gan me his Jarman flute,
   To play bi th' fire at neet!
     So, Mary, link thi arm i' mine.

There's cups an' saucers; porritch-pons,[h]
   An' tables, greyt an' smo'; [i]

[b] My feyther's gan mo forty peawnd] My father's given me forty
pounds
  [c] fowd] fold, i.e. valley
  [d] awhoam] at home
  [e] kist] chest
  [f] clooas] cloths
  [g] woles] walls
  [h] porritch-pons] porridge-pans
  [i] greyt an' smo'] great and small

There's brushes, mugs, an' ladin'-cans;
  An eight-day's clock an' o';
There's a cheer for thee, an' one for me,
  An' one i' every nook'
Thi mother's has a cushion on't,—
  It's th' nicest cheer i'th rook.[j]
    So, Mary, link thi arm i' mine.

My gronny's gan me th' four-post bed,
  Wi' curtains to 't an' o';
An' pillows, sheets, an' bowsters, too,
  As white as driven snow;
It isn't stuffed wi' fither-deawn; [k]
  But th' flocks are clen an' new;
Hoo says there's honest folk i'th teawn
  That's made a warse un [l] do.
    So, Mary, link thi arm i' mine.

Aw peeped into my cot [m] last neet;
  It made me hutchin' fain; [n]
A bonny fire were winkin' breet
  I' every window-pane;
Aw marlocked [o] upo' th' white hearth-stone,
  An' drummed o'th kettle lid;
An' sung, "My neest is snug an' sweet;
  Aw'll go and fotch my brid!"
    So, Mary, link thi arm i' mine.[17]

The narrator's eagerness is well expressed in the lilting
rhyme and refrain, and the details seem natural and realistic. Love and sex, however, are no longer linked meta-
phorically, as in "The Bury New Loom," but are expressed
through the cataloguing of material goods. These objects,
intended to symbolize the narrator's love, become more

----

[j] cheer i'th rook] chair in the collection
[k] fither-deawn] feather down
[l] warse un] worse one
[m] cot] cottage
[n] hutchin' fain] fidgeting glad
[o] marlocked] frolicked

important than the emotions they represent, so that the net effect of the poem is little more than a list of what a good man can offer his wife. Both individuals derive their characters from these objects, rather than from each other or from their respective vocations, as in earlier weaving poems. No effort is made to give Mary a personality beyond that of her tears, a suitable manifestation of happiness in a modest Victorian woman, one assumes; nor does the narrator rise above the conventional expression of anticipation and joy. Although women have traditionally been called to come away to a private place with a lover, here that place is reduced to a "neest," and the woman to a "brid," with all the connotations of domesticity, rather than sexuality, these words imply.

Closely related to this nest-making image is the presence of every member of the narrator's family; each brother and sister is identified by the kind of gift he gives—Tom and Jem are practical, while Charlie and Jack supply art and music. These presents represent the family's responsibilities to the young couple, and are a means of bringing Mary into their circle. The most positive characteristic of this poem is the image of a happy, reasonably well off, and self-sustaining family that it presents. The Lancashire dialect custom of calling individual brothers and sisters within a family "our" instead of "my" will soon embrace Mary, offering her both possessiveness and warmth of feeling. Each member of the family is equally important for his particular contribution to it, and the family as a whole serves as a refuge from a competitive industrial society. Indeed, the personal goods mentioned in this poem are not simply the lover's gifts, but are also representative of individual and family wealth to be shared with Mary. The expression of close family ties and shared goods balances the effect of enumerating material objects.

"The Bury New Loom" and "Come, Mary, Link Thi Arm i' Mine" each came out of well-defined and stable communities, dominant in their respective times. They represent the best works of the Lancashire working-class community, but their appeal was limited to those familiar with the way of life described. More crucial, however, are the changes in attitude and tone to be found in comparing the two poems. "Come, Mary" is more personal and more general than the earlier work. It has a lilt and charm which make courting a pleasure to be savored in the present and in memory, but love has been placed in a thoroughly acceptable social context. The existing institution of marriage is presented as the ideal toward which every working man and woman ought to aspire, and indeed, in the poetry of the time is close to becoming the sole outlet for sexual attraction.

"Come, Mary" is both the summation of local dialect verse and a foreteller of future difficulties. By limiting themselves to a particular kind of poetry and language that could express only a limited range of subjects and emotions, dialect lyricists of the later nineteenth century could not reach beyond the local, even to the symbolic level of earlier rural and weaving songs. The specific details, interesting in themselves as portraits of Lancashire working-class life, are seldom elevated above the particular to speak for a general condition. The endlessly anecdotal style which personifies much working-class verse led to an increasing sentimentalization of the minor details of everyday life, as if they were in themselves central to each reader's major concerns. In the process of mirroring an idealized version of working-class life, Waugh and his contemporaries actually separated poetry as a means of defining this life from daily usage, and made it special and occasional. Poetry for working-class readers came to be a means of expressing and explaining one's emotions on exceptional occasions, such as marriage or death, rather than being integral to one's life. Literature written by and for working-class people could only suffer from this separation.

II

During the nineteenth century working men wrote three types of protest poetry. The most common was occasional verse for a particular movement, written not so much to inform its members as to arouse a wider public. For example, the Ten Hours Movement in its campaign to legislate shorter working hours churned out countless pathetic verses about factory children dying prematurely from overwork. A number of songs, of course, were aimed at the converted. Trade-union hymns, rallying chants, and marching songs were all popular for encouraging flagging spirits. These usually followed a standard format; there was little narrative, so that verses could be sung in whatever order they were remembered. The emphasis was on praising particular leaders, calling for patience and faith in the cause, and condemning the opposition. A catchy refrain was an important means of stirring members to act in unison for the cause. Both of these types were primarily occasional, and seldom survived the event that brought them forth unless a particularly good tune accompanied the song.

"Consolatory verse" was the most important type of protest poetry. Although such verse was usually written during a time of economic distress, the sufferings of starvation and unemployment were such as to raise the best examples above the limitations of a specific occasion. These poems were a remarkably powerful form of consolation because they were true to the conditions and attitudes of those who read them for solace and as an explanation of their plight. They show rather than tell the reader about poverty—in contrast to the "factory child" genre of protest poetry, in which a static picture of suffering is set up and then the reader is admonished to feel pity for the figure portrayed. In consolatory verse the emotions are defined by the actions within the poem and not by an outsider or, as in "Come, Mary," by physical objects. Generally few solutions are offered; indeed, in most cases no solutions were available except the passage of time.

The most famous Lancashire protest poem of the nineteenth century was "Jone o' Grinfilt." In the 1790s, during the first patriotic enthusiasm for the French Wars, a poem was written by a schoolmaster, Joseph Lees, about John of Greenfield, a small village near Oldham. Since the weaving trade was temporarily down, "Jone" decided to enlist in the army and help his country "ha'e battle wi the French." This first publication was enormously popular, and within a short time had over a dozen imitations circulating throughout the North. A discontented weaver who leaves poor conditions at home to find redress or a better life was a loose enough narrative to fit almost any occasion. In the best folk tradition, Jone was soon capable of prodigies of sight-seeing, bravery, and political insight. The Reform Bill of 1832, Queen Caroline's trial, the Crimean War, and the New Poor Law were all excuses for Jone to leave Lancashire.[18]

The version which survived the longest came out of the postwar period of 1815–1819, when political and economic repression were at their greatest. "Jone o' Grinfilt, Jr." was a magnificently sardonic description of the handloom weaver's situation. Versions of the poem were still being sold in the 1860s, and a few years ago Ewan MacColl discovered an old power-loom weaver from Delph, a small village in the Pennines, who sang a starker and harsher version than any we have from the nineteenth century.[19] The following comes from a broadside published in Manchester in the early 1860s:

I'm a poor cotton weaver as many one knows,
I've nowt to eat i'th house and I've worn out my cloas,
You'd hardly give sixpence for all I have on,

My clogs they are brossen [a] and stockings I've none,
You'd think it wur hard to be sent into th' world,
  To clem [b] and do th' best ot you con.

Our church parson kept telling us long,
We should have better times if we'd hold our tongues,
I've houden my tongue till I can hardly draw breath,
I think i' my heart he means to clem me to death;
I know he lives weel by backbiting the de'il,[c]
  But he never picked o'er [d] in his life.

I tarried six week an thought every day wur t' last,
I tarried and shiften till now I'm quite fast,
I lived on nettles while nettles were good,
An Waterloo porridge [e] were best of my food;
I'm telling you true I can find folks enew,
  That are living no better than me.

Old Bill o' Dan's sent bailiffs one day,
For a shop score I owed him that I could not pay,
But he wur too late for old Bill o' Bent,
Had sent tit [f] and cart and taen goods for rent,
We had nou bur a stoo [g], that wur a seat for two,
  And on it cowered Margit and me.

The bailiffs looked round as sly as a mouse,
When they saw aw things were taen [h] out o't house,
Says one to the other all's gone thou may see,
Aw sed lads never fret you're welcome to me;
They made no more ado, but nipp'd up th' owd stoo,
  An we both went wack upoth flags.

I geet howd of Margit for hoo wur strucken sick,
Hoo sed hoo ne'er had such a bang sin hoo wur wick [i]

 [a] brossen] broken
 [b] clem] starve
 [c] de'il] devil
 [d] picked o'er] wove
 [e] Waterloo porridge] porridge made with water
 [f] tit] for it (?)
 [g] nou bur a stoo] nought but a stool
 [h] taen] taken
 [i] wick] born

The bailiffs scoured off with owd stoo on their backs,
They would not have cared had they brook our necks,
They're mad at owd Bent cos he's taen goods for rent,
      And wur ready to flee [j] us alive.

I sed to our Margit as we lay upoth floor,
We shall never be lower in this world I'm sure,
But if we alter I'm sure we mun mend,
For I think in my heart we are both at far end,
For meat we have none nor looms to weave on,
      Egad they're as weel lost as found.

Then I geet up my piece and I took it em back
I scarcely dare speak mester looked so black,
He said you wur o'erpaid last time you coom,
I said if I wur 'twas for weaving bout loom; [k]
In a mind as I'm in I'll ne'er pick o'er again,
      For I've woven mysel thoth' fur end.

Then aw coom out and left him to chew that,
When aw thought again aw wur vext till aw sweat,
To think that we mun work to keep them and awth set,[l]
All the day o' my life and still be in their debt;
So I'll give o'er trade an work with a spade,
      Or go and break stones upoth road.

Our Margit declared if hoo'd cloas to put on,
Hoo'd go up to Lundun an see the big mon [m]
An if things didn't alter when hoo had been,
Hoo swears hoo'd feight blood up toth e'en,[n]
Hoo's nought again th' Queen but likes a fair thing
      An hoo says hoo can tell when hoo's hurt.[20]

Most protest verse, indeed poems by working men, were
awkward in phrasing and veered between a stilted literary
language and the vernacular, giving the work an odd tone

[j] flee] beat
[k] bout loom] without a loom
[l] awth set] all their set
[m] the big mon] the king. Altered to read "the Queen" two lines
later, to fit the date of publication.
[n] e'en] eyes

and inconsistent form. This poem, on the other hand, is taut and flexible in its conversational tone and easy use of the weaver's dialect. A very clear narrative of events is presented, and the available consolation honestly recorded.

There seems, however, to be a break between the seventh and eighth stanzas; whether this is by intention or because all surviving versions read this way is unclear. The weaver declares that things are at "fur end," using a weaving term that means the end of a piece of woven cloth, to describe the plight of himself and his wife. There seems to be no way out of their dilemma of no looms, no furniture, and no money, except to argue as he does, that since they have nothing left, things must improve. Then, the next two stanzas describe an event one would have supposed occurred previous to the confiscation of the furniture. Since he says that he was weaving "bout loom" the previous week, where does the final piece of cloth come from? [21] It may be that these verses come after his comment to Margaret in order to indicate that he could indeed be made lower in the world by means of his master's degrading attitude. Or, his declaration to "ne'er pick o'er again" may be a defiant recognition of the inevitable; accepting poor relief and its required labor of stone breaking or spadework is made to seem a choice by his refusal to work any longer for the putter-out (who has no work for him anyway). Given the combination of melancholy tone and sardonic comment, it seems that the weaver accepts poor relief and all it entails, but as the final stanza indicates, demands justice; indeed, the final three lines became proverbial in Lancashire as a comment on hard times.

A dominant characteristic of this poem is its insistence on the rights and personal dignity of the individual; the weaver knows his position in the world and has no desire to overturn its hierarchic order, but oppression he will not tolerate. The poem combines a highly specific attack on those in power—the church parson, the putter-out, the shopkeeper, and the houseowner—with a general acceptance of economic instability as an uncontrollable factor in life. Thus, the main threat of the poem in the final stanza is based on an if-clause which negates the possibility of ever visiting the king (or queen, as this updated version reads). This stanza comes out of a long tradition of appealing to justice at its source, the crown, and of struggling as individuals. The political unity of the workers was an ideal that only slowly became an integral part of working-class consciousness, although its appeal was always present. The poem conveys no sense of the larger economic forces at work, nor of any revolutionary possibilities for change; rather, it emphasizes the continuation of self-respect—and a willingness to fight for it—in spite of social and economic repression. Both the limits and the strengths of this view partially explain why the English weavers did not rise up violently against their "mesters," but sought redress through appeals to justice and to Parliament, or simply waited for a turn of fate.[22]

After the prolonged depression of the late thirties and early forties, a period of relative economic calm and prosperity characterized the textile districts of Lancashire until the outbreak of the American Civil War. The Northern blockade of Southern ports closed off almost all cotton supplies to Lancashire; only the poor-quality short-fibered "shurat" cotton from India and Egypt was available during the war. The result was almost total unemployment for cotton-mill operatives. By 1862, out of 350,000 operatives, 40,000 were on full time, 135,000 on short time (an undefined amount of work), and 180,000 totally unemployed. In Preston, a typical mill town, poor relief applications rose from 4.6 percent of the population in November 1861 to 47.5 percent one year later.[23] Hard hit by the increase in local rates, levied to pay for relief, small tradesmen and shopkeepers could not extend credit. Rent money was not to be had, so families moved to poorer and poorer quarters;

while there was little outright starvation, deaths from secondary causes rose. Many families were reduced from incomes as high as three and four pounds to less than ten shillings.[24] In such conditions, skilled spinners and power-loom weavers, like Jone o' Grinfilt, Jr., were forced to break stones to earn a shilling a day poor relief.

The four years of suffering brought forth many poems and songs, often written to earn a few extra pence by sing-ing and selling on street corners. A few of these ballads be-came enormously popular, selling thousands of copies as penny broadsides.[25] They were sung widely throughout the country, and snatches can still be heard among weavers dur-ing hard times. Many of these amateur productions bear a marked resemblance to Waugh's most popular works, or to such traditional songs as "Jone o' Grinfilt, Jr.," which continued to be sold. (In spite of the references to hand-loom-weaving conditions, readers obviously felt its story to be applicable to their own situation, and still found com-fort in Margaret's threat.) Most songs expressed solidarity with other unemployed men, emphasizing the need for cheerfulness and confidence that "good toimes" would come again. Little is said about the Civil War and its implica-tions, beyond an ill-defined hope of good will toward all men.[26]

One of the best-known poems of the time was James Bowker's "Hard Toimes, or the Weaver Speaks to his Wife," first published in 1862:

Draw up thy cheer,[a] owd lass, we'n still a bit o' fir,
An' I'm starv't to deoth wi' cummin' throo th' weet an' mire;
He towd a lie o' thee an' me, as said as th' love o' th' poor
Flies out o' th' kitchen window, when clemmin' cums to
    th' door.
Aw'm not ruein'—as thae weel knows—as ever I wed thee,

    ^a cheer] chair

But I've monny a quare thowt [b] as thae mon sometimes
    rue o' me.

I'm mad at them America foos, as never hes enuff
O' quarrelin' an' strugglin', and sich unnat'rel stuff,
An' its ter'ble hard, owd wife, to ceawer bi' th' chimley jam,[c]
An' think if they keep on feightin', as thee an' me mun clam; [d]
An' not aar faut,[e] its like breykin' wer shins o'er th' neighbours'
    stoos,
An' it shows us for one woise mon, ther's welly twenty foos.

But better chaps nor me an' thee has hed to live o' nowt,
An' we'n hed a tidy time on't afoor th' war brok' out;
An' if I'm gerrin' [f] varra thin, it matters nowt o' me,
Th' hardest wark is sittin' here schaming for th' choilt an' thee.
Tha' art gerrin' ter'ble pale too, but fowk wi' nowt to heyt
Con't luk as nice an' weel as them as plenty hes o' meyt.[g]

Ther's lots o'hooams areawnd us whear wot they waste i'
    th' day,
'Ud sarve for thee an' th' choilt an' me, an' some to give away;
An' as I passes by their dooars, I hears their music sweet,
An' I con't but think o' thee till th' teears dim mi seet;
For if I'd lots o' brass,[h] thae shud be diff'rent, never fear,
For th'art nooan so feaw,[i] yet, wench, if thae'd gradely [j] clooas
    to wear.

An' aar bonny little Annie, wi' her pratty een so breet,
Hoo shud sleep o' feathers, and uv angels dreom o neet;
I fancies I con see her monny a weary heawr i' th' day,
As I shud loike her to be sin, if luv mud heve its way; [k]

[b] a quare thowt] a queer thought
[c] to ceawer bi' th' chimley jam] to cower by the chimney side
[d] mun clam] must starve
[e] aar faut] our fault
[f] gerrin] getting
[g] meyt] meat, used generically to mean food
[h] brass] money
[i] feaw] few, i.e. lowly
[j] gradely] proper, decent
[k] if luv mud heve its way] if love would have its way

And if what's i' this heart o' moine cud nobbut cum to pass,
Hoo shud bi' th' happiest woman, as hoo is th' bonniest lass.

I'm a foo wi' clammin' soa, or I shudn't toke like this,
It nobbut meks wer teeth watter to think o' sich like bliss;
An' th' winter cummin' on so fast, wi' th' dark, an' th' snow,
     an' the cowd,
For I heeard th' robin sing to-day as I heeard him sing of owd,
When thee an' me wur younger, an' i' wur soft cooartin days,
An' I cum whistlin' thro' the fields to yoar owd woman's place.

Thea loved me then, an' as wimmen's soft enuff for owt,
I do believe thae loves me neaw, mooar nor ever I'd hae thowt,
An' tha' hes but one excuse, if I'm ragg'd, I'm fond o' thee,
An' times, though hard, I connot think'll change thee or me,
For if we're true an' reet, an' as honest as we're poor,
We's never hev no wos [1] chap nor poverty at th' dooar.[27]

Bowker has absorbed the values implicit in a cash-nexus
relationship, and sees emotional security in terms of money
and the necessities and luxuries it provides a family. As a
man who derived his identity from the sale of labor, the
weaver needs reassurance that his family still loves him
when he cannot fulfill this role. In turn, he promises gifts
in the future as representative of his own love for them.
Although there is the same cataloguing of material goods
as in "Come, Mary, Link Thi Arm i' Mine," the realistic
descriptions of "clemming" and poverty place the desire
for presents and good times into a realistic context. The
poem barely rises above the most platitudinous thoughts,
but it undoubtedly provided solace for Lancashire families
suffering from what seemed like an endless period of un
employment over which nobody but the foolish Americans
had any control.

     Although "Jone o' Grinfilt, Jr." seems more pessimistic
than "Hard Toimes," the latter is more passive and accepting of the status quo. Unlike Jone, Bowker's weaver does

---

[1] wos] worse

not think in terms of economic stability or of deliverance from his plight by outsiders as a right; instead he finds consolation in the continued love of his family. Whereas the earlier poem concentrated on the stripping away of Jone's worldly goods, here the weaver's poverty is brought into focus by means of contrasts with a remembered past and a hoped-for future. The weaver's love of his wife and daughter encompasses these thoughts and gives him strength to face the present. The present, in one incident, is the sharp difference between his own plight and that of the indifferent wealthy who throw away enough food to feed him and his family. But this event is preceded with a comment on others who have suffered even more, and does not lead beyond a statement of obvious injustice. The weaver reduces his insoluble difficulties, the Civil War and his unemployment, to familiar household events to make them manageable and comprehensible. The war is analogous to bumping one's shins on a neighbor's stool, and unemployment is primarily "schaming for th' choilt an' thee." The difficulties of poverty are softened through an emphasis on family love and an avoidance of too deep a consideration of why they are clemming.

Even when we consider that "Hard Toimes" did not have forty years of oral circulation to smooth out its awkward lines, flat clichés, and weak metaphors, the poem lacks precision in comparison with "Jone o' Grinfilt, Jr." Emotions are not integral to the poem itself, but are evoked in the reader by means of familiar phrases and words. The most serious effect of poetry such as "Hard Toimes" is that it forms the vocabulary and ultimately the emotions of the reader. Readers grow to define and describe their emotions in literary language, forcing individual thoughts and feelings into a generalized picture taken from their reading. That which does not fit a format becomes unreal and unacceptable; any variation from the familiar is suspect. Individuals no longer trust their particular feelings, and their own words to describe them, but draw upon external sources. Bad poetry becomes not an explanation of emotions, but a substitute for them.

Fortunately this kind of poetry was not the sole source of language for the working class; the Bible continued to be the most widely and intensively read book. But when we look at other reading matter, the problem is, if anything, worse—the yellow press and Grub Street fiction provided little more than sensationalism, crudely drawn characterization, and simple solutions or evasions of insoluble problems. Indeed, in time the power of the popular press was such that working-class writers were almost universally absorbed into it. By the twentieth century we cannot speak of a working-class poetry separate from popular verse.

In our day numerous writers have predicted an efflorescence of working-class literature. But when sex and protest can be so thoroughly socialized into existing mores, little that is radically new can be expected. The very ability of the English ruling class—in both politics and literature—to absorb and neutralize those aspiring from below has led to an accelerating loss of local and submerged cultures different from the dominant culture. We should not, however, regret the loss of a culture based on qualities we do not wish to see continued, such as poverty, inadequate housing, poor education, and overwork, disabilities under which all working-class writers struggled throughout the nineteenth century. Rather, we must now ask how we can preserve the best of a traditional subculture while still keeping it responsive to new demands and new struggles. For teachers and scholars this involves the preserving and resurrecting of the people's history. For example, the study of dialects has advanced scientifically since the days of Joseph Wright's *English Dialect Dictionary*, but dialects are not yet a part of our literary and historical studies. Literature should be defined so as to include local works, popular culture, songs, hymns, and oral storytelling. Each of these forms of creativity has a claim against the dominant bourgeois culture. The values and autonomy of working-class people can be encouraged and solidified through acceptance of a broader definition of literature and creativity by teachers of English. Indeed, our discipline needs a redefinition of the function of literature in our lives, those of our students—of the working class. *How* and *why* people create both the written and spoken poem, song, anecdote, or story are crucial questions too seldom asked.

NOTES

1 The wealth of working-class literature has scarcely been touched by scholars. For a survey of the poetry, see Martha Vicinus, "The Lowly Harp: Nineteenth Century Working Class Poetry," unpublished Ph.D. dissertation, University of Wisconsin, 1969.

2 The exception to this generalization is A. L. Lloyd's *Folk Song in England* (New York: International Publishing Co., 1967).

3 See Richard D. Altick, *The English Common Reader: A Social History of the Mass Reading Public, 1800–1900* (Chicago: University of Chicago Press, 1957), for a discussion of the problems of literacy and cheap reading matter.

4 For a full discussion of the fight for an unstamped press, see Joel H. Wiener, *The War of the Unstamped: The Movement to Repeal the British Newspaper Tax, 1830–1836* (Ithaca, N.Y.: Cornell University Press, 1969). Ben Brierley (1825–1896), a Lancashire dialect writer, speaks of reading the *Northern Star* to his father and friends in his autobiography, *Home Memories and Recollections of a Life* (Manchester, 1886), p. 21.

5 The most detailed examination of industrial dislocation and its impact upon individual workers and their families is Neil J. Smelser's *Social Change in the Industrial Revolution: An Application of Theory to the British Cotton Industry* (Chicago: University of Chicago Press, 1959). See also Alfred P. Wadsworth and Julia De Lacy Mann, *The Cotton Trade and Industrial Lancashire 1600–1780* (Manchester, 1931; reprint ed., New York: Augustus M. Kelley, Publishers, 1968); R. S. Fitton and A. P. Wadsworth, *The Strutts and the Arkwrights 1785–1830* (New York: Augustus M. Kelley, Publishers, 1958); W. Radcliffe, *The Origin of Power Loom Weaving* (Stockport, 1838); and Andrew Ure, *The Cotton Manufacture of Great Britain*, 2 vols. (London, 1861).

6 The Ten Hours Movement, of course, centered its efforts through the 1830s and 1840s on gaining legal regulations over the working hours and conditions in cotton and woolen factories. See Cecil Driver, *Tory Radical: The Life of Richard Oastler* (New York, 1946; reprint ed., Wilmington, Del.: Mellifont Press, 1970).

7 See John Harland and T. T. Wilkinson, eds., *Ballads and Songs of Lancashire, Ancient and Modern,* 3rd ed. (London, 1882), for examples of Lancashire poetry from medieval times through the nineteenth century.

8 For an idealized account of handloom weaving during the Golden Age, see *The Autobiography of Samuel Bamford,* Vol. 1, *Early Days,* ed. W. H. Chaloner (New York: Augustus M. Kelley, Publishers, 1967), pp. 96–115. The quotation comes from "Hand-Loom v. Power-Loom," by John Grimshaw in Harland and Wilkinson, *Lancashire Ballads and Songs,* pp. 188–89 (emphasis added).

9 The figures are quoted in Ephraim Lipson, *A Short History of Wool and Its Manufacture Mainly in England* (New York: Humanities Press, 1953), p. 162.

10 Sim Schofield, *Short Stories about Failsworth Folk* (Blackpool, 1905), p. 17.

11 Broadside collection, John Johnson Collection, Bodleian Library, Oxford. It should be noted that the weaver is a woman, in a trade traditionally associated with men. See Duncan Bythell, *The Handloom Weavers: A Study in the English Cotton Industry during the Industrial Revolution* (Cambridge: Cambridge University Press, 1969), pp. 60–61, for an analysis of the number of women in the trade. See also Ivy Pinchbeck, *Women Workers and the Industrial Revolution, 1750–1850* (London: George Routledge & Sons, 1930). The John Johnson Collection contains a later version of this poem, making the joiner a steam fitter and the weaver a power-loom weaver.

12 Detailed descriptions of the process of weaving, its technical terms, and an analysis of grades of fiber can be found in earlier poems in the woolen industry. See for example, John Dyer, *The Fleece* (1757).

13 Such performers still exist in the remoter parts of Great Britain, but are generally part-time.

14 Condemnation usually centered on the lack of educational opportunities. See almost any working-class autobiography written in the nineteenth century, but in particular for Lancashire, Ben Brierley, *Home Memories.*

15 For a discussion of Lancashire dialect, see George Milner, Introduction to Edwin Waugh's *Poems and Songs* (Manchester, n.d.

[1892]), pp. xiii–xxxii. See also W. E. A. Axon, *The Literature of the Lancashire Dialect: A Bibliographical Essay* (London, 1870).

16 For the life of Edwin Waugh and his early difficulties, see Edwin Waugh, "Diary: 21 July 1847–10 February 1851," unpublished manuscript, Manchester Central Reference Library; George Milner, Introduction to *Lancashire Sketches*, Vol. I of Edwin Waugh, *Collected Works*, ed. George Milner, 8 vols. (Manchester, n.d. [1892]); and Ben Brierley, *Personal Recollections of the late Edwin Waugh* (Manchester, n.d. [1890]).

17 *Poems and Songs*, ed. George Milner, pp. 16–19.

18 The authorship of the original "Jone o' Grinfilt" is under some dispute. For the best-known account, see Harland and Wilkinson, *Lancashire Ballads and Songs*, pp. 162–75. For a correction of this, see Charles Higson, " 'Jone o' Grinfilt' and 'Oldham Rush-bearing,' " Oldham *Standard*, May 1, 1926.

19 Ewan MacColl, *The Shuttle and Cage* (London: Workers' Music Association, 1954), p. 3.

20 Broadside Collection, Chetham's Library, Manchester.

21 In the West Riding woolen trade a master often gave a weaver his wages in the form of the piece of cloth he had just woven, thus leaving to him the task of selling it in a depressed market.

22 The exception is the early nineteenth-century Luddite and Captain Swing movements, that largely attacked machinery and not men. See Frank Peel, *The Risings of the Luddites, Chartists, and Plug-Drawers*, 4th ed. (London: Frank Cass & Co., 1968), and E. J. Hobsbawm and George Rudé, *Captain Swing* (New York: Pantheon Books, 1968). Harland and Wilkinson reprint a number of poems written during this time protesting the new factory working conditions. See in particular the poem praising the fire that burned a new power-loom factory in 1790, "Grimshaw's Factory Fire," *Lancashire Songs and Ballads*, pp. 202–4.

23 John Watts, *The Facts of the Cotton Famine* (Manchester, 1866), pp. 121ff.

24 For one weaver's personal account of these years, see "The Diary of John Ward of Clitheroe, Weaver, 1860–64," ed. R. Sharpe France, *Transactions of the Historic Society of Lancashire and Cheshire*, Vol. 105 (1955), pp. 137–85.

25 The most famous songs were Samuel Laycock's "Lancashire Lyrics," reprinted in *Warblin's fro' an Owd Songster* (Oldham, n.d. [1893]), pp. 41–66.

26 For working-class reactions to the Cotton Famine, see Edwin Waugh, *Home Life of the Lancashire Factory Folk during the Cotton Famine* (Manchester, 1867); Joseph Ramsbottom, *Phases of Distress: Lancashire Rhymes* (Manchester, 1864); Samuel Lay-

cock, "Lancashire Lyrics," *Warblin's fro' an Owd Songster;* and Harland and Wilkinson, *Lancashire Ballads and Songs,* pp. 489–516. For a brief account of operatives selling broadsides and singing on street corners, see John Watts, *Facts of the Cotton Famine,* pp. 124–27.

27 Harland and Wilkinson, *Lancashire Ballads and Songs,* pp. 512–14.

SUGGESTED READING

Although much working-class literature was occasional and highly local, a number of important primary and secondary works have been published. Lancashire is fortunate in having a long tradition of preserving local artifacts and printed sources; all the major cities have local history collections and specialist librarians. The broadside collections in the Harris Library, Preston, the Brown and Picton Libraries, Liverpool, and the Manchester Central Reference Library, Manchester, are particularly valuable for the study of working-class literature. Unpublished letters, commonplace books, diaries, and manuscripts of local authors are available in all of these libraries.

In addition to the works cited above, the following are recommended:

William Lovett, *Life and Struggles* (London, 1876), and Thomas Cooper, *The Life of Thomas Cooper* (London, 1886; reprint ed., New York: Humanities Press, 1970). Two autobiographies by early Chartist leaders. Both men believed in self-education and self-help, following in their youth a rigorously disciplined reading program in order to teach themselves foreign languages, literary masterpieces, and the rudiments of science.

Friedrich Engels, *The Condition of the Working Class in England,* trans. W. O. Henderson and W. H. Chaloner (Stanford, Calif.: Stanford University Press, 1968). Originally published in 1845, this is a classic study of the condition of the working classes in Manchester in 1844. Although it has been under attack ever since as a biased report (and is treated as such by the translators), its basic findings have not been refuted.

Asa Briggs, *Victorian Cities* (New York: Harper & Row, Publishers, 1965). See particularly the chapter on Manchester. A brilliant description and analysis of the new industrial cities of the nineteenth century.

E. P. Thompson, *The Making of the English Working Class* (New York: Pantheon Books, 1964). The standard work in the field; its basic premise is that the working class made themselves and their industrial culture through the establishment of independent institutions, and were not merely a reactive body to dominant forces of the time. Covers approximately 1780–1825.

J. F. C. Harrison, *Learning and Living, 1790–1960: A Study in the History of the English Adult Education Movement* (Toronto: University of Toronto Press, 1961). A study of the problems of adult education, popular culture, and the function of learning for the working class in northern England.

Richard Altick, *The English Common Reader: A Social History of the Mass Reading Public, 1800–1900* (Chicago: University of Chicago Press, 1957). A standard work. Although it deals largely with the development of Grub Street and writing *for* rather than *by* the working class, the statistical and factual material is invaluable.

A. L. Lloyd, *Folk Song in England* (New York: International Publishing Co., 1967). The best survey of English folk song and working-class traditions in the field. It suffers, however, from the problems inherent in covering so much material, and from a bias toward industrial songs that most closely follow earlier folk traditions.

Raymond Williams, *Culture and Society, 1780–1950* (New York: Columbia University Press, 1958) and *The Long Revolution* (New York: Columbia University Press, 1961). A scholarship boy, Williams has analyzed the development of industrial culture to the present day, arguing for a different "great tradition" from that defined by F. R. Leavis and other more conservative literary critics. Although his work often seems to lack a historical context, he makes the valuable point that creativity does not necessarily find a literary outlet, and that persons in literary professions are too ready to condemn nonverbal institutions.

WHO'S AFRAID OF A ROOM
OF ONE'S OWN?

Lillian S. Robinson

The huckster congratulates me on attaining full humanity. Of course, I made myself ridiculous for a time back there, demanding equal rights and the vote, but now my emancipation is complete, and its badge, like a tiny torch of freedom, glows in my hand:

> You've got your own cigarette now, baby,
> You've come a long, long way.

> Advertising jingle for "Virginia Slims"

Virginia Woolf's *A Room of One's Own* is forty years old this fall,[1] and, by the deplorable sexual analogy that informs our culture, should be approaching the age of irreversible infertility. But the experience of any woman who begins to inquire into her own condition at first recapitulates that of her predecessors, so that "for women writers, as for Negro, what others have said bears down on whatever they can say themselves."[2] New limitations have indeed given me the impatient feeling that our ancestresses "mismanaged their affairs very gravely," but in reopening the subject of Women and Fiction, I find, to reverse the analogy, that Virginia Woolf's essay is still seminal and remains a logical starting place.

Although the cultural condition of woman has not changed in substance, two areas that *A Room of One's Own* mentions only incidentally—the realms of sexuality and politics—have seen the emergence of some new possibilities, possibilities that could radically reshape more than our literature. I may not agree with that other Virginia, the tobacco peddler, about how far my liberty has already taken me, but if I had been alive when *A Room of One's Own* was first published, I could not write about these developments as part of my own formative experience. Virginia Woolf speaks of straining off whatever was personal and accidental in her impressions and so reaching "the pure oil of truth." Thus, the experience of literature itself provides a standard by which to measure the extent and effects of the changes that have already occurred and those I believe are impending.[3]

I

"No age," Virginia Woolf remarks, surveying the wealth of written opinion on the Woman Question, "can ever have been as stridently sex-conscious as our own." In an era of even greater sexual candor, Woolf's notions of sex-consciousness appear quaintly limited. She attributes male writers' preoccupation with the subject and their new desire for self-assertion to a kind of backlash, their defensive response to the militant struggle for women's rights. It is true that the suffrage movement of the last century was popularly identified with "free love." I think this is only partially due to the movement's attack on traditional ideas about "woman's place" or to the sexual liberation campaigns of such radicals as Victoria Woodhull and Frances Wright. It is more likely to have happened because mention of "woman" evokes an immediate association with sexuality—almost despite the context in which it occurs. (Göring used to say, "Whenever I hear the word 'culture' I reach for my gun." The analogy doesn't quite work if I were to say what most men reach for when they hear the word "woman." Yet their response is equally reflexive.) Nonetheless, the sex-consciousness provoked by the struggle for suffrage was but rarely an explicit awareness of sexuality.

By contrast, the "revolution" in sexual mores that had only begun in 1928 makes our own period sex-conscious (even, to square the compound, self-consciously sex-conscious) in a sense whose principal focus *is* the bedroom. Permission to be unchaste has not freed women from the object-role we occupied when it was chastity that was the valued commodity. The standard is still imposed from without, and realization of one's femininity must still be achieved at the sacrifice of a fully liberated personality. Perhaps it is "one of the tokens of the fully developed mind that it does not think specially or separately of sex," yet the contradictory expectations women must live up to make such measured growth impossible. Fuller consideration of both the old chastity taboo and the contemporary free sex ethic will perhaps illuminate our new double standard.

The most striking invention in *A Room of One's Own* is Shakespeare's gifted, doomed sister, who is frustrated and ultimately destroyed by the related limitations of sex and sexuality. Conventional notions of her social role defeat her as an artist, but it is her breach of the chastity taboo that is her final undoing. The poet Judith Shakespeare kills herself after her seduction and impregnation by Nick Greene, but the enforcement of chastity has already done its worst.

> No girl could have walked to London and stood at a stage door and forced her way into the presence of actor-managers without doing herself a violence and suffering an anguish which may have been irrational—for chastity

may be a fetish invented by certain societies for unknown reasons—but were none the less inevitable. Chastity had then, it has even now, a religious importance in a woman's life, and has so wrapped itself around with nerves and instincts that to cut it free and bring it to the light of day demands courage of the rarest.[4]

Today, when it is equally damning to be considered "afraid of sex" (that is, of sexuality), the courage required is far less, but in either case women's sense of identity is still supposed to depend upon sexual conformity.

Virginia Woolf is content to leave unexplored and un-challenged those "unknown reasons" for the chastity fetish. But it is here that the problem begins. According to one of Freud's most widely accepted theories, the communal life of mankind had a twofold foundation: "the compulsion to work, which was created by external necessity, and the power of love, which made the man unwilling to be de-prived of his sexual object—the woman—, and made the woman unwilling to be deprived of the part of herself which had been separated off from her—her child." [5] This is a description of only one way of reconciling erotic drives with the "reality principle." It is the mode characteristic of the stage we may, with Freud, call "civilization," only as long as that term has descriptive rather than normative value. For our ancestors experienced a number of social forms before the establishment of the monogamous family, with its insistence on female chastity. In fact, the earliest communities might not have survived if our forebears had, as Freud suggests, so conflated the experiences of loving and owning as to desire exclusive rights over the "object" of love. "Mutual toleration among the adult males, free-dom from jealousy, was . . . the first condition for the building of those large and enduring groups in the midst of which alone the transition from animal to man could be achieved." [6]

Only when property began to be individually owned

and subject to inheritance was the assignment of children
to particular parents a necessity. As long as the value of
the mother's work entitled her to participate in such ownership, it was necessary to be certain who was a child's
father in order to assure its rights of inheritance. But since
the division of labor made the home the woman's sphere,
while the realm that produced the wealth was the man's
even if she worked in it too, wealth had to descend along
the male line. Thus, Engels maintains that the overthrow
of "mother-right," or inheritance via the female line, was
"the world-historic defeat of the female sex" and the origin
of male supremacy. "Monogamy arose out of the concentration of considerable wealth in the hands of one person—
and that a man—and out of the desire to bequeath . . . [his]
wealth to this man's children and to no one else's. For this
purpose, monogamy was essential on the woman's part, but
not on the man's." [7] It is not difficult to see from this how
the same principle came to be applied to premarital chastity and how female virginity was reified into a commodity.
Virginia Woolf herself accepts the whole sex-family-prop-
erty relation when she speaks of the material deserts of the
gentleman to whom the first "letter" in *Three Guineas* is
addressed and defines his prosperity as consisting in "wife,
children, house." [8]

It was in the Victorian period, when the Woman Question went public, that the contradictions in the female
condition were mostly explicitly identified with both class
and property. The dual functions of physical pleasure and
material security were separated and assigned to different
women. Frigidity in one's wife, interpreted as assurance of
fidelity, was the safeguard of respectability, while seduction (or rape) of a lower-class girl provided the double en-
joyments of sensuality and ownership.[9] Sexual availability
and the concomitant capacity to enjoy it were hallmarks of
lower-class women. This attitude is carried to an extreme
and reduced to unconscious absurdity in the later novels

of Henry James, where the unchaste woman is not a wanton servant girl but a society woman whose poverty is quite relative, noticeable only in the rarefied circles in which she moves. For such women as Kate Croy or Charlotte Stant, their comparative poverty "not only accompanies sexuality, but appears to cause it." [10] Edith Wharton's *House of Mirth* makes this implicit causality more credible. Lily Bart has been forced by her dependent status to use sexual potential as a means of social advancement. But the increasingly compromising situations in which she is entangled are actually the result of her financial need and only superficially of the flirtations that are its symptom. Even where this link between poverty and unsanctioned sexual behavior is not so direct, some man's assumption of the *droit du seigneur* creates a classic situation in the English novel from *Pamela* and *Fanny Hill* on.

Now by 1928, it was no longer possible to objectify a "nice fresh servant" as completely as does the Victorian author of *My Secret Life* when he describes the class as "ready, yielding, hot-arsed, lewd, and lubricious." Nor was it possible to make corollary generalizations about the virtue and unresponsiveness of "ladies." But more than a trace of the attitude remains in Virginia Woolf, as she discusses the widening opportunity for a young woman novelist to observe and describe "the courtesan, the harlot, and the lady with the pug dog." A female writer, she acknowledges, is better fitted than any man to portray these women, but even with the best will in the world, we are not yet ready for her to do so. For some time to come, the writer "will still be encumbered with that self-consciousness in the presence of 'sin' which is the legacy of our sexual barbarity. She will still bear the shoddy old fetters of *class* on her feet." [11] The italics are mine, but it is Woolf who takes it for granted that the difference between a woman who is sexually selective and one who is not is a matter of class.

Well, there, you might say, is one substantive change wrought by the Sexual Revolution—a social pattern so radically altered as to justify leaving off the inverted commas around the word revolution. At first glance, this is certainly true. It is no longer possible to use considerations of class status to draw any conclusions about a particular woman's capacity for sexual enjoyment or the likelihood of her indulging it. In another sense, though, chastity remains as much of a class *determinant* among women today as it ever was. I first realized this by considering a rather bizarre but entirely apt model. A friend (male and black) was describing how, as an isolated civil rights worker confined in a Southern jail, he did serious political work among his fellow prisoners. The focus of his story was the interest he was able to arouse among men whose initial attitude toward him was overtly hostile. As he spoke, I recalled similar stories about prisons that became schools of political action—in Ireland, in Algeria, and increasingly, in our own country. I began romanticizing my own future as a politically aware convict. As I write, I am awaiting trial for two political crimes that could earn me fifteen months behind bars.[12] For a brief moment, I rather relished the image of myself at the House of Detention, helping to define the inmates' awareness of our oppressed condition and focus my sisters' anger. But almost before I began, I felt there were barriers to a sense of sisterhood, barriers that gave the word itself an unfamiliar flavor that even "brotherhood" does not have.

I tried to analyze the obstacles that might prevent me from sharing a basis of trust with other imprisoned women —most of them prostitutes. There is a difference, and it is based ultimately on sexual behavior. My "respectability," or their probable reaction to it, is the only seemingly insuperable barrier. At best, I would benefit from a kindness that says, "You're a 'nice' girl; you don't belong here." At worst, I would be playing a missionary's role and would deserve a missionary's martyrdom. But what really creates this frontier that women themselves police? Education, of course, and my being a teacher. But I am also a working-class New Yorker, and this comes through more clearly than superficial acquisitions of accent and manner. My "idealism" might get in the way, too, since I'd be in jail for what might look like an esoteric *and freely chosen* offense. But I did not opt to be an activist any more than a prostitute has selected her profession. Objective conditions —the same objective conditions—determined both our "choices." Our common situation as women and our shared circumstances would, in the long run, provide grounds for unity that are more persuasive than any divisions among us. But it is interesting that I had even a momentary hesitation and that the word "sister" retains an uneasy ring. The mystification surrounding our sex is so compelling that a woman who is convicted of a "crime" and imprisoned is far more degraded than a man in the same position. It is this same mystique that made me think that the apparent gap between me and my sister inmates would be created by my "respectability," a quality that is defined by the Man, but that women are all too ready to enforce.

My own chastity is at best a relative matter, consisting principally in the exercise of a veto power. What makes the difference—and would continue to do so in a place where no man appeared for weeks on end—is how men treat me, as contrasted with how they treat prostitutes. Or how one *would* treat us if he were present. My self-respect does not depend on some notion of my fancied superiority to other women, but it does to some extent depend on being respected by others. And of course the way others treat you derives in large measure from your own expectations. Mother always said that girls who cheapened themselves (the revealing idiom of the tribe!) lost all self-respect. And so they do—if not in the way she meant it.

Virginia Woolf, musing on the female condition, says,

"I thought how unpleasant it is to be locked out; and I thought how it is worse perhaps to be locked in." My little fantasy about prison life makes her metaphor rather uncomfortably concrete, but still true to the double imprisonment resulting from actual incarceration and from the social condition of women. We are supposed not to like—or to trust—each other, and the basis for our antipathy is our purportedly permanent competition for a mate. The greatest mutual suspicion exists, however, among women with different life-styles, where life-style is a matter of sexual behavior. It has usually been women who maintained the distinctions and created the bitterness, but never we who ordained the system. A couple of generations back, I would have been relegated to the class of whores and excluded from the company of suburban housewives. Now I have a greater latitude—men have made it possible for me to be unchaste and remain in the category of "good women." But although membership has shifted, the classes themselves remain, and my "freedom" does nothing for the women still excluded by male fiat from the ranks of the "respectable."

As I reread what I have written, I realize that I have been playing with the connotations of "class" and "caste." It would be more exact, though clumsier, to say that sexual behavior both constitutes and reflects the material conditions that underlie a class analysis. Certainly, unexamined use of the concepts of caste and class does not much illuminate what remains a vexed question among women attempting to define our situation. Yet it is important to consider how these terms do help describe it.

When Virginia Woolf says that class makes the world of sexual "sin" unfamiliar to her, she is literally correct in that her economic status protects her from having to earn her living as a prostitute. But her class identification is precarious and, as an attribute acquired by association, it differs from the usual factors through which economic relations determine class. In *Three Guineas,* she speaks about the shared "background" that would appear to place her in the same class as her male interlocutor. But there is a gap between them that she at first perceives as a difference in privilege, signaled by her having to use an awkward formula to describe herself. "Our ideology is still so inveterately anthropocentric [*sic*] that it has been necessary to coin this clumsy term—educated man's daughter—to describe the class whose fathers have been educated at public schools and universities. Obviously, if the term 'bourgeois' fits her brother, it is grossly incorrect to use it of one who differs so profoundly in the two prime characteristics of the bourgeoisie—capital and environment." [13]

For this reason, one tendency among present-day feminists is simply to make class coextensive with sex. Theoretical justification for this position is sought in such observations as Engels's that "the first division of labour is that between man and woman for child breeding . . . I can add: The first class antagonism which appears in history coincides with the development of the antagonism between man and woman in monogamous marriage, and the first class oppression with that of the female sex by the male." [14] But coincidence is not identity; it is because the institution of slavery appeared simultaneously with the monogamous family and in response to the same economic conditions that the relation can be made. At least by analogy, a class description can be applied to the family, in which, because of their respective relations to production, the husband is the bourgeois whereas his wife represents the proletariat.[15] To rely on this, however, is once more to elevate metaphor to the status of argument.

At one point, Virginia Woolf goes so far as to address the educated male as a member of an opposed class: "Your class possesses in its own right and not through marriage practically all the capital, all the land, all the valuables, and all the patronage in England. Our class possesses in its own right and not through marriage practically none of the capital, none of the land, none of the valuables, and none of the patronage in England." [16] This comes closer to a materialist definition of class than many that depend on citations of Marxist texts, for it recognizes control of the means of production as the basis of oppressive power. A Radical Feminist position correctly defines all women as oppressed, but does not take into account that, while those few who own the wealth are men, most men do not control any of it. In material terms, it is insufficient merely to allege that all men benefit from a system of male supremacy, and if we are not to use materialist standards, why bring in a term like "class" at all?

The question of caste arises when we admit that women do acquire a class affiliation from their fathers or husbands and that it is functional. This "secondary" affiliation shapes our lives to the extent that Virginia Woolf could, after all, afford to be a writer and not a streetwalker. When Lenin speaks of "women . . . worn out in petty, monotonous household work, their strength and time dissipated and wasted, their minds growing narrow and stale, their hearts beating slowly, their will weakened," he specifically exempts the pampered ladies of the bourgeoisie "who shove onto servants the responsibility for all household work, including the care of children." [17] Yet his description of the psychological effects of women's work is closely echoed in Virginia Woolf's description of the lives of bourgeois women deprived of the privileges of "their" class. As for the exercise of power, she believes that "the daughters of educated men" are at a real disadvantage. "Not only are we incomparably weaker than the men of our own class; we are weaker than the women of the working class. If the working women of the country were to say: 'If you go to war, we will refuse to make munitions or to help in the production of goods,' the difficulty of war-making would be seriously increased." But economic conditions deprive working women of the freedom to exercise this imputed power. The two positions quoted reflect a real antagonism, one that divides women through misapprehension about the meaning of a class situation.

Similarly, many American women today who are themselves educated and who, by paternity or marriage, are "middle-class," hold jobs and receive salaries that are definitely "working-class." Their primary identification is with their acquired status, even when they perceive the frustrating contradiction they are acting out and when they suffer its cultural and material consequences. Among working women, a similar tendency creates an artificial "class" barrier between clerical employees and those who do factory or domestic work. On a level that is personal as well as economic, there is mutual envy and suspicion between women who are "free" to be exploited on a job and those who are "free" to stay home and be exploited there. Of course, when we make use of such notions as status and group identification, we are defining class in sociological terms. In an orthodox Marxist analysis, these factors simply contribute to false consciousness; class is determined by the individual's relations to the means of production. But because a woman's relation to social production is often at one remove, we must consider very carefully what other elements constitute the *material* basis of women's lives.

It is in this sense that forms of sexual behavior create material barriers best understood as class-based. Engels claims that "among women, prostitution degrades only those unfortunates who fall into its clutches; and even these are not degraded to the degree that is generally believed. On the other hand, it degrades the character of the entire male world." [18] On the moral plane, Engels is right, but the transformation into social norm of the economics underlying monogamy has a far more degrading and divisive effect among women. This conflict has a class nature and, as the most cursory glance at "our" literature reveals, is one of the most enduring divisions among women. However, I have sisters who are prostitutes; no man who buys a woman is my brother.

Lenin himself perceived the ways in which all women share a common condition: "We hate, yes hate everything, and will abolish everything which tortures and oppresses the woman worker, the housewife, the peasant woman, the wife of the petty trader, yes, and in many cases the women of the possessing classes." [19] An unexamined "class" division among women becomes like any artificial contradiction imposed upon members of a subject group so that they cannot see that their true interests are identical. Black and white workers, male and female workers, in this country have been so divided as, traditionally, were white workers of different ethnic backgrounds. Withdrawing sexuality from the realm of material considerations and accepting it on its own terms is the only way we can liberate ourselves from destructive isolation. And it is the only way the whole race can begin to realize its full erotic possibilities.

But what does that mean, "sexuality on its own terms"? The erotic dimension of freedom leads to consideration of the other side of the coin, the new morality that is supposed to have liberated me and that has at least allowed me to indulge myself sexually and retain my social standing. What the Sexual Revolution has actually done is to establish a new bartering system, on the premise that one kind of freedom can only be won at the sacrifice of another; fulfillment "as a woman" (orgasm, childbearing, motherhood) is made to substitute for, and is seen as qualitatively different from, fulfillment as a person. The new rules owe a great deal, of course, to Freudian theories and prejudices. Freud attributes the fundamental female conflict to the "momentous discovery which little girls are destined to make," recognition of their own natural inferiority to males because of their lack of a penis. As a

Wellesley undergraduate resignedly observed to one of my students, "That's the way life is. Men have castration complexes and girls have penis envy." [20] Psychic difficulties arise as a result of the two-phase sexual life that women lead, because, as they mature, their focus is supposed to move from the clitoris (a truncated "masculine" organ) to the vagina; the first phase thus "has a masculine character, while only the second is specifically feminine." [21] Two different kinds of orgasms are allegedly experienced in the two zones: clitoral orgasm is immature, reflecting adherence to one's innate masculine qualities, the masculinity complex, and the undeveloped male organ; vaginal orgasm is the reflection of mature femininity. According to Marie Bonaparte, intellectual rejection of this two-orgasm descriptive model is also symptomatic of that pathetic "claimant" (of male privilege), the "clitoridal" woman.[22] They do get us coming and going!

Freud does not, as far as I know, explicitly recommend that women interpret acceptance of femininity as acceptance of a passive *social* role, but he condemns all female efforts to formulate another role. I say "condemns" advisedly, because his strictures do not stop with merely stigmatizing certain behavior as reflecting the castration complex, but develop into normative statements. Thus he says, "behind the envy for the penis, there comes to light the woman's hostile bitterness against the man, which never completely disappears in the relations between the sexes, and which is clearly indicated in the strivings and in the literary productions of 'emancipated' women." [23] (Freud's setting off of "emancipated" is rather like the promiscuous know-nothing use of "so-called" but in this case it is ironically apt; there is indeed no such thing as an emancipated woman.) It does occur to Freud that males also are convinced of the superiority of having a penis and that the oppression of women has something to do with male fear of castration, but he quickly dismisses the idea.

Similarly, he does not consider the ways in which culture reinforces the woman's initial sense of being permanently without something very important. Freud apparently cannot credit that any of the freedoms and privileges of human (that is, masculine) life have intrinsic as well as symbolic value. A little girl may want to be a boy because it seems to her that boys and men have better lives than girls and women; even if it were the castration complex, theirs or ours, that has given the male his dominant role, it could also follow that to someone who envies that role, possession of a penis is symbolic of *it* and not vice versa. In any event, we are "bitter" and again our bitterness has no content; it is only the continuation of our first reaction to not having a penis. (This is as if the authors of *The Mark of Oppression,* a classic psychiatric study of the American Negro, were to conclude their case histories with the remark, "Yup, them nigras sure are bitter against whites—and the worst are the ones who have been striving for social equality." A norm for black people's behavior deriving from this would be for them to relax and accept not only their blackness but all the social conditions it currently implies.)

The most distressing thing about the Freudian attitude is that it disarms criticism by asserting that female attempts to take issue with the theory are merely further demonstrations of the castration complex. Freud anticipates arguments in favor of the male masculinity complex from women analysts and their male colleagues with feminist views, but says that it is "quite natural that the female sex should refuse to accept a view which appears to contradict their eagerly coveted equality with men." Worse yet, the utilization of one's mind to dispute Freud's arguments shows "masculine" aggressiveness and competitiveness. Again, arguments have no content, only form. And "the use of psychoanalysis as a weapon of controversy can clearly lead to no decision." [24] In short, don't show *him* any evidence—particularly if you're a woman and can't be "objective" about the implications of the penis envy theory.

Freudians are thus quick to see the castration complex in female "literary productions" with a positive thrust of any sort; they shake their heads like Virginia Woolf watching the Manx cat and marvel that "it is strange what a difference a tail makes." [25] A woman I know mentioned Carolyn Heilbrun's perceptive *New York Times* review of Mary Ellmann's *Thinking About Women* to her analyst; in it, the reviewer alludes to Freud's responsibility for our present predicament. "She is obviously," snapped the doctor, "a typical neurotic spinster with a castration complex." Since Freud also "freed" us from some of our guilt about sexuality, a new norm of the fulfilled woman appears, such that one can "see" not only penis envy in some women's intellectual efforts but also perhaps frigidity, homosexuality, or virginal frustration. The fact of one's writing in a critical way is often "proof" enough—if one's sex life were all right, one wouldn't need to do so. An extreme (but not isolated) case of this attitude is reflected in a female listener's letter to a radio film-reviewer. Addressing her as "Miss," which she clearly considers an insult in itself, the listener remarks, "I assume you aren't married—one loses that nasty, sharp bite in one's voice when one learns to care about others." Altruism is obviously the result of a satisfactory sex life. "Mrs. John Doe and her sisters who write to me," says the broadcaster,

> seem to interpret Freud to mean that intelligence, like a penis, is a male attribute. The true woman is supposed to be sweet and passive—she shouldn't argue or emphasize an opinion or get excited about a judgment. Sex—or at least regulated marital sex—is supposed to act as a tranquilizer. . . . [In this sense, popular Freudianism goes] beyond Victorianism in its placid assumption that a woman who uses her mind is trying to compete with men. It was bad enough for women who had brains to be

considered freaks like talking dogs; now it's leeringly assumed that they're trying to grow a penis—which any man will tell you is an accomplishment that puts canine conversation in the shadows.[26]

So we are freer to enjoy sexuality but jeopardize our capacity for enjoyment if we try to do anything else as well. Which may explain why the Sexual Revolution is not only a failure but is neither essentially sexual nor a revolution.

In this regard, even considerations of what "free" sexuality might be like reflect a kind of blind spot where women are concerned that makes their projections rather hard to visualize. Herbert Marcuse, for instance, speaks of such freedom as involving "not simply a release but a *transformation* of the libido: from sexuality constrained under genital supremacy to eroticization of the entire personality. . . . The free development of transformed libido within transformed institutions, while eroticizing previously tabooed zones, times, and relations, would *minimize* the manifestations of *mere* sexuality by integrating it into a far larger order, including the order of work." [27]

I fail to see how the social oppression of women can be made consistent with *anyone's* discovery of the liberated Eros in a nonrepressive society, but so it must remain as long as meaningful work for women is interpreted simply as "competition" rather than unalienated production. Marcuse's study ignores this question, which could lead to the comfortable conclusion that when he speaks of a new mode of being for humanity he means all of us. A volume, however, that is subtitled "A Philosophical Inquiry into Freud" must not remain silent if its author rejects one of the good doctor's principal assumptions. As it is, I am uncertain whether I am allowed to imagine myself as part of that potentially free humanity about which Marcuse is so eloquent. Marcuse foresees the release of homoerotic as well as heterosexual feelings, without mentioning women's place at all, or, on the other hand, giving us the sense that we are so completely and necessarily involved in his new structures that it would be superfluous to speak of us separately or specifically.[28] (Virginia Woolf found Woman almost entirely absent from the pages of history and thus felt bewildered as she read. I often fail to recognize myself in psychological or philosophical works in which Woman appears, yet when she is not present at all I sometimes feel like a tactless intruder.)

Freud himself, while encouraging women to live a fully mature (that is, vaginal) sex life, would question our fitness for the broader range of experiences Marcuse postulates, not only because we should eschew self-assertive competition but also because we cannot maintain a moral standard established by and for men. We in the West have a long (though by no means unchallenged) history of maintaining that women have souls and thus have the same degree of final responsibility as men. Our culture has an ambiguous tradition with regard to the relative corruptibility of each sex, and makes some allowances for weakness, but does not apply a double standard to ethical expectations. Freud, however, suggests that "for women the level of what is ethically normal is different from what it is in men." His reasoning is that in boys the Oedipus complex is destroyed by the castration complex, whereas in girls it is preceded and caused by the castration complex. This means that girls lack incentive to destroy the Oedipus complex, with devastating results:

> Their super-ego is never so inexorable, so impersonal, so independent of its emotional origins as we find it in men. Character traits which critics of every epoch have brought up against women—that they show less sense of justice than men, that they are less ready to submit to the great exigencies of life, that they are more often influenced in their judgments by the feelings of affection or hostility— all these would be amply accounted for by the modification in the formation of the super-ego which we have inferred above. We must not allow ourselves to be deflected

from such conclusions by the denials of the feminists, who are anxious to force us to regard the two sexes as completely equal in position and worth; but we shall, of course, willingly agree that the majority of men are also far behind the masculine ideal and that all human individuals, as a result of their bisexual disposition and of cross-inheritance, combine in themselves both masculine and feminine characteristics, so that pure masculinity and femininity remain theoretical constructions of uncertain content.[29]

Here again, as in the case of possible feminist disagreement with his analysis of penis envy, Freud puts into operation a kind of psychic Uncertainty Principle intended to discredit objections. His logic reminds me of the old Jewish joke about the two neighbors who go to court over a broken vase, which ends with the defendant's lawyer trying to prove conclusively "that Schwartz never borrowed from Weiss the vase, that it was cracked when Weiss lent it to him, and anyway he returned it in perfect condition." [30] For if we point out that many women are no more unjust or emotional than many men, a Freudian can always fall back on the master's notion of human bisexuality. The important thing to remember is that the weaker side, the one functioning on the lower ethical level, is the feminine one, so that a woman's strengths come from the masculine admixture in her personality, while a man's flaws are from the presence of feminine traits in his.

In this instance, too, Freud ignores the effects of cultural expectations on character. The weakness and emotionalism of women is encouraged—sometimes we are even taught to use it as a weapon—whereas that of men is suppressed. We are taught to have different ideas about what constitute the great exigencies of life and to respond accordingly. Intuitive judgment is regarded as our natural substitute for reason, and we are brought up to rely on it.

Although I have cited his writings so often, Freud himself is not the culprit we are up against. His ideas are simultaneously a product or symptom of a cultural evil and a force to justify and perpetuate it. But he and his followers have offered women immense and fraudulent sexual rewards for embracing and (womanlike) rearranging all the dollhouse furniture on which Nora Helmer slammed that door.[31]

II

Which brings us back at last to literature. Freud takes it as evidence of his theories that women have been assigned certain traits "in every epoch." We know this, of course, from what men have written about women. And the whole point of *A Room of One's Own* is, after all, that for most of that time women had no literary voice of their own. We do not know how they lived, let alone what they would have considered their own dominant characteristics and those of their men. Even in our own time, a serious female writer delineating a masculine failing is likely to be accused of almost everything but attempting to speak the truth. Woolf mentions her astonishment "when Z, most humane, most modest of men, taking up some book by Rebecca West and reading a passage in it, exclaimed, 'The arrant feminist! She says that men are snobs!'" They are not ready to listen to us, but how often, since finding our tongues, have we had something significant to say about men?

English literature, in the engaging person of Virginia Woolf's Orlando, turned female sometime in the eighteenth century, when the novel became a potent literary force. For the purpose of speaking about a room of one's own is precisely that women writers, confined for both subject matter and a work-space to the common family sitting room, chose the novel as the most appropriate literary medium. And the novel has consistently attracted a wider female audience than any other genre. Our greatest nineteenth-century novelists, Jane Austen and the Brontës, bring women characters to a kind of prominence different from any they previously enjoyed. They have almost nothing to say about men, however—flattering or deprecating—because the male as such was almost an unknown quantity to them. (I say "as such" because they obviously were aware of certain types that exist in the ranks of both sexes.) Mr. Darcy, Mr. Rochester, and Heathcliff—the ones who spring most readily to mind—all represent similar solutions to the problem of depicting a hero. If he is defined a priori as "remote," it is already attractive to the romantic mind, and it becomes unnecessary to put him into quite as many situations that would reveal his creator's ignorance about him. If this sounds flippant, it nonetheless makes more sense than dismissing all such figures as a maiden lady's Byronic masturbation fantasies.

Consider, too, these authors' other male figures. Edgar Linton and St. John Rivers are halfhearted constructions, not merely in contrast to the brooding heroes of the books in which they appear, but also because it is impossible to see around the particular literary functions they serve to a range of human qualities. They are quite as inscrutable as their dark, brooding rivals, but embarrassingly inadequate without the cloak of mystery the others wear. The men good enough for most Jane Austen heroines to marry are similarly undistinguished, especially when measured against the women they eventually win. Her male figures, whether good or bad, are caricatures, what an earlier age would have called humor-characters. Two exceptions, one in each category, are Henry Crawford and Henry Tilney. Crawford is the most interesting man in Jane Austen, but he is also unbalanced, inconsistent, poorly motivated, and hard to believe in. As for Tilney, he is not a fully developed character, but I think his is one portrait the novelist could fill in from her own experience. Although I can't prove it, I suspect that the hero of this novel in which three important brother-sister pairs occur was modeled on the author's own brothers.[32]

I have separated George Eliot from the other three "famous names" with whom Woolf classes her. I did so in part because I could not make the same generalization about her experience of men. More important, I think her male characters should be considered with those of later women novelists. It seems to me that writers as different from each other as George Eliot, Edith Wharton, Doris Lessing, Mary McCarthy, and Virginia Woolf herself succeed with two principal types of men, the womanish and the weak. (And I do not mean to identify these two qualities.) In general, if one had to form a conception of man from his appearances in women's writings, he would turn out a spineless creature, one who needs mothering and whose weakness is yet more sadistic than overt strength. It is the element of sadomasochism, in fact, that puts relationships these women depict in quite another tradition from the Erring-Male-Set-Straight-by-Good-Woman myth that recurs from Dante through Louisa May Alcott to Johnny Cash. This cruel, weak man, whom every woman recognizes as a genuine and familiar type, does not appear in the novels of male authors until quite recently and then as an antihero. Even so, he is treated from a masculine point of view, and we are shown his sufferings rather than what he does to others.

Women novelists not only introduced this man into our literature but have been almost obsessed with him. I can only speculate about some of the reasons for this preoccupation. As I have said, the type is not invented, but readily recognizable. Is it possible that such men are especially attracted and appealing to women who are free enough of their socialization to become writers at all? The parasitic dominance of Doris Lessing's men, for example, could not be fruitfully exercised over a woman who was *not* gifted and "independent." The woman novelist may,

because of those very characteristics that make her a novelist, have even more (extraliterary) experience of this man
than the rest of us. Furthermore, being able to put him in
a book gives her more definitive control over the situation
than she is likely to have in life. Literary treatment of such
a character is also a form of protest against a tradition that
prepared one for almost anything else in a lover but this
preponderant type. I don't mean to imply that a woman's
creation of literature is an aberration whose symptoms may
be deduced from consideration of particular works; the
corollary to such a clinical approach is to discard the
specific work once we have determined the "ailment" it
points to. What I do think is important is that, as Simone
de Beauvoir expresses it, even our greatest women writers
"in men . . . comprehend hardly more than the male."
That is, they are reacting to their experience, and their
reactions have a common imbalance. In this sense, it is
worthwhile for the reader who wishes to know what to
make of a widespread male character-type to inquire about
its real and fictional antecedents. Such inquiry may also
help explain why female novelists have failed to direct
their attention to the full range of masculine possibilities.

But what of women in fiction? Have novelists of their
own sex added to the range of types or the dimensions of
personality presented by men? An answer requires first of
all a glance at male writers' portrayal of women. Virginia
Woolf says that between the reader and a female character
an obtrusive figure always blocks the view, the figure of
the masculine "I." Women do dominate the scene, however, in the writings of some men; the problem is how
they do so, whether the author, in showing us what goes
on in his heroine's mind, is showing us anything like the
mind of an actual human female. As I look for examples
to help answer this question, I am amazed at how many
writers have chosen to evade it by externalizing the psychological situation, using "objective" images that convey

the pattern or content of a woman's thought without actually entering into it. The experiences of Emma Bovary and Anna Karenina, to name two eminently successful literary creations, are realized for us in this way.

In the fiction of Henry James, women are more delicately calibrated instruments for the reception of impressions than men—more so, at least, than any man who is represented as being an active *and sexually potent* participant in events. His women's special sensitivity is reflected in an awareness of social or moral nuances so fine as to be unobserved (in fact, unimagined) by the average person. Although I cannot quite imagine James saying, "Isabel Archer—*c'est moi,*" he does give the impression of strong identification with some of the women he writes about. We so readily see the author himself as the archetypal asexual Jamesian observer that there is a tendency to say that he "doesn't count." But however little he may have counted as a man, he had never had the sexual or psychic experience of being a woman; there is no reason why someone of James's temperament should find it easier than other men to imagine what it would be like to be female in a given situation. (Indeed, the only comparison that can be made along this line is a negative one with the self-consciously masculine novelist who is so uneasy about his virility that he feels it threatened by even attempting such an identification.) Despite the acuteness of James's observations, he does not give his women a wider scope than those who are less perceptive about female psychology. They are still principally shown, as Virginia Woolf claimed most female characters are, in their relations with men.

The question of the author's identification with his character suggests the peculiar problem of point of view. Very few first-person narratives are related by a character whose sex is not the same as the author's. The necessity, in such a case, of delving into a mind of such different configuration from one's own, and of having fewer ways of masking one's ignorance about it, has kept most writers from making the attempt. Almost all the instances I can think of are, for one reason or another, rather special cases. There are the epistolary novels of the eighteenth century, some of which involve the author in psychologizing. Although the novelist does have to adopt the persona of a woman, the letter form still provides some measure of protection, for the most prolix letter writer is holding something back, presenting herself as a character. Moreover, the role assigned such young women as Pamela and Clarissa is not simply exaggerated; it is mythic. A diametrically opposite archetype is embodied in such figures as Fanny Hill (whose narrative is still nominally epistolary) and Moll Flanders. These characters serve their purpose by being women as men wish them to be, not guides to the feminine psyche. To my mind, keener psychological penetration is demonstrated in the letters from women in *Les Liaisons dangereuses*, for these characters—however distinctly "typed" they are—do have as much independence and vigor as the men whose epistles alternate with theirs. The alternating male-female point of view, even when less ambitious, is rarely this successful. Mark Twain's "Diary of Adam and Eve," whose whole point is to demonstrate something about comparative psychology, is an embarrassing failure constructed of platitudes veneered with wit and culminating in a genteel, domestic truism. Another case, Cesare Pavese's *Among Women Only*, succeeds precisely because the female narrator does not pretend to reveal anything about psychology but rather to make a point through the flat recital of events. The tone of the novel is deliberately colorless, and the dominant mood of its characters is alienation. As long as alienation is his subject, it is no *more* ambitious for Pavese to assume the voice of Clelia than, say, for Camus to assume that of Meursault. Another problem is that of the female in a stream-of-consciousness narrative as practiced by Faulkner or Joyce, but here again the identification is incomplete and the narrator, far from being individuated by the author's use of her point of view, is actually *generalized,* mythologized.

Much masculine investigation of women's minds is of this formulaic sort. Speaking as a psychoanalyst, Theodor Reik says, "Why do we men not understand women even though they give us so much material by which to know them? We see them, we hear them, we even smell them, but all this is not enough because we can never be women. We always conclude that women understand men, but men don't understand women. It is one-way traffic." [33] But the heart of Virginia Woolf's objection to male domination of literature is not that female psychology is never explored but rather that so much experience is omitted, women being present in books almost exclusively as the lovers of men. She is delighted to find in a young woman's first novel the typical line "Chloe liked Olivia," because it opens up a whole new realm of literary possibility. Friendship, particularly of the special sort shared by those who work together, is a relationship entirely neglected by men writing about women. It is only partly male ignorance of women's self-contained culture that is responsible for this neglect. More often, it is cultural bias about women's relations with one another: we "don't like" each other and we don't, of course, have work of the kind that provides meaningful experience with one's colleagues. (For some reason, men do not regard women at the village well or the city laundromat as colleagues who share a job.) The typical male assumption is embodied in the remark that arouses Reik's professional chuckle: "She is an exceptional woman. She is beautiful and warm. Even women like her in spite of her qualities." Another of Reik's patients says, "I would like to meet a young woman who is not an exception. Most women I know say they are not like other women, they are exceptions. I would like to know a young

woman who says she thinks and feels just as women do."
But despite the irritation that certain women provoke in
us, I suspect our constant competition is more legend than
fact. The goal that Virginia Woolf ironically articulates,
"the development by the average woman of a prose style
completely expressive of her mind," is not calculated to
place the woman writer in an elite position with respect to
the rest of her sex—nor yet to make a freak of her. Self-
hatred does work to give some women desperate confidence in their uniqueness; but for each one who speaks of
herself as an exception, there are many of us who are
outraged when men tell us how free we are of the stereotyped sins of our sex. (It never occurs to them to alter the
stereotype, and they cannot understand why we are not
flattered by being exempted from it.)

It seems to me that, despite Chloe and Olivia, Virginia
Woolf was premature in her belief that women were now
truly able to expand their literary horizons. She speaks of
being free to explore new subjects, almost free from bitterness about the female role or about men. "She wrote as a
woman," says Woolf of her composite young novelist,
"but as a woman who has forgotten that she is a woman, so
that her pages were full of that curious sexual quality
which comes only when sex is unconscious of itself." The
typical novel of which Virginia Woolf speaks is meaningfully entitled *Life's Adventure,* but in inventing it she
spoke too soon. Literature follows history at least as much
as it shapes it, and the predicament of women has not
allowed us to forget our sex or even to write without
awareness of the Woman Question. The women of whom
we write are still struggling to define themselves *as* women;
life's other adventures are inevitably encompassed in this
experience. Not to write about it would be a betrayal of
our condition.

For a woman to write about a female character's search
for herself does not necessarily mean that she is concerned

with social problems or with feminist ideas. Our modern novelists have been less interested in public conditions and limitations than with their personal effects. In fact, as Simone de Beauvoir observes, women writers "do not contest the human situation because they have hardly begun to assume it." [34] Self-definition, for a woman, still means self-definition in relation to men. Thus, authors of their own sex have limited fictional women almost as narrowly as have men to their role as the lovers of men.

Doris Lessing has expressed her dismay that *The Golden Notebook* is read as a novel about sexual relations or even as a feminist work. She apparently intended it to reflect an entire epoch in intellectual history. But to depict such an epoch through the experiences of a woman is, because of the nature of our society, to give it the coloring of sexuality. To entitle one segment of the novel "Free Women," however ironic the term, and to view relations between the sexes so candidly, is merely to reinforce this interpretation. Or perhaps the "personalism" (Beauvoir calls it narcissism) drilled into the behavior of women is such that "the woman writer will still be speaking of herself even when she is speaking about general topics."

The novels of Colette show a more realistic appreciation of the way that sexuality is always dominant in female identity. Colette's women are not restricted to a single age or type and their decisions are often concerned with an entire life-pattern. But sexuality is always at the heart of the story, whether the subject is adolescence, loneliness, Lesbianism, or sympathy with nature. When Annie in her admittedly slight novel *Claudine s'en va* determines to leave her husband, the reflection of what is in her mind and what she will become is far more vivid than when Ibsen's Nora walks out or James's Isabel decides to stay. And in a more fully realized work like *The Vagabond*, Colette's examination of the meaning to a woman of isolation, work, jealousy, independence, and revived love is both passionate and remorseless. Yet in *Break of Day* the writer herself suggests another, more paradoxical reason for preoccupation with sexual relationships:

> At no time has the catastrophe of love, in all its phases and consequences, formed a part of the true intimate life of a woman. Why do men—writers or so-called writers— still show surprise that a woman should so easily reveal to the public love-secrets and amorous lies and half-truths? By divulging these, she manages to hide other important and obscure secrets which she herself does not understand very well. The spotlight, the shameless eye which she obligingly operates, always explores the same sector of a woman's life. . . . But it is not in the illuminated zone that the darkest plots are woven. . . .

We are so accustomed to *defining* women as enclosed space that the desperate need for privacy, for that room of one's own, is articulated only rarely. The woman writer, says Virginia Woolf, has her scope limited to a cramped but always public territory. Colette adds that within that territory she exhibits what appear to be secrets so as to preserve the real secret. The lives of women are so public that many feel they have no secrets to protect, aside from the false "feminine mystery" that puts us outside the bounds of *human* psychology. Colette seems almost to be making coy reference to that kind of mystery, when actually she is speaking of a much more profound need to pull back and try to establish an independent self. A powerful paradigm of this urge occurs in *Among Women Only,* where everyone crowds into a single (female) life and feeds on it. Brought up where there is no spatial or moral privacy for women, the young Rosetta has to rent a room in an elegant hotel in order to attempt suicide.

The question of how much is revealed appears at first to be a matter of "characterization," since so often the woman writer's only subject is herself. Simone de Beauvoir maintains that most women who write do so in order to charm, and that the selective self-revelation of women's literature is analogous to stripping oneself naked as a form of passive seduction. Women writers "suppose that . . . it is sufficient for expression, communication, to show what one is." The complaint most commonly leveled against women's fiction is that it takes a narcissistic view of private life and thus concentrates on "boring" details of clothing, person, and surroundings. Yet even if the superficial aspects of domestic-sexual life were the sole subject of women writers, their contribution to literature would be a leavening realism. Virginia Woolf lists the great heroines of Western literature with their monumental scale and moral extremes, remarking on the disparity between their larger-than-life fictional quality and the oppressed existence of actual contemporary females. "A very queer, composite being thus emerges. Imaginatively . . . [woman] is of the highest importance; practically she is completely insignificant." The possible reasons for this anomaly are not as interesting to me as the question of whether it is as great as we think. For, however overwhelming the stature of the Clytemnestras and Lady Macbeths, a good case can be made for their inability to initiate a whole action. They do not act, but, like women writers, they react. Less heroically polarized ladies of bourgeois fiction, when the novelist is herself a woman, are freer to act. In this sense, their autonomy is much greater, although the scope of their actions is more limited. Female characters, as well as female authors, come into their own in the novel.

I discussed earlier some positive reasons for women writers' apparent restriction to the personal universe or viewpoint. One need only allude to the areas of experience from which women are excluded to comprehend the negative arguments. As Virginia Woolf constantly reiterates, it is impossible to describe commonplace events one has not seen or participated in. Even her own relative freedom to travel across London unescorted in a public conveyance and lunch alone at a restaurant could not have been enjoyed by her nineteenth-century predecessors. As some man is always ready to point out, the best of them made a literary virtue of those restrictions; but some other man is equally ready to deride the "feminine" touch in modern novels that continue to describe the heroine's costume and coiffure now that both she and her creator are free to experience more important things on that bus. A Jane Austen would have used her opportunity well, and we should certainly be exposed to no more recitals about the sprigged muslin and pelisses of her young ladies than we are while they are restricted to Bath or Highbury. But she would still be a woman riding that bus, and that fact continues to shape what she experiences, how she transforms it into fiction.

Marie Bashkirtsev, quoted in *The Second Sex,* said that in order to be a true artist, she needed "liberty to go walking alone, to come and go, to sit on the benches of the Tuileries Gardens." I am sure this must seem an extravagant excuse for failure—and the "proof" is that woman has done so little now that she has that freedom. The problem is that she can go for a walk, sit on a park bench, but not in such a way as to transcend her sexual identity, much less apprehend whatever lies beyond that.

> Culture must be apprehended through the free action of a transcendence; that is, the free spirit with all its riches must project itself toward an empty heaven that it is to populate; but if a thousand persistent bonds hold it to earth, its surge is broken. To be sure, the young girl can today go out alone and idle in the Tuileries; but . . . [the street is] hostile to her, with eyes and hands lying in wait everywhere; if she wanders carelessly, her mind drifting, if she lights a cigarette in front of a cafe, if she goes alone to the movies, a disagreeable incident is soon bound to happen. She must inspire respect by her costume and manners. But this preoccupation rivets her to the ground and to herself.

So the woman writer whose plot calls for her to take her heroine walking in the park would draw upon what she knows it is like for a woman to walk in the park. Whether or not she decides to expose the heroine to a "disagreeable incident," all her own experience has made her aware of her body, carriage, and clothing on such a walk, and some of that is likely to carry over into what we are told about the heroine.

These "disagreeable incidents"—do you know just how destructive they are to a woman's sense of herself as a person? How intrusively they remind her that her notions about love, work, respect are illusions or are granted her on male sufferance, since her very presence on the street is a sexual act and an implicit challenge? Nor are such incidents an anachronism in this age of Sexual Revolution. While I was writing the first version of this essay, I decided it would be a good idea to reread *Civilization and Its Discontents,* which was not among the works of Freud I'd checked out of the library. It was early evening on a holiday weekend; libraries were closed and the nearest bookstore sold only pornography. I telephoned a friend who lived nearby, and he invited me over to pick up his copy of the book. "Better still: if you've been working all day, you should have a change of scene. I'll make dinner and you can try to write here. Just stop off and buy a can of chili without beans and a head of lettuce." As I set off on this errand, I was full of the books I'd been reading and the myth of social progress. In the immediate circumstances of my life, I was even freer than Virginia Woolf in an omnibus. I could walk through my New York neighborhood after dark, hoping the local supermarket sold chili without beans, and I could do so clad in a version of Mrs. Bloomer's last-century liberation uniform. That the most unliberated devotees of fashion were all wearing the Bloomer costume now was an irony that pleased me, as did the local pornography shop's dubious contribution to social freedom. I was free to bring the chili to the apartment of a single man and to dine with him alone there. Unlike, say, Lily Bart, I would not be inviting lewd assumptions by spending the evening there. Still more remarkable, whereas those untrue assumptions were enough to ruin Edith Wharton's heroine, I knew no one who would censure me if I remained overnight. And I took all this so much for granted that I would not have been thinking about it at all were it not for Virginia Woolf's remarks about how Jane Austen never rode an omnibus.

My realization that my pants suit is a Bloomer costume led me to think about the sociology of dress, the significance of introducing sports into the education of young women, the contribution of the bicycling craze, changing interpretations of hair and skirt lengths. What had begun with thoughts about my own life had taken several steps into generalization. But I was interrupted by the first "disagreeable incident"—a strange man made an obscene remark to me, inspired by nothing more than my presence on the same sidewalk where he was walking. By the time I had traversed the four blocks between my house and my friend's, two other men had accosted me, separately, reaching out for me with their words or hands. It occurred to me that even Virginia Woolf on an omnibus was exposed to the same possibility of insult, the same hint of danger. She could not be "just" a brilliant novelist observing a segment of London life; she was also a piece of female flesh experiencing it. And that had to be part of how she perceived whatever happened to her. My own grandmother used to take a streetcar to her job in a sweatshop. She was free to earn her own miserable living, free to travel alone. Because she spoke no English, she always carried a hatpin to protect herself from the men who pressed close to her to provoke "disagreeable incidents." I have always wondered why the hatpin has become, in family tradition, a substitute for language; what on earth could she have *said* had she all the verbal skill of a Virginia Woolf? For each of us, any escape from the domination of gender is brief and illusory.

I should not like these observations to be so vulgarized that I seem to be saying female novelists concentrate on physical descriptions because of their encounters with strange men in the street. The "disagreeable incident" is only one element in the sexualization of women's whole life and psychology, for almost everything in our experience is translated into sexual terms. Thus the woman writer's tendency to make relations with men her principal subject is a symptom of the same condition that is also responsible for her notorious attention to superficial detail. Mary McCarthy's essay on "The Fact in Fiction" presents a convincing argument about the realistic "information" that novels contain. At one point, she refers to a novel's "documentation" as feminine. Her theory can be usefully related to Virginia Woolf's thesis that the novel is a uniquely appropriate feminine genre; my idea about the sexualization of women's experience is simply a further restriction added to those she adduces to show why women writers write novels. It also helps explain why, if the novel in general is a vehicle for material facts, those written by women dwell on one category of facts: the environmental details that are descriptions or extensions of our own bodies.

In discussions of Women and Fiction, it apparently becomes impossible for many commentators to separate feminine style from feminine subject matter. Mary Ellmann's *Thinking About Women* supplies a great many examples of critics who use sexual analogy to describe both the way women write and the things we write about. They even use it to comment on the laudable absence of these "feminine" habits if they cannot find them where the stereotype insists they should be. And it is always useful as a slur. Wolcott Gibbs, for example, discussing his own editorial idiosyncrasies, says, "I suffer . . . seriously from writers who divide quotes for some kind of ladies' club rhythm, 'I am going,' he said, 'downtown,' is a horror. . . ." It *is* a horror, but it bears no discernible relation to that other male bugaboo, the women's club. What it does sound like is a parody of James. But James's "femininity" is normally seen as a matter of subject, not style; Geismar describes him as "perhaps . . . the greatest feminine novelist of *any* age, the artist who brought the domestic realm of a Jane Austen, say, to the edge (if no further) of world literature."[35] Apparently, it needed a *man* to take it even that far! Yet the very existence of the "Jacobite" cult among male critics belies the notion of a domestic scene as the exclusive province of women writers or readers. What is meant by the domestic realm in this case, anyway, if not that of relations between the sexes? And, although our culture has made that very nearly women's only interest, it has never been only we who were interested in it.

Feminine style remains an elusive notion. In *A Room of One's Own*, Virginia Woolf makes a great point of the "man's sentence" and how uncomfortably the great women writers of the last century used it. Jane Austen alone, she believes, was able to laugh at that sentence, transcend it, and thus develop a perfectly good, serviceable sentence of her own. But what makes it a "woman's sentence" aside from the undeniable fact that Jane Austen was a woman? The blurred distinction between style and subject is brought out when the same notion is applied to Dorothy Richardson in Woolf's *Contemporary Writers*, where she states that the difference between the "psychological sentence of the feminine gender" in the hands of male and female writers is in Richardson's molding of the sentence to explore a woman's consciousness. "It is a woman's sentence, but only in the sense that it is used to describe a woman's mind by a writer who is neither proud nor afraid of anything that she may discover in the psychology of her sex." But then, as Mary Ellmann points out, "the only certain femininity is in Dorothy Richardson's subject." [36]

I have similar impressions from my own experience. When I was an undergraduate, a woman who was very confused about both sex and literature suggested I read the fiction of Anaïs Nin because she writes "like a woman." I found the first book I tried very tedious, not because her style was particularly "feminine," but because of her protagonist's self-conscious hold on neurosis and on conventional female stereotypes. When I castigated my classmate for inflicting this experience on me, she explained that she hadn't meant that Anaïs Nin writes like a woman, but from a distinctly feminine standpoint, a very different thing indeed. On the other hand, a teacher in a "creative writing" course once told a female student to read Grace Paley "because she writes like a man." That one really puzzled us, and the only partially satisfactory explanation we could come up with is that she is straightforward—though not particularly naturalistic—about the pleasures of sexuality. Which means that we are outgrowing a little of our protective hypocrisy. But there is surely nothing that reflects her gender (or that contradicts it) in the shape of Paley's sentences.[37]

Developments in the Sexual Revolution should have made it possible for the first time for female novelists to supply a woman's "style" and viewpoint about sexuality. No man, one would think, could do a very accurate job of describing what it feels like for a woman to have intercourse with a man, and the subject is certainly germane to concern with defining the female condition. But women have concentrated more often on the inward aspects of a sexual affair. I am not arguing that women should strike back at men by objectifying them in dirty books as oppressive as those written by and for men; but not all explicit descriptions of sexuality are dirty and women have not given us such descriptions. In Doris Lessing and Anaïs Nin, we encounter characters who are self-conscious about their femininity, "superior" women whose nerves are very close to the surface. These women have extensive sexual experience, but we learn about what goes on in their minds, mostly in regard to the whole relationship and not its specifically sexual side. Lessing accepts the implications of so doing, rejecting not only mechanical male formulae but nearly all descriptions of sexual scenes. "Women," she claims, "deliberately choose not to think about technical sex. They get irritable when men talk technically, it's out of self preservation: they want to preserve the spontaneous emotion that is essential for their satisfaction." And this emotion is to be apprehended in terms of Freudian mystification:

> A vaginal orgasm is emotion and nothing else, felt as emotion and expressed in sensations that are indistinguishable from emotion. The vaginal orgasm is a dissolving in a vague, dark generalized sensation like being swirled in a warm whirlpool. There are several different sorts of clitoral orgasms, and they are more powerful (that is a male word) than the vaginal orgasm. There can be a thousand thrills, sensations, etc., but there is only one real female orgasm and that is when a man, from the whole of his need and desire, takes a woman and wants all her response.[38]

At the other extreme is Mary McCarthy, whose depiction of sexual scenes is almost invariably ironic. She is detached and clinical, as one must imagine her characters themselves are, and even a pleasurable experience is described in an alienated way. Sexual experience that is more than technically successful and that accompanies feelings of warmth and love arouses the same reticence in McCarthy as in Lessing.

For the most part, we have left it up to men to define women's sensibility in this as in other areas—with pre-

dictable results. Women who read Joyce are naturally impressed with Molly Bloom's soliloquy in the over-all structure of *Ulysses*. But it is normally men who think of
Molly's sexuality as defining a female type that is recognizable realistically as well as mythically; to a woman, she
is only an archetypal male fantasy of woman's inner life.
Despite my recourse to this notion of woman as men wish
she would be, I do not believe there are very many female
characters in literature that are deliberately constructed as
fantasy-ideals for male readers. Outside of pornography,
where the females are no more than stylized orifices, fictional women are not created to provide imaginary lovers
for the men who read about them. It is my general impression, in fact, that men do not realize fiction in that way,
that they rarely encounter a lady in a book with whom
they "fall in love," or liken a woman they meet to some
literary heroine. Women do this constantly—at least adolescent girls do, and adult women without much literary
sophistication. The hero, in these cases, is always the same,
the masterful Byronic figure, never that weak man in
search of Mother who is fully and credibly delineated in
modern novels written by women. In young girls, it is a
phase, and when they outgrow it they remember more of
Wuthering Heights than the dominating personality of
Heathcliff. But the subliterary works intended for older
women supply a continued need that I imagine is the nearest many of these readers get to masturbation. Our grand-
mothers gasped over *The Sheik*, with its overtones of romantic rape, long before Valentino gave the word flesh.
And our mothers reacted the same way to Rhett Butler.

On the next lower level, however, there is no pornography written by or for women, and even the milder sexual
titillations appeal to our narcissism or our aspirations
rather than to more outgoing impulses. After all, a sexy
woman appears every month on the cover of *Cosmopolitan*
as well as *Playboy*. I think there is a whole range of popu-

lar literary forms that cater in this way to culturally in-
duced fantasies. What men seek in those forms—detective,
Western, and adventure stories, as well as pornography—
is a confirmation of the virile ideal, an identification of
themselves as master. What women seek is the force that
we are educated to believe will act upon our "natural"
passivity and bring it to life, fertilize our incompleteness,
and give us an identity, much as the sperm is depicted as
bringing life from an otherwise inert ovum. In pornography, the man is master in fact, not merely "masterful"
as in confession magazines or light romances. But his dominance is necessarily exercised over a being without personality, whose "fulfillment" is in total reification. Women
do not identify with such a figure, and it is not part of our
fantasy life to reverse the politics and make of ourselves
the monstrous master a distorted system recognizes as Man.

I find confirmation of this, rather than an exception,
in *Story of O,* whose author's pseudonym is female and
whose "heroine" degenerates (as the ideogrammatic name
"O" itself implies) into undifferentiated femaleness. This
femaleness is defined as total abdication of personal and
sexual autonomy, degradation of both flesh and spirit. In
an introductory note, André Pieyre de Mandiargues discusses the way the book ends. O, depilated, chained, and
wearing an owl mask, is in the final scene "exposed to
public scorn: the display of a body which is no longer anything but an object, flouted beneath the plumage, offered
to the first comer. Then: death. Inevitably; woman,
through the decline of her flesh, having become pure
spirit." The mystic arithmetic is faulty here: he says you
degrade and then subtract the flesh and what is left is pure
spirit. But what makes him think there is any *spirit* left?

All the commentary I have read about this novel is by
men and follows the lead of Jean Paulhan in describing it
as the absolute apotheosis of female sexuality and the fulfillment of our darkest fantasies. I can hardly imagine its

arousing any woman sexually; women who read it tend to consider it mildly disturbing, but even our revulsion is impersonal, political, not of that overwhelming sort that might reveal some correspondence of O's experience with one's own secret wishes or fears. (I recall Colette's story about herself at age fourteen, fainting when she read Zola's description of labor pains in a volume that had been forbidden her. Or an eighteen-year-old of my own generation who fainted in the office of the doctor teaching her to use her first diaphragm. We are so conditioned that certain natural truths do indeed make us sick, but everything that makes us sick is not, for that reason, the truth.)

I believe a case can be made for Pauline Réage's being a man, none for "her" being a woman. As Paulhan acknowledges, O is a masculine fantasy. Addressing the author, he says:

> That you are a woman I have little doubt. Not so much because of the kind of detail you delight in describing—the green satin dresses, wasp-waist corsets, and skirts rolled up a number of turns (like hair rolled up in a curler)—but rather because of something like this: the day when René abandons O to still further torments, she still manages to have enough presence of mind to notice that her lover's slippers are frayed, and notes that she will have to buy him another pair. To me, such a thought seems almost unimaginable. It is something a man would never have thought of, or at least would never have dared express.[39]

Female authors, the argument runs, observe and report on details of dress and appearance. I have acknowledged that and attempted to explain why it continues to be true when both real and fictional women should have more engrossing subjects on their minds. But precisely because this preoccupation is recognized as part of the feminine value-system, it is subject to imitation and even to parody. Pavese, who comes much closer to depicting woman's world than to assimilating her thoughts, has mastered that habit without the standards that inform it. In an early scene of *Among Women Only*, the female narrator describes a character's slipper-satin dress as "worth more than a lot of words." A few chapters later, Pavese has Clelia tell us about a gathering of shallow young society people and artists: "Then Momina arrived. . . . Her gloves alone were worth more than the whole studio." But Paulhan's argument about Réage is more intricate; it is not merely her trick of observation that is "feminine" but the self-effacing ability to notice homely details, details relating to how she can serve, at such a moment. He uses the book's thesis about female nature as if it were a proved fact. For surely if Réage is a woman that detached remark about the slippers is meant ironically.

Paulhan goes on to reveal why it is so important for him to believe that the creator of such a bizarre lapse into domesticity is female:

> In her own way O expresses a virile ideal. Virile, or at least masculine. At last a woman who admits it! Who admits what? Something that women have always refused till now to admit (and today more than ever before). Something that men have always reproached them for, that they never cease obeying their nature, the call of their blood, that everything in them, even their minds, is sex. That they have constantly to be nourished, constantly washed and made up, constantly beaten. That all they need is a good master . . . that we must, when we go to them, take a whip along. Rare is the man who has not dreamed of possessing Justine. But, so far as I know, no woman has ever dreamed of being Justine. I mean, dreamed aloud, with this same pride at being grieved and in tears, this consuming violence, with this voracious capacity for suffering, and this amazing will, stretched to the breaking point and even beyond.

In short, the supreme masculine fantasy is for the woman to confess that all of it is really *her* fantasy. And that it is not some aberration, but the unconscious female norm.

But which of us is so acute and yet so self-destructive as to pander to this particular male fantasy? To be able to do so demands an unimaginable combination of meretricious intent and freedom. We are not that blindly generous to the madness of others, nor is any of us that free.

III

Once again, I catch myself using the word "freedom" in a paradoxical sense. The only way to escape this and to find a suitable conclusion to my remarks is to speak politically. In *A Room of One's Own,* Virginia Woolf comes very close to it, but the solutions she hints at are restricted by their idiosyncratic nature and their class bias. I suspect that the impossibility of developing a program from her poetic statements has contributed to the work's acceptance. It is just what a romantic plea for freedom should be: eloquent, stirring, and ultimately ineffective. But Virginia Woolf was not wholly satisfied with beautiful language. At least, she felt the need to reopen the Woman Question ten years later and report new, essentially political conclusions.

The resulting volume, *Three Guineas,* has never been as widely read or as well liked. Critics tell us that in this work Virginia Woolf allowed her bitterness at the female condition to distort and overcome the lyric power demonstrated in *A Room of One's Own.* E. M. Forster says that although "feminism inspired . . . the charming and persuasive *A Room of One's Own,*" it is also responsible for what he considers her worst book, "the cantankerous *Three Guineas.*" Carl Woodring is the rare male commentator who apparently relishes the clever blending of earnestness and irony that marks *Three Guineas.* But he destroys the force of his observation by claiming that the author offered the second of her three guineas "to help the daughters of uneducated men enter the professions. The insistence on uneducated fathers, as a way of giving civili-

zation a fresh start, is as shrewd as the financial manipula
tions of Keynes."[40] But there is no such insistence; the
contribution actually goes to those daughters of educated
men who make up the "class" with which Virginia Woolf
identifies and whom she just as accurately describes as the
daughters of uneducated *women*. The difference between
the sexes remains a considerable one, after all, and this
misreading makes one rather wonder at Woodring's earlier
contention that the argument of *A Room of One's Own*
"was already obsolete" when it was written.

The real difference between the two feminist essays has
nothing to do with a subject gone stale or, as Forster suggests, with "grumbling from habit." Rather, it results from
a deepened awareness that makes Virginia Woolf's feminism, that "peculiar side of her," the force that ultimately
alters her entire social outlook. Consideration of the politics of both works reveals a developing analysis and points
the way to future strategies.

The fundamental insight of *A Room of One's Own* is
that psychological and cultural oppression of women is
the result of economic dependency. Thus, possession of the
requisite five hundred pounds a year—bequeathed, or
earned by one's wits—is to her the *sine qua non* of creative
life. Advocating that some women have the opportunity to
earn that five hundred pounds means at best a limited extension of privilege. She does not stop to consider that
women's poverty is an essential part of an entire system, or
what would happen to an economy based on profit if all
adults had remunerative jobs. Extending privilege without
sexual bias but within a small class also means giving a few
women a stake in maintaining the system. Virginia Woolf
acknowledges, with Lady Lovelace, that the price of empire
"was mostly paid by women." She recognizes that it was
women's contribution to the war effort after 1914 that
finally won them some independence, and that "if they
were again dependent upon their fathers and brothers they

would again be consciously and unconsciously in favor of war."[41] Yet, although deliberately rejecting that party, she aligns herself with the masters of empire when she exults that "no force in the world can take from me my five hundred pounds."

In *A Room of One's Own*, Virginia Woolf's central perception about women's need for fiscal independence is presented as something different from politics. She tells of the bequest that she received around the time women were granted suffrage in England: "Of the two—the vote and the money—the money, I own, seemed infinitely the more important." Despite its relative insignificance to herself, she apparently believed that since the enactment of suffrage women were, in fact, politically emancipated. At that time, she did not take the next step and recognize how meaningless are formal political rights in an unfree economic system. The later work, *Three Guineas*, does link economic and political questions. The author discusses the power bourgeois women now have, apart from the old whorish "influence" of the salons.

> For some reason, never satisfactorily explained, the right to vote, in itself by no means negligible, was mysteriously connected with another right of such immense value to the daughters of educated men that almost every word in the dictionary has been changed by it, including the word 'influence.' You will not think these words exaggerated if we explain that they refer to the right to earn one's living.

Once again, Virginia Woolf leaves unexplained a social "mystery" that she is very close to penetrating. For there is no reason to be surprised that economic and political power are related. *Three Guineas* implicitly recognizes this fact whenever its author looks beyond male "attitudes" to the material sources of power. Women now have the opportunity to earn their living; why do so few succeed in attaining financial success and the social influence that accompanies it? Clearly, it is because ours is not a system in which much power is wielded by those who earn their living. In their own right, women still own almost none of the means of production and reap almost none of the profits. Thus, they exercise little power, and only briefly does Virginia Woolf toy with the notion that things would be better for women if there were a female automobile manufacturer to scribble a check and endow, say, a college for women. One woman's elevation to the ranks of privilege could do nothing for the rest of us; even her influence, the writing of the check, could not open the way to the next lower rung of privilege to many women. For under capitalism, there is only so much material power to be had, and those who have it hold on to it. As Virginia Woolf knew, they protect what they own in the name of God, Law, Nature, and Property.

> Behind us lies the patriarchal system; the private house, with its nullity, its immorality, its hypocrisy, its servility. Before us lies the public world, the professional system, with its possessiveness, its jealousy, its pugnacity, its greed. The one shuts us up like slaves in a harem; the other forces us to circle, like caterpillars head to tail, round and round the mulberry tree, the sacred tree, of property.[42]

Virginia Woolf thus arrives at an analysis of her condition and identifies the enemy precisely as a Marxist would. She does it without abandoning her own social identity, but as a means of elucidating it.

On the question of work, Virginia Woolf is less clear. Because her subject in *A Room of One's Own* is the cultural condition of woman, she speaks of the freedom to work at artistic creation. And because that work does not necessarily produce the requisite income, she mentions earning five hundred a year by one's wits. In *Three Guineas,* the subject is wider, and therefore she speaks about women's place in the professions. As the author constantly reiterates, however, we cannot judge or even describe what we do not experience. So, although she knows the drudgery of working merely to eat, she cannot write of what meaningful, unalienated work might be like.

According to *A Room of One's Own*, in a hundred years women "will take part in all the activities and exertions that were once denied them. The nursemaid will heave coal. The shop woman will drive an engine." This is to some extent an attractive image of the future, since the existing division of labor is one cause of both the economic and the psychological oppression of women. Virginia Woolf has it backwards, however, when she claims that making these exertions available to women will mean that womanhood is no longer a "protected occupation" and that we will begin to die off earlier than men. Actually, the idea of having female coal heavers and engine drivers represents freedom from the mystique of feminine frailty, a mystique that Virginia Woolf herself apparently accepts. Moreover, it is a continuation of precisely that phenomenon that brought so many women (and children) onto the labor market in the first place, the technological advances that made brute strength less important in production. When people exist to serve production, rather than production existing to serve them, the labor of women and children is degrading and inhuman. The tragedy of the woman driving an engine and heaving coal is not that she will stagger exhausted to an early grave; rather, it is that she shares both the exploitation and the alienation of the men who do these jobs.

Theodor Reik remarks complacently that "a woman's life is tragically interrupted or even finished when she renounces the desire to please others by her appearance and begins to neglect her looks. A man's life is tragically interrupted or even finished when he renounces work, whether manual or intellectual." [43] It will feel good for women not to have our identity so tied to sexuality, to be able to define ourselves in terms of work, too. But it will be better still when the work itself has meaning. When the process of production exists for the people who do the work, "the fact of the collective working group being composed of individuals of both sexes and all ages must . . . become a source of humane development." [44]

But how can production be for the benefit of the workers while it is for the profit of the owner? How can there be jobs enough for all when maximum profit is the goal of production? That profit depends on the existence of both a marginal labor force and an untabulated army of domestic workers who are "paid" indirectly with the wages from *their husbands'* productive work. "The emancipation of women and their equality with men are impossible and must remain so as long as women are excluded from socially productive work and restricted to housework, which is private." [45] As for the socialization of domestic labor, it is Virginia Woolf and no dialectical materialist who suggests that the state provide "a wage . . . to those whose profession is marriage and motherhood." Addressing a man of the educated class, she tells him:

> If your wife were paid for her work, the work of bearing and bringing up children, a real wage, a money wage, so that it became an attractive profession instead of being as it is now an unpaid profession, an unpensioned profession, and therefore a precarious and dishonored profession, your own slavery would be lightened. No longer need you go to the office at nine-thirty and stay there till six. Work could be equally distributed. Patients could be sent to the patientless. Briefs to the briefless. Articles could be left unwritten. Culture would thus be stimulated. You could see the fruit trees flower in spring. You could share the prime of life with your children. And after that prime was over no longer need you be thrown from the machine on to the scrap heap without any life left or interests surviving. . . . [46]

She attributes society's inability to execute this scheme to the exorbitant amounts spent for what we have since learned to label "defense." But what is it that our armies defend, if not property? Who profits materially from war and the preparation for war? And how is "the state" to pay wages for housework until we all own the means of production in common and state policy is an expression of our ownership?

Virginia Woolf's researches into the comparative poverty of women were prompted, she says, by her visit to Oxbridge. It is the marked contrast between the spacious richness of the men's foundations and the beef-and-prunes atmosphere of Fernham, the women's college, that made her ask why women are poor. The university stands for a whole world of leisure, elegance, and luxury that *A Room of One's Own* treats as essential to the creation and perpetuation of art. In wishing that privileged ethos to be shared with women, she is calling for what our vulgarians have since termed "a piece of the action." The university is the bastion of that "intellectual freedom of which great writings are born," and the important fact about it in *A Room of One's Own* is that in recent times almost all the great writers of England had "procured the means to get the best education England can give."

But whereas *A Room of One's Own* is a book about money, sex, and culture, *Three Guineas* is a book about money, sex, and power. In the later work, the important facts about the university are that "the great majority of men who have ruled England for the past 500 years, who are now ruling England in Parliament and the Civil Service, has received a university education," and that "an immense sum of money . . . has been spent upon education in the past 500 years." These facts lead her to recognition of what the university is really about, whom it really serves, and thence to rejection of the entire aristocratic culture *A Room of One's Own* is so ready to embrace. She envisions, instead, a new kind of institution, one that will foster neither the old culture nor the system whose ve-

hicle she now perceives education to be. In this experimental environment, there is to be no opulence, no museum hush, no permanent decoration.

> Next, what should be taught in the new college, the poor
> college? Not the arts of dominating other people; not
> the arts of ruling, of killing, of acquiring land and capi-
> tal. . . . The poor college must teach only the arts that
> can be taught cheaply and practised by poor people; such
> as medicine, mathematics, music, painting and literature.
> It should teach the arts of human intercourse; the art of
> understanding other people's lives and minds, and the
> little arts of talk, of dress, of cookery that are allied with
> them. The aim of the new college, the cheap college,
> should be not to segregate and specialize, but to combine.
> It should explore the ways in which mind and body can
> be made to co-operate, discover what new combinations
> make good wholes in human life. . . . There would be
> none of the barriers of wealth and ceremony, of adver-
> tisement and competition which now make the old and
> rich universities such uneasy dwelling-places. . . .
> [Artists and scholars] would come to the poor college
> and practise their arts there because it would be a place
> where society was free; not parcelled out into the miser-
> able distinctions of rich and poor, or clever and stupid;
> but where all the different degrees and kinds of mind,
> body and soul merit co-operated. Let us . . . found this
> new college; this poor college; in which learning is sought
> for itself; where advertisement is abolished; and there are
> no degrees and lectures are not given, and sermons are
> not preached, and the old poisoned vanities and parades
> which breed competition and jealousy. . . .[47]

Thus Sir Leslie Stephen's snobbish daughter, detached
"from the working-classes and from Labor," she whose "attitude to society was . . . aloof and angular," paints for us
the People's University. But "reality" intervenes in her
dream, the reality of higher education as a channeling
mechanism for bourgeois society. The college Virginia
Woolf depicts can only flourish in a society where competition is not a norm and where learning and culture are

valued because of what they contribute to the common good, not how they bolster existing power and profit. In short, the People's University is the cultural focus of a free, socialist society.

A free, socialist society—does Virginia Woolf say *that*? Well, no. I can underline her radical analysis of social inequality, her radical vision of a new world. I can point out the close parallels with classic Marxist views. But I can't distort Virginia Woolf into a revolutionary. Her strategy for change has built into it not only defeat but resignation to defeat. That is why it is appropriate to re-examine that strategy and see what new possibilities forty years of history have opened to us. Forster admits that as a man, and an elderly one, he is unfit to judge Virginia Woolf's feminism. "The best judges . . . are neither elderly men nor even elderly women, but young women. If they . . . think that it expresses an existent grievance, they are right." Recent experience shows that they—that we—still do. Our differences lie in how we believe the grievance can be redressed.

Virginia Woolf's solutions are never collective, however much she may talk about social problems and the number of people they affect. She denies Walter Bagehot's claim that most women "are utterly destitute of the disciplined reticence necessary to every sort of cooperation. Two thousand years hence you may have changed it all, but the present women will only flirt with men and quarrel with one another." It is clearly not up to women to make drastic changes in themselves, individually, before changing the system that is responsible for their present "defects." Yet in her own most radical proposals Virginia Woolf is suggesting precisely the same kind of isolated reform.

In *Three Guineas*, she elaborates on the idea of the "poor college" and then, when reminded of the goals of existing colleges, simply "drops out." Action consists in refusing to support institutions that serve a corrupt and vicious system—a withdrawal that is personally cathartic,

perhaps, but socially useless. Similarly, a request for contributions to an organization promoting peace and freedom
is countered by the vision of an Outsiders' Society made up
of "educated men's daughters working in their own class—
how indeed could they work in any other?—and by their
own methods for liberty, equality and peace." Despite her
own arguments, Virginia Woolf is not convinced that the
Woman Question crosses—at times obliterates—class lines.
And what are women's own methods? The enemy and his
institutions are again clearly labeled, for the Outsider "will
bind herself to take no share in patriotic demonstrations, to
assent to no form of national self-praise; to make no part of
any clique or audience that encourages war; to absent herself from military displays, tournaments, tattoos, prize-
givings and all such ceremonies as encourage the desire to
impose 'our' civilization or 'our' dominion upon other
people." She believes that the "psychology of private life"
warrants her conviction that this use of indifference would
help materially to prevent war. "For psychology would
seem to show that it is far harder for human beings to take
action when other people are indifferent and allow them
complete freedom of action, than when their actions are
made the centre of excited emotion." [48] In short, the Outsider is to accept her status as Outsider and work a new
kind of "influence" upon the war-makers of her "own"
class. She is to re-enact Lysistrata as psychological drama.

To do this means to work for change within the isolation of individual female lives; to acknowledge and depend
on the power of those who rule; to refuse reinforcements
from the ranks of other oppressed groups. By contrast, in
this eighth decade of our century, all women's liberation
organizations, whatever their political orientation, seek to
destroy the private, individual battlegrounds that have so
long assured defeat for women's struggles. All reject the
rulers' definition of ourselves and our movement, as we
reject the legitimacy of his authority. All perceive the

analogy between our own situation and that of other oppressed people. Our entire program is based on these differences between our perspective and that of Virginia Woolf.

A similar evangelical note distorts Woolf's description of what our oppression has taught women, our "vocational" education at the hands of "poverty, chastity, derision and freedom from unreal loyalties." Women, she says, must turn these great teachers to advantage and refuse to be separated from them. Thus, practice of poverty means earning only enough to live on independently; chastity means refusal, having earned that much, to sell one's brain for the sake of money; derision means rejection of "all methods of advertising merit," preferring obscurity and censure to praise and fame; and freedom from unreal loyalties means ridding oneself of pride at belonging to a nation, a religion, a family, an institution, or a sex. (She says nothing of class pride.) To be sure, these are the qualities that go into making a fighter for freedom. But developing them does not in itself constitute liberation. The oppressed can find the sources for freeing themselves in the identity shaped by oppression, but, again, that is not the same as being free. Once more the note is one of self-purification rather than social action.

The trouble with taking the next step, with proposing collective solutions, is that it leads to the problem of collective means. So long as the struggle for liberation is kept private, there is no political reason to wrestle with the issue of violence. Virginia Woolf, who passionately hated war and killing, points out that "scarcely a human being in the course of history has fallen to a woman's rifle; the vast majority of birds and beasts have been killed by . . . [men] not by us." [49] It's a beautiful record. Women are only now awakening to question whether it may not also be the means of our enslavement. For if we accept the principle that the oppressed must be the vanguard of a revolution, and if we acknowledge the rhetoric of women's oppression, then how can we let someone else fight for our freedom? And knowing as we do how women have always had to relate to those in power, how can we expect to coax, to legislate, to seduce that power away? How can we participate now in a movement for liberation as it educates and takes limited action—only to drop out when the action escalates? The women who realize that the next struggle for freedom includes us have already enlisted as soldiers in an army we have yet to build. But we have accepted this responsibility with sorrow, not exhilaration, for we have no tradition of *machismo*, of the "fine, manly character" inculcated by war. I don't think women are in danger of developing our own *machismo* cult. If we become soldiers in the next revolution it will be because without that we never can be free. And without us, it would not really be a revolution.

Finally, in the strategy of sexual liberation, there is sexuality, the almost unmentioned realm in both of Virginia Woolf's feminist books. Andrew Sinclair, in *The Emancipation of the American Woman*, deplores the initial tolerance women's suffrage leaders showed for Victoria Woodhull's free-sex movement, a tolerance inspired by no more than the humane feeling that this time it would not be *women* who destroyed the sister who broke sexual taboos. The nineteenth-century radicals were premature, says Sinclair; they "demanded physical freedom outside marriage too soon." Society's unreadiness for this liberation delayed the granting of political rights to a movement associated with "free love." Actually, the free-sex enthusiasts came closer than the suffragettes to naming the enemy. They recognized sexual repression as a form of tyranny and the monogamous family as the institution of oppression. The failure of the early feminist movement was not that "free-lovers" held back suffrage, but rather that the mainstream dismissed their arguments and clung to the campaign for civil rights. Those rights are valuable, but alone they failed to alter the real material basis of women's lives, a basis in which economics and sexuality are inextricably linked. Norms of sexual behavior are different now, but it still remains for us to liberate sexuality from notions of ownership, competition, and domination. In the process of revolution, we have to reinvent love.

A Room of One's Own concludes with an exhortation about the resurrection of "the dead poet who was Shakespeare's sister," in language finer than any I can muster to frame my disagreement. Virginia Woolf speaks of all of us living with the famous five hundred pounds and rooms of our own, with the habit of freedom and the courage to live fully human lives, saying that if we do so, then the poet will finally rise from among us. But she never really means *all* of us and she cannot explain how we each—separately —put on the habit of freedom. The poet, she maintains, "would come if we worked for her, and . . . so to work, even in poverty and obscurity, is worth while." This is itself poetry, but it also embraces private martyrdom and self-effacement, with no clear notion of how that individual austerity will lead to the desired advent. It is self-interest that should make us work, not merely for the conditions that will at last allow a female poet to be a poet, but for the liberation of all people, on which that poet's freedom finally depends. If we do so, who can tell what poetic energies will be released from our ranks to take their part in remaking human life?

NOTES

1 The original version of this essay was written in November of 1968. I revised it in January of 1970. At the time the revision was completed, I had not read Kate Millett's *Sexual Politics* (New York: Doubleday & Co., 1970), which I understand deals with

some of the same material. Our approaches are quite different, however, as are a few of our conclusions. In any event, although we cover the same ground, neither of us regards it as her "turf."

2 Mary Ellmann, *Thinking About Women* (New York: Harcourt, Brace & World, 1968), p. 199. Speaking of acknowledging debts to predecessors, I feel I ought to rationalize my annotations. In general, I agree with Louis Kampf that "the hours one spends in a library should bear better fruit than a footnote." Thus, I have not given a full source description for certain phrases or ideas that I have cited verbatim and marked with inverted commas. But a bibliographical note should not be mere mechanical proof that one has served one's time amid the books; so I have included complete references for citations that the reader—her interest, curiosity, or incredulity aroused—may want to pursue.

3 Throughout this essay, as I speak of mutual dependency between fiction and social reality, I refer to my own experiences as a woman. But the "professional reader's" mind that I have been trained to develop and to trust is not a woman's mind. It is supposed to be neuter, but to the extent that it readily identifies, in reading, with the Ego and not with the Other, it is in fact masculine. I hope to write someday about the gender of the critical mind; I do not do so here because my present subject is prose fiction and I want to explore the problem with regard to the reading of poetry, which is where I feel the greatest psychic dislocation. As a critic and teacher of literature, I am aware that the dislocation is present whenever I read or write. This essay is an exception—one that creates quite different tensions.

4 Virginia Woolf, *A Room of One's Own* (1929; reprint ed., New York: Harcourt, Brace & World, Harbinger Books, 1957), p. 51.

5 Sigmund Freud, *Civilization and Its Discontents* (New York: W. W. Norton & Co., 1962), p. 48.

6 Friedrich Engels, *The Origin of the Family, Private Property and the State* (Moscow: Foreign Languages Publishing House, n.d.), pp. 54–55.

7 *Ibid.*, p. 128.

8 Virginia Woolf, *Three Guineas* (1938; reprint ed., New York: Harcourt, Brace & World, Harbinger Books, 1963), p. 3.

9 In *The Other Victorians* (New York: Basic Books, 1966), Steven Marcus points out the pervasive Victorian identification of sexual domination with capital and with class domination. The same pattern appears throughout "our" literature, but only in nineteenth-century England were both sexual and social categories so rigorously defined in literature.

10 Maxwell Geismar, *Henry James and the Jacobites* (Boston: Houghton Mifflin Co., 1963), p. 6.

11 *A Room of One's Own,* p. 92.

12 Those fifteen months are no longer impending; I got to pay a fine and leave my fingerprints on file. But given conditions in America today, fantasies about what kind of life one would have in prison are by no means idle or unrealistic. (The first week in January, when I wrote this note, it ended here with the quiet reminder that we are living at a time of accelerating political repression. It is now the third week in January, and I am once again facing criminal charges; this time the penalty is sixty days.)

13 *Three Guineas,* p. 146.

14 Engels, *Origin of the Family,* pp. 106–7.

15 *Ibid.,* p. 121.

16 *Three Guineas,* p. 18.

17 Clara Zetkin, *Lenin on the Woman Question* (New York: International Publishers, 1934), p. 19.

18 Engels, *Origin of the Family,* p. 123.

19 Zetkin, *Lenin on the Woman Question,* p. 17.

20 This reduction of psychoanalytic theory is quoted in a Shandyesque work by Paul Superak entitled "Metapsychomorphoses." The section cited is called "A Conversation with a Wellesley Girl of the Inferior Sort, Though Not Without Redeeming Virtues."

21 Sigmund Freud, "Female Sexuality," in *The Complete Psychological Works of Sigmund Freud* (London: The Hogarth Press and The Institute of Psychoanalysis, 1957), Vol. 21, p. 228.

22 Marie Bonaparte, *Female Sexuality* (New York: Grove Press, 1965), p. 7.

23 Sigmund Freud, "The Taboo of Virginity," The Psychology of Love, III, in *Complete Psychological Works,* Vol. 11, p. 205.

24 *Ibid.*

25 *A Room of One's Own,* p. 13. I am wrenching the line out of context, of course, but that is a proper Freudian procedure.

26 Pauline Kael, "Replying to Listeners," in *I Lost It at the Movies* (New York: Bantam Books, 1966), p. 206. Kael's qualification about marital sex is necessary because a "free" sex life can also be suspect: "When a woman has a succession of short-lived sexual affairs the suspicion arises that the woman unconsciously wishes to be a man." (Theodor Reik, *The Many Faces of Sex: Observations of an Old Psychoanalyst* [New York: Farrar, Strauss, & Giroux, Noonday Press, 1966], p. 116.)

27 Herbert Marcuse, *Eros and Civilization: A Philosophical Inquiry into Freud* (New York: Random House, Vintage Books, 1955), pp. 182, 183. Italics are his.

28 In a recent interview (*Guardian*, November 23, 1968) Marcuse observed that he saw no sense to a women's liberation movement that was separate from an integrated movement for human liberation. Despite the political shortsightedness of this remark, it would presumably confirm women's full citizenship in Marcuse's nonrepressive commonwealth. But it is still inexcusable to write a whole book about sexual liberation without explicitly recognizing that there are two sexes and that our problems in the unliberated state are very different.

29 Sigmund Freud, "Some Psychical Consequences of the Anatomical Distinctions Between the Sexes," in *Complete Psychological Works*, Vol. 19, pp. 257–58. Both citations are from this passage.

30 Nearly a year after using this story to epitomize Freud's reasoning process, I was delighted to discover that he himself cites a version of it as a "piece of sophistry which has been much laughed over." (*Jokes and their Relation to the Unconscious* [New York: Norton Library, 1963], p. 62.)

31 One of the freest women in modern literature is Nora inside out. She is Lizzie Hazeldean, the "heroine" of Edith Wharton's novella *New Year's Day*, who feels compelled to assure her dying husband that his illness is not causing her material deprivation. In order to maintain the elegancies that once cemented their love, she enters into an affair with a rich bachelor who makes up the deficit in her income so her husband sees no change in their standard of living. After the death of the husband she "betrayed" as the supreme act of devotion, she lives outside the pale of respectable society, but entirely free of sexual involvements. If human freedom under existing social forms is always a paradox, it is an especially ironic one for a woman.

32 The young Austens' pleasure in satirizing literature is preserved for us in Jane Austen's Juvenilia. Similarities in tone between the sister's *Love and Freindship* and the brothers' essays in *The Loiterer* have often been commented upon. James Austen is the author of a letter from "Sophia Sentiment" (*Loiterer*, No. 9) which discusses the mandatory content of "Novels, Eastern Tales and Dreams," while Henry Austen wrote the catalogue of stylistic devices appropriate to such ventures (No. 59). As I read these attempts, however, it is not the exaggerations of *Love and Freindship* I hear, but the somewhat matured ironies of Tilney himself. Henry Tilney is revealed to us principally through these opinions of his, but it is very likely that what little we see of his actions and character is drawn from the novelist's two brothers, whose views are so much like his own.

33 Reik, *Many Faces of Sex*, p. 102. I wonder about this "under-standing" that women are supposed to have—even when we are neither psychologists nor novelists. How much of what is called understanding is the masculine demand for essentially maternal attentions? How much is the subject's ceaseless, wary observation of the master she has to please?

34 Simone de Beauvoir, *The Second Sex* (New York: Bantam Books, 1961), p. 669. Subsequent quotations from Beauvoir are passages in the same chapter.

35 Geismar, *Henry James and the Jacobites*, p. 49.

36 Ellmann, *Thinking About Women*, p. 172.

37 Theodor Reik, in attempting to explain why there are so few women composers, and none of the first rank, whereas there are many fine women writers, completely confuses aesthetics and psychology of the arts, while creating some new stereotypes for us. He says: "In order to write, for instance, a novel, you take your material mostly from observing others, whereas in musical composition the echo—the reemergence and recapture of one's own emotions—is the essential thing. Most women do not listen to themselves when they speak, sob, or laugh. It seems to me that the average woman has a fine and perceptive ear for others, but almost none for her own emotional experiences." (*Many Faces of Sex*, p. 196.)

38 Doris Lessing, *The Golden Notebook* (New York: Ballantine Books, 1968), pp. 214–16.

39 Jean Paulhan, "Happiness in Slavery," in Pauline Réage, *Story of O* (New York: Grove Press, 1967), pp. xxiv–xxv. The next passage cited is also from this page of the introductory essay.

40 Carl Woodring, *Virginia Woolf* (New York: Columbia University Press, 1966), p. 9.

41 *Three Guineas*, p. 36.

42 *Ibid.*, p. 74.

43 Reik, *Many Faces of Sex*, pp. 75–76.

44 Karl Marx, *Capital*, Vol. I (New York: International Publishers, 1967), p. 490.

45 Engels, *Origin of the Family*, p. 266.

46 *Three Guineas*, pp. 110–11.

47 *Ibid.*, pp. 34–35.

48 *Ibid.*, p. 109.

49 *Ibid.*, p. 6.

ABOUT THE CONTRIBUTORS

ELLEN CANTAROW writes: "I came improbably both to radical politics and to the profession of literature: as a girl I wanted to study small mammals and reptiles and write short stories; politics meant nothing but a new face in the papers every four years. 1958 found me at Wellesley, freeing my last toad, and 1963 at Harvard in comparative literature, with no animals but an occasional nightmare. It was the fact of my womanhood, the war, the American education that made me a radical. Returning to graduate school after a two years' absence, I worked for Resist in late 1958; by 1969 I was deeply involved in the women's movement and participating in the Harvard ROTC strike. Subsequently I was active in Bread and Roses. I have been a member of the New University Conference. Last year I taught at the University of Massachusetts in Boston. This year I am jobless. I spend my time reading, writing, helping in the effort to advance the old mole in her progress, and observing the spider who lives beside the steps in my back yard."

SHEILA DELANY is an assistant professor of English at Simon Fraser University, Burnaby, British Columbia. Her degree (Columbia University, 1967) is in medieval English and comparative literature. She has also taught at Queens College and City University of New York, published articles on medieval and other literature, and edited *Counter-Tradition, the Literature of Dissent and Alternatives.* A study of Chaucer's work, *The Poetics of Skeptical Fideism,* is forthcoming. She has worked with the New University Conference and the Canadian Party of Labour, and is a friend of the Progressive Labor Party.

KATHERINE ELLIS is currently teaching English at Livingston College, Rutgers University. She is active in the women's movement and has published articles on day care and other feminist issues. Prior to working at Livingston, she was a graduate student and teaching assistant at Columbia University. She lives in New Brunswick with her five-year-old son.

BRUCE FRANKLIN is on the Central Committee of Venceremos, a multinational revolutionary organization in the San Francisco Bay Area. He is also a professor of English at Stanford University, though currently (November 1971) suspended from teaching and on academic trial for his political beliefs and activities. His books are *The Wake of the Gods: Melville's Mythology, Future Perfect: American Science Fiction of the Nineteenth Century, Who Should Run the Universities?* (with John A. Howard), and *From the Movement: Toward Revolution.* He has written many articles on politics, education, and literature. Forthcoming are *Red, White, and Other Colors: Communism vs. Capitalism in Russian and Anglo-American Science Fiction* and *Selected Works of Stalin.*

FLORENCE HOWE is consistently late these days, since the women's movement has transformed her from an activist/experimentalist assistant professor of English at Goucher College to an itinerant professor of humanities at State University of New York/College of Old Westbury, a public lecturer, and, imminently, president of the Modern Language Association. In her spare time, she writes essays and books (late again); works as central coordinator and editor for The Feminist Press; coordinates (with Carol Ahlum) a Women's Studies Clearinghouse for the Modern Language Association's Commission on Women; and yearns for the days of young and pure activism and teaching. Her publications include essays on teaching, Doris Lessing, the draft, women, sexual stereotypes in the public schools. With Ellen Bass, she is editing a volume of poems by twentieth-century American women. She has begun a new book on the education of American women.

Louis Kampf has been active in the civil rights and antiwar movements. He has worked in several community organizing projects,
been a member of Students for a Democratic Society and the New
University Conference, and participated in attempts to transform
education. Currently a professor of literature at the Massachusetts
Institute of Technology, he has been president of the Modern Language Association of America, and has written books and articles on
politics, literature, and culture.

Barbara Bailey Kessel has taught English at Hagerstown High School
(Maryland), West Leyden High School (Illinois), and Iowa City
Laboratory High School, in the Manpower Training Program of
the United States Labor Department in Chicago, and at Malcolm X
Community College in Chicago. She has worked for a year as an
organizer–office worker for the New University Conference, and
went to Cuba in August 1969 with a delegation from NUC. For the
past two years she has been organizing for women's liberation and
teaching in the Women's Studies Program at San Diego State College.

William Labov is a professor of linguistics and psychology at the
University of Pennsylvania. Harvard College, B.A. 1948; Columbia
University, M.A. 1963, Ph.D. 1964. He served on the faculty of the
Columbia University Department of Linguistics from 1964 to 1970,
when he moved to the University of Pennsylvania. His research has
been concentrated on the structure and evolution of language in its
social context. He is the author of *The Social Stratification of
English in New York City, The Study of Non-Standard English,* and
many papers dealing with research within the speech community.
From 1965 to 1968, he conducted research for the Office of Education
on the structure and use of black English in inner-city areas. He is
currently conducting research on sound changes in progress in the
United States and England, sponsored by the National Science Foundation. He is a member of the Executive Committee of the Linguistic Society of America, and of the Sociolinguistics Committee of
the Social Science Research Council.

Paul Lauter was most recently fired from the University of Maryland, Baltimore County, allegedly for "subversion of the grading
system." He now works for the United States Servicemen's Fund, a
support organization for the GI antiwar movement. He has followed

that route from college teacher to movement activist before: from Hobart College to the Mississippi Freedom Schools in 1964; from Smith to the American Friends Service Committee and Students for a Democratic Society; from the Antioch-Putney Graduate School to Resist. Along the way he has written about Thoreau and about the draft, about Scott Fitzgerald and about the Washington schools; edited a book, *Theories of Comedy,* and written one, with Florence Howe, *The Conspiracy of the Young.*

RICHARD OHMANN writes that he "is the well-known proletarian metacritic." He has carried on the struggle while laboring as a junior fellow, associate professor, associate provost, consultant, chancellor, acting provost, editor of *College English,* professor, adviser, and alumnus. In each gritty job he has given his bosses reason to quake. Currently he is terrorizing the ruling class at Wesleyan University from his base camp in the English department, the next thing to underground. According to sources, he carries membership in the New University Conference, the Resist Steering Committee, and the Modern Language Association of America.

WAYNE O'NEIL is a professor of linguistics and literature at the Massachusetts Institute of Technology and head of its literature faculty, and a lecturer on education at Harvard University. He has written on linguistics, literary theory, education, Thailand, and the FBI. He is active in several radical organizations, including the People's Coalition for Peace and Justice, Resist, and the New University Conference.

LILLIAN S. ROBINSON writes: "My origins are working-class, my sex female, my education bourgeois; if I am a revolutionary, a feminist, and an intellectual, it is these facts that determine what the labels mean. Brought up in New York City, I am a graduate of Hunter College High School and Brown University, where I earned a B.A. and M.A. in English. I studied at the Sorbonne and the NYU Institute of Fine Arts and am currently completing a Ph.D. in comparative literature at Columbia. Although I always considered myself a radical, it was the 1968 Columbia Strike and the women's liberation movement that helped me pull my politics, my work, and my personal life together. (The essay included in this collection was my first attempt at such a synthesis.) At present, I identify with the women's liberation movement in Boston and the Rosa Luxemburg Committee at MIT. I am Instructor of Literature at MIT, where my elective course is called 'The Sexual Order.' "

MARTHA VICINUS is a member of the New University Conference. A founding member of the Wisconsin Teaching Assistants Association, she participated in unionization efforts on the campus. At Indiana University she is an assistant professor of English and editor of *Victorian Studies,* and is active in the university's women's liberation group. She has written articles on popular and working-class culture in nineteenth-century England, and was editor of *Suffer and Be Still: The Victorian Woman,* a collection of essays. At present she is completing a book on the literature, songs, and music of the Victorian working class.

INDEX

VINTAGE CRITICISM,
LITERATURE, MUSIC, AND ART